THE COVID
CHRONICLES

THE COVID CHRONICLES

The collected diaries
of the Westport, CT Library
advanced writing class
during the COVID-19 pandemic

Edited by
Gina Ryan & Mary-Lou Weisman

Writings and photographs by:
G. Kenneth Bernhard © 2021
Bernadette Hutchings Birney © 2021
Lynn Goldman © 2021
Judith Hamer, PhD © 2021
Deborah Howland Murray © 2021
Morgaine Pauker © 2021
Gina Ryan © 2021
Donna Skolnick © 2021
Polly Tafrate © 2021
Mary-Lou Weisman © 2021
Maria Rossello Zobel © 2021

ISBN-13: 978-1-949122-22-0 (Paperback)

Front illustration by the Centers for Disease Control and Prevention (CDC)
Cover and interior design by Gina Ryan & Alison McBain.

Westport Library—Westport, CT
https://westportlibrary.org/
Fairfield Scribes—Fairfield, CT
https://www.fairfieldscribes.com/
United States of America

First printing April 2023.

"Our minds and souls contain volumes inscribed by our experiences and emotions; each individual's consciousness is a collection of memories we've cataloged and stored inside us, a private library of a life lived. *It is something that no one else can entirely share, one that burns down and disappears when we die.* But if you can take something from that internal collection and share it—with one person or with the larger world, on the page or in a story recited—it takes on a life of its own."

Susan Orlean from *The Library Book*

AUTHOR MARY-LOU WEISMAN WAS IN the early weeks of facilitating her Spring 2020 advanced memoir writing class at the Westport Library in Westport, Connecticut when she found a creative way to deal with literary lockdown.

March 17, 2020

Hi Class—Bored? Nervous? Hostile? Lonely? Personal Essay writers and memoirists unite!

Let's all commit to keeping a diary. What are we doing to deal with the extreme conditions under which we are now obliged to live? If you have one, how are you getting along with your mate? How are you filling your time? Are you transgressing? Do you have some good tips or entertainment ideas for the rest of us that might help to keep us sane?

The benefits should be obvious. First of all, you'll be writing, choosing your words, being productive, maybe even amusing your classmates, doing something worthwhile with your endless time.

As for when "we ten" shall meet again I have no idea, which is another good reason why we should stay connected.

Let me know if you're willing to go viral.

Cheers!
Mary-Lou

● ● ●

DEB: I'm willing, I'm drawing a lot, but writing sounds good.

JUDY: I'm in. Seem to have stopped everything and started sleeping, but I'll get my journal out and go back to what I love—writing.

POLLY: Sounds like a good idea. Should be "fun" and helpful.

MARIA: Thanks, Mary-Lou, for a great way to keep on keeping on. I'll give it a try.

GINA: I will, but I may bore you to tears.

MARY-LOU: Great! You can't bore us to tears. We're already bored to tears.

DONNA: I'll accept the invitation to write and share. I appreciate the incentive. I look forward to reading what others write.

MORGAINE: My first reaction was "NO." The coronavirus is the last thing I want to write about, and then I gave it a shot.

KEN: Sounds good, colleagues, count me in.

BERNADETTE: Quip me in.

Advanced Memoir Writing Class
Masked & Unmasked

G. Kenneth Bernhard: attorney, former elected official, past library trustee, sailor, birder, and humorist. Known as "Cookie Man" for bringing treats to writing class. Enjoyed Covid lockdown baking bread, laughing, and singing with his funny bride of 33 years, and sharing his sense of the ridiculous.

Bernadette Hutchings Birney: yoga studio owner and humorist. Tested negative, negative, negative when early Covid-19 tests were unreliable, unreliable, unreliable. Now recovering from long haul Covid.

Lynn Goldman: former business analyst, current lady of leisure, pre-school teacher, and humorist. Spent lockdown with husband and teenage son. As the youngest class member, Lynn was the last of the writers to be eligible for the vaccine.

Judith Hamer, PhD: grant writer, former Rockefeller Foundation learning officer and professor at Columbia University and New York University. Her life changed when she was widowed for the second time in 2017. During the pandemic, she, and the other isolated residents of Meadow Ridge ate meals in their own apartments rather than in the common dining room.

Deborah Howland Murray: portrait artist, illustrator, and art teacher. Deborah lost her husband of 34 years in 2018 and following his death, put her beloved historic home on the market. Spent lockdown walking dog, Arlo (now deceased) in Winslow Park and chatting with neighbors over fences. Was exposed to guest at the infamous "ground zero" Westport Covid party.

Morgaine Pauker: adventurist, fine art photographer, artist, and gardener. Has generously gifted fellow writers with packaged reams of paper. Spent Covid lockdown with husband, joined by adult daughter and her boyfriend fleeing NYC apartment, and her son who finished his senior year at Syracuse remotely.

Gina Ryan: former nonprofit CEO, organizational consultant, occasional artist, and current analyst for trustees of employee stock ownership plans. Wife/companion to gay ex-husband for 36 years who died in 2000. During pandemic lived in three-generation all female household with daughter and three granddaughters in various hormonal phases.

Donna Skolnick: author, presenter, workshop facilitator and retired Westport teacher. The second oldest of five girls, she Zoomed twice weekly with her sisters in Michigan, Idaho, Texas and Florida during the pandemic.

Polly Tafrate: retired from 25 years of teaching first-grade students just in time to enjoy seven newly-born grandchildren and indulge in hobbies—travel, gardening, volunteering, cooking, and freelance writing for newspapers and magazines. She is a contributor to *Chicken Soup for the Soul* and spent the pandemic recovering physically and mentally from nine days in the hospital with Covid.

Mary-Lou Weisman: author, essayist, writing teacher, gardener, Francophile, and humorist. Still married to Larry after outing him in three books including, *Intensive Care: A Family Love Story, Traveling While Married, and Playing House in Provence: How Two Americans Became a Little Bit French.*

Maria Rossello Zobel: Havana native—emigrated to New York in 1943. Former model, fashion merchandiser, singer, and design assistant. Widowed in 2009 after 38 years of marriage, she enjoyed visits with two children and four grandchildren during lockdown. Maria is a birdwatcher, Spanish language workshop leader, and companion to dog Archie.

THESE COVID CHRONICLES FOLLOW THE *unfolding of the pandemic over the course of seven months preceded by the whisperings of the spreading virus during January and February 2020. They trace the sudden lockdown in March, hospitalizations in April, supply chain shortages in May, a slow reopening in June, cautions celebrations in July, a hurricane in August, and a hybrid back-to-school schedule in September.*

Canceled classes, deaths of parents and pets, family tragedies, strained relationships, racial injustices, postponed weddings, Zoomed memorial services—all colored traditional holiday celebrations and family get-togethers and in some instances, fueled political outrage.

Leadup to Literary Lockdown

December 31, 2019
The China Country Office of The World Health Organization was informed of cases of pneumonia of unknown etiology detected in Wuhan City, Hubei Province of China.
Happy New Year!

January 7, 2020
Chinese health authorities confirmed that this cluster was associated with a novel coronavirus.

January 9, 2020
The first session of this Advanced Personal Essay Writing Class meets at the Westport Library

January 20, 2020
The first US case of coronavirus is reported—a man in Washington State developed symptoms after returning from a trip to Wuhan.

February 11, 2020
The World Health Organization announced a name for the new coronavirus disease: COVID-19.

March 5, 2020
As of this date, Westport, did not have a single known case of the coronavirus. That evening, fifty party-goers gathered at a home in Westport to celebrate a friend's 40th birthday. A writing classmate was one of them.

March 8, 2020
More than 100 countries have reported cases of COVID-19.

Westport Library hosts a COVID-19 information town hall moderated by Mark Cooper, director of health, Westport Westin Health District.

March 10, 2020
Due to the coronavirus the Westport Library has canceled all classes (including this one) for the month of March.

There is a three-hour starting delay in Westport schools so teachers can prepare for possible closure. Connecticut Governor Lamont declares state of emergency.

March 11, 2020
The World Health Organization declares the coronavirus outbreak a pandemic.

March 12, 2020
Westport Library and Westport Public Schools close.

March 2020

Tuesday March 17, 2020
St Patrick's Day

Daniel has been home from college since Saturday. We're on the cusp of the four to five-day window for signs of the coronavirus to rear its ugly head. I feel so bad for him. The last semester of his senior year, quarantined at home with Mom and Dad.

I drove to my mom's house on Long Island this morning. Bright side, no traffic. Tomorrow she turns 85. My two older sister's Dianne and Lorine will join us in celebration.

Is this total stupidity? Visiting my mom when breaking news is telling us the elderly are the most vulnerable. We're three potential carriers, my sisters and I. What the hell are we thinking? Do I have a fever or am I having a hot flash? Is the ache in my lower back a flu symptom or is it from gardening yesterday afternoon? Should I have stayed home? Too late now.

Meanwhile my daughter Michelle, her boyfriend and their cat have just arrived at my house in Connecticut. She's coming from NYC where the governor cautioned all New Yorkers to assume they've been exposed.

Deep breath.

Morgaine

Tuesday, March 17, 2020
Rapunzel, Rapunzel...

But it is not a tower in which I am isolated. It is my garret art studio above the garage, where I spend most of my days working at my easel while removed from human contact. Now there is an actual human in the driveway below, a friend delivering groceries!

1

I throw open the large window, breathe in the air freshened by the morning's rain, and lean out as far as I can.

"Thanks so much, Dede! I really appreciate your help."

"How are you feeling? Are you going to get tested?"

I have been in close contact with someone who tested positive for COVID-19. I have a sore throat, dry cough, headache, and low-grade fever. Tick, tick, tick down the list of possible symptoms.

"I have a video appointment with my doctor tomorrow so I can get a prescription for testing. We'll see what happens. Symptoms are mild, but I'm a cancer survivor and a senior. I'm on the fence, ethically. So few tests... so many people who might be in worse shape than I."

"Got it. And got most of the stuff you wanted. Only two avocados. Trader Joe's is setting a limit of two per customer for any single item. And only one shopping cart to keep folks from hoarding necessities."

These are the conversations we have these days. My daughter in Belgium shares on a family text thread that they are in lockdown and there is no toilet paper anywhere. She and her husband are down to a roll and a half. Many bathroom jokes ensue. Maybe I can sell my roll of Dump Trump paper on eBay for a small fortune. Maybe I should mail it to her. Even the most mundane activity under normal conditions is exceptional now. We, who are accustomed to mountains of convenience, are receiving a huge wake-up call.

My cousin jokes that she is not sure her marriage will survive spending 24/7 together. I wince a little bit, thinking how much I would love to have my husband here.

I do have my beloved dog, Arlo. "Yup. Have the same problem. Arlo and I never have issues, but these days we're constantly fighting over the best spot on the couch. He's threatening to leave me and get his own doghouse."

I am not bored. I work at home on things I love—art and writing. But the classes I teach are suspended, so my scanty income has dried up like a desert. I count on friends, family and getting out in the world to counter the aloneness of the solitary hours of my workday and the twenty-four-hours-a-day of widowhood. Life as I know it has come to a screeching halt for the second time in two years.

Deb

Tuesday, March 17, 2020

It is quiet today, very quiet. The day broke with rain, but now the sun is shining through a cloud-streaked sky. Daylight lingers now that we've pushed the clock an hour forward. I like that.

It is the eve of my 83rd birthday. Two days ago, it was Marvin's turn: the anniversary of his birth. He would have been 86. I wonder what he'd say or do, of the days we are living now?

It is hard to believe that such an impossible thing could happen. But here it is. "It" being the novel coronavirus.

I am one of the lucky ones. My children call to ask for my safety. Both have declared their intention to either commit me if I dare to venture to a place with crowds—I had kiddingly said I was going to Costco—or sealing my door shut. But, not to worry. I've behaved and have remained at home with my little four-legged friend Archie and lots of books. Until just now, I've not been able to write so this virally is a good thing.

One thing worries me (really? only one??). I am fearful for the presidential elections in November. Already we've had a governor cancel primaries. Should this situation worsen and continue into the fall and winter, I would not trust this president to not postpone the elections so as to maintain his tenure in office. Perhaps I am overthinking—I tend to do that—or over-worrying—I tend to do that, too. Maybe tomorrow my spirit will lift.

Maria

3

Tuesday, March 17, 2020

Even though we're starting this journal sharing process tomorrow night (maybe), I'm starting tonight since I want to flex my daily writing muscles. I need some structure. This is a different way of keeping a journal. Usually, I write about the day's happenings or anything that stands out from the day by hand in a specific notebook—Clairefontaine graph paper in a spiral notebook. I like the regularity of the squares on the paper and the smooth feel of the paper and its color. Haven't found the right pen yet that I can afford—something that feels good in my hand, not too thin or too thick, just the right amount of heft and balance and a thin, even, dark line of ink. I know pens exist that fit this description—but I haven't really looked.

I can already see how typing rather than writing and the structure that typing imposes is affecting my writing: I'm going back and editing, which I never do in my handwritten journal. I'm going to try and stop that.

It's been a lazy day—I find I can sleep much more than I should. Last night was the last time that Meadow Ridge residents formally met together for dinner. As of today, we are required to order our food from an extensive menu and pick it up in the lobby of whatever building we live in. I didn't have dinner with anyone last night—hadn't planned to—but at least when I went to our bistro, I saw people and was able to chat with them briefly. Today I haven't been out of the apartment, and I haven't thought about what I'm wearing. All activities are canceled, and visitors are banned.

What did I do? Found out about a Zoom meditation group that my regular Thursday morning group has set up; answered all my emails; watched a series of YouTube videos about the adventures of Stella, a blonde Labrador retriever, that reminded me of the dog we used to have.

Finally decided to do something productive, so I started reading the 32 essays that have been submitted to the TEAM Westport essay contest; the topic is stereotyping. There's a long description of the topic that I won't bore you with. I'm the lead judge; three other people are on the committee. I've read nine— two are spectacular, three are maybes, the rest are not in the running. At this rate I'll be finished in three days. That's okay since we won't be handing out awards for the foreseeable future. Before the virus, the awards ceremony was scheduled for April 2, 2020, at the library.

This seems monumentally boring to even write about—are we sure we want to do this?

Judy

Tuesday, March 17, 2020

Saint Patrick's Day. I put on a green tank top and sweater, setting off the sterling silver good luck shamrock necklace whistle Stan had given me years before. For a Polish husband, he was always clever at finding ways to delight my Irish Celtic sentiments.

Granddaughters home schooling starts in earnest. Teachers will be available online from 8 AM to 3 PM and will be grading assignments.

Find out that my niece's wedding shower is canceled. June 20th wedding is… what?

Dentist's office is closing until further notice.

Watch the White House daily coronavirus briefing. I confess it. I am totally fascinated by ambassador/doctor/US army colonel Deborah Birx. She presents a calm, levelheaded, realistic assessment of what's going on. Plus, I am intrigued by her sense of fashion. Can't wait to see what she'll wear next. She's definitely a scarf person.

Dig into the valuation analysis for a $10 million construction company whose stock price had increased 712% over the past year. Monica and I tried out a Zoom conference call platform that would allow us to set up audio/visual and screen sharing capabilities for us and our clients.

None of us have been out of the house nor have we had any visitors since March 11th. So far, so good. Girls sing, dance, do laundry, vacuum, feed their fish, play games on their iPads, facetime with their friends on their iPhones, make cookies, and sketch. Ryan practices her lines and songs for her part as Dorothy in the Connecticut Music Theater's production of *Wizard of Oz*. Don't know when or if it will be performed. Their dance competitions in March and April are canceled.

Gina

Wednesday, March 18, 2020

Hi all, the first few days of this emergency, I felt lazy, unable to make myself do anything much except touch my face and scold myself while washing my hands and singing "Happy Birthday" twice to myself on the Kazooka. Utterly unfocused, I dragged through the day. I thought vaguely about all the things I might do in the house but did none of them. I felt disappointed in myself. I slumped on the couch. I watched a lot of TV which made me even more disappointed in myself. The only routines I followed were red wine at 5:00 PM, along with salty corn chips.  Dinner was at any time I could bring myself to microwave whatever from the freezer, followed by binge watching TV while binge eating ice cream.

Remember *Bridge on the River Kwai*? Wasn't it Alec Guinness who kept up his troops' morale by making sure they marched information and brushed their teeth daily? So, I've been very good about brushing my teeth, and marching daily, weather permitting, at Sherwood Island, but that's about all I did. The rest of my daily hygiene—except for hand washing through 2 choruses of "Happy Birthday" a few times a day—has gone to hell. I take infrequent showers, don't apply any makeup, wear the same clothes for days, and eat whatever's handy. If this pandemic lasts long enough, I may find how must how much of my hair is still red. I'm learning a lot about myself. When the chips are down, I'm a slob.

After about a week, I came to life. I must have been what they call "depressed," but I'll save how I went sane in tomorrow's virally. (It has something to do with making myself write by convincing my classmates that writing would be good for them.)
Mary-Lou

P.S. Not a bit incidentally, Deborah has told us that she might be infected—we hope only mildly. At the same time, I heard about Deborah, this morning's New York Times' *op ed page featured a piece in which Deborah's and Dave's inspiration, the therapist Esther Perel, was quoted in an article entitled "Marriage During the Coronavirus." I love a coincidence.*
Mary-Lou

Wednesday, March 18, 2020
Abstinence Makes the Heart Grow Fonder—Unless We Get Divorced First

My husband came down with a 102-degree fever and a cough on Friday. The minute that thermometer left his mouth, I left the room and haven't been back since. He has been quarantined for five days, and I've moved to a different floor of the house. Aside from a few business trips that kept us apart, this is the longest we've gone without touching each other since we met.

Now that we can't be in the same room, I am so aware of how physical we are; how much that makes us feel loved.

My husband always likes to intertwine our hands, but his fingers are so bony it hurts, so I curl my fist inside his palm—our bizarre way of holding hands. We give each other friendly shoves to see who can get in the house first. We sit on the couch: our thighs touching, or his feet on my lap, or his arm around me, or my head on his shoulder. He hooks a finger in my belt loop when I try to stand up and pulls me back down to kiss me. I drape myself around him while he pays the bills on his laptop. He comes up behind me when I'm in the kitchen (always at the worst times!) when I'm stir-frying or taking a tray out of the oven, and he bites my ear or snuffles my neck, while I squirm out of his grasp, half-annoyed and half-turned on, saying, "Hot stove! Hot stove!" Even in the car, we touch each other: he grabs my hand and puts it on the nape of his neck. Or he says, "Nobody's checking me," which means, "Take your hand and fluff the hair on the back of my head." When we sleep, we find each other: back-to-back, toes to leg, an arm curled over a chest. He reaches out his hand to me in the morning when his alarm goes off at 5:30, a little squeeze on my shoulder before he leaves. But now there's none of that.

I miss him, but I am also supremely irritated by him now. I have become Beck-and-Call-Nurse-Waitress and I'm sick of it. I go up and down the stairs with water, popsicles, Tylenol, rice, pasta, salad, a hot water bottle, a fruit cup, tea, a thermos, more tea. I knock and run away. He leaves the dishes in the hall, and I put them in the dishwasher and scrub my hands like a surgeon. He asks for charging cables, books, a folding chair, a TV tray. I go up and down the stairs some more.

When his fever was very high, he was kind and grateful and said, "Thank you, thank you, you're so nice," every time he heard me outside his door. But his fever broke on Sunday and now that he's feeling better, he has turned sarcastic and demanding. When I ask how he's feeling, he coughs and says, "How do you *think* I'm feeling?" as if I'm an idiot. He's mad that we're out of bananas and accused me of "poor planning." He's tired of being cooped up in one room. He's tired of talking through the door and me saying, "WHAT?! WHAT?! Okay, Mumbles!" because I can't make out what he's saying. He's tired of texting me, and me not responding because I left my phone in the other room and didn't hear it ping. We are tired of each other. And the longer we don't touch each other, the more we both stop caring.

Through a closed door, I cannot see how cute he is; how his silly expressions always soften my anger and make me laugh, even when I don't want to laugh. I can't kiss the side of his neck or stroke his bristly sideburns. I can't smell his smell, which always reminds me of pencil shavings and hotel soap. I can't put my head on his chest and cry.

So many of our arguments, our temper tantrums, our fears and stress are resolved by our bodies. That "oh, come on," nudge, raised eyebrows and sweet smile; that "you know you want a piece of this!" swagger that makes us giggle. We touch each other and it's all okay. We are okay.

Nine... more... days.

Lynn

Wednesday, March 18, 2020

Running low on milk for girls. Thought I needed more than one supplier to keep us stocked. Re-ignited my account with Fresh Market and got a delivery within the hour. Good to have more than one source. Can't get everything in the same place.

Girls are using up my paper and ink with school homework. Ordered more supplies from Staples (the office supply place, not the high school).

So sad, but not surprising, to see some of my personal service places closed down. Posh Nails in Westport for pedicures, H Salon in Southport for haircuts. Need to get a pair of slacks tailored but hesitate to go to Gino's of Rome (Italy) or Bae's (China) until the crisis passes. These businesses are all fantastic. I also need to get to Renato Jewelers for watch batteries at some point.

Finished another valuation analysis for work, and more reports are flooding in. A busy time for me.

The pregnant niece is sad about canceling her baby shower, as is her sister who was to have a wedding shower this coming weekend.

Monica, the girls, and I went for a long walk around the block for an hour—Bulkley to Greens Farms to Clapboard Hill to Maple, to Post Road and home. Kept our distance from other humans, although one couple thought we were avoiding their dogs.

Girls and I took a lot of photos of spring buds showing up. Grateful for a sunny afternoon.

And yes, Ambassador Birx had another delish scarf at the WH briefing today.

Gina

Wednesday, March 18, 2020
Coping with Corona—at least I think I am.

I like alone time. I used to call these days my "snow days" as I revert to those in the classroom.

Am I enjoying them this week? Yup, but the promise of a month or more, or even more, makes me think: not so much.

Spending this unforeseen amount of time with my husband, (who doesn't always put in his hearing aids), the ubiquitous Fox News, our dog who is hanging onto life by a silver thread, and a blank calendar make me determined not to complain, go out for a walk every day, do custodial things like cleaning out my file cabinet, and finish up writing assignments that I've procrastinated and probably won't get published anyway due to everything closing or, in my case, the newspapers where I'm published going under for lack of advertisers.

Yesterday I thought that that the only stores necessary to sustain life as I know it are grocery stores, bookstores, and wine stores. An owner of a bookstore I'm writing about thinks that Trump will close down ALL retail by the end of the week. Then what?

Polly

Wednesday, March 18, 2020
11:11 PM

Make a wish.

If only it were that simple.

How can I sleep when the suffering of the planet, with no end in sight, is surging through my veins?

Tough day.

Morgaine

Wednesday, March 18, 2020

Quarantine, Day 3. Received more than 100 texts, 26 WhatsApp messages. Two FaceTime calls, four phone calls. Zero personal contact.

It begins very early, with my daughter in Belgium forgetting about the five-hour time difference, or my friend who rises at 5:00 nimbling her fingers for the coming day. My phone is always on and nearby, ready to alert me if my almost 98-year-old mother has an emergency. Each time it dings at an ungodly hour I am convinced that she has been rushed to the emergency room, or worse. Instead, it is the beginning of a string of texts and messages about the absurdities of life in this day and time. It may keep me bleary-eyed, but it also keeps me amused and connected.

The highlight today was a video from my cousin Robbie, age 42. A bright unicorn seemed to mouth words in Robbie's 6'6" deep voice, reminding those he loves to wash their hands for thirty seconds, or in the case of my son, thirty minutes. They are like brothers, and I couldn't stop watching it or laughing. I responded on our family text thread, "Thank god I'm a member of this family."

I mean it. The silliness is balanced by serious and insightful political commentary. They are a socially conscious bunch. Their humor and intelligence are such a safety net always, but especially in this really challenging time.

It is real for me. On Friday I will have a "drive-by testing" to see if I have COVID-19. It will be nearly a week from now before I have results. If positive, I will begin another two weeks or more of quarantine from the day I receive the results. In the meantime, I will not leave my property, nor have personal contact with other people. It is a great time for reflection, for seeing how I can help

in small ways, for practicing self-control in terms of attitude.

And it's a great time for drawing. The portrait attached with this virally entry is about 80% complete. Maybe it will reach 100% tomorrow. It is David in what we called his "mad professor" days, when he was brainstorming furniture designs. It has elicited the same response from every person to whom I have shown it and knew him, "Those hands!" They were distinctive, and equally eloquent as his words. It's why I chose the pose. The little sketchbooks were ubiquitous. I found them in his desk drawers, his night table, in the bathroom vanity with his toothbrush, in a bin on the coffee table in the den. Many of them remain poised for him to continue his musings on the parabolic desks he was designing.

My musings are on the best way to post art projects of interest to all ages. Last night's news reported a spike in gun sales—lines out the doors of gun shops. Many first-time gun buyers feeling they will have to protect their families and food supplies form marauders. Make art, not war, my friends, art not war. Maybe I can help us do so just a little bit.

Deb

Wednesday, March 18, 2020

The day began lazily. Got up at 7:30 and tried to break the habit of a light breakfast and then back to bed for "a minute" which usually means I sleep until the Brian Lehrer 10 AM show starts on NPR. So I had coffee, went for a two mile walk, had breakfast and then succumbed to the bed.

At 9:45 a call from Jill, daughter #3, awakened me. She explained that she was now working from her Manhattan home. She reviews legal documents through a temporary agency. Yesterday she told the agency owner that he should let his 30 lawyers work from home since people were coughing and sneezing around her. Another lawyer threatened to sue the owner if she got sick from the working conditions.

"But my throat hurts and my chest is tight," Jill added. "I'm in the drugstore to buy Ibuprofen."

"No!" I was adamant. "No ibuprofen! If you have the virus, ibuprofen will suppress your white blood cells. Then they won't be able to fight off infection." Hadn't she read the three Covid-19 articles I'd sent to her and her sisters? I had thought that Jill was the most likely to read them since she focuses on detail and logic. It's not the first time I've misjudged a daughter.

I went back to one of the articles about prevention and procedures. What did Jill need that she probably didn't have? An oximeter to measure the percentage of oxygen in the blood. I ordered it from Amazon. I don't usually act so quickly, but I know why I did in this case. An oximeter replaces me and my perceived ability to keep my daughters safe. I am always ready to battle the real and imagined monsters under the bed.

Five minutes later daughter #2, Fern, called from Boston. She's working from home, as is her husband; their two teenaged daughters are home too. It sounded noisy. I mentioned Jill.

"She should go to the hospital," Fern insisted. "I'll find out which one is best. Talk to you later."

Ten minutes later Fern had discovered through her cousin, a Columbia University professor, that Columbia Presbyterian is the preferred hospital. "Stay away from Harlem Hospital," he cautioned. Fern has told the ER that Jill is coming in, and she's told Jill where the entrance is. Jill agrees to go.

Then the oldest daughter, Kim, weighs in from Los Angeles. Kim claims Jill shouldn't go to the ER. If she doesn't have the virus, she's sure to catch it there. Fern counters that breathing difficulties run in the family—she has underlying asthma. I was asthmatic as a child—and therefore Jill needs to be seen. Kim suggests telemedicine; isn't there a way to contact a doctor by Skype or Zoom? Kim and Fern are having a text argument

They exchange six texts in 30 minutes, each arguing for their perspective. At least they're not punching each other as they did as children, and they're not coming to me to resolve the argument. As the texts fly, Jill has found a way to teleconference a doctor who prescribes albuterol. We find that out when there's a lapse in the sister text wars.

Everyone's satisfied: Jill's getting immediate medical care. We'll all be keeping an eye on her. There are secondary satisfactions too. Fern has acted quickly and definitively and has drawn on family contacts. She's the glue for the family as I take a step (well, maybe ½ step) back. Kim has offered a fresh perspective; she's the most technologically savvy of the three. I have seen again that my 50-something daughters can navigate this world without the expertise I imagine I have. They can fight whatever monsters lurk under the bed, in the closets, under the stairs. Jill has seen that her sisters care about her. Two days ago, she'd told me they didn't.

And it's the first time I've seen a text war!

Judy

Wednesday, March 18, 2020

Today began as most days do, normal days that is, although days are not normal now. But I followed the usual routines: shower, let Archie out, feed him, and then my breakfast—coffee at last!

The sun was shining so we went for a walk along the river, the path bordering the library and the Levitt Pavilion. It's so tranquil there. Last year I saw a heron by the riverbank. He was almost hidden among the limbs of a tree that had collapsed into the water's edge. This year only mallards and gulls have ventured onto the mudflats. It's still too chilly for egrets and herons. I'll keep looking.

The incoming tide sent ripples on the surface, and it was a happy thing to see that the water is crystal clear. I wonder if all the timbers that are scattered along the river's edge were once part of homes or bridges? There are so many of them darkened now by their time in the mud.

When I returned home, I received two phone calls conveying birthday wishes. That was nice—being remembered is most often nice. The phone, however, did not seem to be in a jolly mood as it kept cutting out.

Then the CO2 alarm started beeping and when I pulled it away from its plug, thinking to silence it, it instead gave out a continuous shriek that would have woken the dead. To say I am challenged by mechanical things is an understatement, so I called my son, who came over and took out the thing's battery.

The day ended with a delicious meal at my daughter and son-in-law's home. After dinner: short ribs in an incredibly luxurious gravy, roasted potatoes, and salad, we watched a movie: *The Good Liar* with Helen Mirren and Ian McKellen. It's on Amazon and well worth the $$.

At 10:30 Archie and I were back home, snug in our bed. And so until tomorrow. It's been quite a birthday!

Maria

Wednesday, March 18, 2020

Henry Miller speaks to me every morning from the note on my desk. He says what I want to contribute, only much better. So my first contribution to our dialogue is, hopefully, forgivable plagiarism

> *Dear diary, if you are not a cripple or an invalid, if you have your health, if you still enjoy a good walk, a good meal with all the trimmings, if you can sleep without first taking a pill, if the birds and flowers, mountains and sea still inspire you, you are a most fortunate individual and you should get down on your knees morning and night and thank the good Lord. If you can fall in love again and again, if you can forgive your parents for the crime of bringing you into the world, if you are content to get nowhere, just take each day as it comes, if you can forgive as well*

as forget, if you can keep from growing sour, surly, bitter and cynical, MAN you have it made.

I am off to Earth Animal to restock on bird food and then come home to enjoy watching the fat, backyard squirrels invade the overflowing bird feeders.

Ken

Thursday, March 19, 2020

1:15 PM—Waiting for the furniture to arrive. I shall finally have an honest-to-goodness desk. Then I shall busy myself transferring my writing—now and always scattered on the dining room table and in multiple files—to the newly arrived desk, bookcase/file cabinets. It'll be good to have something to do during another day of confinement.

2:35 PM—The two delivery men just left—all went well. No nicks in the walls, no mud prints on the carpet. It will take me a while to get used to the furniture. I'm weird that way, they seem like interlopers. Time will pass and then it'll be okay. I don't like change, even inconsequential as these two pieces may be. I loved the way the guest room looked, but in truth, it was merely an attractive museum. In the almost three years I've been here, the guest bed has been used three times.

My daughter calls me. She's going grocery shopping tomorrow and wants me to send over a list. I take a photo of it and text it to her. For the next two hours I text additions.

I pay a bill and worry about the post office staying open. How to get stamps then? I continue to pay my bills the old-fashion way: write a check, mail it. Paying bills online is not a safe alternative for me; I've been known to transpose numbers and/or place a decimal point where it doesn't belong.

Earth Animal is open and Archie and I drive over and stock up. He's now good for about two weeks. When I pull into the

17

garage, I don't get out of the car immediately. My hands, the steering wheel, and the door handle get swabbed with Clorox wipes.

5:30 PM—I feed Archie, pour myself a glass of wine and have leftovers from my birthday.

7 PM—PBS News Hour. Finish *Marley*—a good book.

10 PM—Bedtime comes and we climb the stairs to my room.

Maria

Thursday, March 19, 2020

The enormity of the 2020 crisis is overpowering me. As a "news junkie," I am comfortable absorbing heaps of information, but the coronavirus is threatening my capacity to navigate through normal life. The trajectory of the virus and its multi-faceted components appear to be more than I can handle emotionally. I am comfortable managing my life, caring for family, taking in the Middle East, learning about climate change, following the primaries, and being worried about how harsh life is for too many people, but having to monitor the health of the world and being a witness to the unraveling of the financial systems is impacting both my psyche and my moods.

I read recently how emotions are the brain's way of responding to a crisis. Historically and most commonly, crisis comes in the form of a single event and the brain constructs an emotional response to it as part of a plan. But, with today's 24/7 news cycle, crises come in waves overpowering our brains capacity to effectively absorb them. The results are often frustration, depression and illness. Until two weeks ago, I thought I was fine. Now, not so sure.

So, on this first day of recording daily life with the coronavirus, I will practice a more focused pattern of thinking, limit my access to reported news, and absorb events in my immediate surroundings. Not an easy thing to do for an addicted multitasker. I will report on my progress tomorrow.

Ken

Thursday, March 19, 2020

Meals have gone haywire: my son and I have fend-for-yourself-breakfast; my husband gets coffee delivered on a tray. Lunch has moved to 3 PM: takeout or left-over takeout, or wilted salad or Top Ramen. *(—If there is Top Ramen, is there Bottom Ramen? That's what it feels like we're eating.)* Dinner has all but disappeared. I think my son is living on fancy Swedish chocolate bars that he has hidden on top of the fridge.

I have never enjoyed cooking and feel even less inclined to do it now. I only make dinner so the three of us can sit down and be together as a family. Since we can't be together, what's the point? My son and I sit in front of the TV at 7 PM. He'll eat an entire box of Triscuits. I have lost my appetite. My husband texts me from upstairs, "When do the animals get fed in the zoo?" Poor thing. Forgotten up there.

Groceries will hopefully be delivered between 2 and 4 PM, but I forgot to order bananas, butter, bagels, bread—as if my brain just forgot the letter B existed. I contemplate going to Stew Leonard's. I also contemplate lying to my husband and telling him Whole Foods was out of bananas, because this time he'd be right: poor planning. Amazon is texting me, more than a dozen times, telling me many of the items I ordered are not in stock anyway. They offer to substitute millet for rice. I decline. *Millet?* I wonder if I will reach a point where I am not so picky.

Lynn

Thursday, March 19, 2020

I'm awake. It's five-thirty AM. I'm in a twin-size bed in my mother's guest room with her cat Rosebud huddled against my thigh. Contact. I lay there for twenty minutes digesting my new reality.

ShopRite opens at six. The six to seven-thirty time slot is reserved for senior citizens. Of which I am, apparently. *Huh.*

At 6:10 I turn on my cell-phone flashlight, I get up and put on the clothes I wore yesterday. I'll strip down when I get home, throw everything in a plastic bag and get right into the shower.

The parking lot is not empty. In gloves, a scarf mask and armed with a list of necessities to get Mom through the next couple of weeks, I grab a cart and enter the semi-stocked supermarket. Dystopia. But I refuse to go there. Get what you need and get out—Quick!

There's an encounter in isle five, with an over friendly stock boy. He insists on showing, rather than telling me, which isle I can find almond butter. I tighten my scarf and keep my distance. There's a line at the *one* open cash register. I take my place and warn the woman behind me that I'll be running back for ice cream as we get closer. We recognize the horror in each other's eyes. She shares her ambivalence in leaving the house.

"I'm here getting supplies for my mother who just turned eighty-five yesterday—surreal!"

Another register opens up. I'm third in line. I run to the freezer to find amongst a whole lot of cookie dough ice cream, the last Neapolitan. Mom's favorite. *Thank you!*

At the register I fill three reusable bags as if my life depends on it. Nothing is going in. The bags only collapse in on themselves. My hands are shaking. *Stop. I must take hold of myself.* Somehow, I do. Before I know it, groceries are loaded and I'm back in my car. I tear off my gloves and scarf and roll them up into a ball of dark wash. There's a tickle in my throat. I can only hope its acid reflux.

Instead of hugging my mother goodbye I rub the back of her bathrobe, while Rosebud circles my feet.

Before getting onto the highway, I stop at the gas station, where gas is $2.19. I pay cash. *Oh shit.* I picked up the gas nozzle without gloves and there are no wipes in my glove compartment. I drive the entire hour and forty-five-minutes back to Westport scratching my itchy nose with my sleeve.

Home!

"Wash your hands," says my daughter the minute I walk in the door.

Morgaine

Thursday, March 19, 2020

If *Westport Now* is a reliable source, then Westporters are taking an especially hard hit from the coronavirus. The news sent me swiftly from denial to acceptance. Along with acceptance came fear, like a tight fist in my chest. Then a few hours later, I watched Trump's press conference and heard him warn viewers that they shouldn't believe anything that they read in *The New York Times, The Washington Post,* or the *Wall Street Journal.* Anger took the place of fear. How dare our liar in chief take on three of the most reliable and esteemed newspapers in our country. It was bad enough when he talked about "fake news" over matters not quite so dire as the threat of global annihilation, but this time he, this man in charge of saving us from ourselves and defeating this pandemic, has, himself, become the "enemy of the people." Perhaps these newspapers will take him to task in some effective way that I cannot imagine as hard as I try, since Trump can rely on his cultish base to blindly believe him, no matter what. Enough of this; I'm getting ranty.

I am no longer dragging my butt around. I am continuing to brush and floss. I have awakened from my torpor. This morning Larry and I put on our vinyl gloves and went shopping. Our emphasis was on purchasing foods that don't need to be frozen or refrigerated, such as spaghetti and meat sauce in jars. We finally get it that we're in this for the long run. We also bought some prepared fresh foods to eat in the next few days, so that we don't have to rely on our freezer, which is full. Then we went home and put away everything but a box of Duncan Hines brownie mix which I baked and ate, ruining my dinner, which is anything that is about to go bad in the fridge. Then, I ordered a bunch of "unavailable, if ever" sanitizing products from Amazon.

I am with you writers who feel overwhelmed by fear and compassion. However threatened, we are the lucky ones. We are inconvenienced, but millions of Americans are or will be ruined, financially and spiritually. We don't have to go to work to unload the groceries that we can afford to buy. We can stay warm, even entertained. I'm with those who are wondering why we should spend billions bailing out huge lobbying, tax-break-receiving corporations or industries like the airlines. Uh oh. I feel another rant coming on.

I'm enjoying keeping this virally—it keeps me writing—and it keeps me in touch with you during this terrible time. Maybe we're writing a book! And, those writers who haven't yet joined in, please do, however brief your messages may be. We want to know what you're thinking and how you're faring.

Mary-Lou

Thursday, March 19, 2020
Virally we roll along, roll along…

I have a friend who loves superlatives. We joke about the differences between us. "Have the bestest, bestest day," she will sign off. "Have a day," is my response.

It's been a day. More like dragging along, than rolling along. Whatever I have, Covid-19 or otherwise, I am tired. I find the hardest thing is making sure my playful labradoodle gets enough exercise. But I resisted wearing the same outfit for the fourth day in a row and varied the sweatshirt. I did spend some time on my hair, only because my kids will each FaceTime at least once a day.

Found some normalcy in getting work done on political commitments. Feels good to be working to end the orange reign of terror. And I'm co-chair of a group promoting census participation. Corona is just another example of why this is so important. Data from the census will determine funding for health clinics, desperately needed in this crisis. I have insurance; many of our most vulnerable people do not and rely on these clinics.

I have conversations with my TV and radio. More like tantrums. The news leaves me yelling at whatever device is reporting the bias and inadequacies of the American response to the virus. I am addicted to it and cannot give it up.

But there are highlights, and personal relationships to balance the global and national pictures. I had a very long phone call with my four-year-old grandson, who had just watched the *Wizard of Oz* for the first time. Usually, he's a little tornado of activity you catch on the fly. But he stayed with that phone call long enough to recount the entire movie, and to ask my opinion about whether the wicked witch of the west could ever come to his house? We discussed the finer points of brooms that breathe fire, monkeys that "definitewy are **not** wike Curious George because he's nice and can't fwy," and most importantly, that you can always find a way home to the safety of mom and dad.

Later, I had a half-hour talk with my son, the little guy's father. My son is bright, extremely politically savvy, and very funny. It is a rare luxury to have so much time to spend communicating with family and friends. In many ways, life has morphed into the tortoise in a region where it is distinctly the hare under normal conditions.

This will bring out the best and the worst in people, as all crises do. I am really moved by the outpouring of offers to shop for what I need while in total quarantine. How can one feel truly alone considering that?

Deb

Thursday, March 19, 2020

A surprise start to my day—a FaceTime visit with my oldest grandson, Langston, who turned 23 yesterday. We had planned to meet at my sister's house in Maryland this week, but you know what happened to those plans. We were all disappointed because we adore Langston.

He and I talked aimlessly as we always do. He's in nursing school after being directionless for a few years—left college (too Republican, he said of the Maine state school), ran a head shop for his ex-girlfriend's father, managed an eyeglasses retail store, went to LA to live with his mother and become an actor, worked construction, thought about joining the Navy, preferably the SEALs. When I pointed out that he might die in a SEAL operation, he replied with 21-year-old bravado.

"Someone has to, Judy."

I pushed back. "You're worth more to this country alive than dead. I know two Navy men that I can introduce you to, but not before you tell your mother about your plans. Or does she already know?" That was the last I heard of the SEALs.

Today we talked about how we read. He listens to audiobooks on the drive to school—mostly science fiction—has racked up 1000 hours in the past two months. I only listen to audiobooks on the treadmill; currently I'm listening to the *Dune* series, a sci fi series he told me about. It's slow going since I walk mostly outside so I can listen to the birds and watch spring come.

Then we moved on to hair. His is long, black and curly.

"What happened to the man tail you wore at Christmas?" I asked.

"That was my hipster look. Now I'm gonna French braid it."

"That'll be your Black look," I commented. A little dangerous, I thought, to advertise your race when you don't have to. But you'll have to figure that out for yourself, kiddo.

I talked about my hair which is now too long. Should have had it cut two weeks ago and now my NYC hairdresser is closed. "Guess I'm letting it grow out. I'll ask your mother what she uses to get hers to curl and crinkle."

"Yeah, she knows everything about hair. She knows everything about everything." He's smirking.

"I know she does, Langston. Even when she doesn't." Now we're laughing outright at the foibles of Kim, his mother, my daughter.

Judy

Thursday, March 19, 2020

Wow! Stop & Shop is setting aside shopping hours from 6 AM to 7:30 AM for seniors only. Only it isn't just the seniors who show up. Are these the same folks who form the lines of first-time gun buyers?

Monica gets a call from Liquor Locker where we haven't shopped since moving to our new neighborhood three years ago. She compassionately places an order and will pick it up curbside.

I participate in two conference calls organized by The ESOP Association (Employee Stock Ownership Plan). It is now operating completely remotely. Folks are ramping up their Zoom skills to facilitate meetings. TEA may be sponsoring more webinars in the future. Meetings will be re-thought and focus along geographic lines… one-day meetings, no overnight hotel stays, no airline flights. No placing the organization in vulnerable hotel contract cancelation clauses. Membership is now the only revenue driver.

I tease my paramedic son about using a bandana for a facemask. He assures me that as a trained firefighter he has his own protective gear. My daughter-in-law is back at her nursing job at Hennepin County Medical Center in Minneapolis. She sounds upbeat.

Gina

Thursday, March 19, 2020

Hi there, yesterday I was walking with a "new" friend in Ridgefield. I've started reaching out to people who are interesting and who I haven't had time to get to know. Now I do. The drive to our meeting place not only gets me out of the house but lets me enjoy the daffodils that are about to burst into bloom, the new buds on the trees and the greening of spring.

During our walk, this new friend mentioned that she and her husband are now ordering curbside takeout from area restaurants. When she was signing the credit card statement the other night, she added a $50 tip. The "waitress" burst into tears.

Then we discussed our respective cleaning ladies. I mean in a world crisis, what could be more important? Should we cancel? Should we allow them in our homes? After some thought my friend said that she probably will cancel but will pay her anyway. This gave me a new awareness of how thin and fragile a line so many are walking today. I'd love your comments,

Polly

Got it, Polly. I'm thinking I may need to support local restaurants. It would be a nice change of pace. Oh! Time to watch Resistance *on PBS for three hours. So unusual to have subtitles, but many of my choices to watch do have them. It just*

means I can't browse through the Sunday Times while I watch, as I do with some shows.

A colder day to walk, but I'm glad I walked the trail again. A friend I saw there told me it's not owned by the town, so the town can't decide to close it as they have every other outdoor places. Wonder what the predicted weather tomorrow will be. May it allow for some outdoor time. That has become essential. May the week ahead bring some positive news about the health crisis and may we all remain healthy and upbeat.

Donna

Missed this one until now, Polly. You're right. It is heartbreaking to think of people who live hand to mouth and do not have resources to weather what might be a long storm. I hope as a society it might break the "all about me" mindset. Ironic that this form of immediate threat might serve to slow us down, to walk and bicycle more and drive less, than the (somewhat) more long-range threat of global warming. Anyway, a hopeful thought.

Deb

Friday, March 20, 2020

Hiya,

Sorry to have been MIA. I made the early decision to do my part to flatten the curve and closed the doors of my yoga studio well over a week ago in order to move all of our yoga classes online.

Frankly it pissed me off to no end that some of my colleagues only closed when the state actually stepped in to shut them down. My business is my sole source of income, and corona is an existential threat to my teeny tiny yoga studio, but it's also an existential threat to millions of people, and people come before dollars every time. So.

I cannot watch the liar in chief and his disgusting hate mongering in terms of the "Chinese" virus. I seethe when I read about GOP senators dumping their stock options and trading on inside information after their private senate briefing on Covid-19 in January. I rage when they bail out corporations while offering small businesses loans to be repaid, and $1000 to citizens. They don't give a single fuck about the constituents they took oaths to serve. I'll refrain from saying that I'd like to lock the entire lot of them in a room with patient zero. (Oops, looks like I accidentally said it.)

On the bright side I'm quarantined with my hunky boyfriend of 8 months—in my postage stamp of an apartment. If we survive corona and each other, I shall continue to update.

Lastly, and said with oceans of love, Mary-Lou—stay the fuck at home. Please. Larry too. Don't go shopping. When you need supplies call me and I'll bring them to you

Stay safe everyone,

Bernadette

Friday, March 20, 2020

Greetings writers, I've been enjoying reading your daily entries. Early on—before we started sharing diaries—Mary-Lou urged us to write and said there was now no excuse for handing in first drafts. Well, I don't think that applies to these reflections, for that's what you're getting. Most important for me, it was fun. Thank you for the push to write. Time becomes infinite when I do.

This is my first day without anything at all on my schedule. I do have a list—that's part of who I am—but the things on my list are all of my own choosing and can easily be put off until a later day. Such as, I want to play the piano, put on music from my college days at Michigan and dance like I'm at a fraternity party, organize the container cupboard that's been in disarray for too long—but the list has nothing pressing. No one else is counting on me to be somewhere at a specific time. There's nothing that *must* get done. Even the clean dishes in the dishwasher are patient and silent.

My goal over the next unknown number of days is to be in *an illusion of infinite time.* I first heard that phrase at a writing conference at Bard back in the 80s and I embraced it as a personal goal. However, I've orchestrated my life in such a way that it doesn't happen as often as I'd like—but I can feel it in my body when it does.

For example, in early February I dropped my daughter at the Westport station for her afternoon train back to the city. As I started to drive home, it was such a lovely day I decided to drive through Compo Beach. Then I felt like a drive around Sherwood Island would also be a treat. I knew as I drove across the bridge toward the beach, that I was in *the illusion of infinite time.* My mind wasn't chiding me with a list of things I had to accomplish. It was as if I'd stumbled into a time/space where I had all the time in the world. Time was abundant. So delicious!

This morning as I walked from opening the blinds in the living room toward the kitchen to make my decaf latte and avocado toast, the piano caught my eye. It's a shiny black baby grand that I bought for myself back in 1987. It's complicated the two moves I've made in the past decade, but I never doubt it's worth the space it takes. Often when I glance at it with the possibility of sitting down to play, I'll feel there's something more important to accomplish. My beautiful piano becomes furniture. This morning—I sat down and played for ten minutes—just enough time to experience the grace of playing before continuing with my day. There was nowhere else I had to be in that moment but seated on the piano bench with my fingers on the beckoning black and white keys. I stopped playing, thanked my beautiful musical friend and headed to the kitchen, confident I'd return later in the day.

In the *illusion of infinite time*, I can stand at the window and marvel at the buds on the trees. There's time to watch the birds flying and darting in the distance and wonder what they're thinking, is there a hierarchy to their flight pattern? I can notice a book on the bookshelf, pull it out and scan a few pages to see what I remember. You get the idea. When I'm fully in the moment, life feels sweeter, somehow expanded. I go from *concrete sequential* to *abstract random.*

Probably many people feel this way on vacation or in the company of beloved friends and family. When I play Canasta with my sisters in Michigan, joking, teasing, loving our precious time together, my familiar sense of structured time melts away. There is nowhere else I would rather be. That feeling of stepping out of time is entering a bubble of wonder.

So, I ask myself why doesn't *the illusion of infinite time* happen more often for me? It is certainly more frequent now than when I was teaching, raising my two children, packing as much as I could into each day. And certainly, in the evening when I settle in to watch a British, French or Italian TV detective series, there's nothing else I must attend to. I'm right there, grateful to have such fine and scenic shows to watch.

Years ago, a friend wrote a book, *Time: A Familiar Stranger.* What an apt title. Now that I've been given this unexpected gift of time, I anticipate the days ahead will offer many opportunities to shift my relationship to time. I intend to stop telling myself I don't have time for the pleasurable little moments. I plan to pay less attention to a looming list and to go with the flow. I hope to nudge myself toward a healthier and more satisfying way of being with Time.

Donna

Friday, March 20, 2020

Being under government orders to stay put, not to mingle, and to remain out of the virus zones, I have today pursued Donna's wise counsel of living with an *"illusion of time."*

I have no obligation to see people. No meetings. No one expects anything from me. What a blessing! So, I watched an episode of *Curb Your Enthusiasm,* thoroughly enjoying the irreverent, quirky personalities.

I found a free backgammon site on the internet and played a few games, deluding myself into thinking I could win against the rascals at the NYC gambling clubs.

A call from a neighbor required me to provide some legal assistance and I was handsomely rewarded with homemade, fried chicken.

And watching the acrobatic squirrels in my backyard circumventing the expensive obstacles intended to prevent them from raiding the birdfeeders was as satisfying as having front row seats to a Cirque de Soleil performance.

All proving that riches come in many forms.

Ken

Friday, March 20, 2020

For someone who hates to cook, who would happily live on chips and coffee, it's odd that so much of my day-to-day revolves around food: getting it, making it, cleaning up after it. It's my albatross. When I get yelled at for running out of bananas or I find my son eating his cereal dry because there's no milk, or at dinnertime when all the expectant eyes are on me—even the cat and guinea pig give me baleful stares—I find myself feeling like some sort of failure on one hand, while feeling enraged on the other. I feed myself! Why can't they?! Why is it always me?!

I don't see anyone else offering to make me a salad or pick up bananas on their way home from work. I don't eat bananas, yet I'm the one who has to make sure we have them. (*I am really hung up on the whole banana thing, apparently. It's funny the things that sting. Ten years post-virus, is this what I'll remember? The bananas?*)

31

I don't see anyone else offering to menu plan or chop a damn vegetable. And not one to ever keep my mouth shut, or suffer in silence, I've asked for help on the dinner front. They look at me like I'm crazy. Like, "This is not part of our arrangement." They go to school and work, and I wield a knife and wipe up crumbs. It's worse now than before, because now everyone is home when they used to be out. I'm on the hook for four extra meals per day.

Since Whole Foods only dropped off milk and an onion, I had to venture out. I went to Stew Leonard's, which I hate. It's the IKEA of grocery stores: a maze of people and food, where you're forced to walk all the way through. There is no surgical strike at Stew Leonard's; it is a hunter-gatherer expedition. I always feel like I should go in there with a spear and a fur-trimmed parka.

I witnessed a few horrifying things at Stew's that would not have been horrifying two weeks ago. A boy, about ten years old, was walking through the store with his mother. He touched EVERYTHING: running his hand along all the cereal boxes, picking up blocks of cheese and putting them back down. He grabbed a pack of cookies, his mother said no, he threw them down on the shelf, and three more packs fell on the floor. He picked them all up. That kid touched EVERYTHING. Suddenly I was completely skeeved out. Then it occurred to me that this must have been happening all the time. Every day. For my entire life. Every item I've ever brought home has already been snotted on and caressed by a grimy child. Oh well.

The other thing that wouldn't have previously given me pause: A man whistling over the fruit display. WHISTLING? Are you kidding me? Please, sir, spit and exhale a little more over my apples. OMG. What is wrong with people?! But two weeks ago, under those same circumstances, I would have smiled and been reminded of my dad who loved to whistle.

Stew's was generously stocked (hooray, rice!), but I don't know if I can endure going there again. I might have no choice.

Stop & Shop is out of the question. I swear that place is built on an ancient burial ground. My shoulders tense whenever I walk through the door. And once they unleashed that aisle-prowling android with the creepy eyes, I began my boycott. My husband drags me there occasionally for late-night ice cream runs and I give the robot the finger and try to get it to run into me so I can get my picture on *WestportNow*: "Woman Tackles Robot in Produce Section." *Come at me, Marty. I dare you.*
Lynn

Lynn, that description of Stew's is hysterical, and I really relate. Going back for an item you forgot is like driving the wrong way on I-95. Deadly. And the bit about the Stop & Shop robot is very funny. It is creepy. Sounds like a good time for healthy frozen dinners unless someone else wants to pitch in. No snotty fruit that way, either.
Deb

Ahh bananas—as in a 1970s rock musical (I'm having a senior moment) that used bananas erotically (use your imagination), as in "You're bananas to do XXX." And wasn't there a Woody Allen joke/film about bananas? I hate bananas—their slimy consistency, their all-encompassing smell, the way they make my tongue itch. But my husband loved them. I'd even hold my nose and eat a bunch if I could buy just a ripe banana for him one more time.
Judy

Friday, March 20, 2020
I woke up in the blissful state that Donna described so beautifully. I stayed in that state through coffee and oatmeal—time stretching endlessly before me. Then I lost it. I am an anxious person. (I don't suppose this revelation will surprise anyone.) I love to write, in part because writing puts me in that focused alpha

state where time disappears. I love to read, when I also lose my sense of time, but why I don't allow myself to read until every trivial chore is done, only attests to my habit of speeding like a water bug on the surface of my life. Listening to Trump does not, yet I can't resist wrestling with the devil. Maybe this forced, prolonged time at home will give me more of the peace I crave.

I walk on Sherwood Island with Larry, every day, weather permitting. When the sun came out at 3:30 today, weather permitted big time. We drove to the beach and immediately found that peace in nature, in watching blues of sky and sea, feeling the warmth of the sun on our backs, of enjoying crunch of shells and sand underneath our feet, and of not even talking.

I am being nourished by everyone's virallies. Now that Bernadette and Donna have joined us, we are all the richer. I'm so impressed by everyone's kindness, generosity, humor, advice, anecdotes, truth telling. Speaking of truth, the brownies are gone.

With the proliferation of virallies, I could spend the whole day just responding to everyone. I love the photos. Is it any surprise that Judy's daughter Kim is beautiful? As for Morgaine's daughter's stash of her daughter's songs, if anyone hasn't heard Michelle's beautiful voice, you should.

Mary-Lou

Friday, March 20, 2020
The desk and bookcase/files await. I begin. My condo has four flights of stairs. The basement, which was finished by the previous owner, is my "den." When I moved in, almost three years ago, I thought I'd write there, but it turns out I don't like writing without some daylight. The computer is in the basement as is the printer and my main library—but there are books everywhere. My files, too, are in the basement and I load my arms and carry them to the second floor (but really the third, counting the basement) and

place them in one of the drawers. I continue with four more trips up and down and must stop—my back really hurts.

Walgreens texts that my two prescriptions are ready. It's a good time for a break and some outdoor time. When I get to Walgreens, I buy some moisturizer and as I walk toward the pharmacy, I spy toilet paper rolls! I don't need them, but my daughter does. There aren't many, so I take four.

After the pharmacy, we head to my daughter's house—it's almost 3:30 and she is back from shopping. I give her the toilet paper and pack my groceries. Then home again.

A few more trips up and down with books and more files and I'm exhausted That's it for today. I watch the PBS News Hour. It's Friday: David Brooks and Mark Shields. They are a treat even though the subject matter is familiarly upsetting. Surfing the channels on the boob-tube, I find a movie I've seen before, but I don't care. Almost everything else seems to be about alien invasions, wars, horror—all things I don't want to watch. The movie I found is lighthearted, romantic, and its two leading actors are eye-candy: Michelle Pfeiffer and George Clooney.

Archie goes out for his last call and finally, we are in bed. I read a bit and when I've read the same sentence four times, it's lights-out time.

Maria

Friday, March 20, 2020

Seven-year-old Frances spies a chubby groundhog ambling around our backyard. Welcome back, Spring!

I watch another White House propaganda briefing, smooching at the TV screen as one secretary after another kisses the ass-in-chief who cruelly turns on a member of the press from NBC. Those of us who will miss watching the Met Gala on TV this year can be grateful for the fashion display of ambassador/doctor/colonel Debbie Birx. Another elegant dress with a scarf draped over one shoulder. I fantasize about a Biden-Birx ticket.

I spend an hour trying to clean out the leaked ink from my printer. Right now, it's telling me that I installed fake cartridges, which I might have gotten from Amazon. I need to read the fine print about the sellers on that site.

I finish another valuation report analysis, this one for a $113 million company that provides residential care for children and adults with cognitive disabilities. This is challenging work with a 63% employee turnover. I wonder how they are coping with the coronavirus.

Gina

Friday, March 20, 2020

I wake to the possibility that I may need emergency dental work as the Governor of NY tightens restrictions and businesses shut down. Connecticut is likely next. I knew eventually I was going to lose the tooth but hoped that the deep cleaning I got last week would delay the inevitable. Instead, it made it worse. My dentist said to give it a couple of days, so until tomorrow....

I work out to an online boot camp video and take a literal run to Fresh Market for 'fat free' this and 'light' that, for my figure conscious daughter, Michelle. I feel calm, compared to my excursion to ShopRite the other day.

Hubby receives a notification on his phone.

Morgaine

Saturday, March 21, 2020

Big outing for me. Went to get tested, exchanged two sentences face-to-face with each of two living, breathing humans, albeit in hazmat suits and masks.

It was a fiasco. Let it be said it is never a good idea to drink a large cup of tea before you leave for an appointment twenty-five minutes from your home, receive the wrong address to which you must report, spend additional time finding the correct location, wait in a line of cars, hear when you reach first in the line that the testing staff are taking their twenty minute lunch break, wait again, think about the five minutes for the test and the twenty-five minute return home, knowing all the while that you are surrounded by medical buildings with clean bathrooms and you can't access them because you're QUARANTINED!

I struggled with the decision to have this test or forego it so someone with worse symptoms or a more vulnerable constitution could use it. This morning there was an article in the *Washington Post* about governors in states with major cities and dense population who are declaring the window to get ahead of this virus has passed. They are moving on to the next phase, which is conservation of items necessary to combat the strain on hospitals already experiencing a shortage of beds, protective clothing, and equipment. It is too late for testing millions of people so those who are virus-free can move about while those with the virus are identified and quarantined. We have reached the point where all people need to shelter-in-place and tests should be reserved for those who have serious symptoms or are hospitalized.

When I called my doctor to get a prescription for the test, there was no clear policy. There still isn't unless you live in states like California, New York, or Maine, which require their residents to remain at home, and limit testing for those whose lives are compromised. Most of Europe is doing this, as well. And yet, last night Trump declared that his administration has acted perfectly, given that they had to build a response team from the ground up because there was nothing when he took office. Bush and Obama had teams in place; he disbanded Obama's pandemic response team that helped bring Ebola to its knees. Gggrrrrrrr.

In contrast, yesterday at home was mostly peaceful and quiet, save the constant dinging of my cell phone. Again, a mix of drawing and working on Census promotion. Two serious stick fetching sessions for Arlo. It was so warm, I had to let his old bones rest for a while and give him a water break in order to let him play as much as he wanted to. He's a good companion. I can wander the property with him and know he will stay with me. He's either in my studio when I am or lying at the base of the stairs to the studio. At night, we snuggle on the couch, which is fine as long as I have at least one hand scratching him. If I'm derelict in this duty, he looks at me woefully and paws my hand. If I pretend not to notice, he reaches over and in gentle retriever fashion, takes my whole hand into the gigantic mouth that can hold three tennis balls at one time. This is Arlo feigning viciousness, attacking me for not doing his bidding. I tell him I'm terrified as he happily wags at the attention.

Deb

Saturday, March 21, 2020

Today is my mother-in-law's birthday. She is alone in Florida. Her husband died four weeks ago. She has been busy throwing out his things. While it's sad for her, it's also empowering. There are things he kept which drove her crazy: a giant box of rusty nails; souvenir baseball caps from every place he'd ever been; papers— some important, most not. Out they all go.

"I got space in the garage now!" she crowed, thrilled. She likes things organized. She gave most of her husband's clothes to the man who cleans her pool. He was so appreciative, my MIL said, they both stood at the edge of the pool crying.

She has been spending time in her garden. She picked up ten bags of mulch at Lowes.

"It took me two trips, but I did it." She's 80. (Meanwhile, I struggle getting 5 pounds of flour in my grocery cart.) When she comes to visit us, she gardens in our garden. No one can dig a hole like my mother-in-law. Once she saw my wimpy arms lifting an inch of dirt with the spade, she rolled her eyes up to the sky and huffed,

"Oh, for god's sakes. Give it here!" She practically shoved me out of the way. She slammed the spade into the ground and forked up two cubic feet of soil. "THAT'S how you dig a hole!" She rolled her eyes again and went back to weeding.

My MIL is a *Good Morning America* junkie and every day she calls us with warnings about what to do or not do, based on what her favorite hosts say. She has been very concerned about her son, my husband. She calls morning and evening, asking for an update. My husband loves to pull her leg. He puts her on speaker phone while he tells her the most outrageous lies. When she asked if he was able to get tested, he said, "Well, they were pretty backed up, so I have to keep the swabs up my nose till I can go back on Tuesday." She believes everything he says.

"What?! That's terrible! That must be so uncomfortable! How do you sleep?" He keeps the story going for as long as he can. He winds her up to the point of cruelty almost. I feel bad for her. I shout to the phone, "Nana, don't listen. He's full of it!" My husband pouts when I spoil his fun. Sometimes right after talking to him, my MIL will call me and fact-check. I'm the Snopes of their relationship: a "well-regarded reference for sorting out myths and rumors."

For my MIL's birthday we sent her a pound of See's chocolates, nuts & chews. She called to thank us, telling us how much she loved them, how beautiful the packaging was, how she ate five pieces and then moved the wrappers around, so it didn't look like she had eaten so many. It is nice to hear her so happy. She has been sad or stressed for so long. She was her husband's caregiver and barely left the house for the last weeks of his life. Now that she is finally able to go places, she is being told not to go out. She keeps talking about the delicious chocolate. I make a mental note to buy her another box at Christmas.

"I have a sweet tooth, you know," she says. I smile. "Yes, I know. Have you tried the coconut one yet?" (Coconut is her favorite.) "There's a COCONUT ONE?! Ohhhhhh! Now I *am* excited!"
Lynn

Saturday, March 21, 2020

Woke up this morning at 10 AM, no doubt a response to having walked 4-plus miles yesterday. (That's one way to make this time fly, but I'm not recommending it.) This weekend we were supposed to visit a friend in Cambridge, MA whose husband had recently died. This friend—who's 88—lives in a small, close-knit neighborhood, so she is well cared for. So is the homeless woman who lives in her car, which she has parked on my friend's street. The neighbors keep her supplied with food.

The sunshine beckoned us outside again today. This time, for a change, we walked all over the beautiful, old, wealthy town of Southport. I'm so glad we did. In contrast to our walks in Sherwood Island, which tended to be brisk, this time we walked slowly, captivated by the gorgeous colonial, Georgian and Victorian architecture including two amazing churches. The sidewalks are made of flagstone.

I was reminded of Donna's entry about time. This walk was her kind of focused time out of time experience. We stopped often to admire the decorative curlicues, the wrought iron railings, budding flowers, ancient oaks—even the fire hydrants that are painted to look like revolutionary soldiers. We spotted a large evergreen bush onto which had been grafted a completely different species of evergreen and located the site of the graft. Weird.

Our conversation primarily took the rueful form of wondering which house we'd like to buy, assuming we had the money. There were quite a few other walkers, but we all kept our distance without any difficulty. It was "heart-warming"—an expression that I realized is both show and tell. That's just where one feels the pleasure that we felt when nearly everyone we passed smiled, waved to us, and called out "hi." How much we need community!

The reason I'm telling you all the above is to tempt you to have the same experience we so enjoyed. Plus, just in case you do, know that there's a well-stocked small store called "Switzers" and a branch of the Sono Bakery which, if you call ahead, will slip you something delicious out their front door.

Mary-Lou

Saturday, March 21, 2020

Saturday is laundry day. This is a hangover from when I worked and the weekends where when chores were done. I guess it's true: old habits are hard to break. And really, who cares? I can do laundry any day I want!!

It is now 6 PM and I've read all the virally entries and marvel at the creative expressions beautifully expressed. Thank you all.

Okay, that's it for today. I haven't anything profound to add and dinner awaits.

Take care and be well.

Maria

Saturday, March 21, 2020

A big ole turkey struts through the yard this morning. I update the Peapod order I placed on March 14 that will be delivered ten days later on March 24th. Monica drives all of us to the Audubon parking area near Sasco Beach. We go for a long walk in the sunshine, keeping our distance from the other HBs (human beings) who are out for some fresh air, too. Glad for the exercise.

Gina

Saturday, March 21, 2020

Morgaine diagrams her first day of spring, outlining all those who are close to, her creative efforts, a toothache, chores....

Morgaine

Saturday, March 21, 2020

I wanted to go to the dog park with my friend, Dede, keeping more than a six-foot difference between myself and others. The last time we did this we laughed over having to shout at one another to have a conversation. It was funny, and fun. Its trails and fields are a great place to watch the daily awakening to spring. Small purple crocuses spread their happy faces across one section of the woods. Little pink buds form on bushes lining one of the trails. They will blossom into tiny grape-like clusters. The stream rushes full of the rain we've had. Dede's dog, Sadie, grabs Arlo's floppy ears and pulls at them until they wrestle and tumble into the stream, happily cooling themselves and lapping up the fresh water.

But I couldn't go. A couple of potential buyers wanted to see my house, and though for their sakes I thought it unwise to let them in, I agreed to have them walk the property and look into windows if they wished. I needed to make sure that any Arlo bombs were removed and some sundry cleanup on the property accomplished. They never showed.

My property is over an acre, but it's beginning to feel very small. I live across from Reichert Circle, a 1950s development, and decided to take Arlo for a walk around Reichert before our usual game of fetching sticks. Big mistake! It was teeming with kids on every sort of wheeled toy, all wanting to approach and pet Arlo, none remembering about social distancing. I scurried back to my property like I'd committed a crime, feeling even more isolated after experiencing the buzzing activity across the street.

My lifelines are two text threads with family, one for the US, and one on the What'sUpApp so we can reach the Belgium crowd. It's hard to describe the irreverence of my family. They are hysterical. This is a text I sent today.

"Feel really bad about not getting tested. Wrangled with whether to cancel because of scarcity of tests, mildness of symptoms, and other things that might have been causing them. Made the wrong decision. Oh god. Not testes. Never had and never will have those. Testes. Did it again. Oh balls!"

My son-in-law commented that even if I didn't have testes, no one would argue that I didn't have balls. My son commented that he was glad I clarified.

Later the text-versation revolved around the correlation between isolation and chocolate to be delivered. Megan always has ice cream on hand for weekends when she and her husband suspend their diets and eat whatever they want. I felt deprived because I didn't have any at all. So, this is what happened…

Deb

Saturday, March 21, 2020

I was profiled at Meadow Ridge yesterday. Again. I thought it would happen. I was assured that it wouldn't. But of course, it did.

Judy

Sunday, March 22, 2020

Random Thought: The Dowager Countess in *Downton Abbey*, played by the wonderful Maggie Smith, utters one of the movie's most memorable lines when she is surrounded by young people making weekend plans. The countess breaks in and, tilting her head with a perplexed look, asks,

"What's a weekend?"

As Monday transitions into Sunday, I am asking the same question. What difference does it make if today is a Wednesday or a Sunday? Following government instructions to stay at home and to practice "social distancing" makes Wednesday feel like a Sunday. The day of the week is no longer defined by what I do in it. It feels unsettling sometimes and liberating at others. There is less to do and more to think about. I could certainly benefit from more of the latter.

Is this what retirement is like?

Ken

Ken asks if this is what retirement is like. Absolutely not! During "normal" times I have trouble fitting everything in—classes on film and a book group reading books of historical significance (we just finished Code Girls by Liza Mandy, which I highly recommend), strength and balance classes at Founders Hall in Ridgefield, volunteer work in the ED one afternoon a week, a writing group with "homework" and my freelance writing for newspapers and magazines. Now it's all come to a pause. I'm learning that you miss what you don't have, especially when it's so abrupt as this.

Polly

I guess TGIF has no relevance now. FOMO—fear of missing out—has also been usurped by Covid-19. There's absolutely nothing to miss out on. My writing conference on Zoom all day yesterday was a splendid diversion. I'm still thinking we should resume meeting on Thursday via Zoom. Right now, I'm intending to set up my Fairfield Library group on Zoom. I look forward to

*seeing their familiar faces tomorrow. What do you think? Ready
for a virtual class?*
Donna

Sunday, March 22, 2020

I'm not really showering, not really sleeping, not really eating. All
the symptoms of depression, but I don't feel depressed. I feel that
stretched-out sense of time we've all been writing about. I stay up
late without even realizing it. I have no concept of how long it has
been since something occurred. I don't *mean* for it to be 12 hours
between meals—the hours just go slippery. I don't *mean* for it to
be three days since I washed my hair—the days just ooze. All the
usual markers are gone. I notice now how much upkeep I did
because of other people: Can't go out looking like *that*. I don't
care if my hair is rumpled and I've worn the same tank top two
days in a row, but I don't want other people to think I don't have
my shit together.

I've been spending a lot of time coloring. Not "adult"
coloring—which is a term I dislike—which makes me think of
people doing untoward things with crayons—but just regular
coloring. Not migraine-inducing mandalas, or those garden scenes
with microscopic spaces either. I'm coloring a kids' book: A Star
Wars Valentine 98-cent jobber my husband picked up on
clearance at Target, a week after the holiday. It has big, easy
shapes, and awful puns which I love: Chewbacca saying, "I
CHEWS you!" Darth Vader saying, "Join the HEART side!" and
the obvious, "YODA one for me!" I color these in and slip them
under the bedroom door. Love notes to my husband. I cannot tell
if he is pleased or rolling his eyes. Day ten of quarantine.

I've also been crocheting again, which is one of those habits I
get very excited about for a short amount of time and then
abandon just as quickly. I did see one baby-sized afghan through

45

to the end, last year. I count it among my greatest achievements and proof that I do have some grit after all.

I am running out of books, now that the library is closed. I love books, but I don't like buying them, especially when I don't know if I'll enjoy the story, or ever want to read it again. I do have shelves of some favorites though. It might be time to return to *Pillars of the Earth*, which is 983 pages. Or *Lonesome Dove*—another tome. I can't stand reading books on Kindle. I have "zombie fingers" and it takes me so many taps to turn a page that my blood pressure rises. I can feel the ghost of my father channeling through me, and I have to take several deep breaths: *"Don't throw the Kindle. Don't smash the Kindle."* That's not reading; that's an exercise in anger management. A cruel test that I am not up for.

Lynn

Lynn, that's adorable, slipping silly coloring book notes to your husband. If he is rolling his eyes, I bet he's smiling, too. Have you tried downloading audiobooks from the library? I love it… having someone read to me. Might go well with the SEE's chocolates. Just sayin'.

It's universal, I guess, this sense of time obscured. It's 2:36. I've eaten a bowl of cereal and managed to tame my hair and get dressed. Everything happens when I feel a pressing need, not because I have a schedule to keep. Starving; eat. Sleep when I'm exhausted. Dinner; so, what if it's 10 at night? Keep coloring—

Deb

Hi Lynn and others, isn't it amazing how the laundry basket takes much longer to fill? I'm beginning to understand how our ancestors wore the same clothes all winter—with maybe a change for Sunday.

Lately I've been listening to books on my library app. When I had my lid lift and my vision was blurry for almost a week, relaxing and being read to by a professional narrator was a lifesaver. I live in Wilton, so my library app is Libby. Westport's must be on their website. Listening to a good book while you crochet might be the trick. It's another literary option for keeping our minds engaged. Unlike Audible—it's free!

I've not thought of the word "doily" in years. Maybe you could make a doily for group members.
Donna

You expressed my feelings so well, Lynn. I am aware though, that this may get old after a few more weeks or months. It's a wait and see mode. For today I'm content.
Polly

Sunday, March 22, 2020

Sex. Not forefront on my mind—until this morning. Could the last time we did it be in the Dominican Republic? Iberostar Grand Bavaro Hotel: pillowed cabanas on a white sandy beach, hot-stone deep tissue massages by Marisol, espresso martinis and an ongoing pool tournament against cousins, Peter and Marla. Ahh the Caribbean!

That was three weeks ago! What is the future of the hotel business now?

Hubby Mark looks great since he dropped fifteen pounds last year and kept it off. Now if only he'd exercise. I suggest to him that he might want to start doing sit-ups and push-ups. Lack of time is no longer an excuse. I stretch, do high knees, squats and lunges and jump rope three times in one hundred intervals.

Late morning, we have Sunday brunch, inspired by Trader Joe's thick-sliced brioche; it makes the best French toast. All hands on deck, even Michelle's boyfriend. Besides French toast with pure maple syrup, there are bagels with smoked salmon and cream cheese, Mark's gently scrambled eggs and a bowl full of plump fresh berries. *How lucky am I?*

While I now have my adult children living with me and my husband home 24/7 (other than food shopping excursions) I still shower daily, make the bed, live in workout clothes, and write nearly every afternoon. It's ingrained.

Morgaine

Sunday, March 22, 2020

The day isn't over, but I'm happy that all my writing books are finally neatly ensconced in the new bookcase. Boy, do they need a thorough culling! But not today. Still working on transferring the files upstairs, but my back is yelling for me to stop. So here I am, writing to all you wonderful writers.

I've spoken to several friends who are far away and on their own: Diana, a friend from our high school days who lives in Tarpon Springs, Florida and who is still going to her volunteering work at the thrift store. She tells me the thrift store provides food for persons in need; cousins in Florida; friend Sarah in California; cousin in Kentucky. It's good to talk with them and sharing what is a common plight.

The pendulum swings from unbelief that this is happening—of course it's happening—to I don't want to hear any more about it while I turn to CNN, PBS, and all the other stations given us the latest update.

The question was posed: what do you do to maintain a semblance of normalcy? Yesterday was laundry, today it was up and down the stairs carrying files and books and taking Archie for a walk in the sunshine. My son stopped over this morning. It's always such a treat to spend time with him. My daughter and I spent a long time chatting while she walked her dog. All in all, not a bad day. I hope the same for all of you.

No deep thoughts or reflections. Just wanting everyone to be safe and stay healthy.

Until tomorrow...

Maria

Sunday, March 22, 2020

Grief is a sneak. It jumps out of the darkness when you least expect it.

Like last night, watching *Little Women* on Masterpiece Theater. How many times did I read the book as a child? How many versions of the movie have I seen? No matter, when Beth died again last night, I fell apart. Not about Beth. About my Murray-man. I couldn't stop the tears.

It has been long enough since I said goodbye to him that although his absence is still very much with me, my life has slowly taken a new form, my own A.D.—After Dave. I had created a tenuous balance constructed out of friends and family, work, volunteer involvements, our writing workshop, and a support group. Above all, if I have not yet wholly learned how to live alone, I have accepted that I must.

Sometimes in cooking shows contestants are thrown a curveball halfway through their allotted time to cook, usually a new ingredient they must use. This virus is our new ingredient, and last night I just couldn't find the recipe to cope with it. Couldn't find the right flavor to counteract the bitterness left by Dave's death. It was simply not OK that he's not here with me. We should be watching *Top Chef* together, playing Ticket to Ride and Backgammon, discussing politics, cooking, just being together, each absorbed in a book, relishing the easy silence.

Once the tears stopped, my reaction to breaking down was what surprised me most. I felt remarkably alive, grateful to feel so deeply, fortunate to have loved him, and to love him still.

Deb

Sunday, March 22, 2020

A short entry tonight. Have been sleeping a lot. Then reviewed 32 essays for TEAM Westport essay contest; we meet on Zoom tomorrow morning.

The most fun—and sobering part of day—was Zoom conversation with family—my sister, her two adult sons, the 11- and 14-year-old grandsons of son #1. Also included were my adult daughters and their children ranging in age from 15 to 23. The three teenaged girls made faces at each other. The grandnephews quickly got bored and drifted away.

The adults, my sister's children and mine, are stressed. Two think they'll lose their jobs. One of them thinks he'll also lose the rental income from the properties he owns. My son-in-law is looking for another project within his company. One nephew, a Columbia University professor, is living in his Vermont house that he and his wife can't rent: they're teaching remotely. I know these are middle class problems; everyone's working remotely.

My sister, her husband, and I don't say much. Our investment portfolios have taken a hit, but that's a long-range problem. We're old now and seem to be less passionate about life's vagaries; we just listen and laugh a lot and marvel at the generations we've produced. They'll find their ways. "It'll all work out in the end. If it doesn't, it's not the end." (*The Marigold Hotel*)
Judy

Sunday, March 22, 2020

Time should be hanging heavy on my hands, but instead it seems to be moving faster than during what we now recognize were our real lives. This slice of life is speedy and surreal. I think that 15 minutes have passed, but when I look at the clock, it's an hour. I have stopped watching Trump's propagandistic news conferences—today's NYTimes had an editorial calling his briefings "propaganda," so I can't claim originality. I used to enjoy talking back at him, but the joy has gone out of that. That he has chosen this crisis to further disparage the press is verging on traitorous. Trump has spent his years in office softening up the American body politic and the press with vicious sucker punches, so that too many think any news but Trump's is "fake." How can we survive this liar-in-chief who, in addition to all the other disasters he has wrought, is now putting the lives of Chinese Americans in danger because he insists upon calling this virus, "the Chinese virus," as if he can rely upon that to deflect from his own deficiencies? I rely instead on governors to get a true sense of what's happening.

Today Larry and I walked on some nature paths in Wilton which are lovely, not at all trafficked and very pleasant. We are intent upon logging at least a couple of miles because the weather report for tomorrow is rain and maybe on Tuesday, snow. Snow? The outdoors is saving our sanity; that, and the coming of Spring.

After our walk we did some shopping at the Wilton Village market where we kept our distance from Ken and his wife Alice, aka "Sam." We had a brief discussion about what day it was. We agreed on Sunday. Then we went home and tried, unsuccessfully for the second evening in a row, to FaceTime with three couples whose company we miss. Larry entered their emails but could only reach two couples. And, to tell the truth—isn't what this is all about?—we were all boring. Something other than the other couple was missing from our get-together. Maybe it was real life. Also, it didn't help that, apparently, we don't know what we're doing. If anyone knows what we should be doing, please tell me. Thanks.

PS I continue to enjoy minding all your business.

Mary-Lou

Monday, March 23, 2020

Being the most guilty of Trump bashing, I've taken on the

responsibility of letting you know that at least one member of our group wishes those of us who are inclined to speak ill of Trump would please stop. This seems to me to be a fair request. This does not mean that we should avoid writing about the coronavirus or whatever difficulties, sorrows or fears we are experiencing. All of that, and anything else, is appropriate virally material. Thanks in advance for your cooperation. I'll be writing my own rant-less virally later today.

Cheers to all,

Mary-Lou

Monday, March 23, 2020

Dear Class—I made a mistake by asking you to avoid writing about Trump. I apologize. Constraining free speech is not my style. I was trying to make peace, but I should not have bowed to anyone's wish to prohibit dissing Trump, even if such free expression causes upset. During this difficult period, and given that Trump is so much a part of our daily virally lives, it is especially ridiculous to ask you to stifle any expression of your feelings. Come to think of it, since we're writers of memoirs and personal essay, and since I encourage the revelation of feelings, both positive and negative, my request was especially thoughtless. In the hope that I have eaten enough crow, please overlook my earlier email and carry on boldly.

Mary-Lou

Monday, March 23, 2020

Finally had that tooth pulled today. It's more like it just fell out. The worst was the novocaine.

Came home and climbed back into bed. Doctor's orders. Rest. Started watching the movie, *Knives Out*, fell asleep ten minutes in. Woke up to Michelle and Greg playing and singing and laughing at the piano.

Read all today's virallies. Thank you all for sharing!
Morgaine

Monday, March 23, 2020

I was going to write something pithy this morning, but this photo says it all………… not knowing which side of me is up.
Ken

Monday, March 23, 2020

While many people are experiencing heightened anxiety, I am experiencing less. For the foreseeable future, I no longer have to endure many of the situations that used to cause me stress: Turning left on busy roads; driving at night; driving in the rain; going to Wal-Mart; crowds; making sure my son gets to his rehearsals and lessons on time; making sure I remember to pick up my son from those places; wondering when my husband will get home from work; being jealous that he spends more time with "work-wife" than he does with me; being alone too much; wondering what I'm supposed to be doing with my life. Huzzah! I don't have to look for a job!

All my general anxiety feelings—and the occasional terror-sweats, panting and heart palpitations—have vanished. I honestly don't remember a time when I've been more relaxed. My husband's quarantine hasn't been *fun*, but aside from worrying about microbes and the banana supply, I have it easy these days.

Now that I have less to think about, I feel like I'm able to think more clearly. I don't walk into a room and forget why. In ten days, I haven't misplaced my keys or sunglasses once. This is a triumph. I no longer feel like I'm getting dementia.

An unfamiliar calmness has overtaken me, and other people too. In this time of social distance, I feel more connected to many people. Everyone I talk to, or text, has a gentler demeanor—there's a lot of well-wishing and sincerity. When people ask, "How are you?" they genuinely want to know. They take time to listen. People check in. Were we all so checked out before? All that rushing—it's done for now. The air is a slow leak from a tire as we come down from our fever-pitch, caffeine-driven craziness. It's weird, but it's nice. Some people feel like this new world is a shock, but I worry about my return to the old one.

Lynn

You expressed my feelings so well, Lynn. I am aware though, that this may get old after a few more weeks or months. It's a wait and see mode. For today I'm content.

Polly

Monday, March 23, 2020

I'm watching the beautiful fluffy snow dance past my window. I can't help but think it's as if someone picked up our earthly snow globe and gave it a good shake. May everything settle back into place before too long, and like Lynn, may we feel stronger and more caring of each other because of it.

Donna

Monday, March 23, 2020

Snow? Really? That was my first thought when I looked out the window this morning. Big, fluffy flakes drifting down.

A bag of ice-melt and a speeder sat by my back door all winter, but it has been a stage prop over this mostly snowless season. Yesterday I picked up the bag and the spreader and put them away in the garage to await next winter.

The universe has a very wicked and perverse sense of humor!

I was on a Zoom meeting this afternoon, but due to my unbelievable ineptitude with machinery of all kinds, I was "late" getting on. It was nice seeing everyone, but nerve racking when you feel all thumbs.

P.S. I received a notice from one of my grandsons about the danger of taking Ibuprofen/Advil in connection with Covid-19. He wrote that the CDC had posted this information although I couldn't find it there. This was checked out by Snopes and seems to have some validity. Apparently, there is some indication that this medication and the coronavirus don't mix well, and that taking ibuprofen might accentuate symptoms. Tylenol seems to be okay.

Take care,

Maria

Monday, March 23, 2020

I keep on thinking about time. Donna started it, now Lynn has made her peace with it, and even I am calming down.

I'm thinking about how, when all of us were young children, we were free of time. Is that the same as free of worry? I went to summer camp for two months in grown-up time, but it felt endless to me as a child. I never worried that that happy time would end. Time simply didn't matter at all. "Time" was an adult word—time to get up, time to stop playing and come to dinner, time to go to bed. This adult preoccupation with time was a bother that we resisted. Then childhood came to an end.

Because of today's requirements to lay low and stay at home, I find myself in a similar child-like kind of free-float. Time has come to a standstill, no countdowns, no destinations. We don't know what the future will bring.

Most of my life I've fretted about time, trying to keep up my usual frenetic pace, as if it were my only choice of how to live. I've been watching too much TV, troubling my mind, thinking up chores that really don't have to be done. Now I've settled in for the duration. Today, aside from over communicating with all of you, I did something I've never done unless being sick in bed permitted the indulgence—I read for hours. Someday this horror will be over, but I hope I can hang on to this bit of childhood timelessness that I've recovered.

Mary-Lou

Monday, March 23, 2020

My mood seems to change by the hour. This morning I felt accomplished: set up and successfully conducted a Zoom meeting to decide on winners of TEAM Westport essay contest. Now I have a new technological skill under my belt—will be ready to Zoom with anyone, anywhere, anytime. Wasn't Zoom the song that introduced the *Electric Company*, a show for older kids who had graduated from *Sesame Street*? "Come on and zoom, zoom, zoom along…" Although my kids loved *Sesame Street*, they never took to the *Electric Company*.

This afternoon I went downstairs to pick up the mail; hadn't collected it since Friday. Residents are nervously congregating. We keep six feet between us while chatting, so when we block passers-by, they don't know whether to go between us or around us. The staff are wearing all sorts of masks—oval, square, pink, yellow, white, even bandanas. I notice that there have been no death notices in the mailroom for a week. Very unusual. Has death taken a holiday, or is the administration hiding bad news from us? I'm beginning to spin out sci-fi fantasies like that old movie, *Cocoon*.

Now I feel sluggish. Listened to a free webinar on finding your voice in memoir writing. I won't know if the tips are useful until I try them. I charge the sluggishness up to age. On second thought, it may be because I ate the best of the dinner that the dining room is now delivering—a roll with lots of butter, a slice of chocolate fudge cake. Also drank the last of the wine. Haven't touched the fish or the veggies. Lots of carbs, lots of sitting. Must go out tomorrow for wine and a walk. Maybe I'll stop and introduce myself to whoever is at the guardhouse.

As for Trump, "God grant me the serenity to accept the things I cannot change / The courage to change the things I can / And the wisdom to know the difference." I can't change what he does as president. I can encourage each housekeeper and maintenance person I see here to register and vote. "Take the action and let go of the results." Al-Anon still works for me although the alcoholic is long gone.

Judy

Monday, March 23, 2020

I wish I had stock in Zoom. Two virtual meetings today, virtual yoga tomorrow and Friday, led by my daughter in Antwerp for me in Westport and my daughter in Boston.

Loved the rainy day. Arlo at my feet in the studio as I worked. Topped off with a long conversation with my son that was so funny I couldn't stop laughing or coughing. This is why.

He and my daughter-in-law are trying to night wean 21-month-old Joah. Towards that end, they've been reading him a book on the subject. It covers such juicy topics as sleeping till the sun comes up and the rooster crows "cock-a-doodle-doo-do." At three o'clock yesterday morning, they were awakened from a deep sleep by Joah standing on their bed screaming "cock-a-doodle-doo-do" at the top of his lungs.

It just so happens that Joah has a stuffed rooster, which is now his new hero and constant companion. He was frustrated at not being able to find a jacket to fit the rooster so the stuffie would be warm when they went outside. So he improvised. My son's favorite hat is now doing double duty as a rooster bunting until the weather is warmer.

They better get a different book.
Deb

Monday, March 23, 2020

Our team had a crisis management meeting to deal with new risks faced by our clients. The value of many of their retirement plans could drastically change from year-end December 31, 2019, given the current coronavirus outbreak. One client with a restaurant group of seven will do curbside delivery from only two of them.

Dismayed to see Dr Anthony Fauci absent from the White House briefing.
Gina

Tuesday, March 24, 2020

Westport got infamous today; we're living in a coronavirus hot spot. The *NYTimes* carried a prominent article about the party of 40 that sickened 20. We received calls from as far away as Provence, inquiring about our well-being. Long ago, when Westport was just plain famous for being a bohemian artists' colony, it was because of a song, the lyrics of which went:

> *'Cause he caught her in the kitchen playing Westport,*
> *A game indigenous to suburban life,*
> *Where you take a wife of whom you're not the husband,*
> *While someone else's husband takes your wife.*

The local lore—perhaps apocryphal—was that partying Westporters put their house keys in a bowl and removed one that was not their own, and took that person to their home and, presumably to bed. These days, if we were to repeat that activity, according to my late friend Tracy Sugarman, Westporters would take that person to a meeting.

Another beautiful day and so Little Endorphin Annie was back at Sherwood Island walking the beach. (In addition to pepping me up, the walk allows me to consume a bowl of Toffee Chocolate Chip ice cream and at least one Toll House cookie at night.) It's a state park and, thank goodness, the state has either chosen not to close it, or forgotten all about it. Walk on the numerous paths, or on the beach. There weren't many people there, but those that were kept their distance and unfailingly waved, smiled, and said, "Hi." We didn't exchange any other words, but just that little wave and that tiny word created the sense of community for which we yearn. I found 3 small heart-shaped stones on the beach—they seemed a good omen. We enjoyed the kids on scooters, people with dogs, two little boys at the water's edge building a sandcastle, an elderly man bravely walking with the aid of two sticks, and a couple sharing a picnic at one of the tables.

Mary-Lou

Yup, that's the party that has me confined to my property, waiting for test results! Two of my friends ran into each other at Sherwood yesterday—at least as much as one can run into someone else while maintaining a 6 ft distance. One had a yellow lab. What a great day to be there!

Deb

Tuesday, March 24, 2020

Where the day goes:

7:20 AM: I wake up grinding my teeth, sweaty from strange dreams and the cat on my chest.

8:00 AM: My phone alarm thankfully reminds me it's garbage day. I drag out one can, half-full. Decreased consumerism.

8:30 AM: My son, Zach, asks if he can borrow one of my books. He holds up Ayn Rand's *The Fountainhead*. I say, "Dude, knock yourself out!" I look for *Atlas Shrugged*, which I thought he might like better, but can't find it.

9:15 AM: Get a text from my friend Mandy, "Talkies?" I grab my coffee and a blanket and sit in my car so we can chat/vent. I find it funny that the only privacy I get now is when I *leave* the house. We had a long catch-up till I ran out of coffee and got too cold.

10:00 AM: I bring Brian a coffee and a yogurt; and a banana even though he didn't ask for one. There are three left, turning very brown on the counter. I think of Goldilocks: These bananas are too many. These bananas are too few. I try not to be angry about this. Maybe I'll make smoothies later.

11:00 AM: Listen to a Moth Radio Hour podcast while I ride the exercise bike. Give up riding after seven minutes and pick up my crochet instead. Four granny squares done.

12:00 PM: My son and I play Rocket League: videogame soccer with cars and a giant ball. We play as a team against two online strangers. I score a goal and my son is so excited, he types, "You just got plowed by my mom!" in the chat box. I am very pleased.

1:00 PM: Make lunch: a recipe from my cookbook makes me smile: "Zach's Old Favorite Lentils." He used to ask me to make it all the time when he was little. He's gigantic now. It seems impossible. I am so glad to have all this extra time with him. Even though yesterday he said, "Gah! Why are you SO annoying?! I mean, like, SOOOOO annoying!" He's not wrong. I completely was being annoying. He has been texting a girl named Jenny, and I sang De La Soul's *Jenifa Taught Me*. And I made Alexa play the song and I floss danced. So annoying! He said of De La Soul, "What is this trash music? Complete Garbo." I love how teenagers talk. (Btw, he hates it when my husband calls him "emo"—whenever my son is in a grumpy, dark mood, my husband will say, "Whoa, whoa! What's with all the emo today?" My son will scowl and say, "OK, boomer." And I shout from the kitchen,

"Hey! We are NOT boomers!" (We are Gen-Xers, thank you very much!)

2:30 PM: My husband wants macaroni and cheese. I bring him some, drop it off and run away like usual. He calls down the stairs, "Is there any pepper?" and suddenly he bursts from his room and stands at the top of the stairs, singing, "Pep-PER, Pep-PER, Pep-PER! Pep-PER, Pep-PER, Pep-PER!" over and over again, doing the floss dance as he sings. After about ten seconds of this, he collapses against the doorway, panting, saying, "Woo. That's tiring!" And he retreats to the bedroom. That's the most exercise he's had in two weeks.

3:00 PM: Ask son to go for a walk with me. He says, "Nah, fam. Ima practice viola." I listen to him play his pieces. When he gets to the scales, I go for a walk by myself, even though I don't really want to. I think of Mary-Lou's morale-march, and that gets me out of the house.

3:10 PM: I walk about half a block and end up (socially distanced) behind a neighbor. I turn around and walk home. Racoons and crows got into my neighbor Danny's garbage (again) and I go around my ¼ acre, picking up a CVS bag, an empty cereal box liner, the plastic from a pack of gym socks and a lot of paper towels.

3:45 PM: I put on my Beats. Thank god for noise canceling headphones: between the viola scales and my husband's conference calls, I just want to listen to music in peace. The Weeknd's new album finally dropped.

4:00 PM: My husband is yelling at the top of his (compromised) lungs because I can't hear him with my headphones on. Coincidentally, I'm listening to The Weeknd sing a song called "I've been the hardest to love." Oh, indeed. My husband begs me to bring in the mail. Fine. I consider myself lucky that I can go outside to get it. There's a padded envelope addressed to him. He opens it like a kid at Christmas, so excited.

"Wow! It came so fast! Yes! This is awesome!" Inside the envelope is a Lego Baby Yoda, one centimeter in size.

4:20 PM: The sun is streaming in my window, and I realize my guitar is getting baked. I play it so rarely, and looking at it, I feel guilty. But I'm certainly not going to pick it up now, with my family lurking and listening. *(Maybe I should play in my car?)* My son and husband are the musical ones. My son is (was?) the concertmaster at Staples and an All-State violist. My husband can play piano by ear. He'll hear a song on the radio and run downstairs and play it. I am, by contrast, very terrible at guitar. I have always wanted to play the cello, but I have no confidence that I'd be any good at that either.

5:00 PM: Finish the NYT crossword and other puzzles. Ask my husband for the fifth time if he got his test results yet. Nope. Dinner tonight is fried eggs. After that I'm going to read, watch one episode of something and I plan to be in bed by 11:00 PM like a normal person. The End.

Lynn

Tuesday, March 24, 2020

I was your typical fifties housewife today, sans the apron. Still wearing my workout clothes even though my exercise is restricted until tomorrow. I dusted, vacuumed, disinfected every surface, and got down on my hands and knees and scrubbed the floor, twice. I even made dinner, a rarity.

Morgaine

Tuesday, March 24, 2020

I am so tired. I woke up at 6:30 AM to receive ten-day old order delivery from Peapod at 7:00 AM. Did not get chicken breasts, asparagus, bratwurst, Dunkin' Donuts French Vanilla Ground Coffee, 100-watt light bulbs, Kleenex, toilet paper (no surprise there), English muffins, tortilla chips and BREAD!!!

A client with a small chain of jewelry stores is closing for now.

Reassured to see both Dr. Anthony Fauci and Dr. Deborah Birx on the platform at the WH briefing this evening. Loved Dr. Birx's scarf construction in addition to her professional, well-thought-out comments on the tri-state area vulnerabilities.

My daughter Maria from Rye relates some of the horror stories faced by a friend having to go to NY Presbyterian for surgery not related to the coronavirus.

Thankful for the leadership of Governor Andrew Como at this critical time.

Gina

Tuesday, March 24, 2020

There are little leaks in the bubble surrounding me. It has seemed as though reality was being held at bay. How to spend my time was entirely a matter of choice rather than one of obligation. A stay-cation of sorts, only with a limited panorama.

As we all adjust to this very bizarre new normal, real stumbling blocks present themselves to me, and most likely everyone else. I am concerned with my finances. It's senseless to look for a job now—on the one hand, a relief from pressure. On the other hand, the small income I have from teaching is a fatality of Covid-19. Will the stimulus package include helping people who have lost some income AND temporarily the ability to find a job?

Then there's my mom. I manage her money—god help her. Her account is getting low. If I sell some of her assets now, it is at a significant loss. The only one who's doing well in this scenario is her aide, who deserves every one of the many, many cents she gets. I may have to ask her to take less pay for now, with the understanding that she will receive the remainder when the market heads northward. There's tightness in my belly at this thought. I'm such a coward.

Flip side. Four-year-old grandson, Silas, FaceTimed yesterday. He received a very basic reading book from a friend. He had never seen it before. I was privy to him reading his first book ever, which he did quite well!

"Oh gee (that's me) did you hear that page? 'Pop had a hat!' "

"Oh yes. And Pop is what you call Mama's daddy."

"Oh yes, I do caw him Pop."

Highbrow stuff.

I also fulfilled a promise to add my little drop in the bucket of things to relieve the boredom of being cooped up. I added a page to my website, for Covid-19, and published the first of 19 art projects that require desire, not talent. Get out that paper and draw!

Deb

Wednesday, March 25, 2020

Dear writers, I can't imagine we're doing much in the way of printing, but if anyone is in need of copy paper I offer curbside pickup. Especially Gina. I also have reams of neon colored copy paper for the little ones, and I'll throw in a bag of tortilla chips.

Morgaine

Wednesday, March 25, 2020

Today my husband came downstairs for the first time in twelve days. He stood in the dining room, looked around, completely bewildered, and said, "Juice?" I said, "On it. But you have to get out of here." He ambled back upstairs. I think he's losing his mind. If only he would stop coughing. Then I would at least let him watch TV with me in the living room. Someone he works with got tested and has been waiting NINE DAYS (and counting) for their results.

Talked to MIL again. On our morning phone call, she said, "I'm going to Publix tomorrow. That's the plan. But I am *NOT* going during senior hours! What a zoo! A line out the door! Plus, those people! They're slow! And they drop things and can't bend over to pick them up! They take forever! And they park their carts across the aisle and stand there and chat! No! Not for me! I'm going at the regular time!"

I love how she says "those people" as if, at 80, she sees herself as a much younger girl. But she is still sashaying around more than she should. I try to politely suggest this, and she says, "They're telling seniors to stay home if they have a CONDITION. I don't have a condition! I'm FINE." And now it's my turn to huff and sigh at her and say, "For god's sakes!" I explain the severity. I explain the spread. I tell her just because the news says only 5 people in her county have it, that probably everybody has it, or will soon. I tell her she really must stay home. She can't be going to my dippy sister-in-law's house, where they're still hosting playdates and happy hours with countless children and neighbors, and nobody washes anything. I said, "Please. Please. Please. This will make you sick. This can kill you." She huffed, basically saying, "Not me. I'm a much younger girl." I am beginning to understand why this whole thing has happened and will likely get worse.

My son came in at that point and said, "Hi, Nana!" and she brightened immediately and said, "How's my Zachy?" They spoke for a few minutes. She told him she found a store in Tampa that sells See's Chocolates. She's going to go over there any day, I know it. I should preemptively send her another box full of coconut ones, just to keep her at home.

Lynn

Wednesday, March 25, 2020

Hello everyone, email function on my computer is on the fritz...

again. I've been reading all your postings and marvel at the ingenuity you are all practicing during this communal lock-in.

Yesterday, March 24, was not one of my better moments. I stayed in my s— clothes all day, no makeup, which always makes me look like I died three days before, and to be honest, I can't remember combing my hair. I managed to use the vacuum, but not too much more. Oh, and I had a phone consultation with the gastroenterologist; we had a nice chat and I was happy to report all is going smoothly!

Today, Wednesday, March 25, I woke with the resolve to climb out of yesterday's trough. So, a little bit of concealer, a bit of blush, lipstick, and a clean shirt, and I felt human again.

My son stopped in with the batteries I requested when he said he was going to Home Depot. The small company he works for has taken a big hit and he has taken a pay cut, but, surprisingly, he is in good spirits.

My daughter continues to shop for her father, her own family, and me. I'm going to investigate Peapod. This will lighten her load a bit. Anyone had experience with this service?

Archie and I picked some meds from the vet—left outside their door—and restocked the wine supply which was running low. Castle Wine in Westport is doing curbside delivery, although I imagine many stores are doing the same.

After dinner I'll check the computer again; maybe it's come to its senses. I hope so cuz typing on the iPad is not the greatest. Time to prepare dinner, so until soon.

Maria

Wednesday, March 25, 2020

The news is there's no news. Heart galloped out of the gate when my doctor's number came up on my cell phone. An answer! Is it better to have a positive result and hope it remains a mild case, or is the more positive really the negative? I crave instant gratification, hate waiting. Now is the moment.

"Hi Deb, it's Amanda." My doctor's PA. She's also a hospice nurse and was so good to us when Dave was dying. All roads seem to lead back to that event. "How are you feeling? I know you talked to Dr. B a week ago and had symptoms of the virus."

"I did." *Yes or no?*

"I'm better than last week. Headache's gone."

"OK, better, but not 100%. Don't hesitate to call if you have a fever again or tightness in your chest. This virus can seem to be on its way out and then suddenly get severe."

"I understand." *Yes or no?*

"Well, I just wanted to check on you. I wish I had your test results, but let's see, you had your test on Friday. We're still waiting for results from last Tuesday. It's taking 8, 10, even 11 days." *Yes nor no?*

"Amanda, how many people get sick of waiting to find out if they're sick, and just start walking around? What a bungled response for the country that's supposed to be the greatest in the world."

"Believe me, I'm with you. It's so frustrating for us. We know what *should* be happening and are face-to-face every day with what *is* happening. I'm so sorry."

Time to get out the apron. Looks like I'm going to need a lot more cookies.

Deb

Wednesday, March 25, 2020

After three days of nursing my printer back to health after an ink spill contamination following a paper jam injury, I am now back in business health. My analysis of business valuation reports depends on printing out 80-120-page documents and marking them up all over the place before putting metrics in Excel spreadsheets and summaries into Word document checklists.

Get an email from Kindred Spirits and Wine. They have free delivery for seniors above 65 on Wednesdays. (I'm above 65 on Wednesdays.) Wow! I email them a list and have three cases of chardonnay and other goodies on my doorstep within the hour.

Attend a Zoom conference call about the impact of the virus on the value of retirement plans. Each company has specific factors to consider. Our clients who are restaurants or jewelry retailers are more vulnerable than those who are small grocery chains or in construction, engineering, or communications.

My two oldest granddaughters spend much of their days in their bedrooms behind closed doors completing assignments for school on their Chromebooks. There is close monitoring by teachers. But the second grader is highly dependent on her mother for home teaching/coaching. A big distraction from my daughter's online work demands.

Dr. Birx has a really wow outfit on the briefing podium this evening, but CNN cuts to the analysts so I miss what she has to say.

Gina

Thursday, March 26, 2020

Mark and I have been working on a 1,500-piece puzzle of Bourbon Street. It has taken over our dining room table. The kids pass by and check on our progress, but they'd rather be on social media.

I did yoga this morning, nothing as impressive as Ken's shared photo, but I can still do a backbend. The afternoon was spent on another rewrite of chapter 11.

I learned today that my daughter's boyfriend wants to go back to their NYC apartment for a few days, pack up some of his belongings (keyboard, speakers, microphone etc.) and come back.

He says he won't leave the apartment while he's there, but there are four door handles, an elevator button, a vestibule and two hallways to navigate.

Is it worth the risk?

Morgaine

Thursday, March 26, 2020

This morning was a new adventure. I joined the seniors at Stop & Shop's early shopping, at 6:00 AM. The streets were empty as I drove in the pre-dawn to Ridgefield. There were about 50 cars in the parking lot when I got there. After putting on my gloves and wiping down my cart I started shopping. Other shoppers kept their distance as did the many workers who were stocking the shelves. I was amazed as to what was there, as opposed to what wasn't.

The produce section was filled, the deli closed, but there were pre-packaged cold cuts to buy, the fish section closed, (maybe these sections open later in the day, but it sure didn't look like it) signs requesting people only take 2 of many items, like the meats and chicken, and they had a few bags of sugar and flour which I haven't been able to find for weeks. They did have some cleaning products like Lysol All-Purpose Cleaner, some boxes of tissues and a few packages of napkins. Before I knew it my cart was filled to the brim.

Of course, I needed to have the regular check-out—this was not a do-it-yourself project, so I waited at a safe distance for my turn. A clerk came over and offered to open his register. He told me I'd have to do the bagging. We had a nice chat. He usually gets to work at 7:00—now it's 6:00.

The best part is yet to come. As I was packing my bags (and I did run out, so I was GIVEN paper ones), a gentleman who had just checked out next to me offered to get me another cart, as he could see that not everything I bought would fit into one cart. He took his groceries to his car, returned, and helped me bag what I hadn't been able to finish.

Let me take this opportunity to say that I'm not trying to hoard, but to limit my shopping to every 10 days to 2 weeks, as everyone in my family is frantic that I might bring home the virus to my husband who is not in good health in anyway. In fact, they want me to find someone to do my shopping and not go into any store, but I'm not there yet. My kindly helper pushed my second cart and followed me to my car, unloaded the bags into its trunk, and they were almost $300 worth of heavy and asked me if I had far to walk to my house once I got home. I assured him I had an attached garage and a husband who could help me unload them. I got the feeling that he would have followed me home to help me unload my bags.

Once home, my husband had a huge breakfast waiting and urged me to eat it while it was still hot. I did.

He unloaded all the bags. We both wiped down each package before putting them away. May we not run out of food soon,

Polly

Thursday, March 26, 2020

Today's theme is COINCIDENCES. The first one comes from a forward. The second coincidence involves Henry the 8th and Donald Trump.

One

A LETTER FROM F. SCOTT FITZGERALD, QUARANTINED IN 1920 IN THE SOUTH OF FRANCE DURING THE SPANISH INFLUENZA OUTBREAK

Dearest Rosemary,

It was a limpid dreary day, hung as in a basket from a single dull star. I thank you for your letter. Outside, I perceive what may

be a collection of fallen leaves tussling against a trash can. It rings like jazz to my ears. The streets are that empty. It seems as though the bulk of the city has retreated to their quarters, rightfully so. At this time, it seems very poignant to avoid all public spaces. Even the bars, as I told Hemingway, but to that he punched me in the stomach, to which I asked if he had washed his hands. He hadn't. He is much the denier, that one. Why, he considers the virus to be just influenza. I'm curious of his sources.

The officials have alerted us to ensure we have a month's worth of necessities. Zelda and I have stocked up on red wine, whiskey, rum, vermouth, absinthe, white wine, sherry, gin, and lord, if we need it, brandy. Please pray for us.

Two

I was reading a review of the last book in Hillary Mantel's trilogy, which is about the court of Henry the Eighth. Here is what the reviewer had to say about the king's court.

"Henry's court is a little world of terror, more Orwellian than antique for of all of Mantel's splendid period ornamentation. Fantastic rumors and royal whim generate its weather. Falls from grace are sudden and frequently fatal. On the throne for a quarter century by now, Henry is a very human Big Brother, not without shame but bathed in self-pity."

What can I say in Trump's favor? At least he didn't decapitate his discarded wives.

Mary-Lou

Thursday, March 26, 2020

Some levity: I think I'm going on a news and Facebook fast. I do this sort of thing all the time: I try 30 days with no gluten; I abandon TV for a season; I'll turn off my cell phone for a week. I even gave up coffee, for a time. I am a cold-turkey kind of person: once I decide not to do something, I won't do it. I excel at deprivation. I behave. That is, until I feel like I've proven the point enough, or get bored and need a new fix. Quitting is my high. I wish I had the other side of that coin, for I am terrible at keeping up streaks, at the doing. Those 100-day challenges to exercise or make something every day? Forget it. Day 3 and I'm out. I can't even manage to take a daily vitamin. This virally is the longest streak I've ever had.

So, I think an information fast is in order. Unless it's "Yay! We're all cured!" or "Boo! We're all gonna die!" I don't need to know. We're somewhere in the middle now and will likely stay in the gray for a while. There's not going to be any big revelations on handwashing in the coming weeks. If my son ever gets on the school bus again, I'll know something has changed. Till then, I need a break. The news is mostly projections, analysis, anticipatory worry. It will come to pass, or it won't. I'll keep following the rules. I'm already taking it all as seriously as I can. Except when I'm not.

I laugh at memes of people wearing dog-cone "lampshades" with the caption: "You have to stop touching your face! It's for your own good!" I laugh at a photo of grocery store shelves, empty except for sad, plant-based meats, with the caption, "We're scared, but we're not TOFU scared!" I laugh at more photos of grocery shelves: "Even in a pandemic, New Englanders refuse to eat Manhattan clam chowder."

And I started playing a (socially distanced) party game today. A friend and I were texting, taking one word of any movie title and replacing it with the words 'Toilet Paper': Gone with the Toilet Paper; Toilet Paper of Endearment; The Toilet Paper Strikes Back! Fried Green Toilet Paper. And my favorite: Indiana Jones and the Last Toilet Paper. OMG. I could do this all day.

Admittedly, a news fast might be harder for me this time. There is such a pull to check the latest, to see what sharks are circling now, but it serves me no good purpose. The only information I want is information I can't get: my husband's test results are still out in the ether. Till then we keep on doing what we're doing. I don't believe that ignorance is bliss, but I believe there are times when it's okay to go to bed with the knowledge you have. For a few days, at least.

Lynn

Thursday, March 26, 2020

I went outside at 1 PM for a two-mile walk, intending to circle the ring road twice. I planned to be back by 1:45—about 20 minutes/mile with a five-minute cool down. Now at 3:30. I'm just returning. This is why:

I met a friend who was sitting in a cupola. We talked about the wonders of Zoom that she and I have just discovered. We both had family conferences on Sunday, three generations chatting together which usually happens only at weddings and funerals. She tells me how she's ordering food online and exploring the wonders of Netflix. She loves new technology; she was a math major. I love it because I like to tinker.

I met a man, formerly a periodontist, who's just lost his wife after an eight-year battle with Alzheimer's. His face is more relaxed than I've seen it before.

"I feel happy... no, not happy, content," he says. "Her life is over, but the love affair lingers on."

I comment, "Two days ago I woke up, sure Bill was beside me. I knew he couldn't be, but I was sure he was. I pictured his profile. When I glanced at his pillow, of course he wasn't there."

"I can't get my head around the finality," he says. I nod. We continue to walk in opposite directions.

At the building that houses the Health Center, I see a friend next to a window talking to someone inside. He was a professor of pre-Columbian art and his wife's field was Spanish literature. We've traded dissertation horror stories. His wife is in the Center with a broken ankle. The health center is under strict quarantine, no one goes in or comes out. So, the couple are chatting through the window. I jump up and down, waving my arms and shouting, "Hi Ginny! Hi Ginny!"

Beyond the building where two roads cross, I see two women walking. We comment on the beauty of the day: some trees are budding, the tulips are out, there are still clumps of snow on the ground.

"How am I going to get my hair cut," one woman wonders. The in-house salon has been closed for two weeks. We shrug. The other one looks at us. We all have gray hair. "No one can get their hair colored, either," she comments. "We're gonna find out who dyes her hair in a couple of weeks. Look for gray roots!" It's catty gossip but still good for a laugh.

"Did you hear about the resident who's been inside for three weeks—no names—with her dog?' he says. "She says her dog is trained to go on paper." We shake our heads and scrunch up our noses, imagining the smell in the apartment. Who is it, our eyes ask?

"No names," he repeats and walks away before we try to change his mind.

At the gardens I see a couple, he a psychiatrist and she a psychotherapist, poking around in a raised bed.

"I just can't wait for spring," she says. "I've planted things but they're not growing." There are several orange plant markers, but she's right. Nothing's growing.

To make conversation, I point and ask, "What's this? And this?" I'm not a plant person; I won't recognize the names even if she tells me, and I can no longer read the markers. Her husband quickly takes over the conversation and talks about the plants they've left at their various houses. They wish they had dug up some and bought them here. One is a jack-in-the-box or is it a jack-o-lantern or is it something else that begins with "Jack"?

"Very rare," he assures me. Then he describes the difficult psychiatric cases he treated while stationed on a nuclear base and how the single men at Meadow Ridge who used to meet for dinner now feel so isolated.

How did he ever help anyone when he talks so much? I wonder. Finally, I break in and explain that I've seen managers refuse to participate in management training sessions only to change their behaviors when their peers started to change. I try to recruit the couple for a five-mile walk that some of us are planning, but they can't walk that far.

I've managed to stimulate my mind and my body in two hours. I knew something would happen today that I could write about.

Judy

Thursday, March 26, 2020

Sunny Thursday greetings. This is too poignant not to share. It also speaks to why our group is so amazing. One more beautiful reflection... One of the founders of Brazilian modernism.

Beautiful poem by Mario de Andrade (Sao Paulo 1893-1945) Poet, novelist, essayist and musicologist.

MY SOUL HAS A HAT
I counted my years & realized that I have less time to live by, than I have lived so far.

I feel like a child who won a pack of candies: at first he ate them with pleasure. But when he realized that there was little left, he began to taste them intensely.

I have no time for endless meetings where the statutes, rules, procedures & internal regulations are discussed, knowing that nothing will be done. I no longer have the patience to stand absurd people who, despite their chronological age, have not grown up.

My time is too short: I want the essence; my spirit is in a hurry. I do not have much candy in the package anymore.

I want to live next to humans, very realistic people who know how to laugh at their mistakes, who are not inflated by their own triumphs & who take responsibility for their actions. In this way, human dignity is defended, and we live in truth and honesty.

It is the essentials that make life useful. I want to surround myself with people who know how to touch the hearts of those whom hard strokes of life have learned to grow with sweet touches of the soul.

Yes, I'm in a hurry. I'm in a hurry to live with the intensity that only maturity can give. I do not intend to waste any of the remaining desserts. I am sure they will be exquisite, much more than those eaten so far.

My goal is to reach the end satisfied and at peace with my loved ones and my conscience. We have two lives & the second begins when you realize you only have one.

Donna

Thursday, March 26, 2020

Humanity! I spent an hour in the dog park, keeping a distance from other people. I was there with a friend, but about 12 feet behind her. It was beautiful in the park and so good to be off my property, but it was also sobering. I sometimes jog through the park. Its hills are nothing for me, but today I was breathing so hard my friend could hear me as I chugged my way behind her. The same thing happens walking up the steep stairs in my house, something I do about thirty times a day, each day. Still, could be allergies, or a cold. If ever I get the test results, I would know!

High points of the day: finished the drawing of "mad professor" Dave. It's safely stashed away until such time as I can get it photographed and then framed.

I am faithfully keeping up with my 19 art projects for Covid-19. A side benefit is that I've remembered how to maneuver around editing my website. Good thing. I still had an address and phone number publicized. Maybe not so smart being a woman living alone. That's about as much concession as I make to distrust, but a necessary one.

My grandson, Aidan, 16, is teaching me graffiti. I am teaching him figurative drawing. My first assignment from him is a graffiti drawing of my initials in "throwie" style. Spent the night watching YouTube videos, then sketching ideas for an alphabet of my own. It's a great chance to be much looser than in portrait work. That said, I will start another portrait tomorrow. Will also schedule a Zoom lesson with Aidan about rendering and basic figure proportions. He's pretty good eyeballing it, so a little training will go a long way.

I revel in this arrangement. When he, his brother and their sister were younger, they used to spend vacations with Dave and me—OhGee/Boppy camp, we called it. Now that they're older and more focused on friends and activities, I must find more sophisticated ways to connect to them. Learning graffiti will be fun; spending time in Aidan's world with him will be sublime.

This slowing down, this shrinking of our worlds, is tremendously opening. There is time to communicate, to enjoy one another even at a distance, to share, to pursue new interests. There is a darkness that lurks outside our doors and causes us to make sure we express our love, on the outside chance that it will cross our thresholds.

Deb

Friday, March 27, 2020

Colleagues in Arms. strike… that… Colleagues with Elbows Connections, putting aside any partisan politics, and knowing there are more important things to do, this is too clever not to share. And lord knows we need to laugh.

Subject: Trump's healthcare package

American Medical Association has weighed in on Trump's healthcare package: The Allergists were in favor of scratching it, but the Dermatologists advised not to make any rash moves. The Gastroenterologists had sort of a gut feeling about it, but the Neurologists thought the Administration had a lot of nerve. Meanwhile, Obstetricians felt certain everyone was laboring under a misconception, while the Ophthalmologists considered the idea shortsighted. Pathologists yelled, "Over my dead body!" while the Pediatricians said, "Oh, grow up!" The Psychiatrists thought the whole idea was madness, while the Radiologists could see right through it. Surgeons decided to wash their hands of the whole thing and the internists claimed it would indeed be a bitter pill to swallow. The Plastic Surgeons opined that this proposal would "put a whole new face on the matter." The Podiatrists thought it was a step forward, but the Urologists were pissed off at the whole idea. Anesthesiologists thought the whole idea was a gas, and those lofty Cardiologists didn't have the heart to say no. In the end, the Proctologists won out, leaving the entire decision up to the assholes in Washington.

One of the iconic TV shows in the 60s was a police drama called *Hill Street Blues*. It started with the police sergeant addressing the street cops on the morning shift. He ended every meeting with, "Be careful out there," which became a familiar thing to say to good friends.

"Be careful out there."

Ken

Friday, March 27, 2020

I hear the mail truck idling outside. I used to send and receive a lot of letters: nearly 500 in and 500 out over the past two and half years. I have pen pals and participate in mail-art swaps. I have friends who send me postcards and presents out of the blue. Some people I correspond with almost weekly. The sound of the mail truck used to be a happy sound: what goodies arrived for me today!

But now? Nobody is mailing anything. Via email, I have "full-disclosure-d" the situation here to all my on-paper friends, and until my husband gets a negative test result (or until the world gets normal again—whichever comes first), no one wants to take a chance on a germy letter from me. I totally get it. Two months ago, I received a letter swap from Singapore. The first sentence was, "Sorry for the delay, but things are pretty crazy here with the Coronavirus." I held that letter by two fingers and grimaced. I held my breath and put it in the bin. Outside.

Logically, biologically, I know that a virus can't survive a journey that long on paper, and the envelope didn't contain any white powder or anything, but still. I had visions of being Patient Zero, with the headline: Pen Pal brings Pandemic to Affluent Suburb. That seems so long ago, and the headlines since then have been just as weird. Now all that's in my mailbox are ads for Tuff Lawn or replacement windows, and it's not even worth the walk down the path. I miss getting letters. I miss writing on paper and reading on paper. Typing is not the same. I miss hearing from my pals. More social distance, this time by mail.

Lynn

Friday, March 27, 2020

Today is my mother-in-law's 85th birthday. Mary-Lou, I couldn't resist sending her your sudsy sing-a-long. The uncombed hair adds to its charm. I attended my first virtual cocktail party in her honor via Zoom, this evening. Donna, I know you've been suggesting our class meet over Zoom, perhaps we start with a virtual social gathering?

The 18" long flexible tube that delivers insulin from a pump to a diabetic's body, makes an excellent cat toy. It's slinky-like curl and sporadic bounce have both Riley and Eloise mesmerized. Riley has been the master of our Westport-size home for 12 years. He seems to be marking his territory, lounging on the settee by my desk instead of outside on this beautiful day chasing a mouse. Eloise, who's five years old and comes from a New York city apartment, is under my bed. We've all had to adjust.

The tooth extraction sight has been acting up. I just started antibiotics. I used to hate taking any kinds of drugs and I'm still not a fan of pharmaceuticals, but they have their time and place. I surrender.

So, has anyone else entertained the thought that this whole coronavirus experience is the universe putting its foot down on how we've been treating each other, the planet and ourselves?

Morgaine

Friday, March 27, 2020

Forays into humanity were short-lived. Health district mandated that dogs must be on-leash at the dog park during the crisis. Arlo, like many dogs, is a different beast on a leash. Once attached to me, he believes I need protection and is defensive with other dogs. So, once again, it's the yard and throwing sticks.

Really such an inconsequential thing in the grand scheme but felt like a sucker punch. Every time I take the boy to the park, I feel as though I'm honoring Dave, who never missed a day, even in terrible weather. Arlo and I have gone through a lot together, and I feel a deep sense of dread as he ages. Arlo's playfulness belies the fact that he is ten, old for a large dog. I sometimes wake him when I can't see his chest rise and fall in his sleep. I am trying to prepare myself for the fact that I will eventually lose him, too. Each time I watch him bound up to a playmate, front legs splayed on the ground and rear end high in a perfect "down dog," tail wagging and barking loudly, I know that eventuality is not yet here.

This evening I had an entire analytic conversation with myself.

"I really want takeout. Want it to feel like it's Friday night." *"OK, go ahead. Restaurants need the business. Will you do delivery or curbside pickup?"*

"Trying to decide. Curbside is risky. It's a popular restaurant, so there may be a lot of other people picking up orders in front of the small shop. But delivery is risky, too. How will I sign the credit card slip and leave a tip that isn't crawling with pathogens?" *"Good question. How would you do that?"*

"Well, I could call the restaurant and tell them that I'm waiting for test results and want to be super careful. So, the driver should leave the food and the slip and move back to his car. I'll put on gloves and sign the bill, leave a tip, and take my food. Then the driver can retrieve the bill and the tip. Done." *"A little complicated but would work."*

"Yuh, but the problem is that I don't think I could explain it to a staff that speaks little English." Ate leftovers, only to find out later from my son that you do the whole thing over the phone or internet, and they just leave the food outside your house and beat a hasty retreat!
Deb

Friday, March 27, 2020
I awoke feeling as if my head was under water, ears stopped up, sinuses congested. It was either a cold or allergies... or a combination. Didn't feel so hot either, so decided to have a Mental Health Day (MHD). I haven't indulged in one of those since

moving back three years ago. Of course, I couldn't help wondering if this was something more than these mundane afflictions.

When I was still living in Florida, I'd give myself permission to have an MHD occasionally. These are days where I do nothing more than read, nap, and eat. And that's pretty much what I did—with interruptions from Archie for food, outdoor breaks, and attention. Early afternoon, my son came over; he wanted to see the new desk and bookcase. The room was lit up with sunshine and we opened the slider and stepped out on the balcony. The ground crew was getting ready to leave and they were parked in front of my condo. We had a chat with them and thanked them for keeping the complex trimmed and neat. When Ron was ready to leave, I refused to hug him, he laughing at me, "Mom, if it were THAT, it's too late." I didn't hug him anyway. I sat on the back steps taking in the warmth of the late afternoon sun and letting Archie roam around smelling every leaf and blade of grass. After dinner, I watched the PBS News Hour and then read some more, went to bed early and read some more before turning out the light.

The book I'm reading is *The Great Influenza: The Epic Story of the Deadliest Plague in History* by John M. Barry. I'd read it when it first came out, 2005, I think. It's about the 1918 pandemic that killed so many, but like many things, I'd forgotten much about it. Given what's going on in our world now, I wanted to revisit it. I came across a word that made me think of one of the critiques Mary-Lou had given me: I often use "big" words, she offered, when simple words will do. The word I came across, which made me run to the OED and Webster is eleemosynary. The definition is: charitable. Here is the sentence in which it is used: "Gates had started working for Rockefeller as a philanthropic adviser, but nothing limited him to eleemosynary concerns." I'm all for using interesting words to illuminate a point, to enhance a meaning, to produce a more elegant phrase, but I'm sure I shall

not ever use eleemosynary in anything I write. It wouldn't be charitable!
Maria

Friday, March 27, 2020

Attend a webinar on the effect of the pandemic on ESOP valuations. Complicated issues. The Employee Stock Ownership Association (TEA) is now operating totally virtually. Over 750 participants Zoom into the conference.

Nice phone conversation with my sister Nell. She lives in Minneapolis but is stuck in Houston where she has been babysitting her youngest granddaughter. Hesitant to fly home.

Watch former VP Joe Biden on CNN Town Hall.
Gina

Saturday, March 28, 2020

Rough morning: Attempted to get groceries. We are a family of vegetarians. I have a teenage boy. He will eat an entire pint of blueberries in one sitting. I have a guinea pig who eats a whole head of lettuce by herself. In two days, we're out of tomatoes. And you already know all about the bananas. We burn through food, even with stocking up and planning. And then there's that rub: Buy too much and you're a hoarder; don't buy enough, you must go out again. I feel I can do nothing right.

I feel like it is not right to ask someone else to do something I'm capable of doing. I am young (ish). I am currently healthy. And I try. I really try. When I go out, I don't speak, lest I "say it and spray it." I smile at cashiers. I nod politely. I wave. I mime. I wear gloves. I do not cough. Ever. I would bite off my own tongue before I let that happen. It is also entirely possible that I am fine and not the insensitive plague-spreader that others might think I am.

Like this morning: I drove to Stew's, found the parking lot jammed like a regular Saturday. I drove right back home. I didn't spread anything anywhere. For going out "a lot," in 16 days I have been to six places: two restaurants, one grocery store, one liquor store, and two trips to the pharmacy. I run in, I run out, like a little mouse. All told, in 16 days, I've spent less than 90 minutes being out in the peopled world. Is that too much? I don't know. And I am angry that, after all this, I still have an empty refrigerator, and might be frowned at when I try to fill it.

Lynn

Saturday, March 28, 2020

The usual Saturday, laundry. It felt normal. It's a good illusion. I do feel better than yesterday, although ears are still not clear. Paid some bills, took a walk with Archie. Maybe I'll watch a movie tonight.

I read all your virally entries and continue to marvel at the writing. Thank you all.

Stay safe,

Maria

Saturday, March 28, 2020

Except when I'm out walking, every day is a mental health day at our house—reading, food prep, eating, less and less TV watching, except at night, and more sleeping. One of the best books I ever read—and I think I'm repeating myself virally—is by a fine writer, Geraldine Books. Its title is *Year of Wonder.* It is impossible to put it down. Try a 17th century plague for a change!

Mary-Lou

Saturday, March 28, 2020

I watched Trevor Noah interview Dr. Fauci on YouTube the other day. He asks the doctor about groceries. The doctor didn't seem

concerned. It's worth watching, just to see the doctor answering questions in simple terms. Our days are so filled with mysteries.
Donna

Saturday, March 28, 2020

Started this gloomy day with a matching mood. I'm very susceptible to changes in light, which is why I bought a light box—a fake sun—into which I was supposed to stare for about 16 minutes each day. It didn't work to elevate my mood, but, along with a 5x mirror and tweezers, it was a good way to pluck my eyebrows. But I digress.

I don't want to be responsible for anyone but myself (and I don't always trust me, either) but I'm skipping the grocery-washing bit. It is so difficult to live in this surreal situation. We must come to terms with not knowing. Given my desire to control everything in sight, by loosening up a bit—just peel and eat the banana—is a big step for me.

We get our Sunday NYTimes on Saturday, which means we get the magazine section, which means we compete to see who can figure out the Spelling Bee near the back of the mag. It's a jumble of letters, all of which you must use at least once to make the mystery word. It's a competition I lose, almost predictably. Today was no exception. The result is that I felt a little worse for trying. I'm supposed to be good with words, but he's better.

I am a sore loser. I like to think that I would have been a good sport if it weren't for my older sister who was better at everything than I was and got to be and do everything 3 years sooner than I did. As far as she was concerned, I existed to be teased. Plus, when it most mattered, when I was awkward, flat chested, freckled and pubescent, she had a peaches and cream complexion, a garter belt, breasts, and boyfriends. How could I compete with that? But I digress.

By now I should have grown up, gotten over her and been able to deal with my word-winning husband. Unlike my sister, he doesn't even gloat. Nevertheless, this day is ruined.

Desperate to make myself feel better, I head for the peanut butter cookies I'd made two days earlier. Larry had gotten there first and finished them.

Can this marriage be saved?

Mary-Lou

Saturday, March 28, 2020

Ordered *Year of Wonder* from Amazon.

Today was one of the least productive days I can recall. I started the day with a number of goals, finished none including taking a nap. I tried to start a new book from my extensive library of highly recommended ones *only* to have successfully littered my desk with several them without reading past a few lines of any of them. I dislike clutter, which is now adding to my annoyance of having been so frivolous with my time.

Tomorrow will be better; I hope. Will it be Sunday or Monday?

Ken

Saturday, March 28, 2020

Advice on hand sanitizers: NO SPIRITS, NOR VODKA, serve. The strongest vodka is 40% alcohol, and you need 65%.

OK, so I printed this out in a large font and gave it to my nine-year-old 4th grade granddaughter who loves science.

At dinner tonight:

"Evelyn, how much alcohol is in vodka?"

"40%, Grama."

My daughter looks at me with incredulity.

"Where did she get that?"

"It's all scientific!"

My nine-year-old granddaughter does know about the 65% effective alcohol level for hand sanitizers. My daughter wants to sanitize me—from what I share with my granddaughters. Monica did muse about the alcohol content in wine, which seems to evaporate at an unprecedented rate at this household. I keep taking corks from garbage and putting them in the recycle bin. Time to screw that.

Gina

"...and a small child shall lead them" straight to the liquor cabinet. Don't waste vodka on countertops and doorknobs.

Mary-Lou

Saturday, March 28, 2020

As the number of virally entries grows, I feel a little like a prisoner-of-war marking the passing days on the wall.

Even so, I had a party today.

A pity party for one. Provisions are running a bit low. Friends who have been helping are stocked up and staying home. When I received a text from my daughter-in-law that my son was headed to the grocery store, I broke my resolve not to ask him to drive to Westport to drop off groceries. He wrote back that he wasn't going out—too dangerous. I'm embarrassed to admit this, but I felt abandoned. Of course, he and my friends were totally right, and their safety is far more important to me than whether I have milk in the house. It wasn't a rational response, just a reaction to the frustration of not getting test results and feeling like my most basic needs are swirling out of my control. Another reminder that I'm alone, whether Covid-19 exists or not. I've gained a sense of strength through that aloneness by resolving large and small life crises on my own, some of which would have been in Dave's wheelhouse. But pandemics are beyond my scope. Grocery store shelves bare, grocery deliveries taking days to arrive, test results delayed, complete physical isolation.

So, I decided that since I was having a party, I would order a special "pity" dinner. It took two hours for the celebration to reach my door, but it was so worth it!

A friend and I discussed the term "social distancing." The connotation is of someone who keeps intimacy at bay. A player protected by an emotional force field. We aren't socially distanced. People are reaching out for contact in every conceivable way. We are physically distanced. At a time when suicide hotlines are buzzing off the hook, and the requests for teletherapy are skyrocketing, when victims of domestic abuse are locked in at home with their abusers, we need to feel as though someone cares. Words make a difference. Socially connected; physically distanced.

Deb

Sunday, March 29, 2020

The lead article in today's the *NYTimes Week in Review* (Ken— today is Sunday) by Maureen Dowd is about the effective, crisis leadership style of New York state's Gov. Andrew Cuomo. While I agreed with her assessment of Cuomo's clear and truthful remarks in contrast to Trump's bumbling and dissembling "leadership," her essay made me fearful. So far, Cuomo has been smart enough to realize that flattering Trump now and again is worth the ventilators. So far, so not so good; it could be worse. What if Trump, who says he doesn't read the "fake news" *Times*, does, in fact read it? And if he does, will he see Cuomo as his enemy rival for being recognized as more presidential than he? And will Trump punish him as he does everyone whose very being casts a shadow on his presidency? And if so, might Trump's shoot-from-the-hip-style revenge take the form of stalling the delivery of ventilators to New York State, or perhaps something even worse that I'm too fearful to consider?

Anything is possible, but what most frightens me right now is the fact that I am even moved to ask myself these conspiratorial questions.

Mary-Lou

Sunday, March 29, 2020

I watch Governor Cuomo's briefing where he describes Sunday dinners with his Italian family. Heartwarming. I am inspired to make spaghetti and hot Italian sausage with ciabatta rolls for our own Sunday dinner.

Gina

Thanks, Gina, for making up for lost time. I'm loving Cuomo. I've heard he's a difficult character, but his words this morning about his brother brought me to tears. Can't help but wish he were in charge. I suspect we wouldn't need constant fact checks.

We haven't sent out for food, yet, because we enjoy cooking. But I'm wondering if maybe we should. We wouldn't mind some nights off and, more to the point, it would be a good way to keep our local markets and restaurants in business.

Mary-Lou

Sunday, March 29, 2020

Mostly Gentle Thoughts on Politics:

My father and stepmother used to go vote together. One election day, over breakfast, my stepmom said, "This is just silly," and they stopped going to cancel each other out. I was raised by three differing views: My father's "I Like Ike" Republicanism, my stepmother's artsy-fartsy-lefty-liberalism, and my mother's "I ain't standin' in a line to vote for some jerk who's richer than God and doesn't give a shit about the rest of us" mentality. (My mother did vote, just once; ironically, for Ross Perot in '92, saying, "Finally! An independent!" I didn't bring up the whole "richer than God" thing.)

I'm somewhere in the middle politically—a blend of all the people who raised me. And I'm fickle. I don't go by party line. I'll vote for who is most sensible, most graceful, most charming, who has a better voice and better speechwriters. I'll pick three of this and two of that, like donuts or bagels. I love to vote. I've never missed an election. I think about places where people have protested and died for the right, and how in other countries, women especially still face difficulties and can't vote safely. I can give up half an hour once a year to take a small stand for something. I feel very proud, very humble, and very powerful when I turn in my ballot. Plus, I'd do anything for a sticker.

The candidates I vote for seldom win. I scored big with Obama and Clinton and that's about it. In 2012, when Mitt Romney was running, his clumsy "binders full of women" comment during a debate basically put an end to his campaign. People were turned off. Four years later, a much less eloquent candidate bragged about sexually assaulting women and went on to win the presidency. If that's not enough to rattle a logical brain, nothing is. That a populace could elect someone after such a comment continues to blow my mind. My world view is based on giving people the benefit of the doubt; on the assumption that everyone is good, even if flawed. But about #45, I am not so sure. (A friend of mine refers to the president only by number, saying that she cannot bear to say his name, like Voldemort.)

Sometimes I wonder what 45 must have been like as a boy. Was he loved? Doted on? Ignored? He was sent away to boarding school at thirteen. Maybe he didn't want to go. He had siblings. Maybe they were mean to him. Did he want to be a chef but Dad forced him into the business instead? Theories abound that he did not form successful attachments to his parents. I do not try to justify, but I try to understand. It helps me to think of him being five years old. He was little, too, once. He wanted the same things we all do; love and security and attention. I imagine him being denied those things, as I remember myself being denied them when I was young. It takes the edge off; it makes me feel compassion rather than disgust when I see how in over his head he is, even though he's able to imperil us all. As much as I wish that someone else were at the helm, the best of men—or women— would likely be struggling these days.

My sister has lost friendships over 45 and is no longer speaking to our cousin who supports him. I think my sister is wrong. I believe in free speech and differences of opinion. I believe that people have their reasons for thinking the way they do, even if I deeply wish they'd think otherwise. People have different religious beliefs, different tastes in music, favorite foods that I can't stand. Getting angry over such things seems foolish. Nobody's 'right.'

I keep in mind that being the president is an impossible job. My family can't even agree on pizza toppings. How is one person supposed to unite 327.2 million of us? For sure, some have done better than others. With 45, the adage, "Expect nothing and you'll never be disappointed" comes to mind. His behavior and rhetoric and wacky mispronunciations have ceased to surprise me. Like the sun rising—there it goes again. Even the late-night hosts' jokes are stale. Circumstances are more serious now and I long for the days of "covfefe," when 45's headlines were silly and harmless. I am forced to view this presidency as I do this pandemic: something I have no control over. Something we all must endure with civility. Something that started one January and will, one day, end.

Yesterday, when 45 rambled about a possible quarantine of Connecticut, even my stoic husband was alarmed: "We should go get the groceries now. Like, right now." Leadership shouldn't be spit-balling ideas at press conferences and scaring people. Or telling lies. Or engaging in vindictive quid-pro-quo, foreign and domestic. I could go on. However, I believe in democracy. I believe that we elect enough donuts and bagels to check and balance whatever goes on in the zoo. At least that is my hope.

Lynn

Sunday, March 29, 2020

My hair looks like I've been struck by lightning. I'm allowed to leave it this way because it's Sunday. In fact, I know it's Sunday because it's late in the day and my hair still looks this way.

This is how I demarcate weekend from weekday. On weekdays I wear real clothes and wet my hair to get my curls back. I'm presentable for Zoom meetings. It doesn't really matter what's going on below my neck, except for psychological impact. On weekends, I can hang out in my sweatpants and let myself go entirely. My FaceTiming family won't care.

Of course, these regulations are entirely self-imposed. I set a schedule and boundaries for myself the way blind people do so they will be on the same day/night, wake/sleep schedule as the sighted. They help me balance on top of the tightrope that is quarantine.

Deb

Sunday, March 29, 2020

Good morning, writers! This morning as I was writing in my journal, I decided to write an acrostic for the word pandemic. My mind shifted from thinking about it to searching for words to describe it. A welcome shift.

Here's my first draft:

P—People quarantined to stay healthy and flatten the curve

A—All of us on planet Earth are involved

N—No one is exempt

I'll show you the rest of mine if you show me yours. Or not. Of course, you don't have to do this. I'd love to see what other wordsmiths come up with. No rush, you have until the end of April (not funny—right?).

Anticipating at least another month at home is disheartening, except for two thoughts:

1. Humans are adaptable and I will get used to this. It won't continue to feel like I'm dragging an anchor around the house.
2. I'm in a space I love with all the conveniences I need and surrounded—on FaceTime and Zoom—with people I love.

I intend to delve into the book *The Pioneers*. I had to laugh to think how I'd fare for a month as a pioneer woman settling in Ohio in the early 1800s. Talk about daunting! It makes being quarantined in 2020 look easy. Or maybe I'd like carrying water from the creek, wearing the same clothes all winter, milking the cow, etc. No. Give me my modern conveniences and tell me to stay at home.

The sun is trying to peek through the clouds. Whether it does or not, may your day be sunny. Here's to health and resilience.

Donna

I'll play!
Population on lockdown.
Anybody got any toilet paper?
No?
Damn!
Every day's the same.
Monday? Sunday? What's the difference?
I would kill to sit in a
Café.
Lynn

Positivity challenge
Anxiety
No end in sight
Death
Evil, egomaniac
Medical supply shortage
Invisible invader
Creative funk
OR
Puzzle mania
Alcohol wipes and spirits
No make up
Daffodils
Elastic waistbands
Michelle and Daniel hugs
Ice cream
Contact friends from far away
Morgaine

Pathogen lurking
Art making
No escaping

Days blending
Eating everything
Mind numbing
Isolation mandating
Connection triumphing
Deb

Passing time with Archie
Anticipating spring
Need more wine
Don't worry, he says—moron!
Early bedtime
Making cookies
Ice cream all gone :-(
Crossword puzzles
Maria

P is for the panic we are feeling
A is for the air we dare not breathe
N is for those "nasty," brave reporters
D is for deceit that makes us seethe
E is for the end of epidemics
M is for the martyrs in our midst
I is for instructions that will save us, and
C is for Gov. Cuomo who is pissed.
(Put it all together, it doesn't spell mother.)
Mary-Lou

Monday, March 30, 2020

Hi writers—I found a new place to walk today—Fairfield. Chilly winds and overcast skies made Sherwood Island seem forbidding. Instead, we walked in the old section of Fairfield, just off the Post Road. If you're looking for new territories to conquer, drive past Fairfield Center and shortly take a right onto Beach Road. That will lead you into the Old Post Road, which is lined with wonderful, old colonial and Victorian houses. The British, we learned, burned down most of the town in the 1700s, but the ones they left standing are covered with plaques and interesting historical information and familiar names: an old tavern where G. Washington, who slept around a lot, crashed for a night, the Burr house, Roger Ludlow, etc. There's even an old cemetery located dead center (pardon the expression) in the old section.

As for Donna's acrostic and then Lynn's, I see we've entered a new writer's territory in which I am eager to play. But first, I must give credit to my husband, the same one who beats me at Scrabble, the Spelling Bee, and crossword puzzles and eats my peanut butter cookies. He's into limericks.

There was a young man from Nome
Who got tired of staying at home.
When you live in an igloo
There's not much you can do.
'Cause life is quite dull in a dome.

This viral insistence
On keeping your distance
Has certainly been quite a bore.
It's very frustrating
To be separating
From others by six feet or more.

How about puns? If Thoreau were alive during this pandemic, he'd feel very walled in.
Mary-Lou

Monday, March 30, 2020

I love all this, especially Larry's limerick and Donna's acrostic.
Polly

Monday, March 30, 2020

Get trash out and do two weeks of laundry. Preoccupied with watching the briefings on CNN. I need to turn off the TV. Attend our weekly six-person team call by Zoom for the first time. I put on makeup and wear a blazer. Attend two Zoom webinars in the afternoon.
Gina

Monday, March 30, 2020

Late afternoon and my daughter left after giving me a much-needed haircut—I feel so much better. I sit down to read last *Sunday's New York Times Magazine*, finally. Dinner is on the stove, a mixture of vegetables from the fridge, some old, some fresh. With a ton of garlic, some shallots, and wine, it'll make a nice dinner over linguini.

I read *Bog Bodies*. Preserved bodies from long, long ago found in northern bogs. Some are thought to have been criminals (one had a rope around its neck), or maybe deposed monarchs. Who knows, really? We can only suppose what happened. Perhaps you read the article, too. I come across a passage that stops me. It stops me because it is speaking of the bog people, but it reaches me as if speaking of today. Here is what I'm referring to, in case you missed it: "Of course, the past does not exist to be explained. It is sovereign, peculiar and particular." And then, a few sentences later: "The past has its own past."

We delve into the past in our memoirs, but our pasts are immutable, immovable, set as if in stone—except in our memories. Why do we revisit what once was? Each of us travels back in time for our own very personal and peculiar reasons. I'm not sure I understand the second quote: "The past has its own past," but I want to think about it.

Hope you are all enduring the present and staying safe. Deb, have you gotten the results of your test back?

I have not read the latest virally group, but I will. Our Spanish group is going to try meeting on Zoom tomorrow afternoon. More on that later. The news is depressing. I turn the TV off.

Maria

Monday, March 30, 2020

The dishwasher stopped working, but I fixed it. That was the extent of today's excitement. I am great with plumbing. I repair running toilets, leaky faucets, plugged-up drains, dishwashers with error messages. My husband and I have an unspoken agreement: water related and I fix it; electrical and he fixes it. Plumbing makes sense to me, but electricity is like magic—a helpful ghost that powers my coffee maker. I do not understand its ways.

Under the electrical heading falls all technology, too. I have put in way too many frantic calls to "tech support" while my husband is at work. "Honey! There's no internet!" or "Lover! The TV! It is not doing what I want it to be doing!" I go through all the reboot steps before I call. When it still doesn't work, I get pissed. Again, I sound like my father, complete with the cursing, "All I want to fucking do is watch a goddamn TV show! Jesus Christ!"

My father believed in a vengeful god, and that god was called the "Get Goldman Office." Whenever my father felt he had been transgressed upon, he would rail, "The Get Goldman Office is at it again!" Every pothole in the road was placed there by the Get Goldman Office. Next time you hit one, blame my dad; it was meant for him. Lost your keys? The GGO was hiding them just to mess with you. Internet down? The GGO was trying to ruin your day. All of life's random inconveniences were the orchestration of the Get Goldman Office. *(I imagine a heavenly kind of King Arthur's round table of hippies, yuppies, senior citizens, small children, and feminists (all groups my father despised), sitting in high-backed chairs, looking down and coming up with ideal ways to torture him. "Let's have the cat puke on the stairs so he steps in it on his way down in the morning!")*

While I doubt my father would blame the GGO for the coronavirus, I've been wondering what he'd make of all this pandemic stuff. He would have been most distressed by the closing of his favorite watering holes and steak houses. I can see him rolling his eyes about the term "social distancing," saying something like, "What are they going on about? The only person I let get close to me is my wife." He would have found delight in the Red Sox's season getting canceled. He would have called to check on me and said, "Daughter Number Three! What's been going on in the 'port?" He would have told me to stay safe and wash my hands, but with swearing and jokes, and he would have reminded me to keep beer in the fridge and not go to any parties. My dad was difficult, and our relationship complicated, but lately I find myself missing him.

Lynn

Monday, March 30, 2020

Four Zoom meetings today and one regular phone meeting. A meeting without video seems so low-tech all of a sudden.

Sadness upon sadness. The first Covid death in Westport that I know of hits close to home. My daughter had a best friend in high school, who practically lived at our house when his parents divorced. I remain friends with him and his mom. Today, her long-term partner became a statistic of the pandemic. Fast. A matter of hours. He had underlying heart disease; was not gifted with many more months, or maybe years, as it was. I think of him dying alone, of his beloved partner unable to be with him to say goodbye.

This physical distancing calls loudly for us to reach out in any way we can. There's the beauty in it.

Deb

Tuesday, March 31, 2020

My husband's test came back negative. It took nine days. Sixteen days, if you count the week, he spent just trying to *get* the test. He looked up all the testing details on the CDC website. He said that for him, hardly any of the protocols were followed. False negatives are upwards of 40%. I think my husband had a Q-tip shoved up his nose for nothing. After all that, it hardly matters. Green light and nowhere to go anyway.

Well, that's bad news, because now he can still get it. I got in my car and went to Target, Trader Joe's, four liquor stores and a Walgreens. Kidding.

My husband has had free range of the house again for a few days. He keeps saying, "I'm feeling much better!" as he stifles a cough, and then another. But he looks better. His color is up.

We finally slept in the same room. It was anticlimactic. He woke me up in the middle of the night, taking a walk-about with the lights on, to check on the cat. When he came back to bed, he put a wall of pillows between us, defeating the purpose of my being there, I felt. And in the morning, he complained, saying I am loud when I sleep. Loud, like Darth Vader. Perhaps we rejoined each other too soon; or perhaps were away too long.

Last night, before bed, he got himself an ice cream out of the freezer—one of those Drumsticks with nuts. He left the wrapper sticky and dripping on the counter, and a trail of nuts on the floor.

I swear to god, it was easier when he just stayed upstairs. Kidding?

We went for a walk today: a one-mile loop around Fillow Street. It was the most steps he's taken in three weeks. We might start going around twice if the sun ever comes out.

Lynn

Lynn, I'm very relieved for you and your husband, despite the doubts about whether he really was negative. This is such a crazy f'd up time. That you have kept your sense of humor is amazing. As a sister humorist, I suspect that what we share is a strong inclination for the comedy side of the mask, when the tragedy side insists upon showing its face.

Mary-Lou

Tuesday, March 31, 2020

The dog has earned his keep. At least I think he did.

No, he did not get my test results for me. I still wait for those. Nor did he go shopping. Good thing, I can imagine what low-hanging fruit he would have helped himself to.

He acted just like a dog, one with a very deep, loud bark.

The story begins last Thursday. That's the night I take my recycling out to be collected.

Usually, I remember to bring the empty bin into the garage when I see it in route to my car. But being quarantined, I haven't used my car. So, I forgot.

Skip to Saturday. I ordered takeout for dinner. A rainy night. I opened one of the garage doors so the delivery person could travel the least distance to leave my food in a sheltered spot. He came up to the front door anyway and left the bag on the veranda. I forgot the garage door was open.

Sunday night. Arlo ran to the door leading from the kitchen to the garage, barking furiously. He's a good watchdog and will bark even if someone arrives at my neighbor's house. And deer on the property seem to be a personal affront to him. They get the same treatment, so I usually assume it's deer. Eventually he stopped barking. Incident forgotten.

Until late Monday night. That's the night I take my garbage out to be collected.

It's also the first time I had cause to be in my garage since the weekend. Damn, the door had been open and the automatic light on since Saturday. Cha-ching, Eversource must be thrilled! I placed the garbage pail outside but didn't see the recycling bin. A glint in the dark beyond the circle of light coming from the garage told me the empty bin must have been blown a little by the heavy winds over the weekend. I went to fetch it.

Not empty! Very, very heavy. ???

I dragged it back to the garage. In it were: 1 power saw, 2 electric drills, 1 Ryobi weed wacker battery, 1 circular drill, 1 charger, 1 small chainsaw and 1 large chainsaw. I was stumped. Had someone borrowed these? Maybe my contractor had them for years and returned them? Why didn't he text or call? Then I looked at the shelves where I store Dave's remaining tools. Empty. Did my bin blow onto my neighbor's property? Did he dump it at the head of my driveway, and weight it down with tools to prevent a repeat performance? Why not just dump it in the garage where it wouldn't blow away?

I closed the car-sized garage door and uncharacteristically, locked the one used by humans. I was more than a little freaked out and had trouble getting to sleep. Whatever the reason, someone had walked into my garage and only Arlo knew it.

Today I was talking to my daughter in Belgium and mentioned it.

"Mom, don't you realize? Someone was stealing that stuff but got scared off by Arlo!"

"Oh my god, you're right, it's the only explanation! Power tools are easy to sell over eBay and Craigslist."

"Yeah, but what I don't understand is how would they know the garage was open?"

"A light comes on when the electric door is opened and stays on until it's closed. It shines onto the top of the driveway and can be seen through the little window. Perfect announcement to anyone on the street to just walk right in and take what you want."

"Did you call the police? I'm worried about you." She's as protective as Arlo, especially since she's so far away.

"I didn't call the police. It never occurred to me that someone tried to rob me. Now I've put everything back and it's probably too late. But I'll lock the garage every night, and when Arlo barks, I'll let him out!"

And with the typing of that last sentence, he is barking right on cue. The landscapers have arrived next door.

Deb

Tuesday, March 31, 2020

Before anyone else is awake I come downstairs to clean the cat box and wipe up whatever crumbs are left on the counter from the night before. I'm pleased to see there aren't many. I walk down the mudroom hallway, open the door to the supply closet and reach in for Riley's pooper scooper. It's gone! *Huh?* I leave a note. "Whoever borrowed the pooper scooper, please return it." I sign it, "Thank you, Management," and go back upstairs.

Upon my return to the kitchen, I see Michelle writing in her notebook. The scooper is still missing, and she hasn't seen the note. She's busy doing her "morning pages," a daily exercise from the book, *The Artist's Way.*

I start grilling her, "What happened to the pooper scooper?"

"Don't ask me." she says and storms up the stairs. My anger has nothing to do with the damn pooper scooper. In all fairness,

I *am* a fanatic regarding housecleaning. Not an easy pressure to live under. I do feel I've made progress in relaxing my standards though.

I feel bad, I'm angry and I take it out on Michelle. But she overreacted, I rationalize. How am I supposed to know she too is struggling with repressed emotions about being quarantined this morning? And that she happened to be writing about those feelings when I bombarded her with questions?

Eventually, Michelle and I hug it out. We agree we're all doing the best we can.

Morgaine

April 2020

Wednesday, April 1, 2020

I go downstairs to the kitchen to get my first cup of coffee. Several of the cupboard doors are hanging open; dishtowels and hot pad mitts are strewn about. Our dining chairs are skewed at awkward angles. Blankets, pillows, and throws are draped all over chairs and heaped in piles on the floor.

"What the?"

I walk into the living room and spy a large sheet of paper with a note sitting on the coffee table.

"April Fool's!" Nine-year-old Evelyn and seven-year-old Frances had gotten up at 2 AM to pull off their prank. We all giggle so hard I almost spill my coffee.

Then my phone pings. A message from my 47-year-old daughter, Maria. I had texted her earlier to ask how her day is going.

"Not great. I just took a pregnancy test." I stare at the phone. She's separated from her husband of 24 years and has been catching up on lost time—*if you know what I mean*. I press the button to call Maria. I don't think Siri would have understood me.

"Was it positive?" I hope Maria can't hear the anxiety in my voice.

A long, long, long pause. Then an explosion of laughter.

"April Fool's, Mom." Oh, my god. I've been completely had. We both roar with laughter for five minutes straight. I haven't laughed that hard in years. It feels wonderful.

Gina

Wednesday, April 1, 2020

When is the last time you pulled your washer dryer away from the

105

wall and got back there with a vacuum and a mop? That was my early morning task after jumping rope 500 times and several other calisthenics. Then I went down to the basement and cleaned out my dark room, which I haven't used since I went digital. Is my "compulsive cleaning" a blessing or a curse? The verdict is still out.

Exhausted, I lay out on the back porch in the sun and closed my eyes.

"Did you hear? Breaking news… Pence has tested positive for the coronavirus."

Michelle and Greg cheer. Greg pulls out his phone to see for himself.

"April Fool's! Gotcha."

Morgaine

Compulsion—To answer Morgaine's dryer challenge, I didn't pull out my dryer because I hate fluff as she does, but because the dryer wasn't getting the clothes totally dry. Turns out there was a hole in the exhaust hose that we fixed with duct tape. Still, I did get kind of turned on by the 2" lint fall I discovered. I gathered some of it in my hands and vacuumed out the rest. I'm definitely a borderline compulsive cleaner.

Mary-Lou

Wednesday, April 1, 2020

Sorry to be offline. I'm down with fever and sleeping day and night.

I shall watch *Les Miserables* and dream delirious dreams of French Revolution style consequences for responsible parties.

Kisses from quarantine,

Bernadette

Wednesday, April 1, 2020

Welcome back, Bernadette. I'm so sorry to hear that you've got a fever—is that a coronavirus fever? I hope not. Write when you can and let us know how you are doing.

Today has been way too typical for any serious consideration—no missing pooper scooper, no family crisis—just the same ol' walk in Sherwood Island, followed by shopping in Wilton, followed by dinner, followed by one-half pint of *Talenti* Coffee Chocolate Chip. (Larry had to wrest the spoon from my hand.) So how about a joke?

Greg, he who fooled me with Pence's bogus health report, reminded me that I'd heard a joke today that just happened to coincide with April Fool's Day. So, blame Greg if he emboldened me to tell this. It is a twinky bit irreverent.

"Five people are on an airplane that is about to crash—Hillary Clinton, Donald Trump, Dr Anthony Fauci, Pope Francis, and Greta Thunberg. Unfortunately, there are only four parachutes. Dr. Fauci says he must have one of them because he's crucial to stopping the coronavirus. The pope believes he must have one because he is needed for spiritual guidance during these troubled times. Donald Trump claims one because, after all, he is the president and leader of the free world. So that leaves Hillary Clinton and Greta Thunberg. Hillary says to Greta, 'You take the last one. You are young. You will do wonders for this world, whereas I have had a full and satisfying life.' Whereupon Greta says to Hillary, 'Actually there are still two parachutes left. Trump jumped out wearing my backpack.' "

Another subject, this one inspired by Polly's interest in corona clichés.

"At the end of the day."
"We'll see what happens."
"Nobody has seen anything like it."

Watch an entire press conference and you'll hear dozens of them. And, by the way, what's with the way Trump moves his hands from side to side as if he's playing an invisible accordion?

Yet another subject. Donna's pandemic acrostic has inspired a couple more in case someone wants to tackle them: Peterpandemic and Pandorasdemic.

Write on and stay safe.

Mary-Lou

Wednesday, April 1, 2020

Since we're on the topic of clichés, I've found one that's helping me:

"One day at a time."

If I wake up in the morning and think, "I'm spending a lovely day at home with my family," then I'm fine. If I wake up and think about the future at all, I feel despondent. If I think, "This?! Till *July*?!" my counting brain starts doing the math and it makes me edgy and snappish. That brings me to my most-hated cliché:

"What doesn't kill you makes you stronger."

To which I retort, "No. What doesn't kill you only makes you wish you were dead." *(There's that comedy mask again, Mary-Lou!)*

I have adjusted to the working from home/schooling from home situation. I have kept a sunny attitude despite my great disappointment over the cancelation of the NBA season, the MLB season, and my 10-day trip to the Baltics. I survived quarantine. I have put up with my people's bullshit. I make meals. I morale-march. I stiff-upper-lip-it. But today, as inconsequential as this might seem, when my son told me they canceled Wimbledon, I had to strangle back a sob. It was enough. I had reached my limit.

My son and I watch Wimbledon together every summer. Ever since he was born, we have had "Breakfast at Wimbledon." We eat strawberries and cream. We have tea. We sit on the sofa and root for people we have never heard of, as well as our favorites. When my son was very small, he loved playing balloon tennis over the back of the couch. He would be Federer. I would be Nadal. He would be Murray. I would be Nadal. He would be Djokovic. You get the picture.

We would bat the balloon back and forth with our hands and try trick shots. He would laugh hysterically and say, "Good one, Mommy!" We would call out the score, "Love, you!" When my son was older, there was one special summer when we were in London while Wimbledon was on, and we went from park to park, watching it on big screens at venues all over the city. We would watch the crowds on the lawn and think about taking the Tube out there, but we never did. We said, "Next time." We are not tennis fans by any stretch, but my son and I always had that one summer week where we pretended together.

Lynn

Wednesday, April 1, 2020

I usually don't comment on other people's posts, but just so you know, I've read every one more than once and truly appreciate our daily contact. To break tradition...

- Mary-Lou, it was I, not Greg, who made the Pence/corona April fool's joke. I've heard the parachute joke before. It's a good one.
- Bernadette, I received your email. YAY!!! Feel better, our thoughts are with you.
- Judy, I too squint to read the titles on the bookshelves of our newscasters. I also examine the artwork on the walls.
- Lynn, get some strawberries and cream on your next outing (since apparently you go out a lot) and a balloon and challenge your son to a match.
- Gina, we've got chips and salsa. Again, curbside pickup: All pickups come with a ream of paper.

- Deb, I have heard about so many break-ins, so glad you were spared. Yay Arlo!!!
- Polly, *Illustrated Guide to Gardening* (right up my alley) curious about the books your son wrote??? Is he published?
- Ken, I miss hearing your innermost thoughts. Enough with the plagiarism—how are you doing?
- Maria, not sure if you prefer red or white, but either way the boxed brand "Sipper" makes a great chardonnay and cabernet.
- Donna, thanks for the acrostic suggestion. Have been enjoying the contributions.

Morgaine

Thursday, April 2, 2020

My social calendar was full.

Five-minute conversation from my garret window with my friend in the driveway below. She had just returned from a mission of mercy to Whole Foods. My neighbor across the street, also a friend, saw her in the driveway and came over. Two live individuals!

That party was topped off by Zoom happy hour with friends from the political group I'm involved with, the Resisters. Unfortunately, the conversation quickly turned to the coronavirus and it turned into unhappy hour. There were two bright spots. The delicious cabernet I was sipping and fixing my attention on a friend wearing a blue beanie, drinking Corona beer and wielding a Trump bottle opener with a huge mouth that bit the cap right off. Now that was fun! Not enough, though. It's the only party I've ever left before the end.

This is getting old. I've been berating myself (it's a personal specialty) for letting my resolve at the beginning of this give way to something somewhere in the cellar of my being. Recently, though, I heard a psychologist talking about the novelty of anything new at its onset, of building new systems and schedules, of not needing to go to work or school, of increased family and reflection time. But eventually it loses what luster it had. We've adapted, and the inconvenience, the pace, and in this case isolation, get to us. The magnitude is frightening and tragic, and many of us find ourselves under-occupied to help distract us from these feelings. Does help to know this, I think.

Here's what I don't know. Why is this test taking so long?

Deb

Deb, I just heard that Quest and Lab Corp took in way more tests than they had the capacity to process. They built up a tremendous backlog and are playing catch up on. I'm guessing your test is among them. : -(

Morgaine

Thursday, April 2, 2020

Morgaine has challenged me to be more reflective and to share more of my inner thoughts. Perhaps I can start with my first thought.

I am so busy with so little to do that every task seems insurmountable. Was it only three weeks ago that the more I had to do, the more I could do, even wanted to do? There was always time for another task, regardless of how time consuming. It is not that I lack for things I want to do; rather it is that I have no pressure to get them done and therefore, I don't do them. I think I am going to think on that and report back soon, if I can find the time.

Overwhelmed,

Ken

Ken, thanks for opening up and trusting your colleagues/friends.

Morgaine

Ken, it's so hard to structure yourself when it seems like you're in a time bubble. In fact, it seems like everything is in a bubble that could burst any second. Such an abrupt and terrifying change in our lives. Overwhelmed is a good word.

Deep breaths.

Deb

Thursday, April 2, 2020

Yesterday I had a Zoom meeting with my four sisters, then a writing group for two hours on Zoom, then a Zoom meeting with my daughter in New York City and my son in California. It almost felt like a normal day. Oh, and I walked 8,500 steps on the trail with a walking friend.

Today was yoga on Zoom and a writers' webinar on revision. If I don't let my mind stray to what's going on in the world—I'm managing.

Tuesday night I had another Zoom session with some former colleagues. One who lives in Brooklyn said she and her husband had not left their apartment for twelve days.

That made me think of "The Twelve Days of Christmas." I started creating "On the first day of quarantine I said to myself, I can do this, it's really not bad. On the second day of quarantine, I said to myself, I'm not complaining, I can do this. It's really not bad." Five golden rings became "This too shall pass." I imagine the singer unraveling as the numbers get higher. You don't have to celebrate Christmas to imagine the silly potential. I offer the idea to you in case you can't fall asleep one night.

It does sound like I've gone Zoom crazy, but there's something about seeing faces I love and hearing familiar voices that soothes my soul. Staying connected feels so necessary.

Your words are also a welcome antidote.

Merci! Merci!

Donna

Thursday, April 2, 2020

I realized last week that I was running out of toilet paper, but figured I'd just go to the store (strongly discouraged here, but Meadow Ridge can only control who comes in, not who goes out). Yesterday I started to panic, so I started calling my contacts.

"You have any?"

"Not that I can spare. Try Carole."

"You have any?"

"Not really. Maybe the manager of the Country Store."

"But they're not open."

"I happen to know that the manager turns up between 1:30 and 2:00 to check inventory."

I positioned myself in front of the store at 1:30. By 1:45 I was feeling that typical New York City impatience. What if she's not coming? What if she came earlier? What if my contact lied to me? Was I waiting for Godot?

At 1:50 another woman named Judy arrived.

"You waiting for Ginny?" I asked.

That Judy didn't seem impatient, so I relaxed. "It would be nice if we had husbands to share this with," she commented. Her husband died a year after Bill.

I nod. "It's hard doing this alone."

"Do you have problems with incontinence?" she asks. "I'm wearing special underwear now."

I shake my head. "Only when I laugh hard. But I guess that's coming."

I have a sudden memory of the booklet I received when I was 12. It explained menstruation and how not to be embarrassed at the drugstore when you had to ask the clerk for pads. "Just say *Modess* quietly," it advised. "It rhymes with 'Oh, yes.'"

What I say to Judy is, "My mother used to complain, 'Pads when you're young, diapers when you're old, always some damn thing between your legs.' I was sixty then. I didn't know what she was talking about."

When Ginny arrives, I ask if she has what I need. She hands me four rolls of toilet paper in a plain brown paper bag.
Judy

Thursday, April 2, 2020

This morning I woke up abruptly, sat up in bed and said to Larry, "Where's Rudy?" Not Waldo; Rudy.

If any of you writers are in the mood to imagine where he might be hiding out—could he still be in Ukraine looking for dirt on Biden?—feel free to speculate. Clearly Trump wants him way out of sight. He could easily spoil Trump's late day campaign rallies.

Which reminds me, in this morning's NYTimes there's a letter to the editor from a guy who suggests that if we want to hear the truth about shortages of masks, ventilators, hospital beds and other life-saving medical equipment, we should have an alternative to Trump's "briefings." I agree. Except for Fauci and Birx we're not getting accurate information. When someone from the "nasty" press asks tough questions, such as, "Why are hospitals and governors panicking because they don't have enough testing kits if you say there are plenty?" he interrupts them so they cannot even finish their question and goes off on a safer tangent about his wonderful relationships with governors. I would so like to respect the presidency if not the president, but I can't.

It would be so healthy for the country if we had a nationwide, Cuomo-type briefing. I'm not sure who should sponsor it. Maybe, since we're so divided anyway, it could be a Democratic briefing. Or, if we could find some Republicans to join in, so much the better. At least it would reflect what's going on in the country. Will the truth set us free? Perhaps not, but it would at least make us more clear-eyed and better able to deal with these bewildering challenges.

Maybe I had a bit of what ails Ken—lots to do and no desire to do it. I feel discouraged about this pandemic. I don't believe things will be better soon, not as soon as the end of April, not soon enough to avoid catastrophe. How about I shut up? It's just me; just today.

Mary-Lou

I am happy to listen to former governor of Ohio, Republican John Kasich.

Gina

No doubt he's good, too. I'm a fan of his.

Mary-Lou

Thursday, April 2, 2020

Our trustee team of six has a Zoom meeting to formalize a process for identifying clients whose businesses are at risk. Two team members are fixated on spreadsheets and processes, while the rest of us are working like mad to help clients apply for Paycheck Protection Program loans. The pair that are fixated are trying to grow their own brand. They have seven clients. We have 100. Are they plotting to take over the business?

I identify risk by keeping my eyes open. I find that a client that makes rigging for entertainment venues is now producing protective face shields. A flag company is making masks. I find out about the diamond company closing from a customer list. I've been tracking data on my own damn spreadsheets for years. I don't need another Johnny-come-lately to dream up a new one instead of using the data that is already there. Am I becoming an old curmudgeon?

Gina

Thursday, April 2, 2020

Today was a day of connections.

I called my neighbor Sue. She's got four grown "kids" at home. Last I heard, her husband was in self-quarantine. His dentist had been exposed. I'm relieved to hear they are both back in circulation. As far as she knows, no one on our block has the Covid cooties.

Out in the sun on the deck, I gave Suzanne and Rosie a call. Suzie and Rosie are the most loving, creative, fun couple I know. When we get together, the whole family joins in; we eat and then play charades. Inevitably, it is an evening of rolling on the floor in laughter. I wonder how charades would work over Zoom.

And then, there was my virtual coffee date with Amy. We have several parallels. Daughters with particular palates, sons who disappear all day to their man caves, showing their bearded faces when hunger strikes, and both husbands are lucky to be able to work from home.

We talk books. She throws out the titles, *Prozac Nation*, *Circe*, and *The Overstory*. I hadn't been reading at all, other than news headlines and virallies, but it just so happens this morning, I took a book off the shelf. It was written in the 1940s by a guy named, Percival. It's titled, *Thinking and Destiny*.

It's a *magnum opus* (900 pages) on the purpose and plan of the universe. It covers such topics as, the law of thought, gods and their religions, varying levels of consciousness and death, to name a few.

Amy is intrigued and says she's going to download it.

"It's not an easy read," I warn her, "It's like learning another language. I had to take notes my first time through. Not *just* notes," I laugh at myself, "I drew pictures and diagrams to help me decipher the books complex ideas. Even with a cheat sheet in my hand, there are still passages that I don't quite get on an intellectual level." Ah, but that's when something extraordinary happens. The mind gives way to the body, and deep within my core I understand the text precisely. I recognize Percival's words as truth.

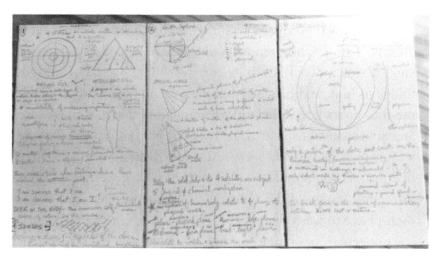

I text Amy my illustrated notes. She texts back, "Wow, you weren't kidding!"

Morgaine

Friday, April 3, 2020

A friend of mine was always thinking about the future: the fun things he looked forward to. If he didn't have anything coming up, he put something on the calendar—plan a trip, or buy concert tickets, or make reservations weeks out at a fancy restaurant, or book a couples' massage. Having something to look forward to always helped him get through all the mundane workaday humdrum. But now? Like the rest of us, he's bummed out. There's nothing fun to look forward to, and there's no indication of when any of us might have fun again. If there was ever a time to legalize marijuana, these are the days.

All the fun I used to have involved going, going, going—going to sporting events, going out to eat, going to parties, going to the movies, going to pickleball, going to the beach, going to museums, going to New York City to see a show. That's what I did for fun. All that going—turned to staying. Stay home. Sit. Stay. Good dog. But, eventually, if too bored or left alone too long, the dog starts gnawing the table legs and chewing the shoes.

My son, who turns 16 next month, has been a trooper through all this. Tonight, he even offered to wash the pots and pans in the sink. It was a conciliatory gesture: earlier in the day I said mean things to him, and he stewed on it and said meaner things back to me four hours later. Then, like a contagion, that meanness spread, and my son and husband argued in their stupid "Who's-the-alpha" way, which drives me crazy. And in my attempt to smooth that over, my husband got annoyed with me. Now we're all hiding in different corners of the house, licking our wounds. But at least I didn't have to wash the pots.

I once saw a woman wearing a sticker: "In Blessed Silence." When people tried to speak to her, she would not answer; she merely smiled and pointed at her sticker. I am thinking of making some for the three of us. I'll do that tomorrow. It will give me something to look forward to.

Lynn

Friday, April 3, 2020
Re Lynn's Digital Diary

It's true. I've always been a go-go girl, and my husband is more so. I think it's been good for me to have my life slowed down, although that it's by an epidemic that slowing some peoples' lives down tragically and sickening others is hardly anything to be grateful for. But the epidemic has had that effect on me. I concentrate better when I'm reading, and I don't always wait until the end of the day to read. Today I spent some time cleaning up the garden. Nature slows me down. So do long walks. Sometimes, when we walk, we don't even talk to one another. But I still did

too much. I have a long way to go before I can let go of go-go.
Mary-Lou

Friday, April 3, 2020

I can't get the thought out of my head, "We're all going to get Covid eventually, it's a matter of the strength of one's immune system."

I have a low white blood cell count. It's "normal" for me, says my doctor at my annual physical each year. What does a low white blood cell count mean regarding fending off the virus? Is that an underlying condition?

I truly don't fear death. It's leaving behind those who rely on me that keeps me up at night. My mother, who I call every day, my daughter, who I remind every day to take her anxiety medication, my husband, who is highly self-sufficient, and can't possibly appreciate all I do to keep our family functioning (and our house clean). In all fairness I'd be lost without him, too.

Can we ever really appreciate how much we rely on each other? All of you who are writing each day and sharing your experiences are keeping me going.

In gratitude,
Morgaine

Morgaine, I don't think we're all going to get Covid. I don't think I'm going to get it and I'm old and practically radioactive. You, on the other hand, can lift 10 reams of copy paper.

We do need one another always, but especially during this terrible time. I don't know how I'd manage if I were alone and couldn't get or give any hugs. My son gives me long-distance comfort. He ends each conversation with, "I love you, Mama." Before this onslaught, he'd say, "I love you, Mom." I read extra love into that. I speak often with my friends, especially to those

who are alone. I love our writers' communications, too.
Mary-Lou

Friday, April 3, 2020

My friend and I were caught red-handed today. Or more accurately, empty-handed. What should have been in each of our hands was the loop end of a dog leash with a dog at the far end. The dog park was empty, save two other people with dogs braving the drizzle, neither of them within sight. We let the dogs off their leashes to play with each other and walked straight into the dog warden.

Plan B. We went to my friend's house and let the dogs play in what had become serious rain. We talked (from an acceptable physical distance) and the dogs completely wore themselves out. There was something very lovely about it. And very comforting. Just that contact with another person, casual and unhurried, regardless of the rain, made up for many hours alone. Watching the dogs, oblivious to viruses, unemployment and death was an encouraging reminder of what life might be after Covid-19. Changed, yes, but not this unnatural enforced isolation and constant awareness of an invisible stalker in our midst.

The damp chill inspired me to finally make turkey soup out of the frozen Thanksgiving carcass and leftover meat. The kitchen warmed from two hours of heat from the cast iron burner and the rich, dark earth smell of broth made from leeks, mushrooms, poultry bones and many herbs.

I sat down to a bowl of soup as Ned Lamont was being interviewed on Firing Line. I've heard him in person several times, and our ReSisters group has discussed how to market him more effectively. He is often ridiculed for his lack of panache. He is far from what you would call eye candy and eschews ten-dollar words for plain talk. Nor is he loud and imposing like Cuomo. But what has always struck me about him is how down-to-earth he is. He comes across like a guy on the street.

I was really impressed with him. He never came close to dodging a question, even when asked if he should have had a Connecticut ventilator company gear up production sooner. His answer was, "Yes, I think I should have." There was no stumbling, no spin. Lots of facts, lots of action being taken, lots of concern for lack of protective equipment. He didn't lay blame, even when discussing the 1,500 ventilators meant for Connecticut that were diverted elsewhere. He referred to himself, Cuomo, and Murphy as the three amigos, constantly working together, and refused to slam Trump when given several opportunities. He was the picture of stable leadership. At the end, the question posed to him concerned whether he was afraid of being seen as overreacting when he issued the stay-at-home order.

"If I overreacted, I could live with that. If there was something I could have done, and didn't, I would never forgive myself."

Watching him was reassuring. We live in a state led by someone who is fully aware that while he appeals directly to Trump and Pence for aid, in the end our lives seem to be in his hands.

Deb

Thank you for your review of our governor. I appreciate knowing we're in good hands at the state level. Today's sun made today feel more like spring and less like the crisis we're in. This morning I told myself I didn't have to be productive in any way. If I thought of something that I might do—such as scrub out the fridge, my reply to myself was "soon." Quite a few things got the same reply, "Soon." I'm wondering when it will be soon.

Donna

Just heard a clip of Trump on NPR saying that he's been in touch with all the leaders, medical and political, in the states and they are all very happy with the equipment they have.

Followed by a report of anger in upstate New York that Cuomo is requiring them to ship 20% of their personal protective equipment and ventilators to New York City because there's such a shortage. Two days after the interview with our governor saying we're desperately in need of more equipment.

Boggles my mind.

Deb

Friday, April 3, 2020

The following letter from my nephew to his father (my brother) brings this home. He's a young man in his forties with two teenagers and wife who live in Granville, Ohio, a small town. I assume he went to the hospital in a city close by. Columbus is an hour's drive. If this is what's happening in Ohio, the message for us in the epicenter is clear.

Dear Dad,

As you know, I had been experiencing some mild symptoms over the past several days related to Covid-19 to include severe aches, fatigue, slight difficulty breathing and a low-grade fever.

This morning I barely could get out of bed, had trouble breathing, and my fever spiked to 100 so I called my doctor. Based on my symptoms he sent me to the ER for evaluation.

I just returned from the ER and didn't really get anywhere with the process. They are not testing anyone unless the person is near death due to test shortages and the ER doc advised testing really doesn't matter anyway as they are treating anyone/all with symptoms as being positive and as he correctly advised, there is no cure or remedy, so you just have to work through it.

I was sent home as bed space is limited and my breathing issues are not to the level where I need constant observation/care or the assistance of an external device. I was advised to self-quarantine for two weeks, meaning not to leave the house and stay away from family members; however all the doctors and nurses I dealt with advised me my immediate family has already likely been exposed and they said the state knows that the virus is everywhere right now so limiting exposure is fairly pointless—they said everyone is going to be exposed at some point and it just will depend on the person's immune system.

So... I'm back at home now and will be here for a while as I work through the illness (whatever illness it is). If my breathing difficulties get to the point where I need assistance, I will return and get admitted; however, to be honest, from my experience today, it would have to be very severe for them to even consider admitting. The ER nurse advised they are just telling everyone to try and take care of themselves at home as aside from ventilator assistance— there is nothing that can be done for persons with the virus— it just must work its way through the body.

Although not healthy, I'm safe and will stay away from other family members and all other persons for the next couple of weeks. I'll keep everyone up to date on how things progress. I feel miserable with zero energy and severe aches, but the Dr. said that should pass in a few days.

I've been questioning the value of the testing. People line up in their cars for hours, get permission from an MD, get tested and then wait forever for their results. From what I've read you can be negative one day and positive the next. I question the reasoning behind this massive testing except for the statistics. If you're positive, the damage to those you live with has already been done.

I'm sorry to have to put it this way, Deb, and Lynn, but what did we know then? Quarantining was necessary.

I also heard this morning that if you have a cardio event and call an ambulance, they'll refuse to come. I hope this is just hearsay as I live with a cardio fragile man who just turned 87.

The good news of today is I found a bucket of disposable gloves!!!! When I volunteered in the ER I would put a few pairs in the pocket of my volunteer's jacket. Yes, there were boxes of gloves in each room, but sometimes they were in an awkward spot, so having a pair in my pocket made it easier. When I was ready to wash my jacket, I'd take the unused gloves out and toss them into a plastic container. I forgot about them, until I was looking for some cleaning supplies and, well, what can bring more joy in this time than a few dozen disposable gloves?

Polly

Thank you for sharing your nephew's experience, Polly. If that's Ohio, what must it be like in NYC?

I can seem fine with my mental health, and then a wave of fear will wash up onto my beach. I'm learning the importance of focus in my life. Perhaps that's a product of my age. I am going to continue to choose my best thoughts, as challenging as that can be at times. Then I need to sit down at the piano, or do a sing-along with a Broadway show, or dance and let the life force flow through me.

I'm so curious—what will be our long-term take-away from this jarring experience?

Stay healthy and keep writing. Creativity is such a Godsend.

Donna

Thank you, Polly for sharing your nephew's story. I can't imagine how he's bearing this with such equanimity. The mere mention of his "breathing problems," of being sent away until he gets better or worse, reminds me of how this country's leadership is failing its citizens, and increases my worry for all of us. I'm even past attacking Trump. What's the point? The press is doing a good job of exposing the weaknesses and dangers in our leadership. There's one of Trump's requests with which I cannot comply: I'm in no mood to thank him.

As I look back on the past weeks of pandemic, I realize that I started out in a "high" mood, as if the danger fired my endorphins and kept me in an "I can do it" fight mode. As this drags on—and it's just begun to drag on—I find myself in Ken's yesterday mood—flat and sinking. I keep reminding myself that I am ridiculously lucky, given what's going on elsewhere. We all watch the news. Reality is undeniable. A "good mood" seems inappropriate.

I'm taking a tip from Donna; instead of sinking into despair, I'll try losing myself in a good book and in beautiful music, and, yes, writing.
Mary-Lou

Polly, that the virus is everywhere is a scary concept to consider. Your nephew appears very calm and I wish him a safe journey through the illness. Chris Cuomo was on CNN the other day recounting his symptoms, and while he didn't have any breathing issues, the symptoms he had were severe. Here's hoping your nephew has a mild case.
Maria

Friday, April 3, 2020

I woke up this morning psychologically convinced that it is Sunday; why else didn't I have something demanding my immediate attention. No matter that it is Friday. I stayed in bed for a moment to ponder the two questions that most bedevil me. What's outside the universe and why, when I have a back itch, is it always located where I can't reach it? Having no success, I delayed a moment more and questioned if future historians will be able to identify the man most responsible for changing the course of mankind, the Chinese bureaucrat who arrested the doctor who tried to warn authorities about Covid-19.

Starting my day, a new question arose. With non-stop news about how the health crisis is overwhelming our capacity to deal with it, how the people who make us safe are themselves becoming incapacitated, how millions are unemployed, and how migrant workers throughout Europe and the US are not available to harvest crops, I wonder if life on this planet will become a re-run of a Mad Max movie. Suddenly, I have a lot of work to do. I am going to watch *Curb Your Enthusiasm.*
Ken

Ken, I think curb your enthusiasm is perfect. In Larry David's world, anything that can go wrong, will go wrong. Sounds appropriate for our current situation. Also, hysterically funny.

Contemplating what's outside the universe might be a bit beyond our control, but hopefully there will be justice for those who could have helped, and for reasons of maintaining their own power, did not. They have a lot of blood on their hands.
Deb

Friday, April 3, 2020
Spend the day organizing digital files and getting credentials updated from valuation firms we engage. The beginning of the month is less pressured with deadlines.
Gina

Saturday, April 4, 2020
Face mask from Larry's fishing garb.
Mary-Lou

Seems like you're ready to tackle the situation!
Deb

"Deborah: Go to your room."
Mary-Lou

I'm already in my room!
Deb

Saturday, April 4, 2020

The sun came out and brightened my mood. I started singing. Larry joined me. Turns out my low times aren't reality based at all; apparently, I'm a slut for sunshine. So off we went to Sherwood Island for a walk, where we greeted and stayed 6 feet away from Ken—slightly bearded—and his wife.

The photo I sent of my "mask" is worth mentioning. (I sent it twice from my iPad but never heard it zip, so figured the image didn't "send." If it did, then you have received three of me which may be at least two more than you need.)

But here's why I sent it. I discovered it among Larry's fishing stuff. Basically, it's a tube, made with two layers of cloth. Unlike regular face masks, no air escapes from anywhere. It does get a bit warm, even sweaty, in there, but once the mask is damp—which doesn't take more than a few minutes—the condensation from your breath turns into a very efficient air-conditioning system. You can find a variety of them on a fishing site. (I'm cc-ing Trump on this.)

Anyone who's read *Intensive Care* knows that we spent too much time at the Esalen Institute in Big Sur, trying to run away from trouble. Instead, we ran into it. Nevertheless, the human potential gurus there were very into the expression, "Stay in the now," which makes a lot of sense since one can't do much about the past, and the future hasn't yet arrived. At an AA meeting I would have received the same message. "One day at a time." Take your pick.

Be safe.

Mary-Lou

Saturday, April 4, 2020

Another technological breakthrough. Have been listening to reports of DJ D'Nice House Party on Saturday night. Figured out how to sign up for Spotify and find his play list—If Michelle Obama and Oprah are listening, so am I. So, I'm now bouncing around in my chair—Ashford and Simpson playing—daughters and I used to dance to their music on a marble coffee table in front of floor-to-ceiling windows at night so we could see a reflection of our moves. I figured marble was indestructible and the "no standing on the furniture" edict had to have an exception or two. Ashford and Simpson used to live in Westport in a compound off Cross Highway. I saw him once driving a Rolls. When he got out, he was wearing a full-length fur coat.

I lied about my age, name, and birthdate to sign up on Spotify—I'm now Goldie and I'm 20 years old—how's that for a do-over? "If I only have one life, let me live it as a Clairol blonde." Seems silly now—wouldn't you want to be a real blonde?—but I felt substandard when the ad first came out. I used to tell Bill that I was going to dye my hair blonde; he'd just look at me with one eyebrow raised. I think his late wife was blonde. He never knew how fraught the topic of hair was for me. Later I thought about returning from my 6-week haircut in New York in a straight, gray wig just to see his face. I imagined his shocked look and then his gasping laughter. Now I wish I'd teased him like that.

Went for a two hour walk today. On my way around the ring road I met a 97-year-old friend. We decided to walk down to a pond on the property. It was silent—no breeze rippling the surface, no geese or goslings, no birds, no fish, no frogs, no dragonflies. The underbrush is greening up, but the trees don't yet have buds except for the red flowers on the maples. We're on the very cusp of spring; not even the virus can stop that rebirth.

We walked back to the buildings, and I continued my way around the road. Met other people, one sitting on a bench, others as passersby. For a while we stood and chatted, keeping six feet between us (although that meant some of us couldn't hear) and asking, "What's new?" No one knows anything although I did learn that some are continuing to play bridge privately despite the ban on "congregating." Further on I met a couple who moved here from Arkansas. When he left to return to their apartment, she began to tell me how depressed he is—87, out of his element, she can't cheer him up. He and I had had a long talk previously about some obscure book in the Bible that predicted an apocalypse. When I googled the book, I discovered that it only occurs in the Catholic Bible, not the Protestant one. Who knew they were different?

Last person to meet was a 97-year-old man sitting in the sun next to the putting green. Our conversation was so animated that someone called from the balcony and asked us what we were talking about. "This and that," I said. We were actually bashing Trump.

The two-mile walk took 3 hours—perfect! Came back and played a Beethoven sonata. Now I'm gonna dance to D'Nice. I still have the table, but no floor to ceiling windows.

Judy

Saturday, April 4, 2020
Sun glowing inside
Watching joyous grandchildren
playing in my yard
Deb

Saturday, April 4, 2020

Spend a good part of the day getting caught up with virally messages. Mary-Lou's facemask is a riot. The afternoon has a patch of sun, so Monica cleans up the patio and pumps up the bouncy house. The girls have a ball tossing themselves around and jumping on the trampoline. Monica makes homemade pizza and scolds me for putting meat in the refrigerator instead of the freezer. We cook up a meal plan for the next few days.

Gina

Saturday, April 4, 2020

Tomorrow, April 5th, I pledge to do nothing!

Morgaine

Sunday, April 5, 2020

One of my favorite quotes is: "If you run into an asshole in the morning, you ran into an asshole. If you run into assholes all day, you're the asshole." After a string of terrible exchanges with my family, I am beginning to wonder if I am the asshole.

My husband got on my case over something minor, which normally I would have barely arched an eyebrow over, but today I exploded in an f-bomb-laced tirade. Maybe because he also got on my case about something minor last night as well. Death by a thousand cuts. Spending time apart lets those cuts heal: talking to other people and enjoying experiences out of the house are like salves. Usually, by the time I encounter my husband again, I have forgotten the slight; but this constant togetherness is a constant reminder, and every slight is an indelible tally-mark.

People talk about the potential Corona-Baby-Boom, but I am wondering if there will also be a Corona-Divorce-Boom. Does seeing someone so up close for so long, warts and all, lead to only seeing warts?

Hours after my invective, we were acting like everything is fine. We got Dunkin Donuts drive-thru and went to Sherwood Island for a few minutes. Sherwood Island is where my husband proposed to me, on bended knee and everything. Sitting there again together, I remembered it's not all warts. I hope he did too.

Lynn

Sunday, April 5, 2020

Bummer day. Woke up this AM with a swelling the size of a golf ball, only a lot more colorful, on the left side of my left foot. It was the size of and as hard as a golf ball. I debated whether to call my doctor. Being prone to panic (thanks Mom) I decided that I either had a quick growing cancer on my foot, or a fiendishly dangerous blood clot that would, if not stopped, make its way into my lungs and kill me. Any of her patients dealing with Covid-19 could just wait a few minutes, while I struggled with my own life and death issues. So, I called.

How many times do I have to feel stupid and embarrassed? Let me count the ways. Never mind. Let's just leave it at "often."

Turns out she thinks that when I walk, the top of my sneaker may have created a hematoma, which is medically fancy for black and blue mark. I should apply ice for 15 minutes 4 times a day. I should not go walking for 2 days. Not go walking? Because of a black and blue mark? Impossible! My doctor walks in Sherwood Island as I do. I'm in danger of getting busted. I am so sorry I called.

Mary-Lou

Sunday, April 5, 2020

Soaking some cotton dishcloths in detergent and bleach. The plan is to use them to make masks. I'm not handy with a needle so this should be interesting. Oh, I can sew on a button and repair a small tear, but not much else. That talent went directly from my mom to

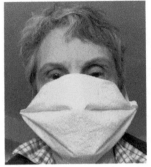

my daughter. There are several videos that illustrate making a mask and I think I can handle the project. They surely won't be the prettiest or neatest things around but hey, what can I lose? Two dishcloths??

Organizing my writing files the other day I found a children's story I'd written a few years ago and sent it to friends with two young boys, one seven, the other not quite two. There are things I can be grateful for even now. I am glad I don't have children at home to supervise schooling or keep entertained.

I am grateful for the sunny days and the warmer temperatures. The daffodils are cheery, and the Andromeda bushes are in their glory. The forsythia has bloomed and the weeping something-or-other in the back is full of white blossoms, so Mother Nature hasn't given up yet!

Stay safe.

Maria

Sunday, April 5, 2020

It seems I am incapable of "not doing." How could I possibly leave crumbs on the floor, not wipe off a sticky countertop or unload the dishwasher? Oh well, I resort to self-acceptance.

I did climb back into bed this afternoon and watched *Knives Out*. Not a great movie but it kept my mind occupied.

Mark and I finished another puzzle. This one is unusual. It's made of mahogany plywood with intricate and unusual shapes. No two pieces are alike. The aroma of the wood and the way the

pieces drop into place is extremely gratifying.
Morgaine

Sunday, April 5, 2020

Even within this state of unusual, normal has crept in around the edges. I've had a lot of work and obligations. Today, I reserved the afternoon just for myself.

The Getty Museum offered a challenge to any who wanted to take it on: choose a famous painting, and using just a few things on hand in your home, recreate the painting. Some of them are funny, some incredible. I love Degas' pastels. I am drawn to his vertical compositions, influenced by Chinese scrolls, and his amazing use of the medium. They break all the rules. So, here is my creation of the afternoon, using my artist's mannequin, toilet paper (appropriate), cloth, and a gray piece of one of my favorite pastel papers.

The day was topped off with a FaceTime dinner with a good friend. Dave and I were close with her and her husband who died five weeks after Dave. We are both physically alone during the Covid era. We both ordered takeout; she had her usual dark beer, I my cabernet, and we talked, sipped, and ate together for two hours thanks to technology.
Deb

Sunday, April 5, 2020
Spend most of the day catching up on compiling the virally

entries. I finally get a chance to write up some of my own doings. The "grand journal" is nearing 100 pages, single spaced. A few of the photos are also included. This is quite the undertaking. If I let it go more than three or four days, I'm done for.

Talk to my son. Northfield Hospital rescinded the budget cuts, so he is back as a manager in the paramedic squad room instead of on the truck. I am SO relieved. Nurse Nancy says same-old-same-old at Hennepin County Medical Center, so I guess that's a good sign for now.

Also talked to my sister, Nell, who is stuck in Houston with her younger daughter Sandra. Nell is waiting for a window of opportunity to fly home to Minneapolis. Her older daughter Sara wants her to stay put and is apoplectic when she finds out Nell went to Costco. Our daughters sure know how to put us in our places.

Monica catches my "be prepared" virus and makes the rounds of Fresh Market and Stop & Shop. Good thing, since I can't get any deliveries scheduled right now. The girls want marshmallows for s'mores now that patio days are coming soon.

Monica comes home with armloads of white roses, yellow tulips, and blue irises. A bounty of beautiful flowers. We'll cook, have a fire in the fireplace and all will be well for tonight.
Gina

Monday, April 6, 2020

The best part of today was outside. The sun shone brightly, which means I did, too. Started the day with a lot of housework—bed-changing, laundry, folding, vacuuming, cleaning the grungy humidifier—the works. Given how much I enjoy physical activity and given that I didn't want to run into my doctor at Sherwood Island and given that my hematoma had reduced in size and color to a plump, purple grape, I relished the work.

Later in the day we took two chairs out of the shed behind the carport and positioned them on the patio. Then we sat together—pooped from housework—and read. For a few minutes all cares disappeared. Spring surrounded us in all its hopeful glory. There is joy and pleasure in the midst of this horror.

I love my house and my yard, even though it qualifies in most realtors' books as a "tear down." We don't even have a garage—just a carport. We bought the place in the mid-1960s to accommodate the needs of our younger son, Peter. Since then, we've added on. After Peter died, we renovated when we probably should have moved, thereby ridding our lives of wheelchair ramps and widened doorways. But we didn't, probably because we didn't want to move away from Peter.

So, here's a funny story about the carport. A while ago, when neighbors could still talk to one another without keeping six feet apart, we took a walk around our block. We encountered a builder whom Larry knew professionally. He was standing outside of an eleven-thousand square foot house he had built. It was located diagonally across the street from ours. The house had been on the market for $3 million and hadn't sold for over 2 years. Of course, the builder was distressed. Most of the houses on our street, like ours, had started out as inexpensive Cape Cods, nearly all of which had been torn down and replaced by McMansions. We asked why wasn't his house selling? It was very attractive, we all agreed.

It wasn't the house, he explained. It was because potential buyers, who were contemplating spending $3 million, did not want their view and their real estate value degraded by looking at a house with a carport. Of course, the builder didn't know he was talking about *our* house, and we were kind enough not to tell him. We waved a cheery goodbye and continued our walk. Eventually the house sold to someone who didn't mind the view, or at least not too much.

Mary-Lou

Monday, April 6, 2020

I said goodbye this morning to Dr. Wong, the ophthalmologist who has treated me for 40 years. He's closing his solo practice to care for his aging parents, filial piety I'm guessing.

I had already talked to his receptionist who admitted that I was one of her favorite patients. She added, "Your husband gave me the book you guys wrote, I've got it somewhere in a box. I've moved a lot since then. Now I'll have time to read it." * Her comment confused me. Had Bill and I written anything together? Then I realized she was talking about Marty. Yes. He was a great self-promoter. Good thing, too. I would never have lined up those book-signing events that he orchestrated.

"He autographed it, too," she added. Of course, he did.

At first my conversation with Doctor Wong was strictly professional. He emphasized that I needed to visit a retinologist regularly to follow the progress of my glaucoma. He mentioned a new operation that's less risky than the one we discussed in November. I made a mental note to keep that in mind. I'm sure my sight will continue to deteriorate. I'm a glass-half-empty kind of person.

Then we took a short walk down memory lane. "It's been a pleasure to work with you," he commented. "Martin too. He was a character."

"Perhaps a better word might be *handful,*" I quipped. "Thank you so much for serving us so well."

There it was. The *us* as in *couple*. I thought I was over that. I thought Bill and I were the only *us* that would be in my mind forever. I thought of the incident that I was sure Dr. Wong was also remembering.

In 1993 I had arranged an alcoholic intervention for Marty. In interventions family and friends of the alcoholic confront him with the effects his drinking has on each of them. A successful intervention depends on surprise, brutal honesty, and a bottom line: if you don't do XX, we will do YY. In my case, I arranged for our three daughters in Boston, my parents, and a couple who were close friends, to meet with alcoholism counselors to prepare what they would say. I found a Black, male alcoholism counselor in White Plains to conduct the meeting since I knew that a white or a female counselor would have no credibility with Marty.

On the appointed day we gathered in the counselor's office. My oldest daughter, Kim, had lured Marty to the meeting by telling him that she had something urgent to discuss with him before she left for a cross country bicycle trip with her boyfriend of the moment. Marty arrived, was shocked to see all of us, listened to the first person's spiel, and left for home and his bottle. When we tried to continue the conversation at home, he locked himself in his study. I explained that we were leaving, left him the name of the rehab facility I'd set up in Chicago, the plane ticket, and the name of the driving service. I'd be back if he went to rehab.

I went to a friend's Wilton home so that they could intercept phone calls for me. When Marty called, they'd ask, "Are you on your way to rehab?" If he answered *No* or the expletive equivalent, they would hang up.

On day two or three, Dr. Wong called. Marty was at his office for an appointment, drunk, disheveled, incoherent. I felt compelled to take the call.

"You should come and get your husband," Dr. Wong said. "He shouldn't be wandering around Norwalk or driving in the state he's in."

"No," I said. "Put him in a cab and bill us."

"You mean you're not coming?" Dr. Wong sounded incredulous.

"I'm not coming. Put him in a cab. Or drive him yourself. I'm not coming." I was sobbing. My friends, watching me trying to talk, were mouthing the word *No*. The husband was making the "stop talking" signal by moving his hand across his neck. Finally, one of them picked up the extension and said, "She's not coming," and hung up.

On day five Marty flew to rehab. I came back to Westport. He stayed in rehab 30 days, came back home sober, attended one AA meeting, one meeting with a therapist and started drinking again. The marriage shifted. I stopped trying to make it work and took a lover. We lived in the house together, but I was no longer present. As far as I was concerned, Judy and Marty Hamer were no longer a couple. There was no *we* or *us*. Eleven years later, Marty died, severing our only remaining bond, the legal one.

I remembered that incident this morning as I said goodbye to Dr. Wong. I think he remembered it too. I blindsided myself by referring to Marty and me as *us*. Where is my head? Where is my heart? Perhaps the real memoir is Judy and Marty's 42-year marriage. I'm not ready to tackle that pain... yet.

Centers of the Self: Short Stories by Black American Women from the Nineteenth Century to the Present, Judith A. and Martin J. Hamer, Hill and Wang, 1994

Judy

Monday, April 6, 2020

Supermarket aisles, like the streets of New York, are now one way. Arrows made of duct tape at each intersection point the way. I was at Stop & Shop this morning at 6:15 AM, wearing one glove, dropped the other one somewhere along the way, improvised with a plastic bag.

Mostly observing the traffic pattern, I came across a fellow senior citizen who had parked his shopping cart with plenty of room for me to pass. I smiled and I wheeled on by.

Peering over his mask he snarls at me, "You're supposed to wait!" I've been housebound for weeks, how was I supposed to know the rules had changed?

I wish I could tell you the day got better from there, but it seems I choose to harbor resentment. It's the pooper scooper. The cat box stinks so bad that my daughter doesn't want to shower in her bathroom and asks to use mine.

It's a gorgeous spring day, I'm out in the garden pulling weeds for an hour or so, stewing over the cat litter.

"Breathe. This too shall pass!"

Morgaine

Monday, April 6, 2020

We can all use a bit of humor, so I thought you might like the following sent to me by a friend.

*I think it's about time we voted for senators with breasts. After all, we've been voting for boobs long enough.—*Clarrie Sargent, Arizona Senatorial Candidate*

*The problem with political jokes is they get elected.—*Henry Cate, VII*

*We hang the petty thieves and appoint the great ones to public office—*Aesop*

*If we got one-tenth of what was promised to us in these acceptance speeches there wouldn't be any inducement to go to heaven.—*Will Rogers*

*Those who are too smart to engage in politics are punished by being governed by those who are dumber.—*Plato*

*Politicians are the same all over. They promise to build a bridge even where there is no river.—*Nikita Khrushchev*

*When I was a boy, I was told that anybody could become president; I'm beginning to believe it.—*Clarence Darrow*

*Why pay money to have your family tree traced; go into politics and your opponents will do it for you.—*Author Unknown*

*If God wanted us to vote, he would have given us candidates.—*Jay Leno*

*Politicians are people who, when they see light at the end of the tunnel, go out and buy some more tunnel.—*John Quinton*

*Politics is the gentle art of getting votes from the poor and campaign funds from the rich, by promising to protect each from the other.—*Oscar Ameringer*

*The Democrats are the party that says government will make you smarter, taller, richer, and remove the crabgrass on your lawn. The Republicans are the party that says government doesn't work and then they get elected and prove it.—*P.J. O'Rourke*

*I offer my opponents a bargain: if they will stop telling lies about us, I will stop telling the truth about them.—*Adlai Stevenson, campaign speech, 1952*

*A politician is a fellow who will lay down your life for his country.—*Texas Guinan*

*Any American who is prepared to run for president should automatically, by definition, be disqualified from ever doing so.—*Gore Vidal*

*I have come to the conclusion that politics is too serious a matter to be left to the politicians.—*Charles de Gaulle*

*Instead of giving a politician the keys to the city, it might be better to change the locks.—*Doug Larson*

*Don't vote, it only encourages them.—*Author Unknown*

*There ought to be one day—just one—when there is open season on senators.—*Will Rogers*

Maria

Monday, April 6, 2020

Glorious sun! I am a glutton for warmth. Arlo and I spent two hours outside at our friends' house. The humans talked; the dogs played. She and I kept a safe distance, the dogs did not.

I understand that physiologically my tendency to run cold has to do with low blood pressure. But the sun seems to penetrate to my bones and just makes me happy. Maybe it's the relief of not having to use so much energy to stay warm that makes these days seem so freeing. Maybe it's the general rebirth as buds form and flowers bloom. The huge forsythia behind the pool looks touched by Midas himself. The front yard is sprayed with yellow daffodils. A spirea bush mocks winter with its snowfall of little white blossoms, which cascade to the deep green leaves and purple blooms of the myrtle carpet below.

When I was riding, this weather marked the transition from the indoor ring to outdoors, from dark to light, from enclosed space to open horizons. Perhaps, because we are somewhat trapped within our own quarters, the arrival of this spring and its invitation to the outdoors seems all the sweeter.

Deb

Monday, April 6, 2020

I take the trash and recyclables out every Monday morning. While the task of getting rid of garbage and trash has a cleansing effect, I feel sad because the Mondays run together too quickly. It is a reminder that another week has gone by, and life is getting shorter. When I was a kid, waiting for three weeks before we'd go on a family vacation seemed like an eternity. Now, anything that is coming in three weeks needs to be prepared for *post haste*.

In early February, I buy a blazer that I plan to wear at an annual conference in Washington DC in May. That meeting is, of course, canceled.

Today we have our weekly Zoom team meeting. All goes well. Focus is on virtual meetings with clients. I also get out a ten-page newsletter for the New York/New Jersey Chapter of the ESOP Association.

Gina

I so relate to your thoughts on time. When I was a child, time was nothing except 3 meals a day.

Now time, even while sequestering, is speeding faster than before the pandemic. With so much "time on our hands" logic tells me that under these conditions, time ought to be slowing down. Should we be grateful?

Mary-Lou

Tuesday, April 7, 2020

Gina, who's been recording our virallies has over 100 pages so far, including submissions, comments, and photos but not videos. So, here's the question. Have we just kept ourselves close and creative during this pandemic, or have we created something that, with editing, could be a published record that others might appreciate? Think about it.

If Gina can download Zoom into my 20th century head, we can proceed on the 16th of April which would have been our last meeting.

Mary-Lou

Thanks, Gina. Just send me the Zoom invite and I'll be there. I've been enjoying meetings with sisters, book group, writing groups, old friends, etc.

Seventy for Easter brunch? Be sure and let us know about how it went.

Donna

Gina, a Zoom class sounds great. We are doing a Zoom Seder on Friday. Midday here for Florida, Boston, Atlanta, and Connecticut; late morning for the Santa Cruz and San Francisco crowd; evening for Belgium and Israel. Could be a free-for-all!! But a fun one.
Deb

Thanks for doing all this, Gina. I've been Zooming with family, meditation group, book group, grandmothers writing group—am beginning to sound like the song, "Come on and zoom, zoom, zoom a zoom." It's from a children's TV program but I can't remember which one.
Judy

The Electric Company!
Gina

Tuesday, April 7, 2020
How to Look Good on Camera, According to Tom Ford

A master class in lighting for your next video conference as told to Maureen Dowd of *The New York Times*:

Step 1

Put the computer up on a stack of books so the camera is slightly higher than your head. Say, about the top of your head. And then point it down into your eyes.

Step 2

Then take a tall lamp and set it next to the computer on the side of your face you feel is best. The lamp should be in line with and slightly behind the computer, so the light falls nicely on your face.

Step 3

Then put a piece of white paper or a white tablecloth on the table you are sitting at but make sure it can't be seen in the frame. It will give you a bit of fill and bounce.

Step 4

Lots of powder, *et voilà!*

Gina

Tuesday, April 7, 2020

Evelyn wants me to get her up at 7 AM to help her try out a secret recipe for French toast. I show her all my secret techniques for measuring the ingredients, soaking the bread, and testing the pan to see if it is hot enough.

I tune into the morning announcements from the Greens Farms School principal with Frances and feel like I am in school again.

Son Chris texts a sky-to-table duck dish he has prepared and is looking for more recipes.

Daughter Maria calls, weeping then laughing as she relates that she has been banned from the Westchester Country Club for being caught on camera pilfering hand sanitizer from the ladies' room. Then she starts a quarantine cookie recipe exchange that I'm supposed to send to 20 friends. Do I even have twenty friends who still bake?

I set up a pro account with Zoom and invite 70 relatives to a virtual Easter Sunday brunch. Already have replies from California and Minnesota. Also trying for a Zoom meeting for what would have been our last writing class on Thursday, April 16th. Mary-Lou and I will have a test meeting tomorrow to see if we can make it work. We could use the session to talk about what we want to do with the virallies.

Gina

Tuesday, April 7, 2020

A quick story. My niece Heather lives in Houston and has 4

daughters. Katie, the oldest, took a job with Disney after college graduation last year. She's been in Shanghai since October. She began a quarantine there the 3rd week in January. Life is back to normal for her, my sister reported after FaceTiming with Katie last night. She can be out, moving about the city, going to her job, meeting friends for meals. That says to me that life really can get back to normal—whatever that will be.

Katie's sister Brittany is home from college. She and Katie share the same favorite author. Brittany bought her latest book, but Katie can't get it yet in Shanghai. So, every night Brittany in Houston reads a chapter to her older sister in Shanghai. Now that's a book club!

Donna

Tuesday, April 7, 2020

I wasn't thrilled to hear my alarm go off at 5:15 AM this morning, but I knew that if I were to accomplish my mission of getting to senior hours at Stop & Shop in Ridgefield by 6:00 AM, this was something I couldn't ignore. Time for a few gulps of coffee, making certain I had my face mask and gloves. Something was blinding my vision as I drove down our short road. When I looked to the left there it was—the biggest, rounded glow of sunrise.

Polly

Tuesday, April 7, 2020

I thought it was funny the other day when the town sent out an email saying the dump was overwhelmed, partly from cardboard from online ordering boxes, but also partly from people cleaning out their homes and garages. Now that we're all staring at the walls, we're realizing that we don't like what's on them. Now that we're spending more time with our stuff, we're realizing we don't want it. Everyone's got their Marie Kondo on. I see it when I walk around my neighborhood: garage doors are up, and people are dragging things out or filling their trash cans.

I liked Marie Kondo, till she started hawking $96 Celebration Ladles. I go through phases where I do what she suggests, and I do feel better afterwards. The only problem is I live with someone else who fills a space as soon as I make one and dirties a surface as soon as I clean it.

My husband and I both grew up poor, with drinky, divorced parents, who didn't buy us toys or pay any attention to us. We didn't have a lot of anything. I find it fascinating that our nearly identical backgrounds led us in completely opposite directions.

I grew up with nothing and I'm comfortable with nothing. Practically everything I own would fit in my car. My husband on the other hand, grew up with nothing and decided, like Scarlett O'Hara, as God as his witness, he'd never have nothing again. And since turning 18, he has gone on a quest to purchase, acquire, store, and admire every single toy, gadget, and gizmo in the entire world. Or so it feels like to me.

This is the gnarliest impasse of our marriage. I said to him today, "I don't know how to handle this. Throwing things out upsets you but having all this crap around upsets me. How do we fix it so one of us isn't upset all the time? And, by the way, I feel like I'm upset a lot more than you are, because—look around," as I Vanna-Whited with my hands, which probably wasn't the nicest way I could have approached it. I feel like I'm battling from the low ground here, because asking him to give things up puts me in league with his mean parents who never took him to Disneyland.

All I want is to take a carload of junk to the dump, like everybody else.

Lynn

"Ta da dump, Ta da dump, Ta da dump, dump, dump" is the song to sing when you're on the way to the dump. Got that out of my

system. (Mary-Lou: Go to your room.)

What to say? I relate to you. I forever want to get rid of most of the stuff that we've stuffed into the attic. Larry likes to hang onto it. Neither of us was as severely emotionally or monetarily deprived as you and your husband. Can't make sense of your dilemma, but I loved reading about it.
Mary-Lou

David was very ADD and Linus personified. We had a deal. his office looked the way it looked, and I said nothing, despite the fact that it was right by the front door. I would go to the library doors that led to it, but not step over the threshold. There was no place for me to sit amidst the clutter anyway. He would clean it up (stuff things in a closet) when we were having a party. The basement (his former office and, theoretically, his showroom) was his also. I hated that he took over the garage and would occasionally clean a path to the garbage pails so I wouldn't break my neck trying to access them, but let it be. I lorded over the rest of the house. I could tell him to put things away, vacuum, wash dishes. As a result, he'd often do those things himself. That was our peace plan.
Deb

Tuesday, April 7, 2020

Hi Bernadette—I hope you're feeling better. Please let me know. We miss you in our virally project. I will totally understand if health, hunk, or yoga makes it impossible to offer your own virally on a daily or even occasional basis. That said, if you're reading our offerings, we'd welcome your reactions, however brief. We're planning to edit and create a book out of both the offerings and the reactions. If we could include you even at a that modest level, you would add a lot to our effort.

Even if you don't want or can't be any part of this, do let us know how you are doing.

Mary-Lou

Tuesday, April 7, 2020

Mary-Lou! Thanks for reaching out.

I've been admitted to the hospital. The latest is that I've developed violent vertigo that leaves me under the impression I've slithered to the floor of one of those horrible spinning teacup carnival rides. The puking starts instantaneously and sometimes lasts hours. It's about the most miserable feeling I've ever experienced—and laws knows, having spent 20 years with the Mingler, I've seen some misery.

I either spend the days sleeping or puking and praying for sleep.

My Covid test came back negative, which surprised me. I suspect a false negative. However, if I don't actually have it, I'm ideally situated to pick it up.

Today I needed a walker AND a babysitter just to take a fricking pee. I'm shaking my fist at some unnamed god.

I don't know when I'll be well enough to participate. Even writing this email required Herculean effort. I miss everyone.

Grumble, grumble, grumble. Stay alive through this shit show please

Love,

Bernadette (...sent from my iPhone... please excuse typos)

Dear God, Bernadette, I'm so very, very, very sorry to read this news. You're in the right place to get the help you need, in spite of corona crowding. My thoughts and hope are with you.

I think I may have gotten IT, also, as I woke up this morning with some of the symptoms. And here my family is so worried

about my husband. I'm thinking, read "hoping," I have a mild case. Stay tuned.
Polly

Oh no, Polly. I hope it's not. If it must be, I pray it may be mild. We are staying tuned.
Mary-Lou

Sending all healing energy I have, Bernadette. Docs suspect a false negative for me also. Really high incidence.
Big virtual hugs—
Deb

Dear Bernadette, I can't tell you how sorry I am to hear your awful news. How, how is this possible? Well, of course it is. I don't know what to say, except that I hope it passes quickly.
Maria

Oh, no to both Bernadette and Polly! So very sorry to hear of your health issues. A real reminder for appreciation for good health. May yours return sooner than expected.
Donna

Polly—you're much on my mind. Let us know how you're doing.
Mary-Lou

So deeply saddened to hear Bernadette's message from the hospital. Bernadette, please know that we send our love and wishes for a speedy, successful recovery. I wish I could help you laugh as much as you have cleverly helped us giggle over time. You have been such a bright presence among us—even as you were going through difficult times.
Gina

Tuesday, April 7, 2020

A good reminder. "How to Edit Your Own Writing." Worth skimming if you have time on your hands. https://www.nytimes.com/2020/04/07/smarter-living/how-to-edit-your-own-writing.html

Donna

Wednesday, April 8, 2020
First day of Passover

Mary-Lou and I use the phone to coach us into a live Zoom meeting. Looks like we can make a "last writing class" session work.

I attend another Zoom meeting with the NY/NJ ESOP chapter officers. They share updates on how their employee-owned companies are managing. Once Again Nut Butter sold out four months inventory in two days because of peanut butter hoarding. Lewis Tree Service has plenty of business clearing vegetation because of tornadoes in the southeast.

Gina

It took weeks, but Gina was generous enough to spend the necessary time with me this AM so now I'm a Zoomer. In a day or two I'll probably need a course in "remedial Zooming" but now, I'm hot. Meanwhile, with Gina's help, I'll let you know what I'd like to have discussed at our meeting. Once I've done that—well before the 16th—grateful if all of you would feed in your ideas.

Mary-Lou

Wednesday, April 8, 2020

It's been a tough day here—not us, but too many others whom we care about, including the death last night of a longtime, close friend.

I had hoped to send out a proposed agenda for our April 16th meeting today but didn't get to it. Know, though, that the "business" of the meeting is to discuss matters closer to home, such as: Do we want to create a virally book after this pandemic is over. (Gina has already created a document of over 100 pages.) If we do choose to do a book, those who have participated in this project, it seems to me, they should be able to withdraw any of their posts that they would not want to share with a Westport audience. That effort could be facilitated at the end of the pandemic at which time Gina will send what will be lots more pages to each of us so that we can skim them and locate anything we want deleted. There's more to think about at that meeting, but the above will give you an idea of what we blithely mentioned when we first started our virallies. Shall we take this off the cuff suggestion seriously?

So, suggested topics should be in that context. Meanwhile, while what I have written above represents some of the ideas Gina and I have had, I'll give the matter further thought and will welcome any ideas you've got.

Mary-Lou

Wednesday, April 8, 2020

I want to write. I don't want to write. Doesn't make sense, but there's where I am. The words tumble in my head as I go around the condo doing mindless but needed things. I clean the counters. I dust. I polish furniture. I do laundry. All those things get done—slowly, but they do get done. And the words keep tumbling. When I sit down to put them on the page, nothing. Whatever I put down, I immediately scratch. So that's why I'm writing about not writing.

I had something prepared for our April meeting. It needed polishing, but the whole of the narrative was down. I wanted to be sure there were no gerunds lurking, although gerunds don't lurk, they are quite bold. Then I wanted to be sure I didn't have any highfaluting words strewn about, and of course, checking for typos, run-on sentences and so forth. But alas, April came and with it came Covid-19, and here we are. I have three pieces started, two or three paragraphs each. One piece is about my father, but I know so little of him. One is my mother's story. The third is what follows what would have been the April submission. I jump from one to the other like a flea from dog to dog, but nothing sticks, and the writing is awful. What to do?

When my husband was sick and I was his caregiver, friends asked, "How do you do it?" You do it because you love him and because it needs to be done. But my answer to that question was always, "I do it one day at a time." And that was the truth. Sometimes it became one thing at a time.

It is dreadful to hear that Bernadette is so ill and that Polly might be stricken, too. I hope not, Polly!! Although I'm not religious, I pray the Universe sends healing to Bernadette and keeps you safe, Polly. Amy, the daughter of my oldest and dearest friend—the one cursed with dementia—has been very ill with Covid-19 but is recovering. Some lighter clouds seem to be on the horizon. China has eased its restrictions although people are continuing to wear masks and I think New York City cases appear to have reached an apex and are now easing downward.

Enough! The PBS News Hour approaches so I shall leave you for today and pour myself a glass of wine.

Be well, my friends. Take good care.

Maria

Maria, I am so engaged in your story. I have not read anything like it. Please send it to me. I long to read it.

Gina

Dear Gina,

Thank you for your kind words. You are always so supportive. When you ask for my story, are you referring to the piece I wrote for what would have been our April 2nd meeting? I'm happy to send you whatever you'd like. I seem to be writing "my life" in bits and pieces. One day, all the pieces will come together, but for now, I write as it comes.

Thank you for all you do to keep our group whole!!
Stay safe.
Maria

Maria, even your writing about not writing strikes a chord. Maybe we all feel at odds, So hard to lose that essential physical presence of other people, and particularly those we know personally.
Deb

Wednesday, April 8, 2020

What can I say that hasn't already been said?

At our Passover dinner tonight, the saltwater in the pitcher that symbolizes tears will be for all those who are suffering and especially Polly and Bernadette.

My heartfelt thoughts are with you!!!
Morgaine

I hope it's not too late to wish you a Happy Passover.
Maria

Wednesday, April 8, 2020

Just to commemorate what we are doing, can each of you send me a short biographical summary introducing who you are, your background, as well as a head shot?
Thanks,
Gina

Wednesday, April 8, 2020

You requested a self-description. My wife and I have talked about doing our own obituaries so when one of us goes, the survivor is not left with the challenge of writing something under pressure while grieving. This assignment is akin to that.

Seventy-five years young. Married to a lovely, funny, engaging wonderful bride of 31 years. Has daughter and grandson who are adored. His brother is younger than daughter and is best friend. Has been an attorney for 50 years endeavoring to help people solve problems from the foolish to the terrifying. Is a protector of animals and an advocate for the environment. Respectable poker player, adequate squash player, and competent sailor. Lover of outdoor adventures and indoor learning. Reads a lot but can't change a light bulb. Enjoys a sense of the ridiculous. The glass is half full.

Ken

Thursday, April 9, 2020
Holy Thursday

When I was a girl, the oldest of six children, our very Catholic family would make the customary rounds of visiting seven churches to earn a plenary indulgence, meaning that all our sins were forgiven and if we died, we'd to straight to heaven with no side trip to purgatory, or even worse, eternal damnation to hell. Church services included the priest washing the feet of twelve men (no women) and the choir singing the *Panis Angelicus*—bread of angels—in Latin. After the mass that commemorated the Last Supper, the altar was stripped bare to symbolize Jesus being stripped naked during the passion. If I were to mention any of this to my children or grandchildren, they would have absolutely no idea what I was talking about.

In later years, I sang in the *a cappella* choir at the Church of Notre Dame in the Morningside Heights section of New York City. I loved the music but not the dogma. It was depressing to realize that I'd lost the faith of my youth but still enjoyed the rituals. I miss doing what I no longer believe in. This year, the churches are all empty, and churchgoers are participating in services via live streaming. The pope stands alone giving a blessing from St. Peter's Square.

I attend a webinar on valuation issues organized by one of our professional partners. I complete a valuation analysis of a financial planning services firm that will likely lose investors.

Gina

Thursday, April 9, 2020

I have been sitting at (or in the proximity of) my desk for about  three hours lamenting how I keep getting distracted from doing what I had planned for the day. On one of my frequent visits to the refrigerator to see if anything new was there or had been overlooked on the previous four or five visits, I returned to my desk to find a cartoon my wife had drawn and left for me, presumably with some kind of relevance. I have recreated it with help from the internet.

High angle shot of a senior salesman sitting at office desk in front of laptop and talking with somebody in his mobile phone.

Mary-Lou, I've accomplished NOTHING......... so I thought I'd keep you posted.

Ken

Thursday, April 9, 2020

I have a family member who is a Trump supporter. Her leaning is nothing new, but this morning I got up the nerve to ask her, via email, if she'd be open to a discussion? I meant on the phone. Instead, she began her defense in writing. I played along.

"He made the economy strong," she says, "and is trying to get manufacturing back in the US, rather than relying on China. And he wants to keep illegal aliens out." She goes on to say how disrespectful the Democrats are of our leader and can't stand Pelosi and Schumer.

My blood is boiling as I type, hoping to open her eyes to his self-interest, money hungry, dangerous policies. To no avail, "We must agree to disagree," she says.

When the conversation ends, I get out my frustration by scrubbing my wood floors with vigor. OH, how they shine.

It's like my mind needs something to obsess about. I go on to start a new puzzle, 2000 pieces. As I search for the edges, I'm thinking of all the arguments I could have made, should have made. Why? I'm not going to change her mind. If only she could convince *me* that Trump is making America great again. If only I could see the world through the Fox News lens. I could be free of the agony I feel whenever I think about what the present administration is doing to our planet, not to mention future generations. It's like a dagger in my heart.

On a lighter note… I woke up this morning to find that Greg, unsolicited, had emptied the dishwasher. Two days in a row. Small victories!

Morgaine

That had to be so frustrating. But there is no discussion with Trump supporters. If they were reasonable, they wouldn't be Trump supporters. Well, at least you have shiny floors!! :-))
Maria

My blood boiled as I read your narrative. Very sorry about the dagger in your heart. It does feel like that.
Mary-Lou

It's really upsetting when there are such rifts in a family. Trump is so extreme, that his politics and personality do not invite common ground for our polarized ends of the spectrum. I would never be able to bite my tongue. Good for you for trying, anyway. Deep breaths.
Deb

Thursday, April 9, 2020

What Maria wrote the other day captured my same feelings: I want to write. I don't want to write. That tug-of-war has extended all through my days: I'm tired, I'm hyper, I'm starving, yet nothing sounds appealing. I'm bored, but don't want to do anything. I want to get out of here, but I'm scared to leave the house. Even the chores are in conflict. Laundry sits in the basket until a new load needs doing, an endless yin-yang cycle of darks and lights. I start and stop and finish nothing. It reminds me of the few times I've driven a stick-shift car: the grinding gears, the stalling, the panic and praying, all that herky-jerky just to get to the next red light.

Mostly, I feel like I am wandering around in a stupor—some sort of delirium. And the rain doesn't help at all.

Like Ken, I go to the fridge too often, hoping some magical food-fairy has filled it. Digging around is depressing: a wrinkly tomato and suspicious-looking cheese. Despite buying two weeks' worth of food last time, in ten days we're already down to the dregs.

I'm not using this downtime well. I'm not learning German or ukulele or making sourdough starter. I'm not exercising or writing anything besides these virallies. I think what I'm doing is a sort of mourning: I liked my life as it was. The few things I wanted to improve about myself require public spaces and social gatherings, so I am leaning towards giving up self-improvement. All winter, I had my moments of being too much of a loner-hermit-homebody, and I would say to myself, "I really should get out more." It almost makes me laugh.

The sun just came out. Time for more morale marching.

Lynn

Thursday, April 9, 2020

Wanted to take a picture with my iPhone and the face ID wouldn't recognize me. Had to search my memory bank for a back-up password. When I looked in the mirror, I didn't recognize me either. I was wearing a mask.

Am trying to write about a friend who died suddenly yesterday, Ken Olshan. Mary-Lou and Larry knew him well. Among many other traits, he loved films and could recall actors, titles, detailed plot lines. We had similar tastes in sarcastic, in-your-face films. He and I thought *Django Unchained*, a farcical look at slavery, was hilarious. Bill and Ken's wife were appalled at our bad taste. "Slavery is nothing to make fun of," they claimed. But I still don't know why Ken loved *The Great Lebowski*. Will go back and watch it for a third time and raise a toast to him.

I seem to be halfway finished with my memoir. Have gone back and outlined what I've written and am beginning to see where the structure doesn't work. I went online, hunting for advice and doubting lots of it. Think I'm learning what questions to ask myself about scenes, character, narrative arc. I'll keep working.

This morning I meditated on Zoom with the sangha I joined a few years ago. After Bill died, I worried that lots of friends here would start dying too and leave me. So, I imitated what my parents did in their 80s—they got younger friends by joining a book group composed of 50- and 60-year-olds. I didn't know then that they were setting an example for me.

Stay well, all of you.

Judy

I agree with you about Django Unchained*!*

So sorry that you, and Mary-Lou, lost such a dear friend, especially at a time when you cannot gather to remember him.
Deb

Thursday, April 9, 2020

I don't have much to say today. I'm feeling sad about the loss of a dear, old friend, whom Judy wrote about today in her virally. I worry about Bernadette and Polly, and this evening, while catching the tail end of the Trump unreality show, I find I am desperately concerned by Trump's desire to prematurely relax and then to put an end to the stringent containment rules we've been following and staking our very lives upon. The time will come— we've seen it happening—when he will run roughshod over Fauci. Trump will adapt a pompous who-do-you want to believe, him or me. Who has the message you most want to hear after who knows how many months of isolation?

Of course, we want to go back to work. Of course, we want to stop wearing masks and staying home. Of course, we want to visit with friends and family. I fear that lives will be sacrificed to Trump's monomaniacal desire to be reelected.

Relaxing the rules plays into our understandable impatience and desire to live free. The longer this lasts the more he is likely to get his way. Psychologically, that impatience will make many people—those who have lost their jobs—more and more likely to believe this unbelievable man. I define the word "unbelievable," not by its pumped up Trumpian meaning, but by its literal meaning—not to be believed.
Mary-Lou

I have the same fear. We've been warned that it has to happen slowly and incrementally.
Deb

Thursday, April 9, 2020

I am losing track. Ironically, too much to do.

This week was dedicated mostly to a) finding out why I'm having trouble breathing and b) Passover.

A conference call with the physician's assistant at my doctor's office resulted in narrowing the breathing/coughing issue down to two possibilities. Either I have walking pneumonia that lingers, or my test for Covid-19 was one of the many false negatives and my lungs are still irritated. She suspects Covid. In that case, it's not only my lungs that are upset. In this era of no hands-on visits, she prescribed antibiotics just in case, and an inhaler in any case.

Passover. My son loves tradition. He spearheaded our family's bi-coastal, international Zoom Seder, and asked me to scan the photocopied pages of the Haggadah we use—46 pages. However, he was too busy with a proposal for work to get to the planning phase. Don't have to be Sherlock to figure out to whom he passed the baton.

I love my family and extended family. We are an irreverent, funny, sensitive, smart, and extremely opinionated clan. Planning anything is a balancing act of opinions that belongs in Cirque de Soleil. The pressure was on.

I tackled scanning the Haggadah as a first step. I have an old printer that doesn't print, but has a document feeder for the scanner that still scans. I tried a couple of test runs with two pages so I would know which way they needed to be fed through the machine, then stacked half of the pages to scan. I haven't heard that they've tested the probability of machines catching Covid-19, but I have anecdotal proof that they do. At that precise moment my scanner succumbed to it. I spent the next three hours using the Tiny Scanner app on my phone to scan the pages one by one and email them to myself. That evening, a conversation with my oldest daughter made it quite clear that she was promoting a Haggadah that her husband had assembled from a make your own Haggadah app. My cousin emailed one that her nephew swore by. The 46 pages never got used.

Today the entire day was devoted to breaking down the service, so everyone had a role, and offering themes to make each section relevant to this moment in history. Well, not the entire day. The inhaler allowed me to take my Yogini daughter's online yoga class, followed by a body scan meditation—a little bit of heaven at 11:00. But I digress.

I ate dinner at 8:30 when I had finally emailed the fruits of my labors to the family. At 11:00 PM I received a text that maybe it would be too long. Well, it may be. And it may be funny. It may feel more significant for sharing it with people who otherwise would be at too far a distance. And just possibly, it will be the most meaningful Seder we've had, when the call to Jews to end suffering and enslavement wherever it exists seems particularly critical.

Deb

Friday, April 10, 2020
Good Friday

When I was growing up, my mother drew all the shades in the house between noon and 3 PM to commemorate the *Tre Ore*—the three hours that Christ hung on the cross. It is a strict day of fast and abstinence. I eat whatever leftovers I can find in the fridge. I have a liver pate sandwich on pumpernickel for lunch. Guess the gates of Hell will be open to me for eating meat.

I finish a valuation analysis for a metal fabrication company in Michigan. I listen to passion week classical music while I work on the spreadsheet. The phone rings. It is my youngest daughter.

"Hi," she says in a low voice. That says it all. I listen and try to talk her up as she sobs through the retelling of the latest fights with her at-home teenagers. Being a single parent cooped up with a couple of ingrates is hell for her. Maybe I should volunteer as a mental health professional as I've been recruited to do with the State of Wisconsin. I'm getting plenty of practice at home.

To deal with my own mental health, I now regularly mute Trump during the daily White House coronavirus task force briefings and wait for someone with moral and professional authority to come to the podium. Dr. Birx's scarf of the day is a sliver of fashion that lifts my spirits.

Gina

Friday, April 10, 2020

Yesterday began with a 911 call.

I'm standing at the bathroom sink; Mark is in the shower. I see his reflection in the mirror. *That's odd,* he's sitting down on the little bench.

I turn toward him, "Are you okay." He mumbles a response. "What's going on Sweetie?" At this point I'm at the shower door. He rises to his feet. His eyes roll to the back of his head, and he falls to the tiled floor. My heart is racing, my hands shaking, as I help him to the bed and wrap him in a towel.

He's conscious but is feeling "brain fog." He goes through a series of stroke test. His smile is even, he can touch his nose with his fingertips and can walk a straight line.

What should we do? He has no Covid symptoms; a trip to the ER is asking for trouble. After a conversation with an on-call doctor, it's decided, he needs to go to the hospital, by ambulance, in case he passes out again.

While we're waiting for the sirens, he sits me down and says, "If anything happens to me, I just want you to know how much I love you, how happy you've made me and what a wonderful wife you've been all these years."

"Nothing is going to happen to you," I assure him, tears streaming down my face. The medics assess his mental state. He is back to his old self joking around and making them laugh. As the ambulance pulls out of the driveway, I feel both relieved and guilty that I'm not going with him. We have *always* been there for each other in any and all emergencies.

After a battery of tests, they believe that the episode was a reaction to a medication known to lower blood pressure. The hot shower was, "pardon my pun," the tipping point.

Morgaine

Oh Morgaine, how terrifying!! Wonderful that it turned out okay, but so hard that in addition to the usual worry, you had to even consider the wisdom of having him checked out. Hope there's nothing more eventful today than not being able to find where a jigsaw piece belongs!

Deb

This? On top of everything thing else? I can only imagine your terror! That you kept your sanity, that you did a stroke check, that you thought through this emergency so clearly—amazing. That Mark summoned up what he must have thought might be his last words, and that they were about loving you—words fail.

Mary-Lou

Oh, my God! What a scare! Your clear head through this incident is heroic. A huge relief that all was okay in the end. You—and Mark—certainly didn't need this on top of everything else. Hope your weekend is serene.

Maria

Oh! What a frightening experience! I can't imagine what you were feeling, Morgaine! I do love the happy ending. At least you were in the bathroom and saw it happen. Finding him on the floor of the shower later—OMG!

Donna

Friday, April 10, 2020

So many people worldwide are put in an ambulance and never return. Morgaine's scary episode is a glaring reminder.

I'm shifting that thought to one that matches the blue sky today. I want to flood myself with gratitude.

Totally different note-G major chord-today I cleaned out and organized the Lazy Susan cupboard in the corner of my kitchen cabinets. (I now wonder who this Susan was and what she did to have a turntable named after her.) Should it really have taken a global pandemic for me to get on the floor and organize that cupboard?

Last week I took out the top-right desk door to see if the papers with all my passwords had slipped behind it. Nope! It's still missing. I've been trying a few times every day to get the damned drawer back in. I hated it sitting on the floor taunting me with my failings. In desperation last night I even asked Google and watched a video for two minutes about desk drawers. How low could I go? This morning on the way to the closet to retrieve a fresh duvet cover, I picked the drawer up from the floor and slid it in, as anyone else would have done on their first try. Such a sense of victory.

This morning I wrote in my journal, "I've thought about this a lot, and I think I overthink things." I had to laugh at myself. I realized I'd stopped "thinking" about how to get the drawer back in and my intuition took over. I just did it.

I'm going to give credit for my drawer success to the relaxing and fun time I had last night. I finally took out my new colored pencils and a "chill out" coloring book. I discovered I loved coloring—-choosing which colors to use, choosing the pattern, etc. I had such a sense of accomplishment as the picture became more and more charming. Coloring took me out of my over-thinking brain for a bit. Being quarantined is certainly the perfect opportunity to over-think. Under ordinary circumstances would I have given that drawer a second thought?

The sun beckons me to go walk on the trail. I'm eager to get back and color. It's the ideal pastime while listening to my Audible book or a podcast. And I feel like I did when I learned to write cursive.

May we all feel safe and protected.

Donna

Friday, April 10, 2020
Zoom seder, seder, seder, Zoom seder, seder...

Today was ours. Perfect that a day off for a Christian holiday made it possible for even those working a regular schedule to participate in our Jewish celebration.

The fact that each of us had to improvise in some way was a perfect testament to the times. I found I had the figs, dates, prunes, oranges, port and nuts for Sephardic charoseth. Even added a little crystallized ginger. It was the best charoseth I have ever made. FedEx did not cooperate in delivering the matzoh mailed to me by my son-in-law, but Carr's water crackers were a decent substitute. The matter of the shank bone for the Seder plate was puzzling, though. No bones on hand whatsoever. I gave my dog a pat as I thought about what to do, and he gave me the answer. Milk Bone! In each of the appropriate depressions on the plate were horseradish, an egg, parsley, charoseth, milk bones, and finally, a tomato. A tomato you ask? In an activist list of Seder plate ingredients, the tomato represents farm workers' rights. I used it to stand for all essential workers who get insufficient pay and do unsung, critical work each day—not just in pandemics.

The service was thoughtful, much of it adlibbed to fit the unusual circumstances. I read the poem that was always my father's favorite, a cousin read the one that is my favorite. Dave's older daughter carried her computer to her music room and led us in Dayenu on the piano, her voice still lovely even when distorted by the tinny computer speaker. We asked the four questions, then asked alternative ones centering around the strength needed, and discovered, in facing the current moment. One of my daughters told a story about learning the quality of resilience from Dave.

This sounds very civilized. But in the midst of all this, my little grandsons were dancing on the table, and despite the mute buttons available to us, eventually we all talked at once until finally someone roared above the din to mute ourselves and get back on track. This added the needed bit of normalcy, the familiar to which we could relate.

I had put a lot of time into organizing the day. It was well worth it. Above all else, it reminded me how very lucky I am to belong to this family.

Deb

Saturday, April 11, 2020
Holy Saturday

As a child, I could hardly wait to dive into the candy I'd given up for Lent. I was allowed to have it after I'd gone to the Easter Vigil mass with my mother. When we arrived at church, the crucifix above the altar was bare. There would be the long litany of saints, the lighting of new fire, the blessing of baptismal water with the Easter candle, and the relighting of the sanctuary lamp signaling the presence of Christ. Altar boys would parade out of the sacristy and remove all the purple shrouds that had covered the statues of Mary and Joseph on the side altars. The priest would intone the Gloria, and the altar boys would ring the consecration bells and bring out huge urns of white lilies and place them on the altar. My mother and I glanced sideways at each other noting the tears on our cheeks.

I could never sing the Gloria at Easter without choking up thinking about my mother. The hymn, "Let There Be Peace on

Earth," had a similar effect.

Monica charges ahead with full-on cleaning and decorating for Easter. I follow suit. I do my own cleaning. I offer to pay my granddaughters to help. They aren't interested—even for money. Anyway, I need what little exercise I can get.

I call Kindred Spirits and Wine to try some different varietals. They wheel my order over in one of their shopping carts in less than an hour. We are so close to the liquor store that they don't even bother to drive.

Monica does errands and returns with more irises, roses, and tulips. The windows and bannisters hang with paper mâché carrots. Bunnies stand sentinel on top of the Steinway. The girls put Easter baskets outside their bedroom doors. Seven-year-old Frances keeps asking about the Easter bunny. The rest of us are coy.

My grand trans Lex calls and chats me up until my hand is so stiff from holding the iPhone that my fingers are numb. Lex rents a room in a house in Eau Claire, Wisconsin that has long since been deserted by the student/roommates who have left campus. Lex's only company is the black cat, Montague. Lex's job as a Starbucks barista has dried up, so he now drives for Instacart. I suggest that he reach out to his Aunt Maria who is lonely in her own house. He does.

I send a bouquet of flowers to my Maria. She texts back, "OMG, they're beautiful. I needed that bit of love."

Gina

Saturday, April 11, 2020

So, this past Wednesday I had a great idea for a humorous essay. It was going to be about Henry David Thoreau, that transcendental guy who practiced self-isolation at Walled In Pond. See? Already I was cooking!

I found my college edition of *Walden* and, sure enough, I had underlined all the most salient lines, such as "Simplicity, simplicity, simplicity," and "I went to the woods because I wanted to live deliberately, to front only the essential facts of life, and see if I could not learn what it had to teach, and not, when I came to die, discover that I had not lived." I was hot. Maybe I'd submit it to The New Yorker. Naw, they take too long. How about an op-ed piece for the Times? They respond right away.

The challenge was to somehow link his experiment in solitude with the shelter in place rules of this pandemic. Maybe the piece would take the form of an interview. I worked on that idea all day Thursday.

On Friday morning, the NYTimes ran a long piece about Thoreau, with photos of his cabin in the woods and what we might learn from him during these pandemic days. I despaired. I re-read what I'd written on Thursday. What had seemed quite promising on Thursday, was a dud—somewhere between funny and not funny.

Larry tried to cheer me up, "The subject of Thoreau was low-hanging fruit. You had to know that. Somebody was bound to write about him in connection with the pandemic. Don't be discouraged. The Times article wasn't a bit humorous. You can still write a funny piece."

So, I spent all day Friday on a new approach. I thought about and dismissed the idea of Thoreau in conversation with Dr. Fauci, or maybe with Trump—too ridiculous. This time Thoreau would simply speak about the virtues of isolation and the temptations of seeking society. Boring. Okay, then, maybe I'd expose Thoreau as a cheat, who snuck into town every other day and dined on key lime pie at the Hawthornes' house. I spent all of Friday on that angle. I knew the result wasn't very good, but I thought maybe there was something to work with.

Larry read what I had written and delivered the coup de grace. "It's feels too forced." "Forced" is the ultimate killer of bad humor writing.

I gave up. Frankly, it was a relief.

Mary-Lou

Saturday, April 11, 2020

I've been missing my dad lately, and this time of year always makes me miss my stepmom too. I used to love celebrating Passover at their house.

Passover was my stepmother's favorite holiday. She used a 1940s Haggadah that she inherited from her grandmother. Over the years, the book acquired dog-ears, stapled-in addendums, pencil-under-linings and stars, wine stains, and charoset sticky spots. My stepmother kept finding quotes, poems, and songs to add; she was especially fond of putting an orange on the Seder plate in honor of women's rights. She'd also frequently say Goddess instead of God when she read the prayers, which made my father roll his eyes and cringe. My dad was not a fan of Passover, or large get-togethers in general, and always said, "Let's get this damn thing over with. I'm hungry!"

Over the years, my father condensed my stepmother's beloved holiday into 'The Speed Seder': he'd skip whole paragraphs on one page and give you the Cliff Notes version of the next as he thumbed through the Haggadah like it was a waiting room magazine. He'd reach the end of a line and say, "And we all know what happened next. Amen!" Another page would get turned, and we'd down another glass of wine. When it was time for guests to participate, he'd behave as if he was teaching his high school accounting class. He'd bark a name, point a finger and holler, "You! Page seven! Second paragraph. Go!" If you didn't read fast enough, he'd cut you off and assign your part to somebody else. He'd say, "Okay, XX. That's enough! Let's give someone else a try," then he'd freeze out poor slow-talking XX for the remainder of the Seder.

We did have a few traditions: For twenty years it was my job to read The Four Questions and make the charoset in my great-great-grandmother's wooden bowl. My oldest sister always got to open the door for Elijah. My sister's Jewish husband was the Wise Son. My Protestant husband was the son who didn't know to ask. My stepmom was in charge of reciting the plagues. We liked to see who could make the best wine-drop designs on our dishes and we'd display our handiwork across the table. My dad would scowl and say in his teacher-voice, "Put your plates down. Moving on!"

But we did have fun, and the food was delicious, and it was familiar and lively.

One year, my grandmother was taking farfel muffins out of the oven and touched her ancient oven-mitt to the burner, lighting it on fire. She stood there frozen, watching the flame, with her arm above her head like the Statue of Liberty with her torch. My cousin yelled, "HOLY SHIT!" and shoved my grandmother's smoldering arm under the kitchen faucet while the rest of us watched from the dining room. Totally deadpan and serious, my middle sister leaned over and whispered to me, "Why on this night, but not all other nights, does Grandma catch on fire?" We held our sides and cried from laughing.

Every year, my stepmother would invite, as she called them, "strays," so at the table there was always some artist or student or ex-pat or Seder-newbie who didn't know what they were in for, so we all, for the most part, behaved ourselves.

My family did the Afikomen backwards, which I never knew until recently. My dad put the matzo, wrapped in a paper napkin, behind a pillow on his chair. Sometime during the Seder, my son would steal the Afikomen and hide it in the house, and my dad was supposed to find it in a game of hot-and-cold. However, at the end of the Seder my dad always refused to look for it. He'd sit at the head of the table and bark my son's name, "Zachary! Get over here!" My six-year-old son would dutifully stand next to my dad's chair and try not to tremble in fear as my dad fished a twenty-dollar bill out of his wallet and said, "Here's the money. Enough fuckin' around. Go get the mutzy." (My dad always called matzoh 'mutzy.') My son would trot away with the money, disappointed that he didn't get to show off the clever hiding place—which was never clever, and usually made a hell of a mess that I would have to clean up before my dad found all the crumbs and freaked out.

After dessert, while the rest of us scattered to help wash up or play cards, my stepmom would clear the table and pat my dad gently on the shoulder as she went past him on her way to the kitchen. My dad would linger at the dining table. He liked to sit alone and survey the empty chairs and plates. He'd look at the mantle clock and polish off the Ring-Jells when he thought no one was looking.

Lynn

I loved being a guest at your Seder past, with all its quirks—the speed reading, the orange, the flaming grandmother.
Mary-Lou

A delightful rendering of the Passover Seder with your family. The picture of your grandmother with her arm in flames high above her head reads like a funny skit...but not.

We also celebrated Passover with a Seder of sorts with friends. Peggy and I would get together a couple of days before, plan and cook, all the while fueling our creativity with wine. Marvin, my husband, and Howard, Peggy's husband, liked to run through the Haggadah, stopping at each place where wine drinking was indicated.

When we moved to Connecticut, I made gefilte fish from scratch two years in a row. I had no idea fish could be so greasy.

171

Good memories.

Happy Passover everyone. Happy Easter, too.
Maria

Saturday, April 11, 2020

"What's this?" he says. Engaged in a 2000-piece puzzle in the formal dining room, I overhear my husband in the kitchen coaching my daughter on her relationship. I strain to hear but can't make out exactly what he's saying. I can, however, tell that his tone is thoughtful, caring and diplomatic, and that she is open and appreciative of his advice. I feel my love for him welling up inside me.

When the conversation ends, he comes into the dining room to join me in puzzling. I run to him, throw my arms around his broad shoulders, and press my body against his.

"I'm just happy you're alive!"
Morgaine

Saturday, April 11, 2020

By evening my spirits were very high. It was a perfect day.

The CT Society of Portrait Artists were invited to an online drawing session with a "live" model. I have missed the 5-hour Friday sessions at Silvermine. These drawing opportunities are like exercise class for portraiture. Over the years, they have helped me hone my ability to see proportion, angles, light and shadow. Creating a likeness takes my entire concentration, and for the one hour of today's session I was oblivious to everything else in my life. The drawing wasn't great, but I felt elated by the experience.

I met my friend with her dog for a long walk at Sherwood Island. It just feels so normal being there, strolling at a safe distance, talking, taking in the glorious sun. The sight of facemasks is becoming commonplace, and soon enough it will seem odd to see an uncovered face, just as it is now to see someone smoking in public. I can imagine the summer, with only the scantiest excuses for bathing suits at the beach but faces fully clothed.

Late in the day I created my Superpower Emblem for posting my art activity of the day on my website and Facebook. I instructed folks to think of a personality trait or a pastime that is the Superpower helping them during this unusual time, and then to create an emblem for their Superpower cape. This is mine.

Then I made the mistake of getting into bed and watching *Hatchi, A Dog's Tale*. It wasn't a great movie, so the effect it had on me came as a surprise. Based on a true story, it is about an Akita puppy found at a train station. The bond between he and his new owner becomes exceptional. Hatchi accompanies his master to the train station every morning, trots home, and returns in time to meet him as he arrives home on the 5:00 train. When his master dies suddenly, Hatchi cannot be contained, even though he has been taken in by his deceased master's daughter. He becomes feral, fed and cared for by the townspeople, and returns every day for 10 years until his death to meet the 5:00 train.

After two years, grief is often overpowered by the joys in my life. But once in a while, it rises through the bedrock and erupts. Tonight, I was undone by this movie. Arlo adored Dave, and Dave who did not want a dog, became totally attached to Arlo. That Arlo was upset by Dave's disappearance was evident in his hours spent waiting by the doors to the house and his aggression in the park. He and I have endured the past two years together, and his connection to Dave is part of why he means so much to me. We have healed together. Everything about this movie struck a deep nerve, it wrenched my heart the way a wrong move can send your back into unrelenting spasm. But I also had the most visceral sense that Dave was there, lying on his side of the bed next to me, and that feeling was as persistent as my grief over losing him. I could FEEL him there, the warmth of his body, the depression in the mattress where he lay. I didn't try to conjure him. He was just there. I don't know how. Just there.

Deb

Deb,

There's so much I want to say about this perfect day. Getting lost in that perfect creative space, when time and ego disappear, is such a relief from being a regular, run of the mill human.

Your emblem is wonderful—so evocative of superpowers—the heraldic shield and the paint brush as sword.

And then the movie: The Lassie Come Homeless of Arlo melted me. That the raw grief you suffered was rewarded by a sense of Dave's presence did me in.

Mary-Lou

Saturday, April 11, 2020

I talked to my three daughters last night, conference call rather than Zoom. Why not Zoom? Jill, the youngest, is on Zoom all day for work and is sick of it; she promised to phone in if we met on Zoom. She also couldn't do it on Thursday; as an alternative, Kim, the oldest, suggested Friday at 8 which I thought we'd all agreed to. By 7:00 I had no confirmation on the media or the time for the meeting. So, I texted Kim, the initiator of the call. Turns out she's annoyed at Jill who never confirmed the time with her.

"Yes, she did," I said. "I've got her text right here." Probably not the best strategy because their long-standing displeasure with each other goes back to childhood. It's not based on logic.

"You wanna set up the call, Mom?" she asks me. I know that turn around trick from years of management. It's called, the monkey's on your back now. But I agree to take the monkey. I text the other two daughters and say that I'll call Kim at 8 and she'll conference in the others.

I call Kim when the PBS Evening News ends. "Sorry I didn't answer right away," she says. "You're early." I always suspected that the PBS show ended early. So sue me!

She calls Fern. "The call's going to voicemail," Kim says. I can hear that she's ready to give up. "Call Michael," I say. He's Fern husband; I know his phone never leaves his side.

When Kim gets to Jill, we're all connected and talk amiably for a few minutes—hair and hair products (we wear different kinds of natural hair—afros, twists, braids—and the salons we use are closed), jobs (two are looking, one seriously and the other one's taking her time), exercise routines. Then the gloves come off.

"I thought you wanted to talk, Jill, about whether or not to rent the new apartment," says Kim. "But you didn't take any responsibility for setting up the call so we could discuss it."

"Oh, I settled that. Mom and Fern said not to take it, so I didn't."

"I didn't know you two had talked." Kim's pissed.

"We didn't really talk," Fern, the peacemaker, interrupts. "We just texted. Your text helped, Kim. You laid out all the reasons not to do it. Mom and Michael and I just said, 'Don't do it.' "

Jill adds, "I'd appreciate it Kim if you didn't lecture me in writing. If you have something to say, just call me and say it."

Kim agrees. "And Jill, I'd like it if you'd let me know next time when you've made a decision that I thought you wanted my help with."

"Done," says Jill.

"I'm really glad you consulted us before deciding," I say to Jill, trying to head off an argument

Jill adds, "Kim, you know I stayed in that last apartment for 14 years. I'm pretty stable, not going from place to place as you claimed. I moved around last year when I was trying to reduce my rent by finding a roommate. I know now that that was a mistake."

Kim relents. "I'd forgotten that, Jill. You're right."

"On a lighter note," Fern adds. She tells a funny story—I've already forgotten it—that refocuses the conversation. That's exactly how she used to handle Marty. She knew how to redirect his anger. I tried to dissect her method, but I couldn't figure it out. Jill couldn't either; her lawyerly logic would enrage him more. Kim smiled her beautiful smile and walked away from him. I sulked or cried.

After the dust has settled, the call continues for another 40 minutes. I've noticed that Zoom meetings and phone calls seem to have a natural rhythm. In the middle there's often a pause for reflection. Later the call reaches another pause that usually signals its natural end.

At the second pause Kim says, "That was fun, you guys. We should do it on a regular basis."

Fern adds, "Yes. Same time next week?"

Jill says, "Maybe not that regular."

Laughing, I say, "Good night, lovely ladies," and hang up.

Judy

Judy,

Such a great exposé of family hierarchies. One thing is for sure; you never get done with being a mother.

Mary-Lou

Family! Sometimes I'm happy to have been an only child although, I imagine, growing with siblings teaches one many lessons.

Maria

I find it's so hard sometimes to extricate myself from the middle of these situations. So true that once a mother, always a mother. Anyone who says it's an eighteen-year commitment until they're on their own either needs to take a math class or never has had kids!
Deb

Sunday, April 12, 2020
Easter Sunday

The girls squeal as they explore their Easter baskets. The bunny has left huge silver eggs filled with nail polish, false eyelashes, makeup remover, crazy socks, hair bands, slippers and, of course, Frances' favorite, CANDEEE! Monica must have been up all night helping the bunny. The girls are anxious for her to wake up so they can hunt for eggs in the backyard.

They start outdoors, finding colorful plastic eggs filled with Hershey's kisses or $2 bills.

Then they find some eggs cracked open with the wrappers torn and the chocolate gone. The animals have sniffed out the treats. Was it the groundhog who lives under the back porch?

Squirrels? Racoons? Skunks? Crows? Turkeys? Something with a smallish mouth. Certainly not the ever-present deer.

At two o'clock in the afternoon I begin to host a Zoom session for our family virtual Easter brunch. Thirty-six of us join in. My daughter Monica is already engaged with her three daughters. My brother Mickey wears a top hat, and his wife Jane, a black fascinator. I wear a wreath of paper flowers that the girls had made for a past birthday. Three of Mickey's kids and two of his grandkids join. My sister Nell and her two daughters and three granddaughters sign in. My sister Maggie and four of her kids and five grandkids come on, including her youngest son, Jeffrey who is a quadriplegic living independently in Louisville, Kentucky. My brother Terry shows his face from Florida and then leaves to play golf with his son and grandson who are holed up in the Villages rather than being home confined in Wisconsin. We talk about the missed baby and wedding showers and a postponed wedding as well as maternity care in Michigan and expired maternity leave in Oregon. A niece's husband has an employee who died from the virus.

Nobody talks about religion or the Resurrection. Of my siblings, one is an ethicist whose three grandkids attend Catholic schools, one a semi-believer with five of six atheistic children, one is a post-denominationalist who attends Fritz Mondale's Presbyterian church in Minneapolis and whose daughters have no interest in religion (and whose father had been an ex-Catholic seminarian) but whose stepdaughter is a Presbyterian minister, and a brother who has been an atheist since second grade. His kids are too. I'd call myself an agnostic these days. Two of my three kids are atheist and the youngest Catholic for social reasons. My cynical grandson says he got confirmed because all the Jews in Rye get Bar Mitzvahs, and the Catholics get Confirmation. He's now a Sigma Chi frat boy who spends spring break on the beaches in Florida. No one in our family cares about going to church on Easter anymore.

We have ham sliders and scalloped potatoes like my mother used to make.

Gina

Sunday, April 12, 2020

Seder and Easter are linked by the fact that they share the themes of Spring and rebirth and renewal. I hope your Easter celebrations were safe and as rewarding as virtual can be. No dog bones. I'd love to know how my classmates celebrated.

I'll keep this short. Rebirth has not been the theme around our house. We lost 2 friends—a couple—to corona this past week.

Other friends are sick. Two, maybe 3 members of our class have been stricken, probably with this virus.

My dear friend Al Jaffee, now 99 years old, is fighting illness—probably not corona—and his wife, my good friend Joyce—died a while ago, leaving him alone and grieving. That I couldn't and can't get close to my friends is painful.

I know that everyone is comfortable with calling our metaphorical response to the pandemic a war, even a war against an "invisible enemy." Like many metaphors it is apt enough, but it's very overused, and while it invokes fear, it is ultimately meaningless. Real wars are fought between two enemies who, for whatever reason, are intent upon vanquishing one another, but the coronavirus knows no intent. It's not out to get us. It's not out to win. It has no soldiers or generals. It has no strategy. We are not its enemy. I suppose there's no harm in calling the virus our "enemy" and our response to this pandemic a "war." It's a metaphor we've used frequently—the war on drugs, cancer, crime, drugs, science, Christmas, guns, truth, AIDS, you name it. But when this pandemic is over, and the dead number in the millions, will we have "won?"

I think that's the point. It's a muddled issue, but it bothers me. War bothers me and making it heroic really bothers me.

Mary-Lou

Sunday, April 12, 2020

We celebrated both Passover and Easter like we celebrate any holiday at the Pauker home—with food.

For Passover we pulled off a traditional Seder, shopping and preparing in a matter of hours rather than the usual days of preparation. This morning, for Easter, we had brunch. The table was set with pastel-colored linens, daffodils and napkins folded to look like bunny ears. The main course was matzo brei.

The discussion at the breakfast table was about helping out around the house. We have all realized we will most likely be living together for another couple of months—at least! We needed some long-term strategies.

It's so strange how the reality of the situation tends to come in waves. Today it hit me like a tsunami.

Morgaine

Sunday, April 12, 2020

My yard was the scene of incredible joy. My son and daughter-in-law, Galen and Meghan, brought my toddler grandsons, Silas and Joah, to Westport for their Easter Egg hunt. They also brought the T-ball set and soccer net that were the boys' holiday gifts. Silas raced around the perimeter of the yard with his not quite two-year-old brother trailing after him. They found the brightly dyed eggs they had made, as well as two-piece plastic eggs filled with popcorn and chocolate chips. Silas made his mom hide the eggs three or four times so the moment would last—and last, and last. The sports gifts were a great hit. Both boys are very active and coordinated, and whenever possible, Galen stretches the limited screen time rule so they can root for their favorite baseball and basketball teams together.

Arlo and I remained on the other side of the fence, keeping our physical distance. Silas and Joah love him and were very upset that they couldn't play with him but found their own solution. My yard is strewn with segments of once-large sticks chewed to smaller bits by Arlo. The boys amused themselves and Arlo by jettisoning sticks across the fence for Arlo to chase and chew.

These visits remind me how much I miss holding their small bodies and kissing them up and down, top to bottom. It is a sweet missing, born of my adoration of them. I adore their parents, too, and to see them in person is a sweet balm.

Another walk at Sherwood Island with Arlo, even though the bright sunshine had been scared away by cold gray. We didn't see Mary-Lou, though I looked for her. But we did see a good friend with her yellow lab, Becca. Somehow, despite their leashes, Arlo managed to coax Becca into a wrestling match. This is as joyous for my furry buddy as seeing the kids is for me.

Settled down with a lovely dinner and *Call the Midwife*, one of my favorite series. All in all, a good day.

Deb

Monday, April 13, 2020

Back to business with a Zoom team call. I refresh all the water in the flower vases. I can't find any of the Cadbury Creme Eggs I bought at Stop & Shop weeks ago; did the girls already eat all of them or did Monica hide them?

Power goes out briefly in the afternoon. Almost as quickly as I let our team members know that we have no Internet, the power comes back on. We are lucky to be on a grid so close to Stop & Shop.

I call my daughter Maria who confesses she didn't join the Easter Zoom brunch because she was in bed all-day with pre-menopausal cramps and her two teenagers did not wake up until 4:00 PM. Don't know why my son Chris wasn't there, but his offspring Lex was a most welcome presence with the rest of the family. I am disgusted and disappointed with Chris and Maria, but my default mode is to have no expectations. On a bright note, Lex and Maria are now Zoom cooking together.

Gina

Monday, April 13, 2020

At 1:30 the power went out. I'd been anticipating an outage all day since the wind was rattling the screens and creeping through the not-so-well sealed windows. I heard the sound of the generator quitting, like a low grunt, and the beep of the modem just before the lights flickered out. I turned off my devices—iPhone, iPad, Kindle, computer—to save the batteries. I wondered again why one person needs four devices, but I didn't have time to figure out an answer.

Then I made preparations for an outage that might last more than a few hours. I retrieved a large, square flashlight whose batteries I test every few months, checked on the smaller flashlights, one each in our bedside drawers, and turned on the battery-operated radio to see if I could get a local station and find out how widespread the blackout was. I picked up only static and figured I'd go to one of the hallway windows later to see if the reception was any better.

I rummaged around in the cabinet in Bill's bathroom and found two cans of Sterno, a metal holder that flips and twists and whose handle slides—probably for the Sterno, but I didn't know how to use it. Also found a Coleman lantern with a dial that I thought would turn it on, but I couldn't make it light. With some twisting and turning I managed to pull out the bottom that was heavy enough to be a battery pack, but I couldn't open it any further to see if there were batteries. I put on one of the headlamps that was under the cabinet. "I can read as the light fades," I concluded.

And I remembered Bill. He had bought all this equipment after the first blackout at Meadow Ridge. It had snowed that October while the trees still had leaves. The leaves iced over, the tree branches downed the power lines, and we were in the dark for four days in increasingly chilly weather. One night we had an ice cream party in the hall with our neighbors; we shared our stash so it wouldn't go bad. Another night we played games in the hall—charades, Pictionary. A third night I figured out how to hook up our electric powered fireplace to batteries—I'd seen a maintenance man do it—so that we could get a little extra heat. Eventually we were so cold that we slept with our clothes on and piled the bed with the blankets he'd kept from his house; I'd left mine behind.

After power was restored that fall, Bill methodically bought all the gear that I tried to use today. So much of him remains with me.
Judy

Monday, April 13, 2020

Hibernating in the house today while sheets of rain and high winds batter the natural world outside my walls. I set myself the project of planning the remaining art projects for "19 for Covid-19," which I have been posting on Facebook and my website.

One of them is an activity I used to do when leading workshops as a diversity educator. I asked participants to trace or draw their hands and then decorate them to reveal the artists' sense of their identities—on the one hand, social identity, and on the other, personal identity. In the workshops, we would number them, but no names. Then we would display them on the walls, and we'd each try to identify which participant belonged to which set of hands. Students were often quite correct, having listened carefully to what each of them had revealed during the workshop thus far.

It was one of my favorite exercises, and I knew that somewhere I had my own set of hands, and perhaps several from middle and high school students. Most likely they were in the attic, which is my least favorite place to spend time. But at one point, I knew I had brought a few files from those days downstairs for a project. I hauled them out, and there were four sets of hands! It caused me to reflect on the decade I spent focusing on diversity issues. I loved it. Leading workshops was terrifying at first, but I grew good at it, and the results were always moving. I was adding my little drop to the bucket, or maybe more precisely, the melting pot. And, of course, Dave was there in those memories, building a continuous counter desk around the perimeter of my office, helping me attach a round conference tabletop to a beautiful cast iron base we found at United House Wrecking. Painting. Helping me move into the office when I was made Executive Director and moved out of my home office to one that could accommodate employees.

It was the time in our marriage that we were the most financially flush. He had a good reputation as a commercial interior designer and a small, thriving business. I was pulling in a decent salary. We could ski, travel a little bit, relax. But I hated being an ED, training people to do the work I loved and spending most of my time fundraising. He was supportive when I couldn't take it anymore.

Now I am visiting the best part of that era, and it is nostalgic and satisfying. One day, I will find the vestiges of this era, maybe these writings. What seems interminable and unbearable will be remembered not only by hardship and sorrow, but by what joy there was to find in it, what lessons learned.

Deb

Monday, April 13, 2020

A moment in time.

Who am I, to be sitting at my desk in front of the window, writing, to the hum of a generator, while 300+ families in Louisiana are now displaced by a tornado, while people in cages are forgotten by the media, while grocery clerks put themselves in harm's way for eleven dollars an hour, while millions of people struggle to breathe and medical workers respond, around the clock, to a pandemic for which our nation is ill prepared?

Was it something I did in a past life? Or is my time yet to come? This is not a morbid question, merely a practical one.

I sit here knowing at this moment I am privileged!

Morgaine

Monday, April 13, 2020

This will be a short one. I've spent most of my day in front of the computer emailing.

My subject today is binging. I love it. I need it. I'm addicted to it. It's like chocolate chip cookies but it lasts even longer. Plus, I can eat chocolate chip cookies while I'm binging. If there's ever a time to put on weight—pandemic pounds—now is the time.

I have strange tastes. Long ago I became addicted to Poldark. But that was just the beginning. After that I needed more and more episodes in my life. Given this pandemic, I can't control myself. My tastes are various. They go from the low to the high-minded. I love hating Nazis, so I'll watch anything with a Nazi in it. *A French Village* was both classy, touching, and memorable. Today my friend Lucie turned me on to *Deutchland 83*. I can't wait. I also love cowboys who ride into town. I cry when they ride off into the sunset. I also love Indians—they go with cowboys. My appetite for 18th century romantic dramas with great costumes, ridiculous hairdos and high bosom dramas cannot be sated. I've seen them all. I'm hanging by my thumbs waiting for more episodes of *Outlander* and *Homeland*. Right now, I've been caught up in *Restaurant*. Frankly, it's a piece of what the French call "*ca ca*," but I have come to understand that I will sink lower than low if there are lots of episodes, especially if they include a test of family loyalties, romance, sex, money, food, a miscarriage and an evil brother. I hear that *Little Fires Everywhere* is supposed to be really good, not intellectually insulting. It's on my list.

I would be grateful if all of you would send me your favorites. Be sure to include whether it's on Amazon Prime, Netflix, Hulu, or LuLu Lemon. Quality, as you must know by now, is not a prerequisite.

Mary-Lou

For your Nazi obsession—The Plot Against America, *HBO*—

185

rewrites history with Charles Lindbergh ousting Roosevelt as WWII gains steam.

Julian Fellowes has a new series, Belgravia, *that is starting this weekend on Epix, but can be streamed on Amazon Prime and Hulu.*

Sanditon, *based on an unfinished Jane Austen novel—Masterpiece channel on Prime Video, or you can also purchase individual episodes of* Sanditon *or the whole season on Amazon, iTunes, Vudu, YouTube, Google Play, or wherever you purchase SVOD. The whole season costs $19.99.*

I will not admit the nadir of my viewing habits.
Deb

The Man in the High Castle—*Prime (Nazi theme)*
Better Call Saul, *assuming you saw* Breaking Bad. *If not watch the latter first.*
Barry—*HBO*
Ozark—*Netflix*
Billions—*Showtime*
Morgaine

Monday, April 13, 2020

Hello writer friends,

I received an email early today from Polly seeking some perspective since we are in somewhat the same situation. She had tested negative for Covid-19 despite having a terrible cough, fever, etc. Her doctor suspected a false negative and placed her on a similar regimen to mine—antibiotics and a stronger cough suppressant.

Tonight, I received a second email. She was admitted to the hospital and is still waiting for a room while they determine whether she should be in the ICU. She again tested negative, though her doctor believes she has Covid-induced pneumonia. In any case, it most certainly is pneumonia and it's a relief to know she's in the right place to get good care.

It's with her permission that I'm spreading the news to you. As she wrote, "positive thoughts are always appreciated. 🙏"

Sending her half of all the positive thoughts that I can muster. The others are for you, Bernadette.

Deb

Thank you, Deb, for letting us know the news about Polly. This is so awful!! What can one say? I hope and pray for Polly, Bernadette, and you. All blessings to all of you.

I learned yesterday that my deceased aunt's husband was at the hospital waiting to be admitted. He had not yet been tested, but they thought he had pneumonia. Since he works at the hospital and told me that the hospital has a number of Covid-19 cases, it is likely that he will add to that number. What a horrible situation. My prayers for you.

Maria

Tuesday, April 14, 2020

NY/NJ ESOP chapters officer's check-in call. I finish the evaluation analysis for a custom pallet operation with a lot of food service clients. Hope they aren't affected by interruptions in the food supply chain.

Monica, Frances, and I take a drive to make sure the battery in the "Swagger Wagon" minivan is still operating. We go to Cross Highway, over to Intensity in Norwalk, up Main Street in Westport and look at all the shuttered places. It is a shocking ghost town.

Gina

Tuesday, April 14, 2020

These are dark days. I am so sorry for your loss, Mary-Lou. It is sad to lose friends, especially when it happens because of something that might have been avoidable. No one wins in a war. The victors may crow, but they have lost something, too. Humanity seems bent on being, no, staying, in conflict with one another. Will we ever learn? I think that question has been asked down through time. Will it ever be answered?

When gloom gets the better of me, I try to think of all that I can truly be grateful for, and there is much of that. Somedays it's difficult to stay positive, but what usually gets me through is the thought that this too shall pass. I just wish it would hurry!

My Easter/Passover went by barely noticed. No gefilte fish, no charoset, no Easter ham, no dyed eggs. We did hold a meeting of our book club on Sunday and since I was the hostess, I made lunch. It was disappointing that my grandson and Pattie (my daughter's stepmom, and my friend), both felt the same about the book we were supposed to have read for this meeting: *Wolf Hall* by Hilary Mantel. I have a running love affair with old English history and had read the book when it first appeared. Because the third and final book of this trilogy just came out, I thought it a good idea to reread the first two books since it's been eight years since the second book. I enthusiastically proposed *Wolf Hall* for our April read. Alas, neither Quinn nor Pattie liked the book. The book for our May meeting is *The Authenticity Project* by Clare Pooley... more of that in May.

Yesterday, Monday the 13th, I mopped floors and then made bread pudding in the afternoon. The recipe I use calls for one-day old French baguette, but it comes out creamier when made with challah and I had gotten one from Gold's Deli.

Today our Spanish group will meet via Zoom and I'm nervous again over being able to succeed in connecting. I hate machines! I love machines!

If anyone has news of Bernadette, please share. I've read about Polly from Deb. Dark days, indeed.

Stay safe.

Maria

Tuesday, April 14, 2020

Colleagues in Seclusion,

I haven't been keeping up with the daily postings, but not for lack of thought. It takes some of us longer to think things through before memorializing them. I always try to abide by the sage advice someone smarter than I proffered… something along, "It is better to be thought a fool, then open your mouth and prove it." Too often I have forgotten that rule, hopefully not now.

So here the thoughts of the past few days.

First, by the hour, I reflect on the tragedy unfolding around us and how incredibly fortunate my family is. Our good fortune is substantive and substantial and none of it is taken for granted. It is easy to feel undeserving as there is nothing to make us more entitled than others. If we have our health, we are rich indeed. Polly and Bernadette**, please, please** get better.

But there has been time for more thinking.

Second, our class is a treasured audience. Our coming together at this time is most fortunate. I can't recall another time when there were people, particularly strangers, who were interested and waiting for me to say/write anything. What a rare happenstance is this!

Third, any moping on my part is sloppy, pointless, and undignified. On reflection, when this crisis is over and things are back to normal, I know for certain that I will miss this time. It is such a rare opportunity to be ordered to stay away from people, rely on yourself, and challenge yourself in unexplored ways. The peace and quiet it brings is enticing and rich with newness. How often does that happen? Never has and won't again.

Below I have extracted a couple of sentences from the book I am reading. These lines are from the very beginning and describe the main character's mood, something to be avoided in this time. The story takes place during the 17th century. Black Plague.

"The memories of happiness are fleeting things, reflections in a stream, glimpsed all broken for a second and then swept away in the current of grief that is our life now. I can't say that I ever feel what it felt like then when I was happy. But sometimes something will touch the place where that feeling was, a touch as slight and swift as the brush of a moth's wind in the dark." Good writing, no?

Year of Wonders by Geraldine Brooks is "based on a true story; this novel explores love and learning, fear and fanaticism, and the struggles of seventeenth-century science and religion to interpret the world at the cusp of the modern era." It got very good reviews and seemed timely.

Fourth, I need to get out of the house if only to stay solvent. I am writing checks to every not-for-profit I ever supported as well as the ones that family and friends have asked me to help.

Fifth, thank goodness it is spring and not winter. On nice days, I am exploring all the parks and open spaces in and about Westport and its environs. All the properties managed by the Aseptic Land Trust are open and inviting. I don't know yet about Audubon properties. Today, I went to Haskins Park, little known, little explored and delightful, just off Compo South. For an hour, I had its 15 acres +/– to myself and sat on a bench overlooking a pond reading my book. On not so nice days, I explore streets and check out the neighborhoods in Westport that I had no reason to visit before now. With no traffic, I can meander without frustrating drivers behind me. Check out Dogwood and Green Acre off of Haskins.

Sixth, there are more thoughts but for another time.

Hugs to all of you, particularly Bernadette and Polly.

Ken

Tuesday, April 14, 2020

For all of us, today started with worry; Polly and Bernadette. I've written to Bernadette but haven't yet received an answer. If I don't by tomorrow, I'll call her. As for Polly, I'm sure she'll let us know how she is doing when she is able. Until then, hope and worry take turns presiding in my mind.

A walk on Sherwood Island helped enough so that when I got home I decided to attack the chore I had put off doing yesterday and for good reason. I didn't want to do it. I was already sorry that long ago, at the beginning of the pandemic, I'd bought a bagful of semi-sweet Ghirardelli bits with which I was planning to make Toll House cookies. By now, I had already polished off some store-bought ones recently purchased from Wilton's Village shop, and they were very good, so I eyed the Ghirardelli bits with annoyance. They eyed me back, so I went to work. I knew there would be trouble. It came in many forms—frozen butter and rock hard brown sugar, and a batter so sticky that it took more than one-half hour to blend the ingredients. If you're still reading, I had to use a grater on that brick of brown sugar in order to create the required 3/4 of a cup. The whole business was messy and difficult. They do taste pretty good, but not worth the trouble. I could have been bingeing. (By the way, thanks to whomever set me straight on how to spell that.)

So here's the less boring part. I made so many cookies that I'm offering them gratis to anyone who would like to do a drive-by pickup at my house (the one with the carport). Rest assured that I wore a mask and gloves while walking on the island, that I sang "Happy Birthday" twice upon entering my home, that my kitchen counters have been washed with a dilute mixture of Clorox and water and then washed with soap. While wearing vinyl clad gloves, I will insert the cookies, how many depending on the orders, in little plastic bags. I will place the bags on the swing next to the front door. Just for fun, I will insert an inspiring literary message into each bag. That's how much I want to get rid of these cookies. I've already eaten my fill and I never want to see them again.

If you would like to take some of these cookies off my hands, please email me, telling me your approximate time of arrival and I'll pack up your goodie bag. If you want to say, "Hi," then ring the doorbell and I'll wave to you from 6 feet away. Thanks.

Cookie Girl

Aka *Mary-Lou*

Tuesday, April 14, 2020

I couldn't get warm today, no matter how I tried. I increased my usual three layers to five, added a fuzzy blanket and a beanie hat, even resorted to alcohol, which usually gets me flushed. None of it worked. My bones felt colder today than they did through most of January. The vernal chill, rain, wind, and damp: sad rewards for surviving winter—and 30 days of lockdown. Though this spring is the worst in memory, I've decided I don't like spring in general. I always expect more from it than I ought to.

The magnolia tree in my front yard was gorgeous and the pride of the neighborhood—people kept stopping to take pictures of it on their walks—a firework of pink blossoms—for five days. After yesterday's rain, it has turned slimy and brown and slicks my driveway with treacherous muck.

Over the past weeks, I've gone on a baking/sugar bender like everybody else, but I make unsophisticated things that take no time and no skill: Rice Krispy Treats, 7-layer bars, 3-ingredient peanut butter cookies. My husband is burning through Girl Scout Tagalongs while I've eaten my share of Mallomars. This kind of behavior too is more winter-like than spring-like. So was spending the weekend curled up on the couch watching movies. (Zach picked *Knives Out*. I picked *Parasite*. My husband picked a strange French animated film about a severed hand trying to get back to its owner. It was surprisingly not bad.)

I've had nothing much to say around the house for the past few days. My whole family has gone into a kind of "blessed silence." I didn't even need to make the sticker; I just needed to be patient. We've run out of words well before we've run out of toilet paper. We're communicating solely with shrugs and eyebrow waggles now.

Here's hoping for warmer, happier days. Sending good thoughts to all of you.

Lynn

Tuesday, April 14, 2020

I could write about my lack of motivation, or how hard the news about Polly and Bernadette hit me, but since my entries have been leaning toward the dark side lately, I'll spare you.

There was one thing that I did do today that was meaningful. I contributed, along with every household on my block, to purchase three meals for 20 healthcare workers at Norwalk Hospital.

Made my day!

Morgaine

Tuesday, April 14, 2020

My son-in-law adores bathroom humor. Last night and today had much to do with bathrooms, but I found none of it humorous. Got hit with the dreaded side effect of antibiotics.

By the afternoon I felt it was safe to leave the house. It was the last day dogs could be walked at Sherwood Island, and the weather had turned sunny. I met my friend and her dog, and we explored a part of the park neither of us had seen before, eventually taking us down to the connector before curving back toward the beach. It was lovely—marshy grass, no people. We dropped the ends of the dogs' leashes and let them wrestle around us, safely out of sight of park officials. On the way back we saw a deer so still that I asked my friend if it was real. The deer, a doe, was soon joined by her two fawns.

My dog is not a bird or squirrel chaser, but deer are another story. Despite his furious barking and menacing growls, those deer just looked at us. They were calm; I was not. Struggling to keep hold of Arlo was no small feat. I've been on horses easier to control when spooked by deer!

Today I had my first curbside Petco drop-off, including a pair of nail clippers. I had given mine to my mom. Once, while trying to clip Arlo's nails, I hit the quick and he bled. A tsunami of guilt washed over me, and I gave up nail clipping. My mistake was Petco's gain. But now... no choice. Proud to say, I managed a totally successful doggie manicure.

For the past two years I have been digging deep to deal with tasks, large and small, that would have fallen to Dave. Covid-19 adds a new layer to the sense of "if it needs to be done, there's no choice but to do it." Each time I cope on my own with an inherited task, it's another drop in the bucket of self-confidence that grief had emptied.

Deb

Wednesday, April 15, 2020

I'm going to go out soon—it's almost 1:00 PM—for a walk, but I'll leave cookies for Gina and Ken, who let me know they wanted some, and a couple of other bags and inspirational messages just in case. Stay safe.

Mary-Lou

Thanks for the cookie offer, Mary-Lou. I'm delayed in reading emails at the moment, or I probably would have driven over, just for the excitement of an outing. I'm looking forward to the friendly faces tomorrow.

Donna

Wednesday, April 15, 2020
Tax Day

No taxes to file until July 15th. What a relief! I am nowhere near ready to have my receipts sorted and tallied so I can meet with the tax preparation ladies.

I wake up sweating thinking about a client whose grocery store chain features Smithfield Meats. That South Dakota meat packing plant closes after becoming a hot spot for the coronavirus.

I bite on Mary-Lou's cookie offer. Monica drives me over. I see the lovely china plate with baggies of cookies on the porch swing. I pick it up. When would I return the plate? I put it down and scoop up the cookies with the aluminum foil resting on top of the plate. I get halfway to the minivan when Mary-Lou calls after me. One of the bags was for "Cookie Man." I am such an idiot. I didn't even read the labels. Mary-Lou tucks inspirational sayings in with the chocolate chip cookies. The girls and I eat them before bedtime.

Gina

Whew… that was close. I will be there around 1:45.
Thanks,
Ken

Wednesday, April 15, 2020

Dear All—I phoned Bernadette at noon today. She was not at home. Her message box was full. I was able to leave my number but not a message. I wish I had something more optimistic to report. I'll keep trying.

Also, I just got off a call with Polly. She's been tested 5 times for Covid-19 but the tests all come back negative. She is in "serious" condition and in isolation at Norwalk Hospital. They continue not to know what's wrong with her, but as of today they are putting her on the strongest antibiotic they've got and think they should know if it's working by tomorrow.

She sounds like the Polly we all know—straightforward, matter of fact, ironically humorous, and stoic. She remarked that if she comes out of this, "I'll have plenty to write about." When I asked her if she wanted me to tell you all how she is, she said, "Tell them that I'm doing my best." Her voice sounded strong, but she said that she chose this time to call because later in the evening she coughs a lot. She told me that what we see on TV in terms of what goes on in hospitals is accurate. Norwalk Hospital, she assures me, has all the equipment they need. There are no shortages. While she isn't up to writing, she very much enjoys hearing from us via our daily journal. She wants us to send her our prayers, and all the healing, positive thoughts we can summon. She will continue to send us news of how she's doing when she is able. I'm touched by how much our pandemic journal has brought us even closer together.

Just finished talking with Bernadette. She, too, is a medical mystery. She spent four days in the hospital. She's okay-ish. I'll write more about her later this evening, but her first words to me were typical Bernadette.

"I'm finally out of the crypt."

Bernadette's illness is not yet diagnosed. First, she suffered from severe vertigo and vomiting. An MRI indicated a "problematic" area in her brain. Was it a stroke? An embolism? They don't yet know. She is at home now, sometimes thinking she is feeling better, and then sometimes feeling worse. She has trouble reading or concentrating. She is going back to the hospital in a week for another MRI to see if whatever is showing up has changed in any way. She said that she doubted they would have sent her home for a week if they were fearful about her condition. Our conversation was full of laughter and joking around.

Nevertheless, she's very worried and in a very scary limbo, as is Polly.

See you all tomorrow at 12:30 on Zoom.

Mary-Lou

So good to hear about Polly! Definitely holding her in the light. Tried seeing if there was any kind of notice about her condition on Bernadette's website, but afraid not. Was a long shot. Do we know if she was in Norwalk Hospital or Stamford?

Deb

This news is guarded and worrisome, but there is still a hopeful glimmer that it is not Covid-19 for Polly. Still, whatever it is, it sounds serious. Thank you for passing this news along, Mary-Lou. Both Polly and Bernadette are in my prayers with hope that they will heal soon. Deb, too, for it is still a question as to whether "19" is lurking.

It's so true what you say at the end of your news, Mary-Lou, about this pandemic bringing us even closer together. I am a relative newcomer to the group, but I feel a kinship with you all. I know you will convey all our hopes and prayers to Polly and to Bernadette.

Maria

Thank you for the news about Polly and Bernadette. Wish it were better news, but at least we have an update. Both certainly need our light and love sent their way.

Just finished Zooming with my four sisters. We meet twice a week, which is much more than what it would be normally. One of the silver linings.

See you tomorrow at 12:30. Maybe Ken could drive around and deliver cookies before we meet. Shouldn't take more than an hour or two. Sort of like the Easter Bunny.

Halfway through April.
Donna

Donna,
Good idea... who wants/needs a class cookie? (M-L, your delicious cookies are already accounted for).
For my classmates who are unlikely to remember the TV Western, Paladin *(I used to watch the show just before* Gun Smoke *on Saturday evenings when I was in sixth-seventh grade)... "Have cookie, Will travel."*
Ken

Is this for real? Ken delivering cookies??
Maria

Great idea for Ken to deliver cookies before Zoom Meeting.
Gina

Send addresses... like the postal service, through thick and thin, the cookies must be delivered.
Ken

A Thousand to One
by Berton Braley (1882–1966)
an American poet.

There's a thousand "Can't-be-done-ers"
For the one who says "It can!"
But the whole amount of deeds that count
Is done by the latter clan.
For the "Can't-be-done-ers" grumble,
And hamper, oppose and doubt,

While the daring man who says "It can!"
Proceeds to work it out.
There isn't a new invention
Beneath the shining sun,
That was ever wrought by the deed or thought
Of the tribe of "Can't-be-done."
For the "Can't-be-done-ers" mutter
While the "Can-be's" cool, sublime,
Make their "notions" work till the others smirk.
"Oh, we knew it all the time!"

"Oh, the "Can-be's" clan is meager,
Its membership is small,
And it's mighty few who see their dreams come true
Or hear fame's trumpet call;
But it's better to be a "Can-be,"
And labor and dream—and die,
Than one who runs with the "Can't-be-done's"
Who haven't the pluck to try.

Ken

Wednesday, April 15, 2020

What a difference a day can make!

While I did watch the news while dyeing my hair, an hour-long process from start to finish, I decided, for today, I would let the propaganda go. Gone with it is the silvery gray strip that parted my scalp.

I got out in the garden for as long as my sore back could take. *I miss my chiropractor.* I chatted loudly across property lines with my neighbor, a fellow DYI gardener, about peonies, the deer population and pool openings.

I learned via email, that through the generosity of the neighborhood we will feed 40 medical workers instead of twenty.

Go Neighbors!

At two o'clock I sat at my computer to write. I wound up editing chapter 11 "The Inner Circle." I hadn't looked at it for at least a week. What fun, to revisit a piece that had been put aside as "polished" and scrutinize it further to make every word count. I'm still working on the last line and will most likely revisit it again before Mary-Lou gives me a due date. I expect nothing less than for all you to tear it apart.

Morgaine

Wednesday, April 15, 2020

These days I cry for no good reason. That's not factually true, because God knows there is plenty to cry about. I think I'm doing fine, keeping myself busy, taking walks with Archie when the weather permits, even cooking up some tasty meals, and then, while making the bed this morning, I just began to cry. When my husband was ill—dying, really—I'd take our dog for a walk around the neighborhood (we were in Florida then) and I'd cry all the way. I'd clean up my face on my return not wanting to upset Marvin any further. He had so much to contend with, he didn't need a weepy wife to console. I know I hold a lot inside, but these days it's impossible to escape the tragedy that is everywhere around us. I see pictures of our healthcare workers with faces ravaged by what they're dealing with, their faces scarred by the need to wear masks for such long periods of time.

My granddaughter, Callie, is an investigative reporter for *The Bangor Daily News* and she's been doing ongoing reporting on the homeless in Bangor. She goes out to see them firsthand and talks with them. She sent me a photo of an older woman cradled in the arms of a young man, both homeless. What does one do for her, for him, for countless others? I worry about my granddaughter out on the street in what I envision is not the healthiest environment. She tells me she wears a mask and disposable gloves, but still, I worry. I send money to the Bridgeport Mission, and other organizations that feed the needy, the homeless, the ones who have no resources. But writing a check is easy.

Today I spent much of the day completing a project I began earlier in the week. I have half-siblings in Puerto Rico. We speak on the phone every now and then and they are always very affectionate towards me. They wanted to know more about our father and his life before they were born. I've put together a few pages with information about him and his parents, siblings, and a few anecdotes that my uncle, my father's brother, told me when I was last in Cuba in 1996. This afternoon I copied some photos and will put it in the mail later this week. It was a good project. It engaged my interest and I forgot for a while the reality of our world.

Sorry to be so down-in-the-mouth. Tomorrow will be better.

Maria

Wednesday, April 15, 2020

Was this the day that the rain came down in sheets, pelting my window so loudly I thought water was dripping onto the wood floors? I think so. Whichever day it was, my heart dropped at the thought of a leaky roof but got lucky this time.

I cannot keep track of the days anymore. I've been off all week. And for some reason, my computer clock seems to feel the same way. It has decided to estimate the time. As a result, I have been unfashionably late to a number of Zoom meetings.

I heard today from the publisher of *Art Times* for whom I had written an article before she disappeared into thin air. She's re-emerged and will publish my article within the week. I tried to remember when I submitted the piece. It was in the beginning of February. Might as well have been another century.

Today daughter Megan is cooking coq au vin, a tribute to the fact that she, her husband and my three grandchildren would have

been arriving in Paris before continuing to Belgium. On Friday, she'll make mussels cooked in beer, with Belgian waffles for dessert. It's what they would have been eating with daughter Ariel and her husband the first night of a week-long visit.
Deb

Thursday, April 16, 2020

"Cookie Man," Ken, had started the custom of bringing cookies to our writing classes at the Westport Library. Today, he offers to drop off cookies before our Zoom class at 12:30. He makes the well-distanced rounds to Judy, Deb, Morgaine, Maria Z, Mary-Lou and me just in time. His cookies are stuffed with heavenly chocolate mousse.
Gina

ALMOST just like our usual meetings! Ken, you're a mensch!
Deb

Wait! I wasn't serious about Ken driving hither and yon! Although driving is still one of our privileges. See you all in an hour. Parking should be easy.
Donna

Thursday, April 16, 2020

I get a text from Bernadette. She is home from the hospital and in bed with a migraine. Deb has heard from Polly. She is in the hospital. Deb, Lynn's husband, Polly, and Bernadette have all tested negative for the coronavirus. We all wonder about the accuracy of the tests.

Mary-Lou facilitates our Zoom class. It is great to see everyone's faces and get a glimpse of their writing spaces. We can see Judy and Maria's books, Deb's exposed brick wall, Mary-Lou's posters, Lynn's art hung on a colorful red background,

Ken's hanging rug, Morgaine's four poster bed and Donna's place of serenity. We decide to go forward with the virallies. We might do a conversational performance—reading excerpts at the Westport Library someday. The compiled journal might be a record for posterity. Ken is a former board member of the Westport Historical Society. He will see if they are interested. They are!

Mary-Lou, and I will work together to give shape to the document. For now, I will catch up with compiling.

Today my grandson turns 20. He poses with a mask pulled down to his neck and holds a Corona beer. If he'd been on our Easter virtual Zoom brunch, he'd know I'd already pulled that stunt.

I do valuation analysis for a marketing firm that focuses on agriculture. What will happen now that their clients are dumping milk and plowing produce back into the ground?

I use the Uber Eats app for the first time in weeks. I order thin crust pizza and sides from Sammy's in Southport. I like the pizza, Ryan likes the mozzarella sticks, and I throw out the inedible chicken wings. Monica is so disgusted she never wants me to order from them again.

Gina

Thursday, April 16, 2020

That was a great Zoom session. Good to see all of you—as you know, I like seeing everyone's habitat—rather like seeing wild elephants on the savannah instead of in a zoo, although I don't know why that comparison comes to mind.

Living such a solitary life reveals more of me to myself. For example, my preference for creating messes and ignoring them until the point comes when I can't stand the mess for one more minute. Then I clean it up, saying to myself, "See, that wasn't so bad after all, was it?"

I was thinking about messes as we talked today. I haven't been keeping up with our virally submissions—not writing regularly or reading regularly. In that case, the mess is my email. I read it all at once and then go a few days without looking, so I'm just catching up with the distressing news about Polly and Bernadette. I have 10,000 emails dating back to 2010—I do know how to delete them and now would be a good time to do that—but knowing me...

There's also a reading mess on my coffee table. Mostly magazines—*New Yorkers* folded over to short stories, *NYT Magazine* sections folded over to multiple *Spelling Bees* and *The Atlantic Monthly* folded over to whatever caught my attention but didn't manage to keep it. The reading nook in my den does not contain bookmarked books because most of what I read is on a Kindle. It keeps a digital marker of half completed books—*Overstory*, *The Color of Law*, *The Collected Letters of Ralph Ellison*. Of course, the Kindle is on top of a stack of books sitting on a low shelf. I don't intend to read those books; I don't even know what they are, but I do know that I don't leave reading matter on the floor. Except for a French dictionary. The small book that I need the dictionary for is on top of the pile of books under the Kindle.

The kitchen goes through messy / clean cycles too. I'm lucky that Meadow Ridge delivers the dinners we select. Right now there's an unpacked bag (I've been writing and I'm not hungry), several plastic containers from previous meals, dishes that need to go in the dishwasher (I think it's empty), and a half unpacked bag from the local grocery that delivers (I didn't order anything perishable). If I get a delivery of wine, I'll have to put something away to make space. Or I'll have to put the wine away. If there were mice or rodents my kitchen wouldn't look like this. I know how to keep it clean—never lived like this with Marty or Bill just out of common courtesy—but I don't choose to at the moment. Does this sound like the alcoholic's response, "I can stop any time

I want to; I just don't want to now"?

The bedroom is probably the neatest. I try to keep my clothes put away. The *New Yorkers* on Bill's bedside chest of drawers have turned-over pages too, but they're neatly stacked and topped with an exercise routine from a 2014 NYT and two 2 lb. weights on top of them. I don't leave items on chairs in any room. I don't know exactly why; it's not a rule that I've ever articulated before now.

I realize this is not new behavior and it's probably not age related. When my daughters were in high school and I was working on my dissertation, our yellow Labrador retriever, Buttercup, would sometimes try to visit me in my study. I think she got lonely during the day without her playmates and the commotion they generated. She'd stand at the door and look at me, forlorn. She wanted to sit under my desk and nestle her head on my feet, but I had stacked papers on the file cabinets and bookcases and, when I ran out of those spaces, all over the floor. She didn't want to step on them; she didn't whimper or bark; she didn't sit or lie down patiently and wait. She just stood at the doorway, looking sad with her lovely brown eyes and yellow lashes. I knew it was time to clean up the mess.

Judy

Thursday, April 16, 2020

So lovely to see you today! I missed your faces. (And we all missed you, Polly and Bernadette!)

Here's today's entry for possible historical posterity. ☺

The other day one of my pen-pals sent me a homemade mask: hot pink with polka dots. She said she made it neon bright on purpose, so I could be spotted leaving the house.

The mask came in handy though, because the no-sew ones go shooting off my face like a sling shot. As if I didn't have enough to worry about, now I spend an inordinate amount of time wondering if my ears are deformed.

My husband and I went out yesterday because he ran out of cough drops and I ran out of dishwasher detergent. As he drove, we noticed there were more cars on the road than usual. We pulled into the Walmart parking lot and drove right out again; the line was down the length of the store. We drove to the other Walmart; same thing. I said, "Today is day 30. Maybe everybody is celebrating."

We drove to ShopRite. It was fairly quiet. I picked up a few things, but no dish detergent. The entire aisle was empty. I was beginning to panic. Hand-wash dishes? How much does God think I can bear?

We drove to Walgreens. This time my husband went in. He is particular about his cough drop choices and doesn't trust me. He wore a mask that I sewed, and if you think my cooking skills are subpar, you should see me with a sewing machine. It took me three hours of swearing to make it. I used the only fabric I had: a pattern of stylized lemons. He looked ridiculous—like a kitchen towel turned bank-robber. He bought cough drops and a fifteen pack of dish-detergent pods, which I normally don't use and don't like, but that was all they had. I was reminded of what I wrote a month ago about being picky, substituting millet for rice.

At Walgreens, my husband witnessed an almost-fist-fight. Two men got into it over a social-distancing breach. A masked man accused a barefaced man of getting too close. The barefaced man pointed to the mark on the floor and said, "It's six feet. Shut up." The masked man yelled, "You are too close!" The bare man said, "You wanna go?" and took a step over the X. The Walgreens cashier, a nice lady, said, "Hey! Not in my store! You want to fight, take it outside!" One of them called the other an asshole. I was reminded of "Asshole in the morning/Assholes all day." But after thirty days of stress, people are maybe not their best selves.

We got drive-thru iced coffee, then we went home. All told, less than two hours out of the house and it was completely exhausting and barely worth it.
Lynn

Lynn, you are hysterical. I will be walking around with the image of a man I haven't ever seen, but feel like I know, with a dishtowel wrapped around his face! My imagination takes it further—scenes of washed hands being wiped across his face to dry them

Soon to try Stop & Shop. Hope I fare better… just found out that the bleach on which I was relying for disinfecting loses efficacy after a year, and the solution after 24 hours. I've been using 2-year-old bleach and made the solution a couple of weeks ago. Um, oops. Have been unable to find any spray or wipes, so may have to plan a shopping cart heist if I see a stash someone else has collected. Thank God I'll have my mask on!
Deb

Thursday, April 16, 2020

We weren't complete without Polly and Bernadette, but it was great seeing all of you. Great discussion on how to go forward with the virallies.

I, too, had been needing dishwashing soap and, like everyone else, found nothing. My daughter went online and bought dishwasher tablets and gave me a box. The brand is If You Care and underneath that it says: "Quality with Integrity." Tablets come 40 to a box, are super concentrated, and eco-friendly. Can't tell you how much the cost because Marissa wouldn't tell me. They do a great job.
Maria

I have dishwasher soap. Will trade half a box for some disinfect-

ing anything.
Deb

Ammonia is another great disinfectant. Check under your sink. Be sure to dilute.
Morgaine

Thursday, April 16, 2020

Funny event of the day: a video of my 21-month-old grandson, Joah. He's sitting in a pint-sized armchair, holding a cup of seltzer, with one foot propped on a pillow. His mother has asked him if he wants to come play.

"No, not pyaying. I'm b'ing Dad."

"You're going to sit there and drink your seltzer?"

"Yuhhh. I'm just b'ing Dad."

What's hysterical is that his dad has a badly broken toe, and has been keeping his foot propped up in the evening, usually with a beer in his hand. Joah managed a great impersonation!

Serious thought of the day: I'm getting really worked up about the pandemic being referred to as the cause of our economic situation. It's not that I have any soft place in my heart for this silent killer. But what it really has done is point up how fragile our economy is, with its extremes of wealth and poverty. These extremes are the reason for the collapse. If people earned enough to save, rather than living paycheck to paycheck, they would be better able to weather this tornado tossing their lives asunder. For all the daily ways in which lack of privilege impacts lives, this kind of crisis writes the story of inequality in huge, bold strokes. I'm pissed about it anew. Will we go back to life as usual, or actually build a strong economy by eradicating the poverty that in the end hurts us all? I hope so.
Deb

Thursday, April 16, 2020,

Below is a quick draft of my note to the Westport Historical Society (now called the Westport Museum of History and Culture).

Ramin, I am part of a writing group, which can no longer meet because of the quarantine. That has not stopped us from writing. We have been sharing our thoughts daily and have created a fairly extensive record of moods, events, and thoughts during the crisis. If I say so myself, the writing is well done, interesting, funny, and poignant. We are thinking of organizing our work and compiling it into some kind of record.

I have been asked by our group of 10 Westporters (three of whom have been personally affected by the virus) to see if the Museum would be interested in our final compilation for inclusion in the Museum's effort to memorialize personal histories during the pandemic. If you encourage us, I will submit a proposal with some excerpts so you can get an idea of what we have produced.
Ken

Ken, sounds like a worthy project and of course we would be interested—absolutely. Thank you for thinking of us.
  Thanks!
Ramin

Friday, April 17, 2020

I complete the valuation analysis for a holding company and five subsidiaries. It has taken the better part of the week. I am worried about one subsidiary that does wireless communications for events like state fairs and other mass gatherings. I suggest that we put them on our watch list.

I have read almost no emails that are not work related this week.

I order pizza and sides from Golden's in Westport for the first time since February 25th. The driver rings the doorbell and leaves the bag and boxes on the front steps. He's gone before I can open the door. The familiar taste is comforting. Everyone is happy.

Gina

Friday, April 17, 2020

Fellow Scribner's,

I do a lot of thinking between the hours of 2 & 4 AM and while I am in the shower. Yesterday's teleconference has caused me to lose sleep and waste a lot of water. If this note is more of a "tell" than a "show," it is the result of an affliction M-L identified when she initially rejected my application to be in her class and with which you are now burdened. It is one of those "warts" that Lynn identified in relationships like the one that seems to be developing among us.

I share with you some of last evening's tells:

1. As a group, we have expanded our mission, an intriguing development. I look forward to where it will take us as long as we retain the intimacy that has made it special.

2. Notwithstanding # 1, should we expand our submissions to include thoughts beyond our personal stories? I probably won't be able not to (double negative).

3. Lynn's account of the two men quarrelling in CVS caused me to recall a life axiom, "Freedom to swing your arms ends at the tip of someone else's nose" and to ask the question, "How long are my arms and where is someone else's nose?"

4. I read a story that zoos are running out of money. In Germany, they are thinking of feeding the animals to each other as a food source. Has one of the world's most developed countries unraveled that quickly? (Read *Babylon's Ark*, the wartime story of the rescue of the

Baghdad Zoo. Fascinating, well written, totally engaging and thankfully has a better-than-expected ending.)

5. I also read a story that the sudden drop in the economy has caused almost all of the residents in a New Hampshire town with a population of 1500 to lose their jobs. It made me think of *Grapes of Wrath* and the desperation of its characters. Is this the new future for too many of us?

6. In client conferences I can remember everything I am told without taking notes. In social settings, five minutes later I can barely remember names. Accordingly, I confess that until yesterday, in our classes, I connected with your faces, but not so much with your names. In our subsequent email exchanges, I connected with your stories but not so much with your faces. Yesterday helped. But I have a new problem. We have shared personal stories without providing context. Beyond what I know about you, who are you? Maybe it isn't important or perhaps it is too soon, or it could be, ironically, too personal, but at some point, I would like to exchange one paragraph summaries to put the stories into a setting. I need a nap.

Ken

Friday, April 17, 2020

"What Historians Will See When They Look Back on the Covid-19 Pandemic of 2020" https://www.nytimes.com/2020/04/15/us/coronavirus-pandemic-historians-archive.html. Did you see this? Looks like we're on the right track. Thanks, Ken for getting the ball rolling and Gina, who suggested the idea.

Donna

Friday, April 17, 2020

Get out of bed at 6:30 AM for "Senior Hour" at ShopRite. I hit the jackpot. They have both toilet paper *and* paper towels. Cheddar cheese is another reward for my early rising. We're a cheese family, from packaged cheddar, which is melted over nachos, inside burritos and on top of any warm sandwich, to Artisan varieties, such as truffle, goat, and aged Gouda. And who *doesn't* love triple cream Brie? No one at our house!

For two years in a row, which makes it a tradition, we've had a cheese tasting party. Mary-Lou attended in 2019. For the record, if a group of fifty is allowed to gather, you're all invited this year. The wine and cheese theme was inspired by a sale at Whole Foods. While everyone loves to save money, my hubby is the ultimate bargain hunter. His love of saving a buck is matched by his generosity.

In the month of December, Whole Foods holds an event they call, The Twelve Days of Cheese. On each of the twelve days before Christmas they offer a unique variety for half price. Mark calls in the morning and has them put a generous wedge aside for him to pick up after work. He wouldn't dare miss a day!

Having gotten most everything on my ShopRite list and then some, the grand total comes to $97.92. With blue-gloved hands and my facemask still in place I stop for gas on the Post Road. Two dollars and five cents per gallon, *Wow!* The oil and gas companies must be hurting, undoubtedly the reason that Trump just relaxed regulations on mercury emissions.

Last stop—Trader Joe's. Sixty-two dollars and fifty cents later I'm on my way home. Even though my hands were covered I wash them with hot soapy water, while singing happy birthday twice for Mary-Lou. I wipe down my steering wheel, doorknobs and handles and wash all produce, and begin prepping for dinner, arugula, and sweet onion quiche. I figure I'll fry the onions now and assemble the pie right before it goes into the oven. I stage the ingredients on the kitchen island: eggs, arugula, pie crusts and...

"Oh shit! I forgot the feta."

Morgaine

Yum, Morgaine! That quiche sounds amazing. Share the recipe? I am a cheese addict, too, so appreciate your family's love affair with all things cheese. Tomorrow I am making the walnut & cheese Gruyere recipe that was in the NYT magazine this past Sunday. Will let you know how it turns out.

Maria

Friday, April 17, 2020

I too am a cheese addict. Every October I go away to the Cape for a week with a group of friends, and every day on that vacation we take turns making The Cheese Plate. It is a gigantic board of different flavors, shapes, olives, crudité etc. And you can tell who made it by how it's organized. Mine are in very neatly presented fans, and I (of course) count to make sure each flavor has the same number of pieces. Mandy just throws down "Cheese Heaps." Tina will go heavy on her favorite flavor and skimp on the rest. Karen likes the smelliest cheese but is kind enough to keep it separate— off to the side like it's been punished. Carroll likes the cheese that tastes like nothing. Havarti, I think?

On the last day, we clean out the fridge, and line up all the packages like a cheese battalion, and we go CYOC (cut your own cheese). After our vacation and we return to our homes, we text each other photos of our small, sad, cheese-plates-for-one, and talk about how we miss our giant cheese-plates-for-5—and each other.

The Dairy Board needs a new slogan: "Cheese: It's What Unites Us."

Lynn

If you "guys" (I hope I can use this collective referral to our group without offending anyone) keep up this discussion about food treats, I offer my delivery service to accommodate those of us drooling.
Ken

I live in an all-female household of five. We have a lot of "Hey Guys" moments. Same with my girlfriends.
Gina

Friday, April 17, 2020

Just saw the Westport Country Playhouse two-hour presentation of Young Artists, live performances of high school students from Fairfield County schools singing songs of their choosing, some from musicals that were canceled, some just tunes that they liked. It was hosted by the Westport actress, Kelli O'Hara. The viewers were supposed to know who she was, but I didn't. I enjoyed the distraction from the news, and I liked seeing unpolished but eager talent.

Bill and I used to sing jazz songs together. We'd go to his sister-in-law's house in Vermont every Thanksgiving, always a wonderful ride. Once I outran a snowstorm when everyone told us to stay home; another time we sang jazz songs all the way there since one song inevitably reminded us of another. We hadn't exhausted our repertoire by the time we got to Montpelier. I learned the songs mostly from my mother. I didn't go to nursery school when I was little; instead, I spent lots of time following her around the house as she cooked and cleaned and ironed—and sang! I didn't know I was learning jazz; I was just imitating her. Bill learned the songs from records and going to performances.

I've stopped singing now that he's gone. Instead, I've gone back to playing Beethoven and Bach and Chopin, the pieces I played between the ages of 12 and 18. In some cases the scores are the old ones with my piano teacher's notes on them. They are technical instructions about fingering and pedaling and tempo, a reminder of the technique I used to have that is now gone.

Mr. Brown came to our house every week. Once my family and I went to visit him somewhere. I remember he had a "roommate" that seemed to stand unusually close to him. Now I realize they were probably a gay couple, but I didn't know the word or the concept then. He was a good and gentle teacher. Occasionally he'd say, "Judy, Judy, Judy" which I came to understand was a quote from an old movie. I think Jimmy Stewart said it. I still haven't seen it.

Playing the piano is a great comfort. It requires total physical and mental concentration. When my mind wanders, things I think I know automatically go haywire. Usually, a wandering mind means that my hands are tired, or my mind is spent; it's time to stop. At least I'm not playing with a goal in mind. No more recitals that terrified me, no audience to hear me; I close the patio doors if they're open. I don't have to play a sonata from beginning to end so I fool around with sections that I like. I didn't play today. That means I will tomorrow.

Judy

Judy, I think you mean Kelli O'Hara, James Naughton's daughter-in-law and Broadway star. Both are very connected with the playhouse. Naughton, besides being a great actor, is very outspoken in favor of death with dignity.

Deb

Judy, my wife Sam LOVES to sing and does it all the time everywhere... thankfully she has a lovely voice and can carry a tune beautifully. She seems to know every song I have ever heard of and songs from shows I have never heard of. When I hear her singing in the shower, it makes me smile that someone is that happy doing such a simple thing. If she is ever in a coma, her instructions are that I am to bring show tunes to the hospital, and she is confident it will lead to her recovery. I, on the other hand, was told by the high school choir director that he would prefer it if I just mouthed the words during performances, which I was happy to do because I could never remember the lyrics accurately.

"Judy, Judy, Judy" was sung by Cary Grant.

Ken

Friday, April 17, 2020

The philosopher, William James, brother of the writer Henry James, is at least famous for saying that if you're in a bad mood, you'll feel better if you smile. Maybe he was one of the first to philosophize about the "body/mind" connection. When I was in my early 40s I discovered running and endorphins. Soon after, I started swimming and found the kind of peace that so many others achieved through meditation. During this pandemic, I've discovered the benefits of singing. Before the pandemic, I sometimes sang in the shower. With water pounding on my head and my voice bouncing off the tiles, I sounded better to me than it did on dry land.

My pandemic repertoire, not counting "Happy Birthday," starts with the songs that first engaged my teenaged emotions. Misery spoke to my condition in those days. One of the songs I favor, since no one is listening, is the Billy Williams quartet singing "Pour Me a Glass of Tear Drops." It's embarrassingly corny, verging on disgusting, but it nevertheless reached deep into my teenaged, romantic heart. I'd play it on the victrola until my parents made me stop. "I'll Walk Alone"—wasn't that Jane Froman?—was definitely classier and produced the same romantic effect. Later, I became addicted to "Lost in the Stars," a serious piece of music by Kurt Weill, with tender, sob-worthy lyrics by Sherwood Anderson. Ultimately, when real love did come my way, I cheered up and began to savor musicals. I can still sing all the lyrics to "Life Upon the Wicked Stage." I mourned the death of Gower Champion.

Larry remembers the same music that I do. We sing together, *a Capella*, unless I accompany him on my kazoo. We do not sing together in the shower. We can sort of carry a tune, and we entertain each other enormously and loudly. If you haven't already folded singing into your daily pandemic activity, I recommend it. Like smiling, it makes you happy.

Mary-Lou

Many thanks for the pandemic tip, Mary-Lou. Singing probably is also good for the lungs. I'm thinking I may feature a musical a day. I'll start with songs from Oklahoma today and move on South

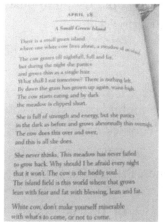

Pacific tomorrow.

Time to put clothes in the dryer as I belt, "Oh, what a beautiful morning!"

We'll raise our voices in writing and song. Tra-la! ♫

Donna

A friend I have loved for a thousand lifetimes sent me this poem. I pass it along to you with love and gratitude.

Donna

Friday, April 17, 2020

Solitude is helping me to focus. So when I received the YMCA email newsletter today and saw that it was full of ideas for keeping entertained while locked down, a light bulb went off. I immediately emailed the director of teen and children's activities at the Y and offered my 19 Projects for Covid-19 for them to use in future newsletters. I thought people would enjoy doing them. I also thought of the size of the Y's mailing list and my name and website going out to every person on it.

She wrote back to me in minutes. The upshot is that she is deciding how to best use what I have to offer. Webinar classes, perhaps.

I am so content working in my little studio. I have eclectic taste in music, and what I choose to play at any given moment depends on the mood and tempo of what I am drawing. My dog has his own bed behind my easel. There's just enough room to dance around when I need a break, or the music is just too inviting to stand still.

But promoting myself is another story. I liked meeting with editors and art directors when showing my illustration portfolio. It was a designated time to talk about my work. It felt very different from today's "networking," with a bunch of people trying to push their abilities to the forefront of the conversation. Ugh.

Deb

Saturday, April 18, 2020

I flatten six pizza boxes from the past two nights and toss all the wilted Easter flowers. I order Girl Scout cookies and a bunch of non-medical designer masks from Amazon. The masks will arrive by June 22nd. The cookies will come sooner. Printer ink is hard to come by on Amazon. I turn to Staples.

The first delivery slot I can get from Fresh Market is April 23. I reserve it. A friend from Weston can get Peapod in three days; I can't get a Peapod delivery slot at all. Monica will go to Stop & Shop for milk. We go through six half gallons a week.

A totally isolated ex-boyfriend of Monica's comes over to help her refresh the rotting pantry door. They go to Home Depot for supplies. It takes forever to navigate the long lines and social distancing. They sand and paint. He grills burgers and hot dogs for us. It's nice to have his company. I love the sound of laughter and

the rhythm of ping-pong balls batting back and forth.
Gina

Saturday, April 18, 2020

More and more often these days, I find myself returning to childhood memories, an activity particular to memoirists, personal essayists, and old people.

This morning, while reading about Trump's calls to "LIBERATE," I heard my childish, sing-song voice say, "You'll be sorry."

The object of my playground taunt was not directed at Trump, our two-faced Janus leader who talks "safety first" at his press conferences and then encourages dangerous behavior in his tweets by playing to many people's worst instincts. But Trump will never be sorry.

That schoolyard taunt was directed at Trump's base. It's pathetic kid stuff, hardly worthy of this situation. They might not even be sorry if every screaming, flag-waving one of them contracts the virus, to which my childhood self would have taken pleasure in saying, "Told ya so."
Mary-Lou

Saturday, April 18, 2020

Since music seems to be the anthem for the latest virallies. Here's my "song."

Music was once a huge part of my life. Starting in my sophomore year in high school, I began voice lessons with Mme. Urbach at the Washington Heights Conservatory of Music. I had always enjoyed singing and as a youngster, amused my family with my gyrations and warbling. I fell in love with opera after seeing Mario Lanza and Kathryn Grayson in *The Toast of New Orleans*. My local library had musical scores—operas among them—and each week I borrowed whichever opera was to be transmitted from the stage of the Metropolitan Opera that Saturday. The first aria/duet I learned was "Libiamo" the drinking song from La Traviata. In my room I followed along singing loudly and forcefully, both parts.

After three years with Mme. Urbach, my piano teacher suggested that I needed to study with a more challenging vocal teacher. I auditioned with Samuel Margolis in Manhattan. Until that audition, I hadn't known that palms could sweat, but when I rang Mr. Margolis' doorbell, my hands were not only wet, but icy cold.

I began my lessons the following week and for two years took the elevator to his studio—the living room of the spacious apartment he shared with his wife. Mrs. M. was never seen, although once in a while, muted sounds came from what I imagined was their kitchen. A brief but thrilling moment came when, during one of my lessons, Mr. Margolis introduced me to Robert Merrill who had dropped in to visit.

I left my lessons and my music behind when I married my first husband and moved to the Midwest where he was stationed at Chanute Air Force Base in Illinois.

Vocal lessons resumed at the New England Conservatory of Music when my husband was transferred to Boston. After his discharge, and our subsequent move to Connecticut, I became active in community theater and sang on many local stages.

Now I sing no more. My voice is shattered. I try very hard not to think about it, but every now and then, I'm ambushed by someone singing an aria I'd studied long ago—my intended music, the one I'd abandoned. In my unfeeling youth I had not thought of the consequences of that denial. I am mute now, only able to listen.

This may sound dark and gloomy, but only for moments, every now and then. There were other songs in my life shared with my husband Marvin (no, not the one in the Air Force). Marvin loved the artists and songs that are part of the American Songbook: Ella Fitzgerald, Frank Sinatra, Count Basie and many others. On Saturday mornings we'd turn on the radio to Jonathan Schwartz: four hours of Sinatra songs, history and anecdotes. We'd dance in the kitchen, where the radio sat, until Barney, our mini dachshund, began pulling on Marvin's pant leg, wanting to be included. He was not content until we picked him up and continued dancing with the small dog between us.

Maria

Saturday, April 18, 2020

Conflict. I hate it, and yet there are times I just can't avoid it. I have to open my big mouth.

Mark made *osso bucco* (braised veal shank.) The cut of the meat was thinner than usual, so when he mixed it in with a pound of pasta the meat was scarce. Michelle, who avoids carbohydrates, dished herself a bowl of what looked to me to be all veal. Of course, it wasn't *all* meat, there were maybe 6-8 noodles in her bowl, but it was definitely a disproportionate amount of veal to noodle, which meant the next person in line was basically eating a pasta dish.

I called her on it and she reacted.

Damn! We had been doing so well for the past month living under one roof. Why couldn't I just let it go? Mark (and probably Daniel) don't care if they have a pasta dish with an *osso bucco* flavored sauce.

Now she isn't talking to me. She feels unappreciated and slighted. She storms off to her bedroom. Greg, who is helping me unload the dishwasher at the time says, "Don't worry, it'll be all right."

He's right. We'll make up, but at the moment it feels yucky. I hate conflict and yet I had to open my big mouth.

Morgaine

Saturday, April 18, 2020

I've been incommunicado. Not because I'm tired of you all or writing. I've been too busy to do much but work. Worked all day on graphics for a friend who is running for State Representative. Progress goes slowly as I learn/remember Photoshop and Illustrator. It's fun, and consuming.

Maybe it rained, maybe it didn't, and I went to the park briefly with Arlo. Don't remember.

Deb

Sunday, April 19, 2020

Low Sunday—so called because it follows the glorious feast of Easter. Didn't realize it was the week of Earth Day until I turned on the TV.

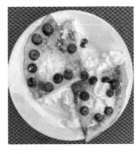

Ryan cooks crepes for breakfast with a little coaching from her mother. They are stuffed with Nutella. Evelyn decorates them with whipped cream, blueberries, and powdered sugar.

Monica's boyfriend comes back to help paint and rehang the pantry door. He and Monica are off to Home Depot again.

I try to update my shopping cart from Fresh Market. I can't. I have to place a new order. It will come before the order I placed yesterday. Go figure. I plan to make split pea soup and 15 bean soup later this week with all the leftover ham from Easter.

I am so homesick for Wisconsin that I order five pounds of fudge and chocolate turtles from Tremblay's in Eagle River.

Gina

Sunday, April 19, 2020

Here's my idea du jour. It's not original, but I think it's a good one. Why don't reporters skip Trump's press briefings? He lies to them. He abuses them verbally. He cuts them off in mid-question when he senses that the questions will annoy him. When he does respond to a question, he uses the opportunity to avoid answering and instead uses the opportunity to aggrandize himself. These so-called press briefs are political rallies. This is a travesty.

Reporters should simply stop attending. They can do their jobs just as well by watching him on TV in real time from another location. They serve no purpose other than as Trump's unwilling victims. One of the most aggressive, on point questioners, Yamiche Alcindor, hasn't been seen at these rallies for days. Did she quit or did Trump ban her? I suspect the latter.

As for Doctors Fauci and Birx, I hope that they would quit his stage as medical advisors. It is evident that Trump does what he can to undercut their message, while they do their best not to upset him while continuing to dispense accurate information. Their discomfort with their nearly proscribed roles is increasingly evident. Why don't they pack up their models and estimates and dispense their critical information in any number of venues that would be happy to have them.

Mary-Lou

YESSSS!
Gina

Sunday, April 19, 2020

Since lockdown began, I have been playing Rocket League almost every day. It's a videogame, like soccer with a giant ball and racecars. My husband and son have been playing it for years. When my husband was quarantined, Zach didn't have anyone to play with, so I volunteered. Zach made it his mission to train me. I have been playing for a solid month and I still can't hit the ball with any semblance of accuracy—it's not Zach's fault—he's a good teacher; I just suck at driving. Now that my husband is back on the videogame scene, Rocket League has become our nightly family activity, even though I am deadweight and a drain on our win percentage.

My family is so patient; they say "Good try, Mom!" and "Ooooh! Almost!" By accident, I often shoot at my own goal, earning me the nickname 'Wrong-way.' Some days I don't mind being terrible, but some days I want to strangle the controller. I had said that I had sworn off self-improvement, but I lied: I really want to master this game! Some nights, I sneak downstairs and do tutorials and trainings online, and I think I must be the only mom in Westport trying to get better at Xbox.

This afternoon, we played League and ended up in a competitive overtime match, with our team rank on the line. My husband made a mistake, and my son made another mistake, and they started arguing about whose fault our imminent loss was. I said, "It's fine! We'll fix it!" and on the next kick-off, my husband missed, but I recovered the ball and scored the game-winning goal. Even a blind pig finds a truffle once in a while. I got high-fives, smiles, and laughs... after the shock wore off. ☺

Lynn

Sunday, April 19, 2020

Worked. My son's family came for a short time to play in the yard. We know the drill now—me and Arlo on one side of the fence, Galen, Meg, Silas and Joah on the other. Silas didn't feel well, which broke my heart. They left after a half hour to take him home.

He was feeling better by the time the family gathered on Zoom to wish my mother a happy 98th birthday. She can do little more than say hello and I love you, but she smiled as her family bantered together. I think she recognizes our voices, though she no longer remembers the connections to her. But she knows we are hers in some way.

I usually visit her every other day. In some ways it's torturous. She's so diminished. But it also feels good to be there, and I feel very disconnected not being able to visit. This is perhaps the deepest way the magnitude of corona is reaching that compartment of my brain where I store my worries about the changes in our lives. My mother is very frail and could die, and I would not have seen her in months, and would not be with her.

It was good to have the Zoom party. We will do more calls just to contact her.

Deb

Monday, April 20, 2020

Oddly enough I feel like the weeks are flying by. The buds on the dogwood tree in the backyard are now little cups of salmon pink. The tomato plant sprouts number eight, and we've had our fourth family Sunday brunch in quarantine.

For my mother who turned 85 last month the days and hours drag on. She was bored before the coronavirus hit, when there were weekly bingo games at the senior center, endless doctor appointments, grocery shopping outings and programs on television to look forward to. Now all she hears are pandemic updates, which are a daily reminder that remind that her age, irritable bowel syndrome, high blood pressure and anxiety put her in the high-risk category. Like me, she's a clean freak, but she barely has the energy or strength to the change the sheets on her bed.

Pre-corona I would visit her, on average, once a month. I'd drive to her mobile home at 6:30 in the morning to beat the commuter traffic on the LIE, get there by 9 AM and leave the next evening after dinner. Spending 36 hours with my mother is not an easy task. She complains a lot! Everything hurts, she's hot, she's cold, she doesn't sleep well and the "damn cat won't stop crying." Poor little Rosebud only wants attention.

My last visit was just about a month ago; I'm feeling the pull. Since then, other than the occasional grocery drop by family members who live closer than I, she's been shut in and alone. I don't consider myself to be a risk since the only place I've been is the grocery store wearing gloves and an N95 mask. *Wait, don't judge! I came by the medical grade face mask honestly.*

On April 10th I received an email from a close friend who is, how can I put this nicely, somewhat neurotic when it comes to being prepared. For example, when she travels, she carries an extra suitcase full of pharmaceuticals and she was wiping down tray tables before it was vogue. In her April email she reminded us of her 50th birthday party back in March of 2013. Making light of her neurosis her husband distributed "End of the World Backpacks" as party favors. In the front zippered pocket were 2 N95 masks.

Anyway, if Mom agrees I'll be making a trip to Long Island in the near future and won't have to get up at the crack of dawn to beat the traffic.

Morgaine

Monday, April 20, 2020

My Trip to Traitor Joe's. All I needed were dried wild blueberries and a bagged salad that I love. Both items, as far as I know, are exclusive to Trader Joe's. I didn't need to have either, but I wanted them. I hadn't driven my car in weeks, and a quick round trip was appealing. I didn't take into account that it was Monday.

When I arrived, I was met a line of about 20 people dressed as bandits waiting to operate, standing behind red carts that stretched from the store's door well past the flower shop. For reasons that I can only ascribe to my very determined nature, I decided to wait. Or maybe it was just masochism.

My entertainment included listening to a guy on his iPhone recite his credit card number, expiration date and code loudly, no less than 3 times, but I didn't have a pencil or paper with me. Not that I would have stolen his number, but I could have gotten a rise out of the guy if I recited it back to him.

A clerk from TJ's made her way down the line, handing out free chocolate candy bars. For as long as it took me to eat it, I entertained kind thoughts.

As the line moved forward, I progressed from the sidewalk to the ramp. My spirits soared.

25 minutes later I entered the store, which had been converted into a children's activity book. There was a maze drawn on the floor, a brief portion of which foot traffic had turned into a follow-the-dots. The lines and dots purported to lead you from aisle to aisle. At the end of each aisle, a curved arrow directed you to take a left or right down the next aisle. Since I only needed my salad bag and my blueberries, both of which were immediately available, I turned my cart around and headed for the check out. On my way, I was arrested by a TJ clerk who explained that I had to continue through the maze, even though I was done shopping. Given my hostage shopping status, I figured I'd buy one of the nice little French pizzas and asked her in what lane I might find them. I waited in that line behind about 8 people for about 10 minutes and then gave up. I didn't want a pizza that much. So, I retraced my way in the maze, left the line and steered over to the last aisle where they have those little yellow blow-up sponges I like—you can never have enough—and then headed to the last cashier, who was just a few steps away. Lucky me! There was only one person checking out. Just as I was about to queue up— I'd made it through the maze!!—another TJ cop sent me back to the pizza aisle which turned out to also be the checkout line. No one told me that! Of course, I'd lost my place. Now there were about 10 people in line, including the guy right ahead of me, who was pushing two carts filled to overflowing. Another 20-minute wait.

Maybe this daily virally will at least give you some idea of what you're up against if you decide to shop at TJ @ 2 PM on a pandemic Monday.

Mary-Lou

The 8-9 AM senior hour is the way to go. Show up at 7:50 and you'll get in when the doors open.

Morgaine

M-L, I had to shop today as well in order to re-supply my neighbor's pantry and his food supplies as he doesn't have a car and is down on his very bad luck. I drove by Trader Joe's at the same time that you were standing in line, and I thought, "My goodness! Those people must REALLY need something at Trader Joe's. How could it be worth it?"

And I kept on driving and went to Fresh Market. There were very few people, and I was out in ten minutes. There is a plastic screen between the clerk and patron, which I thought made good sense. The food is not cheap at Fresh Market, but I have to give them credit for their well-stocked inventory and the caliber of the fresh food. I don't know how they survive because it is almost never crowded. But my neighbor was very happy I didn't come home with just Trader Joe's frozen meals, because when I went by Fresh Market's meat department, I felt obliged to buy him steaks. When I brought them to him, he was thrilled, actually ecstatic. Made my day and I saved a lot of time.

Ken

I can feel something akin to road rage festering inside me—aisle rage! My experience today was at Whole Foods. Should be good, I thought. It's a very civilized place. It seems that wearing masks has given folks a false sense of security. Combined with only the most meager traffic directions, I might as well have been stuffed

into an elevator with 20 other people.
Deb

Monday, April 20, 2020

About shopping: I've had the best luck at Whole Foods, mid-week and late in the day, 5:30 PM or later. Not too crowded, stocked enough. It did occur to me that by that time of the day the store is at its germiest after the constant parade of shoppers have left their slime-trails. I try not to dwell on this.

I almost went out today, mainly because the guinea pig is out of lettuce, but I figured everyone has to make sacrifices—pets included. Instead of shopping, I took a 2-mile walk around my neighborhood loop.

On a happier note, yesterday I made a Wacky Cake—a childhood favorite. It's also called Depression Cake—named for the era, not the affliction. Tonight for dessert, I smeared a piece with raspberry jam, coconut, and drippy buttercream frosting. I might do the same thing for breakfast tomorrow.

Lynn

Monday, April 20, 2020

I finish a valuation analysis for an engineering services firm. Their revenue projections are so outlandish that the valuation firm does not rely on them.

I order sushi and noodles from The Little Kitchen for dinner. It's delicious. The delivery man wears an American flag mask and offers to sign the receipt for me. I tell him to add a tip.

Gina

Monday, April 20, 2020

Zoom in the morning, Zoom in the evening, Zoom around suppertime. Meetings and work. Walk Arlo and work.

Deb

Tuesday, April 21, 2020

By sheer good fortune, I am a ¾'s glass-full person. I am also more cerebral than emotional; although I cry in movies, weep when witness to abuse, and laugh more than most. I am feeling otherwise this morning. Something is different. As the tea kettle whistled, the constant drumbeat of depressing news caught up with me. It is obvious this virus is not just a "bump" in our collective futures, but is, rather, a detour fraught with uncertainty for the world, none of which is encouraging. My instinctive optimism is faltering. I hope the hot tea and refilling the bird feeder will help.

Ken

Tuesday, April 21, 2020

Yay! The fudge and chocolate truffles from Tremblay's in Eagle River, Wisconsin has arrived. That was quick. There is nothing like fresh fudge. Frances is hooked on the maple walnut.

My 12-year-old granddaughter Ryan is in her bedroom singing "When dreams do come true." She has a lovely voice. She had been cast as Dorothy in the *Wizard of Oz* at the Music Theater of Connecticut. Who knows if or when that will be performed?

The sky looks really soupy. I put down my work at 4:15 PM to cook. I made a double batch of chili and a pot of spaghetti. Baked cornbread with jalapeno and shredded cheddar.

Gina

Tuesday, April 21, 2020

I think there are times when the worst possible outcomes from this pandemic hit full force. It may be that the pandemic has blunted your lifelong service to actively serve others and left you feeling helpless. I think it's also true that the human spirit cannot stay in that dreadful place for long. The vital, life-loving you will not have it. Apocalypse now or never? WE JUST DON'T KNOW.

Not knowing is also emotionally destabilizing. So far I haven't told you anything you don't already know. I wish I could. Although I don't even play one on TV, you're probably depressed. Or, to make it less clinical, how about sad or despairing. Has anyone in our writing group avoided falling into that darkness? All I can think of to say is that this terrible sadness will end. It doesn't help that it's a gloomy day. One thing I think you can count on— the tea pot, the bird feeder, and that your own optimism will kick in.

I'm writing this virally while on hold with Apple help and while 2 sticks of frozen unsalted butter are softening on the kitchen counter. The Toll House cookies await. I suspect the butter will soften before I get any tech help. There should be chocolate chip cookies by the end of the day, unless I'm still awaiting Apple, in which case, tomorrow.

This has been a tough day. I received email news that a very close New York friend is in Langone Hospital with Covid-19. His wife had it and is still in recovery in their apartment. He is in isolation. So, of course, is she. What makes her husband's virus especially dangerous, besides his age, is that he has been afflicted for years with a form of leukemia that has been very well controlled, and allowed him to live a relatively active life, although he has made it his business to avoid crowds, such as restaurants, movie theaters, and gyms for the past several years. How ironic is that? When we get together, we always eat dinner at their place. Now that chronic condition will only undermine his chances for recovery. So, "What can I say?

I called into her isolation although I knew that both of us wouldn't know what to say. "What can I say?" took up too much of the conversation. Sometimes, words do fail me. "I'm sure he'll get better," won't do.

"I'm so sorry; this is a horror."

"Yes," she repeated, "A horror."

"I love you," I said.

"I love you," she said. We were both at a loss.

"Call me when you want to talk. Anytime."

At times this pandemic feels surreal. I know that it's real, but for the most part I can hold it emotionally at arms' length. I'm good at denial. Not today.

My email is back in order. The butter is softened. The Toll House cookies await. Doing something helps. Sweetness of any kind does, too.

Mary-Lou

If I had time to bake, this is what I'd do:
Gina's Oatmeal Cookies

1 c shortening

1 ½ c brown sugar

2 eggs

½ c buttermilk

1 ¾ c flour

1 t baking soda

3 c oats

1 c chopped walnuts

1 ½ c raisins

1 t vanilla

Directions:

Heat oven to 400 degrees. Cream together shortening and brown sugar. Add eggs and buttermilk, mixing well. Combine rest of ingredients and drop by teaspoonfuls on greased cookie sheets and bake for 8 minutes until lightly brown. Do not overbake.

Yield: 5 dozen small cookies.

Gina

My favorite cookies: oatmeal raisin. Thanks! For the recipe. I made another bread pudding yesterday from a brioche bread that I almost threw out because it had been at the back of the fridge for so long, I was sure it couldn't be any good. But it was—meaning it wasn't green—and the pudding turned out fine.
Maria

Tuesday, April 21, 2020

My sister-in-law's brother died last week. He had cancer, stroke, and pneumonia as underlying conditions. He was 70. Memorial services will have to be held at a later date. My cousin's son, a truck driver, is positive and in the hospital. My nephew is home from the hospital and on oxygen after catching Covid-19 at his son's basketball game where no one was masked.

I am glad the weather is gloomy. It makes it easier to work.
Gina

Wow, Gina. So sorry to hear the sad news. Am afraid to bake cookies—no one to eat them but me and I'd snuff them all down until I got sick, or they disappeared, whichever happened first.
Judy

I'm sure you know this, Mary-Lou, but it's not the words, it's the caring behind them. Cookies sound like a good plan and baking them has brought the sun out.
Deb

Mary-Lou, in a situation such as your friends' you are so right, words fail. Sometimes just being there, as you surely are, is all you can do and it's what gets a lot of us through. I wish him well.
Maria

Tuesday, April 21, 2020

Well, isn't this a bit of foreshadowing!

Gina

Yes, he's an idiot with zero common sense, and no social skills, but he IS my son. I just hope he never goes into politics. He'd be a disaster.

– Mary Anne Trump

Gina—Is this statement by Trump's mother for real? What's the source? If it's real, it's very valuable. Let me know.
Mary-Lou

Don't know. Came from my younger daughter, Maria.
Gina

Tuesday, April 21, 2020

Weekends are easier for me during The Great Isolation than they were before it. I need alone time, and since Dave's death have learned to cope with far more of it than I could ever have wanted. But weekends are different. I thrive on a balance between time for myself and gettin' out there and partying. Truth is, I often spend at least one, and sometimes both weekend nights alone. It's much harder on those nights to amuse—distract—myself. I hear the traffic and know that there are people who have somewhere to go.

It's a pity party, and I recognize I'm bitter that the couples who were always ready to get together with Deb and Dave seem to have overlooked that half of that whole is still alive. But it's also just sadness. Sadness that Dave and I would have been dancing, or going to a movie and dinner with friends, or hosting one of our many parties. Enter Covid-19. Now no one's going anywhere on the weekends and for me it's a relief. There's no feeling of missing out, of being more alone than anyone else.

I sound like a terrible person. It's not that I don't want other people to have fun. It's just hard not to be as much a part of it as I would like, or once was. I'm sure I'll go to hell or come back as a tsetse fly, but we said we'd tell the uncensored truth.

Deb

Wednesday, April 22, 2020

(Part 1)

Yesterday was my toughest day yet, and to hear that Ken was struggling (our glass almost full guy) didn't help. Although I did ask for you to share your feelings.

Today the sun is shining, and the news is silenced. Mark and I stayed in bed until almost eight o'clock talking. I spewed out all the fears that consumed my being over the last twenty-four hours. Having emptied my vessel, today I choose to fill it with yoga, hugs, French toast, dancing, and writing.

(Part 2)

It's three o'clock in the afternoon, writing time. I now have **two** chapters of my memoir ready for review: "Fireworks" and "The Inner Circle." *A tease.* On to Chapter 12, "Harry."

Harry and I met in 1980, at Cabrillo College in Redwood City. I was sitting on a bench in the sun contemplating my spring schedule thus far: fiber arts, sculpture, calligraphy, and nutrition. I needed one more liberal arts class to be enrolled full time.

I look up. Across the courtyard I see this guy staring at me. *He's cute, but kinda creepy at the same time.* I smile politely then look away. He's still staring; I can feel it. Compelled to look up again, I glare at him. Our eyes are locked as he walks toward me. *Who does this guy think he is? He could be a nutcase.* My defenses are up.

"I'm Harry," he says and then goes on to tell me, accurately, what I'm thinking. He suggests a class I might like under the heading of Ethnic Studies and then walks away. It just so happens

the class fulfills my requirements and fits in my schedule perfectly. Needless to say, I sign up, and another adventure begins.
Morgaine

Wednesday, April 22, 2020

Get a hassle-free delivery from Fresh Market. At long last!!!
Gina

Wednesday, April 22, 2020

Today is my husband's 49th birthday. I rarely buy my husband presents, but I always make him a card. He saves all of them, scattered around the house in his junk piles. His birthday usually passes without much fanfare, but this year people have gone all out: his co-workers Uber-Eats'd us a giant breakfast surprise; his boss is bringing over lunch from Shake Shack; his mother insists we get takeout tonight. For dessert I bought three kinds of super-hero ice cream pints, "Perfect for birthdays!" say their labels. Even our son has gone above and beyond, buying thoughtful gifts: a book of Nintendo comic strips and anti-pet cord wrap (since the cat has taken to chewing on all my husband's monitor cables since working from home began).

My husband is usually aloof, but he has been grinning all morning, like a little kid. Normally meticulous about shaving, he has given it up since he got sick, so he now sports a beard, somewhere between Grizzly Adams and Father Time. With the beard and the smiling, I barely recognize him. He is having a good day and that makes me happy.
Lynn

Wednesday, April 22, 2020
Which side of the bed do you sleep on?

When I was single and living at home, I slept on the right side of the bed when the left side was against the wall. Later I switched the room around and slept on the left side since the right side was against the wall. I'm not a wall-sleeper; I want to be able to make a quick exit from the bed and, if necessary, from the room.

When I married Marty, he slept on the left side in our one bedroom fifth floor walk-up. Since the bed was in the middle of the room with equal access to the floor, it made no difference to me who slept where. I don't remember discussing preferences; it may have made no difference to him either. We kept the same sleeping preferences when we moved to a larger co-op apartment in the Bronx and then to Westport.

The night after he died, I moved to his side of the bed, the left side. I remember answering condolence calls from that side of the bed although I don't know who called. That move took me further away from the skylight in our bedroom and the doors to our deck, further away from the light in the morning and the rising moon in the evening. The move had the advantage of putting me closer to the bathroom, but that was not the reason for it. I moved so I could begin to erase my memory of him—his rage, the smell of Drambuie that his pores exuded. That move didn't work, of course. I had nightmares about his returning years after I married Bill.

When Bill and I got together and I stayed at his house, I slept on the left side of the bed, against the wall. His bedroom was off the living room and next to a den; Ellie, his wife, had apparently slept in another wing of the house where there were three bedrooms. I never asked about those sleeping arrangements; hadn't really occurred to me until now. But I didn't mind sleeping against the wall when he was next to me. I felt safe and protected rather than trapped. Besides, he needed to get to the bathroom in the middle of the night and I didn't. In the morning he got up and made coffee without disturbing me.

We kept the same sleeping arrangements at Meadow Ridge. They weren't logical. His sleeping on the right side meant he was further from the bathroom. It also meant he could lie on his good shoulder, his left shoulder, and hug me. I've continued to sleep on my side of the bed since he died. My side table is littered with eye drops, the telephone, a decorative oil lamp, a working lamp, and a picture of the two of us. His side is carefully arranged and only touched when it's dusted.

I think it's time to change my habits. The mattress on my side is indented and increasingly uncomfortable. It's been slept on and sat on every day for three years longer than his side. I've tried lying on his side of the bed on top of the bedspread; it's obviously not as worn as my side and it's logically the right move to make unless I want to buy a new mattress. But I hesitate. I've gone as far as compromising and sleeping in the middle of the bed. I fear I'll lose another memory of him if/when I move. I won't be able to half-wake up and, turning my head to the right, dream, imagine, hope, insist, with my eyes half closed and my senses dulled, that I will catch a glimpse of him, just a ghost, a fragment, a whiff, a mirage, some essence of him.

Maybe I'll just buy a new mattress pad.

Judy

Your bedtime story is so wonderfully telling. Mine isn't. Our bed is dead center on a wall. I sleep on the right. I have no idea why. The bathroom is equally distant for both of us. What is slightly interesting is that we insist upon replicating that positioning when we stay in hotel beds.

Mary-Lou

Judy, for the thirty-three years we lived together in our Westport home, I slept on the left, Dave on the right. In later years, Arlo and I slept on the left, Dave on the right. Arlo and I still sleep on the left, and I guess as far as we're both concerned, Dave still sleeps on the right. I reach out and stroke his pillow before going

to sleep just in case he's somehow there. Memory foam is aptly named. It helps preserve your memories, while going easy on your back. Get a foam topper.
Deb

I am still sleeping on the same side of the bed that I have slept on since first moving in with Marvin. My side of the mattress is still okay—no indentation. I think about using his side of the bed—it still is "his" side, but like you, my night table is piled with books, pens, backscratcher, a lamp, the blood pressure apparatus, a few boxes from my collection, a notepad, my jewelry box—the night table is pretty large. Archie sleeps with me most nights and he allows me a sliver of the mattress so no chance I'd use Marvin's side, even if I wanted to.
Maria

I always slept on Stan's right (the left side of the bed). Didn't think much about it at the time. I came from a single bunk bed when we married. Now it's a matter of sleeping on the side nearest to the bathroom door.
Gina

You could also flip the mattress over.
Morgaine

Wednesday, April 22, 2020

The report of the day from the "liberal fake news" is that the virus may be worse this winter, with a rebound and its coupling with the regular flu. Oh me! Last week, I did an estate plan for a fellow who had a premonition. We did it using the internet and Zoom. His partner called to tell me that he was taken to the hospital and may be on life support. Oh me! And, regarding the pup I told you about who has been in complete isolation since last November, the

Dept. of Agriculture advised that it had postponed our hearing until the end of summer. Oh me! I need to find some uplifting distractions. I am going to make a cup of tea and go buy more birdseed.

Ken

Wednesday, April 22, 2020

Just when I was feeling flat, Deb's inspiring virally gave me my subject—inspiration. Where does it come from? These moments of inspiration seem to come unbidden. When people ask me, "Where do you get your ideas?" I can't answer. They come to me, and probably to you, from "out of the blue." They come when we are most "in touch" but how do we get "in touch?" I used to be able to enter that illusive place while swimming, or running, or now that I'm older, from walking. Could "out of the blue" mean out of the sky?

Ted Kooser, a Pulitzer Prize winning poet from Iowa, said this when interviewed about inspiration: "You've got to be there when the geese come flyin' in." He saw inspiration as matter of being in a state of readiness to receive it, sitting patiently at your desk, awaiting that honk, that flock, flying in the sky in arrow-shaped formation, heading for its destination.

The poet Mary Oliver who found her inspiration in nature, also used geese as a source leading to creativity.

"Meanwhile the wild geese, high in the clean blue air,
are heading home again.
Whoever you are, no matter how lonely,
the world offers itself to your imagination,
calls to you like the wild geese, harsh and exciting—
over and over announcing your place
in the family of things."

Mary-Lou

Wednesday, April 22, 2020

My AOL account is frustrating me. It's long past time I moved to Gmail, but I'm intimidated by what that might mean. At this point, I keep getting the AOL message that my address or password are incorrect. So, like a tech fool, I spend time putting in a new password on my phone and laptop wherever it asks for one. The next time I go online, I get the same message about incorrect password. When I start a Zoom meeting—as I will in a few minutes with my sisters, I can't invite them on AOL because it won't send anything from my email address. I'm typing this in hopes that the eight hundred times I put in my password earlier today has cured the problem.

OK, so you didn't need my whining today. At least, I'm aware that I can't blame AOL frustrations on Covid-19. A good reminder for me that the world wasn't perfect before and that was fine.

Mary-Lou, I loved your description of Trader Joe's. It was so accurate. I had gone on Good Friday thinking I knew where everything I need is—this can be fast. The half-hour wait outside didn't really faze me. But once I got inside—I wanted to change my mind. As you described, we had to do the conga line through the store. It's silly, but if I usually go down an aisle from back to front of the store, switching directions and making me go front to back made me disoriented about exactly where an item would be and took forever!

Yesterday I ventured out to Wilton's Stop & Shop and was dismayed there were no fresh greens, none or those sweet little clementines, and other items I didn't know were in demand. I left there determined to stay away. I do have food for the time being and maybe I'll be more accepting when I have to go again. I think I might take Ken's advice and try Fresh Market.

I'm about 200 pages into Eric Larson's new book, *The Splendid and the Vile,* about Churchill and the war in 1940-41. The other night I read until 1:30. I realized that even though I know what is going to happen with the blitz, the characters don't know. There's something enticing about that. I guess it's why some people can read a book over and over. It makes me wonder about the relationship between readers and the characters created in what I write. I'm also amazed at how well the British dealt with that tragic time. It reminds me that staying home isn't such a terrible fate.

Time to Zoom with sisters.

Donna

Wednesday, April 22, 2020

The Splendid and the Vile is waiting for me. Anything Churchillian fascinates me. He was a tower of a man, flawed like all of us, but perfect for the time. As soon as I finish *The Great Influenza* that will be my next read.

My daughter, who does the grocery shopping for her father, me and her own household, found mandarins at Stop & Shop in Westport. These are really small, but oh so sweet and tart. Make a great finish to a meal instead of ice cream. I have not ventured out to Trader Joe's and am missing having those French pizza-like pies. I like his cereals too. My favorite the Maple Pecan.

I, too, am having trouble with emails. When I try to send some—not all—the machine tells me it can't send it using AOL, but then—sometimes—when I check in the "sent" list, the email is there. I need to call our tech guy and see if he can figure out not only that, but a few other hiccups that seem very prevalent these days. I wonder if it's because so many of us are on the airwaves.

Maria

Wednesday, April 22, 2020

What day was it? Wednesday. Unpressured. Caught up on virally entries. Looked at the fur balls floating around my floor and thought about vacuuming them. Thinking was as far as I got. A friend suggested I use them to get back into knitting. Not a bad idea.

When I think of this moment in a narrow way, I can handle it. I can place it in a box small enough to get my mind to wrap around it. I can even look at it as offering personal opportunity for growth. When I think of me, I can applaud my resiliency, my ability to cope. But when numbers like 45,000 dead are nailed into my brain, when I hear that we should expect a second, worse, wave in the fall when Covid-19 will coincide with the flu, when I witness the political maneuvering that speaks to vile opportunism while people can't put food on the table, I despair. If this can't unite us, what can? Where is the humanity when multi-billion-dollar corporations can claim that each of their stores/restaurants are small businesses to gobble up relief funds that would mean life and death for ma and pa businesses? I hate feeling apocalyptic like this. I hate feeling as though the cup is 7/8 empty.

This group fits into my small box. Saluting the essential workers with noise and fanfare fits into the box. So do humor, Zoom class offerings, small kindnesses and favors. Responsible political leaders and people who respectfully maintain physical distance are there too. I fill it with positive vibes by donating and giving what I can. These things bring me back to the manageable, the comprehensible, even the hopeful.

Deb

You so speak to my condition. If I think small—and "small" includes my wellbeing as well as my family and friends, Covid workers—I can stay in a tentative equilibrium. The minute I go global, I sink. The struggle between good and evil, between humanity and inhumanity is the fundamental drama of mankind. Right now, I fear we're tilting toward inhumanity.

Mary-Lou

Deborah and M-L, I agree with your thoughtful, healthy perspectives. Thank you!

My small contribution to your solid, personal reasoning is to quote from Shakespeare in Hamlet. *The phase has been overworked but we all know the line, "This above all: to thine own self be true..." I frequently remind myself of this good advice. It encourages me to ensure that I identify and then focus on what is important to me, knowing that if I don't do it, I won't be good to anyone else or for anything else. I don't believe I am being selfish protecting my sanity, which in turn makes me more capable of protecting/helping my family and friends and then others who come within my orbit.*

Enough philosophical stuff. I have tea to brew and birds to feed.

Ken

Here's what does me in: 59 thousand homeless people in LA. How did we let that happen? We've known about homelessness for decades. Why couldn't we have dealt successfully with that? Not inadequate "shelters"—HOMES!

Mary-Lou

I agree. It's what I wrote earlier—this crisis has brought to the fore all the inequities in our society. And cynically, I believe that the only reason it makes the news is that it threatens not only those at the marginalized edges of our society—if they're at increased risk of the virus maintaining traction, everyone is.

As Ken would say, time for tea.

Deb

Thursday, April 23, 2020
VanGogh Unmasked
Shared by Mary-Lou

244

My 7- and 9-year-old granddaughters howled. They knew exactly what this was about, including the story behind the ear. The deep laughter felt so wonderful. Thanks, Mary-Lou!
Gina

Thursday, April 23, 2020
Dear Bernadette and Polly—

If you are able to do so, please let us know how you are feeling. We worry about you, and we crave news and hope that it's good news.
Mary-Lou

Bernadette sent me a text yesterday. Was glad that I checked in with her. She is "freaking out" with all the CAT scans and brain MRIs. How she's doing depends on the day. SO GLAD to hear from Bernadette. No reply yet from Polly.
Gina

Thursday, April 23, 2020
Update: I came home yesterday to a fully equipped private bedroom with large windows and a deck where I can enjoy spring whenever it chooses to come. My husband and kids arranged everything so we can live separately for two weeks.

It was planned for me to come home with oxygen, but at the last minute my oxygen levels were good enough not to need that. 🔬✿

I am still weak. A visiting nurse is coming three times a week. On heavy prednisone and antibiotics and lots of hope. As I hear more of my case, read more and process what happened I am grateful to be alive.

God is good. 🙏
Polly

Dear Polly —I'm so grateful that you're home and on your way to complete recovery. Thanks for letting us know. Rest well. Heal fast.
Love,
Mary-Lou

Polly, that's so good to hear! It sounds like your family shares your sentiment, and I do, too. You'll have lots to write about!
Hugs,
Deb

Oh, Polly! It is such a relief to get your email! So happy you are recovering at home. Take extremely good care of yourself as your body works hard to heal. Your email brought the sun out for today.
Fondly,
Donna

Oh, Polly, so glad to hear from you and that you are back home— that is surely a good sign. We are all pulling for you!! Hugs!
Maria

Thursday, April 23, 2020

Get another hassle-free delivery from Fresh Market. Finish valuation analysis for a hospitality group that had to close its seven restaurants and event spaces.

Watch another jaw dropping White House briefing yesterday. Dr. Birx sits on the sidelines blinking and staring at her feet.

As a follow up, I write this in jest… I am going to take the unlicensed medical advice of the doctor-in-chief and call Kindred Spirits and Wine to order some ingestible disinfectant. Then I will crawl into my tanning bed for a cleansing nap. Beautiful! All set with this virus thingy. Have ordered a dozen Hermès scarves to cover my face when I fly to Georgia for a pedicure. Going with the 1970s trend of shag haircut. Cheers!

What I am really feeling is white rage! When I was a medical social worker at Milwaukee County General Hospital on the pediatrics unit, a sweet little boy came in for dilation of his esophagus. He'd gotten into cleaning supplies under the kitchen sink and ingested Lysol. I never forgot the horror of his injury. I just want to go to my backyard and scream at the top of my lungs, "Dammit to hell" to that imposter of a president.

The least he could do would be to apply tinted foundation to the white raccoon spots around his tan bedded eyes.

Gina

Thursday, April 23, 2020

Sequestered Classmates,

The tea is hot, and the birds are devouring their food. I have two real estate deals tomorrow, which the staff is on top of, so time to write something today. (I am surprised at how many real property transactions are still being done. March and perhaps this month will be two of the busiest in years.)

First things first… for Bernadette and Polly. Hang in there.

Reluctantly, knowing full well that nothing good could come of it, Sam and I watched Trump at his press conference yesterday. He argued and disagreed and contradicted his medical advisors in front of the world leaving everyone scratching their heads. I could feel my blood pressure rise. It went something like this.

Dr. Fauci, "The virus will come back in the fall."

Trump, "It could be done, done in the fall."

Head of the CDC, "The virus will come back in the fall."

Trump, "No one knows what will happen. It could go away in the fall."

Dr. Fauci, "It will definitely come back in the fall."

Trump glares.

WHAT THE HELL? It was a spoiled adolescent brat pretending to be a leader. Grrr!

We decided to watch a movie. It was Sam's turn to pick one. She does well finding movies that are not the Hollywood commercial ones, but fun to watch. Last night it was *The Commitments* about a bunch of poor kids in Dublin who want to form a soulful band. Lively, entertaining and lots of fun. Music was terrific. It inspired us to take out Sam's Spotify selections, turn out the lights except for candles, and blast away. Sorry if we kept you awake to midnight with Aretha Franklin, Otis Redding, Wilson Picket with songs like "Mustang Sally," "Chain-Chain-Chain," and the like. Great fun and I didn't think about the virus or Trump the entire time, which by itself was a blessing.

Ken

You and your wife must have graduated from college about the time I did—1967. The tunes you danced to were all my favorites senior year. Haven't heard some of those names in years. Those college days were a great time for music and dancing.

Just back from a friend's deck in Trumbull. We'd had a picnic like royalty—at opposite ends of the table. So lovely in the sunshine with the extensive bird song.

Donna

Thursday, April 23, 2020

Larry and I took a long, gray walk at Sherwood Island this morning. At least it wasn't windy. Hardly anyone was there. Then we headed home where I was bombarded yet again with an inbox full of requests for money, as well as juvenile surveys masquerading as requests for donations. Most are political. I understand that this is the 21st century's fund-raising strategy. It makes sense. No postage required. Plus, we're sitting prey poised at our computers much of the day. (The remote, digital 21st century offends me in many ways, but that's another story.) I am panicked by their hyperbolic subject lines—Trump is winning!—that are intended not only to get my attention, but to frighten me and, while they're at it, raise my cortisone level, thereby increasing my anxiety. The more you give, even in tiny amounts, the more they ask for more. That, too, makes sense. Still, they infuriate me. I spend a lot of time deleting their hysterical lines before I can get to the day's virallies, or message from people I know.

Since I can't stop them, I've worked out a strategy to stop me. Yesterday I gave the Biden campaign a lot of money, not the measly $10s and $25s I contribute piecemeal over a long period of time. Instead, I gave $100.00 all at once. Of course, they thanked me, as enthusiastically as they thank me when I click on $5 and "no tip." I wasn't expecting a specialized, personalized, gusher of thanks for my unusual generosity. What I was expecting was a change in my own attitude. Now, every time my box fills with requests for money, I feel entitled to delete them without paying the slightest attention. Having overspent once, I've been able to banish all feelings of guilt, although I'm still offended.

I'm curious. Do any of you share these feelings?

Mary-Lou

When I was more flush I "adopted" a child through Save the Children Foundation. As a result, I got so much printed material from them I couldn't stand it. I know what that material cost. One day I stormed into their offices and told them I was discontinuing my contribution, because the printed materials I got from them cost more per month than what I was donating to feed a child.

Deb

I too made a $100 contribution to Joe Biden last week, but that doesn't seem to stop the emails from asking for a $5 or $10 *contribution. Not only is my incoming mailbox full of these requests, but my snail mail is mostly requests for money. There are many worthy causes out there, but I can't help feeling irked at this bombardment. And yes, I receive those stupid so-called surveys, over and over again. I give to those I've always given and the rest—sorry.*

Maria

Thursday, April 23, 2020

I'm off the hook for some of the donating. Because of my husband's job, I am forbidden to contribute to most political campaigns. (I really wanted to slip Pete Buttigieg an anonymous $20, but I am too law-abiding and too paranoid.)

I think campaign finance reform is in order anyway. Candidates shouldn't be begging for dimes from the pockets of the common (wo)man, nor should they be taking what basically amounts to bribes from big spending special interest groups. But I digress.

As for other charities, my husband and I usually pick the one at the top of our minds that year: the library, the animal shelter, this year the food bank.

I used to donate to my college alumnae fund. They were generous to me when I needed it, and I tried to give back so another hopeful Smithie could have a chance. Even when I was still in student-loan-debt up to my neck, I'd throw them $25 or $50 every year. One January, I got a bonus at work and sent in $100. That was a mistake. Once you pony up three figures you end up on the high-roller list, and they started chasing me down all the time. Asking for more and more and more, via snail mail, and worse, by phone. One of the hopeful girls I had wanted to help would ring me up and earnestly ask me to give as much as I could. Some version of, "We're sure you could dig a little deeper. Have you checked your couch cushions? Sell your kidney if you have to!

The Alumnae Fund needs you!" I found it insulting and I asked to be removed from their list. The college has changed so much since I went there: it's not the same and I don't like the direction they've gone anyway. I should give $100 to rival Wellesley. That would show them.

But my favorite give is to street performers: buskers, singers, saxophonists, paint bucket drummers, contortionists, trompe l'oeil chalk artists, break-dancers, clowns blowing giant bubbles, subway violinists, the people who stand like painted statues. I love them all. I put money in their hats every time and I look forward to the days when I can again.

Lynn

Thursday, April 23, 2020

Woke up this morning with a headache after a Covid nightmare. Pulled into Trader Joe's at 8 AM to find the store amid a shut down. I'm told they have a possible positive employee. How responsible of Trader Joe's to close the store with one pending test result and how damn inconvenient! We know all too well it could be weeks before they know the outcome.

As far as giving goes, we are local supporters: the library, the art center (now MoCA), Temple Israel, Gillespie Center, and public radio. Baldwin Wallace Musical Conservatory and Antioch College in Ohio are on the list as well. As for email solicitations, I'm constantly unsubscribing and for the most part they leave me alone.

Let me join the ranks in welcoming Polly home and sending heartfelt wishes for a full recovery to both her and Bernadette.

Morgaine

What a great list of informal charities! I share some of them with you, primarily subway violinists. A writer friend of mine who had very little money herself used to leave her NY apartment with a

pocketful of quarters. She gave indiscriminately to anyone begging on the street. She assumed that anyone sitting on the sidewalk with a cardboard sign was a worthy charity—drunk or sober—I agree with her.
Mary-Lou

Homeless man sleeping in the entryway to a luxury store on Madison Avenue.
Gina

Thursday, April 23, 2020

I've done everything I could think of to avoid writing. My silver shines, my plants are all fed—the outdoor ones, too. But here I am. You all seem to write so prolifically and with such great feeling and humor. I salute you!!

I awoke this morning and for a few seconds I forgot. Then, panic arrived. What in heavens name was I going to fill my day with? I work at keeping the darkness away, but it hovers at the fringe of my mind. Denial seems the best course, but it makes me feel like a coward, a piker. Facing reality of this global catastrophe is just too damn much! And yet, the awful reality of what continues, will not be denied. I turn on the news, I cry, I turn off the news and then, turn it back on. Like everyone else I ask, when will this end? But I know no one can answer that. It will take its time.

It was good to hear from Polly and to learn she is home and that her family made such a good welcome. Bernadette is still undergoing tests to find out what was causing such awful symptoms. I hope they find the cause and it turns out to be something, if not trivial, but a passing something.
Maria

Friday, April 24, 2020

Taking the easy way out and tagging onto Maria's entry. Each day I feel a little bit better, well it's only day three, and then I don't. Quarantine is easy for me, hard for Ray.

I've so enjoyed reading your virallies about how you're coping, or not, during this virus. They remind me there is life and good boredom to return to, rather than being consumed with oxygen levels, pill taking and everything medical.

Perhaps my entries now won't fit. I am fine with that. Please let me know your honest thoughts! Once I was able to get my hands on some paper and a pen in the hospital, I started taking notes. I have plenty to say and once I feel stronger will return to writing.

Thank you for your kind words and thoughts.

Polly

How wonderful to hear from you! How could your entries not fit? Here are my honest thoughts: You speak with an authority about this virus and its treatment that none of us, thank goodness, can match. And you took notes from the jaws of hell? Amazing. Please, when you're up to it, share it all.

Mary-Lou

Polly, we need to hear your voice! There's no fitting or not fitting. Just whatever's on your mind. So good to have you back, and stronger each day.

Deb

I absolutely agree with Deb. Your voice is welcome and important. So glad you're back with us. Your words offer a different perspective that we need. While we were writing about life on the home front, you were experiencing the war.

Donna

Can't wait to read your experience Polly. Cliché of the day—
"We're all in this together!"
Morgaine

Friday, April 24, 2020

Finish a valuation analysis for a company that makes fans and blowers. It's gotten a Payroll Protection Program loan via the Small Business Administration to keep their staff employed.

Have a nice phone chat with grand trans Lex who is delivering groceries to customers via Instacart. Have shrimp cocktail, Brie, and buttermilk blue cheese for supper. Lex's mom is now working on the coronavirus service night shift at Hennepin County Medical Center. Total hazmat suit-up for her.

Place a FaceTime call with daughter Maria. She is not in Rye. She is in Cortland, New York with her boyfriend on an overnight visit with his mother. She is giggling. I don't ask any questions regarding the whereabouts of her 20-year-old son and 16-year-old daughter.

Gina

Friday, April 24, 2020

Woke up this morning at 10 AM. Felt a slight stab of guilt, but quickly recovered, remembering that Judy has confessed to "sleeping in," and when she first wrote about it, I thought "*Why not?*" This pandemic could last for months.

Even though I managed to lop a couple of hours off this soggy day, I quickly pulled myself together and set myself 4 goals to accomplish today. First, get dressed; then rewrite the "bequests" section of my will. (I spend more time on the Bequeath section of my will than I do on my "Do Not Resuscitate" orders, all six pages of which are affixed to the refrigerator door. It covers every life-threatening eventuality up to and including a persistent hangnail.)

Next on my list was to conduct extensive online research to

find perennial flowers to augment my 3 little gardens. (Since my right wrist is shot, I figure I'd best switch to perennials so that from now on I can just watch it all happen from May through October. I googled "perennial flowers, zone 6, long-blooming, various heights." Got a huge result, from which I made a list. Maybe I'll even order them.) Fourth and last, remember to inject myself twice a day with Lysol. (How silly of me to be using it on my kitchen counters, when I could be protecting myself in a far more targeted and effective way—straight into the lungs.)

1) Exercises, shower and get dressed— accomplished at 1:30 PM
2) Bequest review—accomplished by 2:00 PM
3) Search for perennial flowers—accomplished by 3:15, but can't be ordered because of pandemic.
4) Didn't inject Lysol. Trump said he was only fooling

Mary-Lou

Friday, April 24, 2020

Am activating body, mind and soul today, all through video conferencing, primarily Zoom.

Began morning with exercise videos produced by Meadow Ridge intra-net: stretch and strength for ½ hour and core workout for ½ hour. Then took hour and a half break, read mail (threw it out or filed it—no checks, no bills).

At noon joined a meditation group that Bill's acupuncturist introduced to me, all women, mostly therapists—we check in and meditate briefly. When we meet in person, we usually eat lunch together.

At 1:30 joined a conference that started last night, Revolutionary Love—speakers roughly united by progressive work in faith (very flexible) based communities. Was supposed to take place in Washington, DC—I wouldn't have gone. My sister, chair of board of Fetzer Foundation (check it out) had 2 tickets for conference that had to migrate to online. I started watching last night—liked the people of all hues and religious persuasions and good will so I came back for more in afternoon.

My sister and I texted each other about reactions to talks as we watched them—a Muslim woman talking about community organizing; another Muslim woman, 26, talking about her family's migration from a southern state after a lynching to California which included the search for LBGTQ freedom; a Native American from Libo tribe of North Carolina discussing decolonializing wealth, a rabbi from Tikkun organization describing what revolutionary love means. Then I joined a discussion group on how to counteract voter suppression.

In between sessions there was a dance session led by an Alvin Ailey dancer—he described himself as "approaching adulthood"—maybe he's the age of my youngest grandson, 18?—yes, I danced, that's why I walk and take cardio fitness classes. There was also a 15-minute meditation led by an India or Pakistani man. Did that too.

And in between that I talked to my hairdresser in NYC—no one else touches my hair—with the result that it's getting long enough to braid. She's still in business (Whew!) and will open eventually. Also got some documents—copies of my father's draft card from WWII (he never served, too old, married with one child—me!) and census records for grandfather and great grandfather in North Carolina.

We've broken for dinner. At 6:30 I'm going to check out cutie pie's free dance class on YouTube (Mathew Johnson Harris, Ailey dancer). Conference resumes at 7:00. If I get tired, I'll stop.

I've learned how to contextualize the changes that I want to push for at Meadow Ridge and I've found an online source for independent bookstores, a small way to counter Amazon's monopoly. I may be a radical at heart, but I'm too old to march.

Judy

Friday, April 24, 2020

Hiya,

Polly, I'm so glad that you're home with a good prognosis. Good news is so very welcome. Rest up and keep feeling better.

My apologies to everyone for being incommunicado. Honesty—I'm struggling. Even responding to email requires Herculean efforts. I don't know how much of this malaise is physical and how much is mental, but like our democracy I'm hanging on by my fingernails.

Moving the yoga studio's classes online before I got sick was an adrenaline overdose, and I'm not at all confident that my tiny business will survive. The thought of having to start over makes me want to take to bed indefinitely and swap my morning coffee for sauvignon blanc.

I can barely pry my eyeballs off Twitter, which is not good for my anger management.

Are we great yet? Blurgh. Let's all inject some Clorox up the ass and call it a day,

Bernadette

Saturday, April 25, 2020

Finish a valuation analysis for a company that rents diagnostic equipment to hospitals.

Marinate chicken thighs, jumbo shrimp, and asparagus for Monica to grill. The sunny hours of the beautiful day disappear as she social distances with a wannabe boyfriend on the back patio. The food gets charred in the dark. I sit on the edge of my chair clenching my white knuckled fists while watching *China Syndrome* on PBS with Jane Fonda, Jack Lemon, and Michael Douglas.

Gina

Saturday, April 25, 2020

We've been having a string of good days. I scored more goals in Rocket League last night. My son declared, "Mom, you're on FIRE!"

I spent yesterday making ridiculous masks. A red one that I taped white paper teeth on: I call it The Hannibal. When I go out in public, I might remove the teeth, but I enjoyed wearing it around the house for a few minutes. I made an army-green one I call the M*A*S*H. I made a bunch of other failures. One of them was so big it covered most of my head and neck. I call it the Oil Change Funnel. Never in my life did I think I'd own more pandemic masks than bras.

The prettiest mask I have is the neon polka dot one my friend made. When I wear it, my husband calls me The Pink Hoodlum. I imagine us on an old Western poster, or like Bonnie and Clyde: "WANTED: The Pink Hoodlum and the Kitchen Towel: Last seen getting coffee at Dunkies in Southport. Beware! Armed with dangerous wit!"

This morning my husband and I sat outside in the sun with our coffee and donuts. It was warm. The birds were chirping. He smiled at me with his dopey beard and his crinkly eye wrinkles and my heart swelled with love. I think he is the cutest person in the world. I thought, *"What else could anyone want out of life?"* As if reading my mind, my husband said, "It's weird, but I think I could get used to this."

Shut-in life has made him less anxious as well. He no longer has a commute he hates; he can take more breaks; he eats better and more often; he sleeps later. We go for a 30-minute walk in the afternoon sometimes. If the weather's not good, or if he can't spare that much time, he'll sneak upstairs and read a few comic books instead. It's sad that it took a pandemic to get the poor guy some work-life balance.

Lynn

Lynn,, these might give some ideas for your home mask production endeavors...

Ken

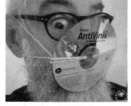  

Thanks, Ken! What fun! What creativity!

Lynn

Saturday, April 25, 2020

I'm currently lounging by the pool with the family—minus one.

My 22-year-old son Daniel, as usual, is in what I call "his office," the room above the three-car garage. It used to be the playroom. The Ping-Pong table survived the transition, however the train set, buckets of Lego's and mound of stuffed animals have been replaced with a high-tech computer, multiple monitors and a mouse that lights up. Daniel will be a Covid graduate from Syracuse in May with a degree in computer art and animation.

I'm hoping the 3D animation field will not only survive but thrive in a world of social distancing. Anyone have any contacts at Disney?

Next to his workstation sits his keyboard, where he taught himself to play piano, and if you spin around on his high back swivel chair you'll see a VR setup all ready to take you to another dimension. From the future to the past... beyond the VR goggles and headphones, a giant green Yogibo sits in front of an old tube TV, surrounded by shelving units lined with old video games and various gaming consoles from the 1980s.

Sorry Lynn no Xbox, but if anyone is interested in Mario Cart for the Switch, Daniel's your guy.

Morgaine

Sunday, April 26, 2020

What a glorious day today! Or, as my wacky Uncle Milton used to say, "This is the kind of day that makes you wish you were alive." So of course, we, and lots of others, walked at Sherwood Island. A couple of days ago I wrote rapturously about how the honking of geese caused two great poets to use wild geese as a metaphor for inspiration. Today, the hundreds of squawking geese that inhabit Sherwood Island played a far less lofty role—that of shit machines. Trying not to step on their prolific poops reminded me of playing hopscotch.

On a more pleasant note, we were intrigued by a game called "disc golf" in which one follows a "par" course and tries to sink the disc into metal contraptions placed in orderly distances from one another around the part. Unlike Frisbees, the discs are of various colors and sizes, and depending upon how far you need to send the disc, just as golfers must match their iron to the distance they are from the hole, disc golfers must do the same. We followed a couple of guys around the course, chatting from six feet away, learning about the game.

When we left the park we donned our masks and gloves and stopped off at Balducci's to buy Larry's favorite "steak bacon" and 4 pints of Talenti ice cream in various flavors, all of which involved chocolate, or peanut butter, or chocolate and peanut butter. A walk of almost 4 miles, we've learned, will offset one-half a pint of ice cream, our dinner dessert.

Larry's been waiting for a sunny day so that I could cut his hair outside, instead of trying not to send it all down the bathroom drain. He came equipped with a "buzzer," with several missing teeth, a brush, a scissors, and a comb, as well as a bushy head of wavy hair. I'm used to "buzzing" the back of his neck between haircuts, but I've never taken on his entire head. He actually looked me dead in the eye and said, "Not too short on the sides."

When I was done, it was a bit too short in the back, but he was pleased.

Apparently, Trump has made such a fool of himself—he peaked the day before yesterday when he suggested that Lysol, injected directly into the lungs, might be an effective way to kill the coronavirus—that his advisors cut short his evening rally last night, and canceled it for tonight. Meanwhile, he's trailing Biden in the polls.

Mary-Lou

Sunday, April 26, 2020

Another rainy Sunday.

Sleep late with the cool air coming in through the open windows. Ryan and Evelyn make omelets; I show them how to clean up the kitchen. Work on a valuation analysis for a pharmaceutical lab. Hope they have customers that are developing Covid-19 diagnostic tests, treatments, antibody screenings, and vaccines. The company gets paid royalties when new drugs are FDA approved and taken to market. Monica and ex-boyfriend paint the kitchen cupboards flanking the refrigerator. I try to catch up on compiling virallies. My ingestible disinfectants are delivered *post haste* from Kindred Spirits. Two kinds of chardonnay and a bottle of Scotch. They are doing a brisk business. *Watch Call the Midwife* on PBS while supping on homemade chili and cornbread.

Gina

Sunday, April 26, 2020

Dear Fellow Sunday-Stay-at-Homers,

As the sun set last evening, having backyard birdfeeders paid a handsome reward. They attracted flights of birds competing to get in the food line. With Mendelsohn playing, we were witness to an extraordinary ballet of winged creatures of all sizes, shapes and colors, and for thirty minutes, they whizzed about in complex patterns with acrobatic squirrels darting underneath to retrieve whatever they casually discarded. It was blissful.

My wife is reading Adam Gopnick's book, *At the Stranger's Gate*. She shared his observation on page 98 about writing, which I found to be insightful. I love the last line, making his point.

"All writers ever do is take pre-existing units, words, arrange them, and insert them into other people's consciousness. Words are always arranged, never invented... The essential magic of writing is elemental—and unlike any other art form. You're not really making something so much as assembling something and once the assembly is completed, you hope it gives the illusion of originality. Like my professor's Renaissance man dressing in the morning, you reach into the sock drawer of words hoping to find an interesting, mated pair among the many choices of mismatched socks, some mismatched socks match surprising well. The socks, or words, exist already. The eloquence of their mismatch is your own to make."

Ken

Sunday, April 26, 2020

I tuned in to Chuck Todd's *Week in Review* this morning, just long enough to see and hear Dr. Birx fail to answer any question that Todd asked of her. She ducked and double-talked her way past questions that called for a simple yes or no answer—including the one about ingesting Lysol—with a lot of extraneous medical information. She's playing the Trump card and is no longer reliable. She serves her master and not the public.

I have written about how I'm able to live in my surreal bubble of denial, even as I am sane enough to recognize that others all around me are sickened by and have died from by the coronavirus. I have mourned those deaths and worried about those who are sick, but nevertheless, their impact is less than it would be if I could be at their bedside, or at their funeral. Not to be able to hug or talk directly keeps me at an emotional distance. But so does my capacity to deny and I've learned in the last two nights that my ability to deny has its limits. The terrible reality lives in my dreams. Two nights ago, in a panic, I dreamed that I "tore the house apart," looking for my passport. I never found it. I don't think we need to spend much time analyzing that. Then last night, I dreamed that our bedroom was struck twice, a minute apart, by lightening. The entire bedroom was red with flames. We burned.

One way or another, the truth will out.

Mary-Lou

These days are real food for subconscious thought! Sounds like two pretty scary nights' sleep, speaking to a pretty scary reality. I'm not so sure that denial is a negative. It sounds like compartmentalizing for self-preservation. so much pain, sorrow and fear. How can one let all of it in at once? Wishing you a great night's sleep.

Deb

Take a look at SNL…
You've got to love Brad Pitt!!!
https://apple.news/A3Bm9-z2bSYCqxcs_wTuroQ

Morgaine

Sunday, April 26, 2020

Lynn and her husband are the good fairies of the East. On a trip to Target they scored not one, but two forms of disinfectant for me, AND my favorite Yasso frozen yogurt bars! The bars I will eat as they are, maybe to cool off while sitting for hours under sunlamps as our orange leader has suggested. The disinfectant came just in time to pour over my morning cereal. Joking aside, emergency dispatchers are receiving many calls from people who have tried

45's novel remedy for novel corona. Reports of extreme esophageal burning are the results.

Yesterday friends assembled to wish our friend Cathy a wonderful new life in California. Covid era drive-by celebration with honking horns and colorful sign-bedecked cars. It was fun, but very sad not to give her a big  hug goodbye. How hard it must be for her to spend these final days in the now empty house she shared with her late husband. So many memories of raising our children together as our parade passes her house.

Binge watched *Unorthodox* on Friday. Couldn't stop watching until I finished the series at 2:00 AM. The story of the trials faced by a young woman breaking away from her ultra-orthodox Jewish community in many ways parallels that of my younger stepdaughter. Dave read the book years ago. It is a memoir. Like the main character, my stepdaughter was seen as a villain by her community when she left. In Israel, Rabbinical law takes precedence over civil law, and she lost her children, her money, the apartment she had paid for. Thinking about this brought me back to my ambivalent relationship with religion. I identify as a Jew and admire some of the precepts of the religion, while at the same time I feel strongly that religion is often a mask for oppression of women and violent cultural chauvinism.

Deb

Monday, April 27, 2020

Monica puts her energy into re-painting a section of the kitchen cupboards. The first coat was too light, so she gets a darker shade. Wow what a difference! She adds sparkly handles to the light gray cupboard doors.

I have a mess to deal with… I leave a Kleenex tissue up the sleeve of a top that goes through the laundry. All my clothes are coated with flecks of the remains. Order pizza from Domino's for the first time in two months. Yay! Contactless comfort food.
Gina

Monday, April 27, 2020

I am feeling a bit better and want to contribute a few virallies. How shall I do this? I want to send them to the group and save at same time. I do not have access to a printer or my desktop computer. Any ideas? Do I set up a whole new link or always piggyback on someone else's? Running out of steam this morning.
Polly

Monday, April 27, 2020

My stepmother, Renee, died last Thursday. She had late-stage Alzheimer's and had been suffering in a nursing home for several years. Whether she died of Covid-19 or something else, I do not know.

I met Renee when I was four years old, when she and my father were dating. They moved in together a year after that and got married when I was ten. Renee didn't like the Cinderella connotation of being called stepmother, so instead she and my father came up with MamaHaha—the word for stepmother in Japanese. Renee taught me about birds, art, opera, ballet. She was always reading, painting, birdwatching, or doing a crossword puzzle. I have no memories of her ever raising her voice or being irritated. She nicknamed me Daffodil when I was little, for my yellow, blonde hair. She used to pat my cheeks and kiss my forehead, and she always wanted to hold hands with me, even when I was an adult. She frequently mailed me postcards, cheering me on through tough times and offering sage advice. She signed most of her notes with, "Remember to be good to yourself! Love, Mama H." My real mother never showed me that sort of affection, and my father's behavior was erratic at best. MamaHaha was my most loving and stable parent for almost thirty years.

Ten years ago, Renee started exhibiting signs of dementia. She asked the same questions over and over. She could not retain information. She lost her ability to make decisions. She started wandering off; my father would have to call the police to find her. She spoke less and less. She would often stand frozen in a room and stare like she could not make any sense of what she was seeing. My father would give her bifocals to her and she would hold them in her hands and turn them over and over, but she wouldn't put them on. She no longer went into her studio to paint. She started having violent outbursts. Eventually she stopped talking entirely.

The last conversation Renee and I had was six years ago. We were at my sister's house for Passover, Renee's favorite holiday. Throughout the Seder, Renee barely spoke. She folded her Haggadah in her lap; she couldn't read. She did not eat or drink. After the sad meal, I was loading the dishwasher when Renee came up to me. She took my face in her hands like she used to when I was young. She said, "I've known you since you were a little girl, you know." I said, "Yes. I know." She stared at me, holding my cheeks for an uncomfortable length of time before saying, "You had blonde hair when you were a little girl." I said,

"Yes. That's true." She said, "I've known you since you were a little girl and I have always loved you very much." I hugged her and said I loved her too. Then she wandered out of the kitchen, looking dazed and running her hands along all the cupboards.

After that, I didn't visit often; the trip up to Boston was too far and too draining. Renee's dementia worsened, as did my father's health—physical and mental. My parents declined and became as unrecognizable to me as I was to them. Seeing them like that was horrible; now they are both gone and that is horrible too.

I have been working on writing this for two days, trying to capture what Renee meant to me; what she and my father meant to each other; writing and deleting too many details of a dementia horror story; struggling with memories that are too complicated to put into sentences. I have tried to come up with some wise words on grieving. At first, writing was cathartic, but now I am exhausted, and I have no wise words. I am just so sad.

Lynn

Lynn, every time you write about or reference your dad and stepmom, whatever the narrative, your love for them, as well as some of the anguish, is evident. All child-parent relationships are complicated, but if it is any consolation from a writing buddy, your affection, sincerity, and goodness are a constant and recognizable to the reader. I am sorry for your loss, but it sounds as if she left a long time ago and she has now only arrived. Hugs,

Ken

What a sad, but ultimately beautiful ode to your MamaHaha. You made her very real. You made us love her too. Dementia is a terrible thief. It robs us of our loved ones before that final leave-taking. All we can do is keep the love close and memories help. Hugs to you, Lynn.

Maria

Hi Lynn—I remember your artistic stepmother from that trip to the beach. The contrast you drew between her and your father was striking. She was the person who made you feel loved, comforted, and valued. That dementia distanced her from you was a kind of slow dying. There are words to describe your grief. I think you've found them. Such a great loss will call upon you often to find even more words that can hold your sorrow. Know, too, that you were lucky to be so well loved.

Mary-Lou

Lynn, it's obvious how much MamaHaHa meant to you, and how great your loss is. My cousin sent this poem when my husband died.

> *These things I know:*
> *How the living go on living*
> *And how the dead go on living with them*
> *So that in the forest*
> *Even a dead tree casts a shadow*
> *And the leaves fall one by one*
> *And the branches break in the wind*
> *And the bark peels off slowly*
> *And the trunk cracks*
> *And the rain seeps in through the cracks*
> *And the trunk falls to the ground*
> *And the moss covers it*
> *And in spring the rabbits find it*
> *And build their nest*
> *Inside the dead tree*
> *so that nothing is wasted in nature*
> *or in love.*
> *—Laura Gilpin*

Sending love. It's the only thing that heals.

Deb

Monday, April 27, 2020

One of the things I am thankful for—odd as it might seem—is being with my mother when she died. So many, now in this time of the coronavirus, die without being able to have their loved ones with them. I can't imagine that pain, awful. Gruesome. When my mother died, I was there, holding her hand, thanking her for everything she'd done for me, telling her how much I loved her. My daughter was there too, as was my son and daughter-in-law.

My mother's constant complaint had always been that she was alone—although much of that was of her own choosing. I believe that loneliness was true for her when she was very young, and it never left her. But, in the end, she was not alone. I think she heard it; I hope she felt it. The slight pressure of her hand in mine leads me to believe she did.

Maria

Monday, April 27, 2020

Do I dare say I'm getting used to the new abnormal? The house is running smoothly. All hands are on deck in both helping out and respecting one another's space. I'm realizing what excellent communication skills my family has. If someone has a problem, we talk it out and more importantly we listen to each other. Of course, it helps to have a home that's over 5000 square feet, where everyone has his or her personal space.

Michelle has received several acrylic painting commissions and has been after me to paint with her. I'm more comfortable with watercolor, so I've been procrastinating. This morning when I woke up, I decided, today is the day. My canvas is a panoramic (16 x 40) to be hung above our flat screen TV. Michelle and I scrolled through the Pinterest app for inspiration (a site you can get lost in for days). I finally chose to paint an abstract cityscape. We stood at the kitchen table covered in newspaper and painted all afternoon. I was totally absorbed and really enjoyed the process. I haven't finished the piece yet, but I like where it's going.

Today the news, what little I saw of it, was actually encouraging. Trump's poll numbers are plummeting, Amy McGrath raised significantly more money than Senate Majority Leader Mitch McConnell in the first three months of 2020 and Kim Jong-Un is presumed dead.

The bad news... my 95-year-old father who lives in Florida tells me when things open up the first place he'll be going to is the bowling alley.

Morgaine's Leek and Arugula Quiche
Ingredients:

1 9-inch pie crust
2 large leeks, white parts only, cut vertically in half, and slice into 1/2-inch strips, wash and drain
1 1/2 cup fresh baby arugula
2 tablespoons unsalted butter
4 large eggs, plus 1 egg white
1 cup whipping cream
3/4 cup grated mild cheddar
1/2 cup feta cheese
1/4 teaspoon nutmeg
1 teaspoon dried oregano
1 teaspoon dried basil
Salt and pepper to taste

Directions:

Preheat the oven to 350 F. Roll out pie crust on a floured surface and line 9-inch pie pan with the crust. Using a sharp knife, trim the excess crust from the edges of the pan. Brush the bottom and sides with egg white.

Melt the butter in a skillet. Add leeks and cook until wilted and cooked through. Remove skillet from the heat and cool completely. Transfer leeks into the pie pan and spread evenly on the bottom of the pan. Cover leeks with arugula and set aside.

In a large mixing bowl, beat eggs and cream until creamy. Add nutmeg, oregano, basil, and grated cheddar, mix thoroughly. Season with salt and pepper. Pour egg mixture into the pie pan. Sprinkle feta cheese on top. Bake quiche in the oven for about 45 minutes or until brown on top and cooked through. The quiche will still be jiggly when you take it out of the oven. Cool down for about 30 minutes before cutting and serving.

Morgaine

Monday, April 27, 2020

Feel like I've been off the grid for days—probably not that long. Am completely discombobulated after 2 ½ days of conference, *Revolutionary Lov*e, basically a social justice conference with a rainbow of people who represent the world as it could be but know it isn't.

Last night I discovered that my external hard disk is no longer "talking" to my computer. Everything is on it—finances, years of writing (I have hard copy of the memoir but very little else). Managed to get my ancient 2010 laptop up and running—no connection there either for the disk drive. The in-house computer guy has taken the old computer and will install Linux which may enable me to recover what's on the disk, but it may not work. I know the disk drive works—I can hear it humming and feel its slight vibration—but can't get to its contents. Of course, I've been on Google all afternoon searching "How to recover information on external Seagate disk drive," but I'm afraid I'll make it worse. Can't believe I didn't do a backup of the drive. Grrrr!

Judy

Monday, April 27, 2020

This evening I watched the new and unimproved Trump show. What was I expecting? I can't explain what evil magnetism draws me to the TV at 5:30 PM, only to lose my appetite for dinner. It's "unbelievable." He's so "fantastically" repetitive, so "incredibly" stupid, so "amazingly" boring, so "beautifully" short on vocabulary. Do I really think he will change?

"We'll see what happens."

It was Albert Einstein who said, "The definition of insanity is doing the same thing over and over again, but expecting different results." That's what I'm doing.

Who could argue with Einstein? He's like "really smart, a very stable genius."

Mary-Lou

Monday, April 27, 2020

Gray and gloomy day. But the rain stopped just when I had a window to take Arlo to the park, so we went. I didn't really want to, but yesterday's crappy weather kept us inside. Almost no one at the park. The chill of the weather, and the chilling news of the day made me suddenly want to run. I did. Arlo loved it. We jogged through the park until we reached Dave's bench. It was wet and possibly Covid covered, so I just stood in front of it, my hand over the plaque with its message and Dave's name in raised capital letters. Like reading braille, I usually rub those letters with my eyes closed. Today when I did, I began to cry. For Dave, for Lynn's stepmom, for my friend's cousin and employee, for my friend who lost her long-time partner, and everyone suffering with Covid, and everyone suffering with the more common illnesses that take people every day. For all the losses known and unknown. Then I kissed my hand and touched it to the plaque and ran on.

Deb

Tuesday, April 28, 2020

Deborah's virally from yesterday, in which she runs her fingers over Dave's name has suggested mine of today—naming. Some of you know that our second son, Peter, died in 1980. I do not believe in heaven, but whenever I'm on a beach I write his name in the sand. When I'm finished with my shower, I write his name in the fog of the glass shower door. "Peter." He lives inside his name.

Names are power. Naming is powerful. Biblical Adam names all the creatures in Genesis. When a child is born, choosing his or her name is, at least for the parents, an important decision that may take months of debate. For a child learning to speak, to be able to name something is to own it. For a writer, finding the right title for a book is crucial, because it represents the book itself. You may like your name, or you may not, but either way, it stands for you.

Years ago, I visited Yad Vashem, the Holocaust Museum in Jerusalem. There are many exhibits—mounds of hair, photos of people holding blankets around their skeletal frames, piles of bodies, a cattle car—horror after horror—but what I remember best is the Hall of Names. The dome of the hall is papered with hundreds of photographs—a mere sampling of those who had died—so many, and so high up that that I couldn't focus on any single one, but in the aggregate the display was powerful and overwhelming.

As I walked through the hall, a voice from out of nowhere I could determine softly intoned the names of those who had been murdered in the concentration camps. A name; then a moment of silence, then another name. In the previous exhibits I'd seen the unspeakable. In the Hall of Names, the spoken names pierced my heart and brought tears to my eyes as no human or other image could. I walked and walked through corridor after corridor hearing name after name, a roll call of the murdered. It was in that hall that

I felt the full impact of the six million murdered. What's in a name?

Mary-Lou

So true. and so with the reading of the 9/11 victims. When I'm at Sherwood Island I make sure to place stones on the names of the two people I was connected to who were on one of the planes. Names mean we were here, claimed as part of the living, remembered as part of dead.

Deb

Yes. I imagine that naming to be similar to the Vietnam War memorial in D.C.—a seemingly endless river of names that at its peak/depth embraces and overpowers you.

Judy

Tuesday, April 28, 2020

I sleep soundly with the heat off and windows open and don't wake up until 15 minutes before a NY/NJ chapter officers Zoom meeting. Pull on yesterday's black top and pants, add an animal print blazer, slap on eyeliner and lipstick, plug in earring studs, and brew a cup of coffee. Whee! I make it just in time.

Check the Fresh Market website, and *voila...* I can get a delivery within five hours. The groceries are on my doorstep in two—with about 2/3 of what I'd ordered. They rest is out of stock.

A college friend sends me a link to a parody of the singing nuns from the *Sound of Music*. A really funny little gem. https://www.facebook.com/MaryDoo255/videos/10156771645117063/

Make Chicken Marbella with prunes and olives for myself. The rest of the family isn't interested. It's a high carb day for the girls. Ryan eats an entire box of French croissants. Evelyn has plain spaghetti. Frances has several slices of sourdough baguette.

Monica goes out for socially distanced drinks around someone's pool with three of her tennis partners. Not being able to play hard at tennis several times a week is getting to her.

What the fuck? Vice President Mike Pence visits the Mayo Clinic in Rochester, Minnesota and doesn't comply with the institutional policy of wearing a mask when interacting with patients and medical caregivers. Why didn't Mayo enforce its own policies? Are they afraid to speak truth to power?

Gina

Tuesday, April 28, 2020
The Sound of Silence

When the words don't come, I choose to say nothing
Know that I am here
I've read your writings and they have made an impact on my heart

In silence I hear
The hum of the refrigerator
The rippling waterfall from the hot tub into the pool
The muffled voice of Mark's coworker on speakerphone
The rumble of hunger
The silent screams from the front lines
The gasp of the last breath
The beating of my heart

I pull a Tarot card from the deck...
Wheel of Fortune

Divinatory Meaning according to *The Book of Tarot*, by Susan Gerulskis-Estes: Fate, chance, and destiny. Cause and Effect. Karma. The future depends on that which has been done before. The laws of nature and probability. The continuation of an ongoing pattern.

Will we ever learn?

Morgaine

Tuesday, April 28, 2020

The sun was energizing. I even felt inspired to do a bit of straightening up, and that takes a lot!

The sunniest event of the day was a visit from daughter-in-law Meghan, and grands Silas and Joah. They were like colts being let out to play in my large yard. I was treated to a unique concert of music from *The Lion King*, and a piece of the birthday cake they made for their mom several days ago.

In the afternoon Arlo and I looped through the park. I planned a long walk to take advantage of the weather. As we approached Dave's bench, there were two women there—one sitting on the bench, and the other reading her the inscription on the plaque:

Sit. Meditate. Converse.

In memory of our beloved DAVID MURRAY, "mayor of the dog park" and best friend to his loyal Arlo. May you enjoy sojourning here as he would have done.

The woman finished reading, looked my way, and smiled. As I came closer, she said, "I was just reading this plaque. It's really beautiful."

"Thanks. Dave was my husband, and this is Arlo."

For the next hour and a half, we strolled together, talking, fully enjoying each other. They have just moved to Stamford from Florida and were excited to hear about the ReSisters political group in which I'm active. Barbara asked to be included on the list for next Monday's Zoom meeting.

Some things just seem providential. To have been brought together by Dave's bench—Dave?—is particularly meaningful. Years ago, Dave and I had simultaneously bought newish used cars. As I was backing out of the driveway, Dave was arriving home. Not hard to guess what happened. We laughed that it seemed there was some great puppeteer with a sick sense of humor orchestrating the collision. Today's meeting seemed just as orchestrated, but with much happier results.

Worrisome end to the day. Just heard that North Carolina had the first case of a dog testing positive for Covid-19.

Deb

Tuesday, April 28, 2020
Hello everyone,

Gina has been kind enough to agree to keep these little entries I hope to be sending. I do not have access to a printer in my quarantine room at home, so I appreciate her help. These thoughts will probably not be in sequential order, but they may be. This will read in draft form.

Tuesday, April 8, the day before my 79th birthday, everything was fine. I went before dawn shopping at Stop & Shop, bought $300 worth of groceries. My husband and I unloaded them, wiped them down, put them away. Guess I made lunch, but I do remember I wasn't hungry. Then I met a friend in Ridgefield for a social-distance walk, made dinner and that was that.

Upon awakening on Wednesday morning I knew something was wrong. Very wrong. I remembered that my young nephew in Ohio had flu-like Covid symptoms, went to the hospital and they sent him home. Not sick enough. Tylenol. Come back if you can't breathe. I could breathe, cough but felt lousy, so I called my MD who said to rest, take Tylenol and drink lots of water. I insisted she arrange for a test.

I was to be tested on Friday at Greenwich Hospital parking garage. My husband was tested at Norwalk Hospital the same day.

My symptoms were presenting more and more Covid-like; his were not.

The tests came back Sunday, Easter. We were both negative. I still thought I could ride this out at home with Tylenol. I had all the symptoms except the fever. I met my neighbor at the mailbox that morning and she loaned us an Oximeter. It ended up saving my life.

Fading: Stay tuned until another time.
Polly

Thanks so much for this submission. Your story, from the get-go, is a real cliff-hanger. Even though we know it has a happy ending—"happy" in the sense that you recovered—I read it with a feeling of fear and suspense. That you had the energy to write as much as you did is, in itself, great news.
Mary-Lou

Wednesday, April 29, 2020

I've long ago settled comfortably into my pandemic way of life. I wake up when I wake up. While nursing a mug of coffee and eating my oatmeal flavored with blueberries, bananas, and maple syrup, I read the newspaper. TV news and the newspaper are my only contacts with the world outside my world. When I go shopping, I don my costume, keep my distance, and feel safe. If something in the news particularly distresses me or makes me angry, I go into my office and spend an hour or two writing a letter to the editor of the op-ed page. Invariably, it will not see print. That's okay with me. Today's was about Trump and opening up the meat packing plants. He's worried that Americans might not get enough protein. Maria expresses her stress in tears; I write my heart out. The effect is the same. Temporary calm. For the first time I know what mellow feels like.

The real world is a sad, dangerous, and chaotic. But inside my world, life is peaceful. I have all the time in the world, and if I don't do it today, I'll do it tomorrow. Most days I get dressed by noon. I go about what has become my routine in an unusually leisurely manner. I answer and delete emails, do household chores, fold wash, take walks, add to the shopping list, talk on the phone with friends, read, and defrost. When I remember, I do my exercises. We might play Scrabble at the end of the day. I don't care if I lose, which is often. I am nicer. I am more thoughtful. Dinner is followed by ice cream, binge watching, more reading and bed. Oh, and somewhere during that now familiar, benign routine, I write my virally.

I'm a very lucky lady of leisure, living on the edge of a cliff.
Mary-Lou

Thursday, April 30, 2020

When I was young, I believed that the extreme views I held were right, and right for all people. I still hold those views, but know that they are right for me, not for everyone. I've grown to distrust and dislike extremism. As we know, nature has extremes enough, over which we would do well to unite, not divide.

Last night I saw the scenes of thousands of Hasidic Jews crammed like cattle in the streets of Brooklyn to mourn a dead Rebbe. I'll admit to a general prejudice against the Jewish ultra-orthodox, given the experience of my stepdaughter. But my thought was, how is this different from any and all fanaticism based on religion and justifying murder? Thousands of people flaunting social distancing. How many essential workers will risk and lose their lives trying to save those people who marched last night?

I fear that as we relax just a little, people will turn that inch of freedom into a mile of partying and lax adherence to the rules.

Despite my outrage and the once again gray sky, today was really good. Busy. A good deed, researching something for one of my students at the senior living center. I decided on my next art activity to post—drawing with your non-dominant hand. Perfect timing. I spent the hour Zoom live model session drawing a portrait with my left hand. Awkward! Realized I'd set up as usual, with my computer and materials to the right! But it was a great exercise, and I found myself adjusting after a bit. Tomorrow I'll photograph my drawing as an example for the activity.

Had a short Zoom meeting to decide on some graphics for Will Haskell, my State Senator. Then, Arlo and I took to the park. When he saw his heartthrob, Sadie, he was so excited I had to let go of the leash before being dragged along behind him. He knew she was there long before we saw her.

When I got home, Meghan, Joah and Silas were already playing in the yard. The thing I miss most is being able to touch their little furnace bodies, their fur-soft skin, juicy kisses, feet so small they fit entirely in my own small hand.

A good dinner, a glass of cabernet while writing get out the vote postcards. Finally, writing my virally.

Drawing, writing, happy beloved dog, darling grandkids and daughter-in-law, productive work. Cabernet. A good day.

Deb

I share your feelings about the Hassidic Jews. I was a child during the Rosenberg spy trial. I remember my parents remarking that it wasn't "good for the Jews." That's a constant refrain when someone of the Jewish faith behaves badly. These Hassids make me cringe. Worse, they feed into the rise of anti-Semitism we're all experiencing.

Mary-Lou

Thursday, April 30, 2020

The past few days I walked a bunch of miles while talking to friends on the phone. I walked on the sunny day, but even more yesterday in the gray and the cold. I couldn't be in my house any longer. I needed air. The conversations with my friends weren't very uplifting. The same song on repeat; all variations of: "I'm going crazy. Trump is an idiot. I'm worried for others. I'm worried that things won't ever be normal again. I'm realizing normal was maybe not so great for a lot of people. I have such little control."

The more my friends talked, the more I walked and listened. Loop after loop, for miles. I kept saying, "Yep. Yep. Yep," and I kept walking. I returned home, very tired, and sat in my backyard, watching the squirrels and robins, until it was time to make dinner.

My grief over my stepmother is easing. I have put my feelings back in the box where I usually keep them. Self-preservation. I have mixed feelings on crying: I usually feel like shit after I do it—hung over; nauseated; constricted. Usually, my crying sneaks up on me. I get about a second's warning to fight it off. My reflexes have to be on point to stop it. I cry like water sloshing out of a bucket—a glug, maybe two, and that's it. The whole bucket never goes over all at once.

I gave the men in my life 1 ½ haircuts: One very successful! For my first attempt, with subpar equipment, my son and I were both impressed with the results. The ½ haircut was not at all successful, but it's not my fault. My husband lost his patience with my slow going, nudged me aside and disarmed me. He ran the clippers roughshod over his head. At one point he gave himself a mullet, and I laughed so hard, I slid down onto the bathroom floor. I held my side and howled! It was a much better release than crying. His pride would not let him let me fix it. He currently looks like the professor from the Simpsons.

Lynn

Thursday, April 30, 2020

I'm not sure what's been going on with me over the past few days. If I had to name it… I feel lost. There have been outbursts of tears behind my mask at Trader Joe's, in the arms of my daughter and as I sit here and type. I'm mourning the lifestyle I took for granted, working up a sweat at the gym, cappuccino at Shearwater with a girlfriend, dinner parties, writing deadlines and even the obligatory overnighters at Mom's. I mourn democracy, alone time with my husband, and my children's future.

Morgaine

Sounds as if what's going on with you is a full force hit of reality. Bound to happen. There is so much to mourn. I don't think a person can stay in that too real place for long. Here's hoping your psyche will return you to the "new normal." Whatever makes you feel good, do it.

Mary-Lou

Thursday, April 30, 2020

Since Tuesday afternoon, I have been ricocheting from horror to incredulity to rage. Our Spanish conversation group meets every week and this week one of our members reported that her father, a gastroenterologist, has a patient in ICU who drank bleach to stave off the coronavirus; he has double pneumonia from inhaling the bleach fumes as he drank, among other problems. It is a horrible thing to imagine someone enduring the agonies that such an act could bring on. The doctor thinks the patient will recover, but what will that recovery look like? His esophagus cannot ever be the same. My horror immediately turned to rage at the monumental monster that is our president. (And how I abhor having to call him that.) And so it has gone since Tuesday, but I said that, didn't I?

Is this what his base is like? There must be some right-thinking persons among that crowd, no? But is that an oxymoron? How can one believe in this ignoramus and still be right-thinking? And who in their right mind would think that drinking any disinfectant would cure anything? It just boggles the mind, and it is difficult to continue thinking in any sort of coherent way when we hear these so-called briefings. I don't tune in to the "briefings" themselves, but inevitably, hear enough about them on the news.

I'm ranting so I'll stop now. Maybe the sun will be out tomorrow. Take good care and stay safe.

Maria

And yes, I already shared the story of the sweet little boy who swallowed Lysol. He was my patient when I was a medical social worker. When you have direct experience with this, the emotional turmoil goes deep. White rage is my constant companion.

Gina

Oh Maria!—Are there enough sane, caring people to save our democracy and the world? Like you, I despair. Just reading your "rant." Really, it's a cry from the heart.

Mary-Lou

Maria, no wonder you are ranting! It's one thing to hear that phone calls to poison control hotlines have escalated. It's another to know of an actual case. The reality hits like a ton of bricks.

Deb

Thursday, April 30, 2020

Here's what's going on. I've been using an external hard drive for my documents since the laptop I'm working on doesn't have much memory. On Saturday I discovered that I could no longer connect to that external drive. The drive was working—I could feel the vibrations—but it wasn't talking to the computer or vice versa. (You can be sure I was talking to both—thank goodness they don't have ears—or do they?)

On Monday, I started troubleshooting... talked to drive manufacturer and nothing worked. Then talked to computer consultant at Meadow Ridge—we worked on it together, tried to connect drive to 2010 laptop that still runs—no luck. Then he did what he's not supposed to do—he took my old computer and installed Linux, a free operating system, on the old computer with the thought that the Linux operating system might make the connection possible. Meanwhile I'd contacted the external consultant that Bill and I often used; they suggested taking disc to a repair shop.

But which one? I'd begun a Google search when one of Bill's sons called. He suggested a nationwide organization where his friend works, so I called them. I've sent the drive to them; it was like releasing a child to the unknown world. They'll look at it and call me with an estimate that I'll probably accept—ballpark is $300—$1200.

I can't remember what exactly is on the disk except for the memoir (I have hard copies of that) and tax documents. I think I'll realize the complexity of what I've lost gradually—like today when I intended to update my spreadsheet of passwords and realized that the original is on the disk.

Of course, I've spent the morning trying to figure out how to do things differently whether or not I get the information back. I've been reading about backup options vs. file storage until my head spins from the acronyms and my eyes ache from the anxiety. I've concluded that I should do both, but I'm still confused about which media to use. At first, I thought I'd just stop writing, but that's not really an option for me—I can't stop.

So that's where I am—trying to get back on track. Think I'll go and read—enough computer for one day.

Judy

What a nightmare! You are one brave lady, and a pretty savvy one also. Kudos to you! Computers scare the… out of me and I'm paranoid enough to keep hard copies of everything I think I might want. My kids laugh at me, but I don't care. I tell them it'll give

them plenty of fodder for the party I want them to have after I die—so they can tell all these stories and laugh.
Maria

Thursday, April 30, 2020

Dear Writing Buddies,

For the past thirty days, the "Weisman Group" has created and shared and improvised wonderful friendships. Because of it, I share what I just thought sitting down at the computer.

Your collective notes this week are touching, distressing, and wonderful all at the same time. I am touched by their sincerity; I am distressed because I commiserate with the emotional pain some of you have shared; and they are wonderful because I marvel at how open, intimate and (because we are a writing class) how well written they all are. I know I will remember these exchanges with great fondness, appreciation, and respect for all of you. Let's stay with it.

As for me, I find myself settling in. The days are not rushing by so much as time is becoming inconsequential. It doesn't really matter what time it is. Time is just something to note, not something that controls. As an example, I spend an inordinate amount of time looking at the birds at the bird feeders. Before the quarantine, I would see the birds, note them for about a minute, and then rush off to something else requiring my attention. Now I enjoy them and there is nothing that demands that I can't. I took out the *Guide for Eastern Birds* book and, very atypically, started identifying the visitors just outside my office window. Great fun. Hugs,
Ken

Thursday, April 30, 2020

Dear Writers,

Like Ken, I have been noticing the birds that flock to my

neighbor's feeder. In my eight years living here, I don't think I've ever seen a goldfinch. I'm guessing I never took the time to watch out the window for them.

I'm still living with my usual and annoying relationship to time. I occasionally wander into that lovely state of illusion of infinite time, but more lately I've felt I don't have enough time to do what I need/want to do during the day. I'm trying to decide if that's just my *familiar* and therefor gravitate back to that whatever the situation. I think about the term *spend time* and it sounds different lately. I do have a To Do list most days, but what I do isn't actually on the list. Just now I spent way too long getting my beach sticker for Compo—but it felt like such a priority. When that parking lot opens—May 15th—I want to drive in, park, and walk. That sounds so exciting!

I seem to get hung up on computer glitches—nothing as serious as Judy's—but I'll try different solutions over and over— way past the time I should have just closed the laptop. I still can't get AOL to recognize the passwords I've installed on my phone and laptop, no matter how many different ways I try. For a doctor's visit (video) next week I have to download the app My Chart. I can't do that because it asks for my AOL password. This would annoy me even without being in the 7th week of quarantine. In the past I would have called AOL and spoken to a kind young man in Bangalore. Now I feel like they have bigger issues to deal with.

I wonder what we Earthlings are learning from Covid-19. It's scary to me that it seems to bring out the anger and frustration in some who want to end the lockdowns, etc. On the other hand, I am hopeful that it's highlighting ancient inequities that need to be resolved.

I read *Water Dance,* by Ta-Nehisi Coates in February. The main character, Hiram, manages to escape to Philadelphia from his plantation in Virginia. He wants to help with the Underground

Railroad organization but is told he is not ready yet. What he realizes over the course of the book, is that wanting his own freedom is too small a goal. Until he desires freedom for all slaves, he hasn't realized his potential. I see a parallel to where we are in society. Until we see that everyone deserves a certain quality of life, we are not awake to what's going on for too many. It seems the virus has the potential to helps us see the truth about our relationships to each other. We are indeed in this together.
Donna

Thursday, April 30, 2020

Well, it was bound to happen. If anyone was annoyed by my virally yesterday, I don't blame them. I sounded so smug, so complacent, so way too content, so removed from the horrors going on around me. Today I felt the full force of what's going on. Terror. Panic. Anger. Grief. Maybe our nation can recover from this monster who has brought us so low. Maybe the November elections will bring about the beginnings of our salvation. This must happen. Hope.
Mary-Lou

Thursday, April 30, 2020

It feels as though our group is more connected than we thought. As the graphs of the virus climbs in casualties our emotions drop to new lows. Let's stay with it everyone. The sun will come out again. Thinking of and appreciating each and every one of you!
Morgaine

Thursday, April 30, 2020
Maybe I'm a freak.

I was walking with a friend today when she asked me how I was doing with isolation. I'm quite sure she meant this as an opening to express my worry, impatience, general malaise about the situation.

"I like it," was my answer. From her position 6' in front of me I saw her shake her head.

I had failed her. She loves to socialize, and will remain responsible, though is growing more depressed at remaining home.

"I mean, I do miss human contact. I miss nights out or simple gatherings. But I don't feel isolated." The implication that I didn't need others struck a nerve. Am I not in need of human contact enough? I do love socializing, and deeply love those in my orbit. But this is a retreat of sorts, a 2-month meditation for me, a challenge to find the internal resources I thought I would never uncover when Dave died. Now I feel content in my home, with more time for the things that are truly important to me.

I suppose I'm lucky. The pastimes I love are within these walls. I have Arlo. I'd become accustomed to being alone before coronavirus hit the scene. But most of all, I love the simplicity. I'm not running around. I'm spending time sitting with my feelings, and digging deep for the real meaning of, and confidence in, relying on myself. Each small accomplishment feels like a real achievement—showering, planning a nice dinner, making good use of everything, stocking my larder, talking with friends and family. I'm remembering birthdays without consulting a calendar. Part of my busyness is leaving time for yoga, longer walks with Arlo, following artistic whims.

Maybe I should feel more profoundly lonely, but I don't. The playing field is leveled. We're all in the same fix. Homebound, left to the devices of our imaginations to find ways to fill the day. Life is distilled to its most important, and in some ways, choice is greater without many of the usual outside pressures. The truth is, I fear going back to what I thought of as normal more than continuing like this.

Deb

Thursday, April 30, 2020

I am so disoriented; I wake up thinking it's May 1st and wishing the rain would just stop! I know, I know, *April showers bring May flowers*, but still…

The girls and I have not left the yard since we went for a beach walk on March 21st, except for my quick cookie pickup at Mary-Lou's house on April 15th to which Monica drove me. Monica has done lots of unaccompanied errands. Wannabe boyfriend brought her some masks which she keeps in the car.

I have not read anything but the *New York Times* and the *Wall Street Journal* since I started *The Signature of All Things* by Elizabeth Gilbert when I was in Key West from February 21-24th. It sits on a table with the bookmark at 20% read.

The girls don't ask to go anywhere. Besides schoolwork and Zoom acting and voice classes, they enjoy creating characters with wigs, costumes, and makeup. Evelyn's piano compositions are getting more creative. The girls can go for days and nights in the same sets of pajamas. I change my clothes every day and wear business casual, makeup, and jewelry for professional Zoom meetings. My niece's wedding is postponed until July 2021. I am focusing day to day and not itching to make any plans. I've been invited to visit my sisters in northern Wisconsin, co-host an awards ceremony in New York in August, and attend a Wisconsin wedding in September but am not holding my breath.

I get regular emails from the clothing stylists at Stitch Fix and Nordstrom's Trunk Club. The enticements are entertaining, but my closets overflow with outfits that I have no occasion to wear.

I miss the days when I would go to downtown Westport and make the rounds of the library, the Y, and the art center—my three anchors. I kept a locker at the Y and sometimes went twice a day. I'd top it off with Oscar's or Java *al fresco*. It felt so vibrant. The library, restaurants and shops are all that's left from my old haunts. Even 323 is gone. Most of this happened before the pandemic. I'm not sure I even care anymore. I'm orienting more to Southport where someday I can again walk between the hair salon, Chico's, outdoor restaurants, the Fairfield Library, and the Fairfield Y.

My grandkids and my work are my life. I even got my April bills out to clients already.

Can any of you still find the scar from your smallpox vaccination? I can. Just barely.

Gina

I enjoy hearing about your day-by-day life—so busy, so varied. Ditto re rage at Pence. Interesting that so many of us are missing normal life. It must be that many of us have reached our patience peak, but Main Street will have to wait, assuming it will be there when it's safe to walk about. It's not just impatience; it's rage.

Mary-Lou

May 2020

Friday, May 1, 2020

May first… Mayday! When my mother was at the University of Wisconsin in the 1930s, the sororities had a tradition of dancing around a Maypole in front of Langdon Hall. When I was a kid in the 1950s, we acknowledged Mayday by praying for the conversion of Russia from communism. When I was in college in the 1960s, I was chosen to crown a statue of Mary with flowers in Milwaukee's Cathedral of St John the Evangelist. A couple of years ago, I surprised an old high school classmate with a May basket on May 1st. I like the May basket tradition best.

Time to support a local merchant during this pandemic by ordering some flowers from Compo Farm Flowers.

Gina

I attended Bryn Mawr College, an all-girl's school for 2 years— the first two—where dancing around the maypole was a May Day tradition. Many years ago, the then president of the college was alleged to have said, "Only our failures marry." Perhaps she wasn't aware that maypole dancing was a fertility rite.

Mary-Lou

My mom graduated from Bryn Mawr. She talked about the maypole. Maybe that's why I'm here.

Deb

Friday, May 1, 2020

Dogwood and Amaryllis in full bloom… Michelle and I made banana bread today. Recipe attached.

*Note: it took close to an hour to bake.

Morgaine

Friday, May 1, 2020

This morning I asked myself, "What's today going to be like?" The Sunrise Rotary Zoom meeting was over at 9:00. I knew I had to tie up client issues. A real estate closing, a client's estate planning questions, and some business matters needed attending to, but none of it would take long. Around 1:00 PM, I was ready for "me." "House chores, Check! Bird feeder, Check! ...Food supplies, Check! ...Email correspondence, Check! ...Bills and taxes paid, Check! ...Music playing, Check! ...Stretching and Exercising (knee hurts and can't take a walk), Check!

For the very first time, I had nothing on my *To Do* list. What now? I got this notion to send **Harry and David's** delicious pears to family and friends with a note "*Happy Quarantine. Hang in there!*" It took 40 minutes.

Thank goodness tomorrow is Saturday. I need a rest.

Ken

Friday, May 1, 2020

I am not planning to liberate myself after May 20th no matter what Gov. Lamont allows, although my hair is turning pink.

"*May 20 openings include outdoor areas of restaurants and bars, outdoor museums and zoos, offices and retail outlets. Barber shops, hair salons and other personal care businesses were types of businesses specifically mentioned."*

I don't know if these openings are premature or not. I fear that Trump's impatience to get on the road again may have influenced nearly everyone's understandable impatience. People have had enough, but I'm not convinced that the virus has.

So, here's my plan. After May 20th, I'm going to wait a full two weeks or more to see if the number of new cases increases in our area. If it does, I'll continue to hunker down. It's not that I don't feel sorry for our local merchants, but when it comes down to my money, i.e., lasagna al fresco at Penne e Bene, or my life, I can be patient.

Mary-Lou

Saturday, May 2, 2020

I'm making my peace with the lost documents. It's not as if someone died—I know that because I have a friend who is dying. She's just accepted at-home hospice. Each week two other Black women and I meet her on a Zoom meeting to discuss a movie that we've decided on seeing. This week it'll be *Black Panther*. It doesn't matter that this will be the 4th time I've seen it; the point is to see Sonja for two hours and laugh a bit and cry later. We'll only know in hindsight which time would be the last time.

I took yesterday off. It would have been Bill's 92nd birthday. There are lots of people here over 90—but he's not one of them. I can't ask WHY because there's no answer.

Today I'm gritting my teeth and retyping the memoir, one chapter at a time. If I stop berating myself for being so incredibly stupid/arrogant/la de da/ add another adjective, it would probably go faster. But I haven't managed yet to turn off that voice in my head.

Walked for a mile this morning, then did an hour Pilates class, then did the chapter. I'm going to walk again as a reward for my angst. Will watch *Black Panther* tonight, holding on to the expectation that we'll see Sonja on Tuesday.

Judy

Saturday, May 2, 2020

Throughout this rainy week, we'd been looking forward to the predicted sunny Saturday. Seventy degrees! We had planned to visit a Westport couple we'd known for years. It would be our first outdoor social call of the pandemic. We were crossing over to freedom. They had been healthy and careful. So had we.

Before leaving our house, I showered, worked hard at making my hair look decent, and changed my outfit 3 times—a modest dressing frenzy. I felt my pre-pandemic anxiety tighten in my chest. For the past 40 days I had been enjoying an unfamiliar calm. Who would see me besides my husband? Having no dates, no obligations, I had relaxed into a state of serenity that I had never known in my real life. Now, suddenly, I needed to look my best, despite my apricot-colored hair with a white skunk strip at my part. I felt hollow and inadequate. The woman we were visiting always looks as if she just stepped out of a (cliché alert!) band box—neat, fashionable, totally put together. She's expert at eye shadow and eye liner. Her hair is always shiny and beautifully coiffed. Her outfits are perfectly coordinated. I would hate her if I didn't like her so much. Finally, somewhat satisfied with my choice of white trousers and a blue and white striped blouse, I applied lipstick for the first time in 40 days. Then, not satisfied, I returned to the bathroom mirror, drew on some eyebrows, and took a couple of swipes at my eyelashes with a mascara wand. Still not satisfied, I gave up and—we left.

We drove to their home and followed the flagstone path to their patio, where they had set up four chaises lounges at least 8 feet apart. He came out of the house first, carrying two bottles of chilled water. Then she arrived. Her hair was tangled, the roots showing. She was wearing no makeup—not even lipstick—no bra, a pair of trousers with bagged out knees, a faded black tee shirt. I'm still trying to figure out the point of this story.

Mary-Lou

Saturday, May 2, 2020

Today was strange. While down on my hands and knees scrubbing the kitchen floor, I was thinking about how lucky I've been to have had both house cleaners and au pairs during my child rearing days. I was a stay-at-home mom, with a pair of extra hands. Boy, could I use those hands now. Every morning I come downstairs to the kitchen, wipe the crumbs from the counter, sweep and then scrub the wood floors with a damp cloth. Combined with the gratitude I feel for having had the luxury of hired help all those years, I feel resentment.

I'm envious of Ken's walk down memory lane, Mary-Lou's daily jaunts, Donna's loving Zoom reunions with her sisters. I too have four sisters, but I don't look forward to our virtual meetings due to our differing political views.

Once the housework is done, the yard work calls to me. There are seven garden beds to weed, mulch to be laid and what feels like an arboretum of plants to be pruned and cared for. Don't get me wrong, I love being in my garden, but it's difficult to surrender to the moment when I know someone is in the kitchen slicing an everything bagel and sesame and poppy seeds are scattering across my nice clean floors. How long can I keep up the pace?

Today was my best day yet. After an hour of yoga, I spent  most of the day in my garden. There was no thought of coronavirus. I dug out two dead shrubs and a tree, weeded the bed near the street and seeded the bare spots in the lawn. Mark fixed my handicapped wheelbarrow;

it had a bolt missing. He took the whole damn thing apart and realigned the frame, then he sawed off the dead branches of a huge shrub and I loaded it into the truck for a trip to the transfer station on Monday.

A day in the garden gives me the feeling of accomplishment, even though there is a ton more work to do. Spring has only begun. My tree peonies are blooming. Ahhh!

Morgaine

Saturday, May 2, 2020

Oh! I envy Morgaine's garden! I know it's hard work, but the physical effort outside sounds ideal right now.

I woke up determined to find the joy in the day but feel a melancholy. Once I write morning pages, I'll perk myself up. A writing course I took several times through the years was proprioceptive writing. The teacher wrote an inspiring book, *Writing Your Mind Alive*. Writing can help me get out of my little thoughts and appreciate the larger world. Writing and a latte on my deck will be good for my spirits. A walk on the trail in nature will also provide a boost.

A question I read in the pandemic diaries in the Times yesterday was "When did this become real for you?" I think for me it was inside Trader Joe's on Good Friday. I was fine waiting in line outside for 30 minutes, but once in the store with the new rules and restrictions, I wanted to just to shout, "Fuck this!" This wasn't what shopping at Trader Joe's was supposed to be.

I never thought I'd have a grocery store anxiety, but now I do. I'm okay going to the Village Market, but I don't run over and pick things up the way I used to. I keep a list and it has to get quite long before I'm ready to make my move. Maybe that will pass with practice. And I do miss insignificant chats with folks at the deli counter and check-out. Hell, I miss casual greetings with strangers everywhere.

Enough complaining. I am grateful for so much! Writing in my journal—my form of meditation, will help remind me of the goodness around me. Sipping a decaf latte and watching the noisy birds in the trees will also soothe me. I guess starting week eight of quarantine requires me to dig deeper. I can do that. Time to put on Pavarotti.

Donna

Saturday, May 2, 2020

I spend most of the day consolidating the daily virallies into our journal and tucking photos into the text. Also research the timeline leading up to our incarceration and the cancelation of our writing classes.

Monica and I clear out all the upper kitchen cupboards before her ex-boyfriend helps her remove all the doors and they begin to paint.

The girls set up the sprinkler in the backyard, put on swimsuits, and hop through the spray holding umbrellas to ditch the water.

My congressional stimulus check arrives today. Spend some of it on a delivery from Golden Pizza—pepperoni pies, French fries, onion rings, fried calamari, and hot chicken wings. I could tell from the voice on the other end of the phone that the restaurant was very grateful for the order.

Gina

Sunday, May 3, 2020

https://m.facebook.com/story.php?story_fbid=2904759752939639&id=826415330774102

If you're on Facebook a lot, you may have seen this. A worthy watch.

Donna

Sunday, May 3, 2020

Last evening was too lovely to stay in the present. Sam and I decided to resurrect memories of other times, starting with when we chartered a sailboat in British Virgin Islands, one of the best holidays of our marriage. To do it successfully, we needed to mix a pitcher of Caribbean Painkillers (Pusser's Rum, pineapple juice and coconut juice mixed in a blender and poured over ice) and to find Ronnie Laws' music, which we played incessantly while cruising among the islands at 8 knots. There was a lot to recall, the perfect sailing weather, the snorkeling, our onboard feasts and the island restaurants, mid-afternoon naps, cozy anchorages, and beautiful sunsets. It was a welcome break from current events.

As our evening progressed, we conjured up other memories, which inspired us to relate them to music playing at the time they occurred. Spotify is terrific resource, which Sam has mastered.

I wanted to hear "Walk Don't Run" by the Ventures, which I remember playing as loud as I could while driving, and sometimes drag racing my grandmother's 1956 black Corvette with the top down. I was 17. Sam recalled a time in college when she was a waitress at the Dial Tone (a Westport pickup bar where you could call other patrons with a house phone on every table... I am surprised I didn't meet her then) which got us to disco, and Donna Summer's "Hot Stuff" and "Last Dance" and Gloria Gaynor's "I Will Survive."

Living in Greenwich Village in the 60s brought up Neil Young's "Harvest Moon," Dion's "Run Around Sue," Dylan's "Knockin' on Heaven's Door" and "Blowing in The Wind," and one of my favorites (to the embarrassment of both my daughter and wife) Neil Diamond's "Love on the Rocks" and "Kentucky Woman." By then we had emptied the second pitcher of the overly sweet Painkillers and headed to bed at the late hour of 9:30. We finished the excitement with the music of Rossini (The William

Tell Overture) and Rimsky-Korsakov (Flight of the Bumblebee), which to be clear were written before our times.

Sunday is another challenge… perhaps we will work our way into the 80s and 90s.

Ken

That sounds like a great evening, Ken. Could it have happened without Covid or does the virus get the credit? Music certainly plays a huge part in my memories, too. I'm so grateful for that.

Donna

What a romantic way to spend lockdown. A lovely description of how wonderful marriage can be. I can taste that delicious drink and feel the wind in my hair driving in that Corvette (what a cool grandmother). Nostalgia can be painful, or sweet, depending on whether you're as content in the present as in the past. This felt sweet.

Deb

Sunday, May 3, 2020

Today my husband suggested we "work on the garage"—meaning we shuffle around his collection of crap and empty cardboard boxes he refuses to throw away. Not my idea of a good time. We have rarely managed to "work on the garage" without yelling at each other. The amount of hostility we are capable of unleashing is sometimes worrisome.

We did okay today though, mostly because I kept my yap shut. I've learned you can't get into too much trouble if you only shrug or smile and nod approvingly. I posted a bunch of garage-junk to the Westport Facebook free-cycle site and have already dispatched a lamp, some toys, and a janky hamster cage to other homes.

Since many of my friends have been texting me pictures of their loaves of homemade bread, I decided to indulge my masochistic side and try it. I've attempted bread a few times before, never with any success. If anything makes me believe in the Get Goldman Office, it's bread-making. My son still has memories of me rage-baking: literally throwing a loaf of failed bread out the kitchen door while I swore the worst swears in a string without  pause. He was probably about seven at the time. I remember him staring at me, agape. He said, "Wow, Mom! Calm down!" I'm surprised he didn't say, "Calm the fuck down!" I'm hoping this time will be different, considering the wellspring of Zen patience I've tapped into lately. The loaf is in the oven now. It looks pretty, but it doesn't smell great. Worst case, the blue jays will enjoy it. I promise to toss it outside, quietly, and gently instead of hurling it with all my might.

Lynn

By all means, let us know how the bread comes out. A mound of butter on a warm slice can make almost any bread good enough. I've yet to venture down that road, except for foolproof breads such as banana bread.

Donna

I'm with Donna. Banana bread is my limit. But I admire your pluck. Please let us know how it turns out.

Mary-Lou

I love bread-making. Kneading dough is just like wedging clay, which reminds me of sleeping overnight in the kiln room with a bunch of college friends while our pieces were firing. And ditto Donna. Butter was one of Dave's 3B's food groups, and

homemade bread disappeared in a flash. I bet this more Zen effort comes out great!
Deb

Sunday, May 3, 2020

Baking is a challenge I have yet to master. My mom didn't bake so I never grew up with that tradition. We had a great bakery on Broadway a block from our apartment so no need to ever learn to bake. I finally was able to produce a fairly good pie crust, thanks to Martha Stewart's Quick Cookbook when I was in my 30s. This past week I tried baking Chocolate Rye Cookies, a recipe from Jamie Oliver's *5 Ingredients* cookbook. Instead of flour, it used rye bread you blitz in the food processor along with eggs, butter, superfine sugar and 70% chocolate. I had the rye bread, eggs, and butter, but my sugar was the regular kind and my chocolate chips were only 60%. But, hey, what the heck, I thought I'd try them. How bad could they be? Pretty bad. They never spread like the book said they should, and they tasted pretty mealy. Don't worry, Ken, you aren't getting any cookie competition from me!!

Lynn, how did the bread come out? And what kind was it?
Maria

Ten years from now, when someone says, "Remember the pandemic?" I can say, "Oh yes! I learned how to make bread then!" 😊 *The blue jays will see none of it. It's almost all gone already! Delicious!*
Lynn

Sunday, May 3, 2020

I text classmate Bernadette to let her know I'm thinking of her. No reply.

Monica's ex-boyfriend, Jeff, shows up and helps sand and paint more of the kitchen cupboards. It involves removing all the hinges, handles, and interior trays and slides. They are both very handy, but Monica even more so. They make numerous trips to Home Depot for paint and supplies. Jeff lives alone and is totally isolated other than visiting us occasionally. He's the only company we've had in two months. I like having him around.

Gina

Sunday, May 3, 2020

The NYT Magazine feature article, "Who Lives? Who Dies? How Covid-19 revealed the deadly realities of a racially polarized America." I'd heard the statistics for the past two weeks: African-Americans make up 33% of Louisiana's population and 70% of the Covid-19 dead, in Michigan, we're 14% of the population and 40% of the dead; in Wisconsin, 7% of the population, 33% dead; in Mississippi, 38% and 61% dead.

Judy

Sunday, May 3, 2020

Spilling a mug of coffee on your bedclothes can ruin your day. I suppose wine would have been worse. First you run a tub. Then you alternate soaking the sheets (I missed the pillowcases). Then toss in the quilt, the bedspread, and the cotton blanket. When that doesn't work—and it doesn't—hit the light brown coffee stains with OxiClean Max Spray. When, after waiting a couple of hours that doesn't work well enough, shake a can of Comet on the offending stains and rub in the powder in with a stiff brush. That works. Then, spend much of the rest of the day washing and drying the sheets, the bedspread, the quilt, the cotton blanket. It's nearly 8 PM and I've missed an entire lovely day. To add insult to injury, now I must make the bed.

Mary-Lou

Monday, May 4, 2020

Because of our quarantine, my hair is longer than it has ever been. Much longer. And, because I have more free time, I am taking longer showers, call it one of the benefits of our ordeal. Last week, while enjoying the hot water and looking for an excuse to stay under it longer, I took note of the bottle of hair conditioner that has been there for years and which I always overlooked. Having never used conditioner (I never bother with the ones in hotels and even wonder why they are there), I thought I would get advice from Sam. I don't suspect any of you would be surprised to learn how simple it is to use. I am now using it frequently and I have to say my hair is much, much softer. I find I am running my hands through my hair more often than before and each time I reflect on how nice it is to touch. And, the best thing is Sam also likes to run her hands through my long, soft locks. It just goes to prove that there is always something good to be found, even in a shower during a quarantine.

Ken

Monday, May 4, 2020

When I came down this morning, I opened the glass slider to let Archie out. There, on one of the wicker chairs on the back porch was a little yellow bird, a goldfinch—so beautiful. He/she didn't seem to pay any attention to us, even when I snuck a little closer to take a better look. It seemed a funny place for her to be, its beak snuggled into the corner of the chair. But okay, we all have our own peculiar sleeping poses. While I fed Archie and had my own breakfast, I kept checking on the little yellow bird and noticed it had not moved. Was it hurt? Was it dead? But no, a little rest was all she needed and off she flew to join her mate.

Then came the robin red breast who has constructed a nest in the bush right next to the back of the house. It flits in and out of there although, yet there isn't any movement in the nest. I am thrilled to have this visitation from our avian friend. I've noticed much more bird activity lately and I wonder, could it be that without so much noise—and fumes—from traffic the area is much friendlier? I dug my binoculars out and I have my bird guidebooks out so am all set. Watching the birds is a calming activity. Well, their activity, not mine. I've had a cardinal pair come visit and the ever-present crows, or grackles—black birds, anyway. I keep the birdbath filled with fresh water. Everyone is welcome.

I have proposed a couple of activities for our community and hope I haven't bitten off more than I can chew. One of the proposals is to have outdoor book readings by the pool where there is plenty of room for safe distancing. We are an age-restricted community and many of our residents are elderly—no, not me!!—and some are handicapped so can't get around too easily. But isolation makes afflictions so much worse, and I thought this was a way to get out safely and do something together. I've already thought of five books that I think would leave the reader—and listener—feeling good. We don't want any doom and gloom—enough of that in real life!! The books, in no preferred order, are: *The Little Paris Bookshop*, *The Authenticity Project*, and the three books of The Wayfarer Trilogy. Suggestions are sure to come in from the audience.
Maria

I think your reading groups are a great idea! We, too, seem to have more birds and nests around than formerly. You reminded me of the canary in the coal mine that warns the miners when the air is dangerous to breathe. The increase in bird life may well mean that our air is safer to breathe, that nature is ready to assert herself. But are we?
Mary-Lou

Are we? I have a sinking feeling that we'll go back to the same-old-same-old. The air has become cleaner because there has been little or no traffic and yet, the minute we open things up a bit, we forget. Cars are back in greater numbers and soon the skies will be tainted with the refuse of our "success." It's hard to change. I don't think Nature is done teaching us quite yet.

Maria

Monday, May 4, 2020

You've all inspired me to get out of the house and off my well-groomed property. Mark and I took a vigorous walk around Compo this morning before the clouds moved in. We trespassed up Blue Water Hill; a private road lined in driveway pavers and long-stemmed tulips. By the time I enjoyed my morning coffee, took a long hot shower, and threw in a load of wash, the wind had picked up and heat of the day was over. Perfect weather for writing!

Not today, however.

Not yesterday or the day before. I'm referring to my memoir writing. Even virallies have been a struggle to commit to recently. I used to be so disciplined. Cold days and/or wet dreary weather were the perfect excuse to spend the afternoon hovered over my keyboard, to delve into my adventurous past and to play with words. It appears that quarantine is the perfect excuse to avoid such indulgences. The drive to write escapes me.

Perhaps tomorrow.

Morgaine

Tuesday, May 5, 2020

I haven't felt like writing memoir at all. I think the pandemic is to blame; not because it's upsetting me (though it is), but because it has anchored me to the present. Memoir is all about revisiting the past, and lately my mind is not cooperating. For the first time in my adult life, I'm spending a little time thinking about the future, but mostly I'm not thinking at all. I walk, I bake, I sit in the sun with a blank mind. I don't analyze any of it. Then I wake up and do it all over again. When today is so much like the day before, the past becomes irrelevant.

There is a great peacefulness to it, but at the same time I wonder if I'm losing my edge, or my grip, a little. I used to think about the past all the time. So much of my identity was wrapped up in my past too: sad, little, neglected waif turns 20-year-old wild-child. If I stop thinking about it, am I not that person anymore? I feel like I have shed it all somehow. Since I'm not giving them any attention, my memories seem to be withering, like houseplants drying out on a sill. This might be good for my emotional state, but I'm not going to be cranking out a lot of pages anytime soon. Maybe it's time to try fiction.

Lynn

Tuesday, May 5, 2020

An interesting day in politics. Trump will not let Fauci testify to Congress. If I had my way, Fauci would resign in protest and then make himself available to any network where his scientific acumen is valued. It was a good idea to quit the briefings, a boring spectacle of monotone readings, lies, misrepresentations, and self-aggrandizement, accompanied by pained looks from Fauci and Birx. The briefings couldn't compare with the MAGA rallies on which his voracious ego feeds.

Plus, he was losing his audience. More to the point, the precipitous rise in the death toll made him look even worse than he looked before, so abandoning the Coronavirus Task Force was another good idea, given that he had abandoned the task.

Not so coincidentally Rick Bright publicly blew the whistle alleging that Trump insisted upon giving contracts to corporations who favored his fake cures over real science. As Deb put it a while ago, Trump has blood on his hands.

It seems as if Trump has stopped being president—which is fine by me—and has started campaigning for president, which is not fine by me.

Mary-Lou

Tuesday, May 5, 2020

Spent Cinco de Mayo in the garden. Replaced the dead shrubbery with colorful new growth. At four-fifteen I poured myself a Michellarita and spent the evening with a smile on my face. No news is good news.

Morgaine

Tuesday, May 5, 2020

Saturday night I instigated a Zoom "Dinner In" with members of my bereavement group. One of the good deeds. Some of the members do not have as much support and have lost their spouses more recently than I have. Each of us ordered takeout, and we shared dinner. Three of us, without coordinating, ordered from the same restaurant. It was nice, a chance to step outside of bereavement and exchange normal news, recommended shows and books, trivial and much appreciated banter.

This has been a time of deep reflection. In yoga today, my daughter asked us during Shiva asana to think of who we trust. I startled myself. Immediately I thought, I trust myself. I feel as though this terrible, tragic pandemic has left me alone to decide whether to appreciate or berate myself. Today I answered that question.

One of the side effects of grief is loss of self-confidence and self-esteem. Perhaps today's answer to myself marks a step into a new phase of life after Dave. I still miss him, tell him often he wouldn't believe what has transpired in the world right now. I tell him because I want him here with me. We would have so much to talk about, so much time to be together.

This poem/exercise comes to mind when I think of reflection. I used it many times in the workshops I led.

I Am from People, Places, Things

I am from
Brilliant and narcissistic divorced parents, more alike than
    unalike.
A large cord of aunts, uncles, cousins, twisted into a strong
    whole.
A grandmother whom I adored and encouraged me always.
A husband who showed me what I didn't want, and one who
    gave me what I did.

I am from
A small brick house in the country on a dirt road, creek, and
    pond in the back,
In a town that thrived on the arts and where I could roam free,
    swim, skate, ride.
Summers on a lake with an aunt and uncle who modeled
    committed parenting.
A home century old, where my husband and children and I and
    memories lived.

I am from
A leftist leaning, a passion for justice and a need to make a
    difference.
Pastels and charcoal, easels and pencils for drawing and writing.
Barns and horses, the thrill of suspension in the air before hooves
    land.

The jasmine, curry, red dirt, red ants, white toothy smiles, and
colors of India.

Deb

Wednesday, May 6, 2020

I wash my sweaty pajamas and change my sheets.

I finish an analysis of a valuation report for a business of home
builders.

Frances asks if she can sleep with me tonight. I tell her yes, if
she takes a shower and changes the jammies she's been wearing
day and night for a week.

Gina

I love the way you mix business with domesticity.
Mary-Lou

Wednesday, May 6, 2020

I walked down to the pond at Meadow Ridge yesterday because
I'd heard that there were six just hatched goslings parented by two
geese. The path down is winding and steep at some places, paved
with stones that turn dark gray and slippery after a rain.

I think of the pond as "wild," but it's not. Benches are placed
at strategic places where one might want to rest. There's one
picnic table with benches, speckled with white lichen (at least,
that's what I call it.) There's even an octagonal, screened-in
gazebo with chairs and tables at the edge of the water. I've thought
about sleeping there overnight in the summer when the moon's
full and I'm feeling brave. It may be just a thought.

I tried to walk quietly along the path that encircles the pond,
hoping to sneak up on the goose family. Before I could spot them,
they heard my sneakered feet dislodge a stone. All I could see was
the concentric circles made as they paddled away into a shady,
camouflaged section of the pond.

"Sit and wait," I told myself. I perched on a rock outcropping that gave me an unobstructed view of the pond. A turtle swam by. Next to me a frog plopped into the water, escaping my gaze before I had a chance to see him.

Then I heard one of the geese, honking and splashing on the far side of the pond. I saw it extend and flap its wings as it chased two other geese away. The goose's partner quickly led their goslings away from the commotion and potential danger. The intruder geese paddled in my direction until they noticed me and changed direction.

That was the drama for the day.

Judy

Wednesday, May 6, 2020

Maybe the news late last night that RBG was in the hospital should have clued me in that today would not be good. But I don't think it's ever good when a day starts with a call from the IRS. To be accurate, three calls from the IRS. Last fall I spent thousands of dollars to hire a tax accountant to get the IRS to concede that their 10-year attempt to collect $135,000 from me was a mistake. I owed them nothing, and I have the letter from them to prove it.

Hence the calls this morning were jarring, to say the least. How could this issue have risen its ugly and ill-advised head again? I was livid to the extreme. Will it take the full $135,000 in legal fees before they get off my innocent back?

Perhaps my rage frightened the squirrel chomping on my house into pausing for a brief lull, but it quickly resumed its attack on the 150-year-old wood.

Even my mindless break to play Spider Solitaire went wrong. Lost several games before, as I am convinced, the computer deduced it better give me an easy game before I deleted the link from my bookmarks bar.

It rained on my walk with Arlo.

They were out of vitamin C at the store.

Was finally involved in a project I wanted to finish when my neighbor called, and I knew it would be tomorrow before I could put the project to rest.

Just one of those days. Tomorrow will be better, because up is the only direction possible.

Deb

Wednesday, May 6, 2020

Today's accomplishment. A gift for my mom for Mothers' Day. Acrylic on canvas.

Morgaine

Oh! I love the cat—the colors, the patterns! Fantastic!
Donna

Thursday, May 7, 2020

I bit the bullet yesterday and agreed to the tech guy's price to recover the information on the disk. It's costing me as much as a new computer—there goes that plan for the year—every five years I buy a new one. Now have to figure out reasonable back up; will do Carbonite in the cloud because one daughter told me their customer service was wonderful. I'll probably need that service with an older computer. Need to decide on another storage mechanism that I can hold in my hand—another external drive?

As a consolation prize, I took myself for a long walk down to the pond again. The frogs were their usual invisible "plopping" selves. I couldn't find the goose family, but I found lots of poop—big ones from the parents, little ones from the chicks. It was silent; the waters were still.

Then I took the car for a ride. Since we're not supposed to go off campus, I haven't been driving. I got into it and immediately felt the need to escape—go to Boston for Mother's Day, go to the beach, just GO! I remembered how to drive and circled the ring road twice—I remember how to ride a bike, too, and haven't done that in a while either—hope it won't be that long before I drive again.

Oh, and on my walk, I found the rabbit. Someone has been moving him around in the woods leading to the pond for years. There's never any telling where he'll turn up, hidden in plain sight.

Judy

Thursday, May 7, 2020

This'll be a quick virally. I've be out in the garden weeding, trying to untangle, rearrange and guide the clematis upwards on 2 iron trellises. About as much fun as trying to get chewing gum out of your hair. Since I've been gardening for 3 days in a row—taking time out for rain—I'm sore everywhere. Everything hurts. Standing, leaning against a wall, is the best option. That, and bed.

This afternoon, having quit the garden, I went into the sunroom and tried to sit down. It was so painful that I didn't dare continue. Stuck in mid-crouch, I heard myself cry out, "Help, help, I'm standing, and I can't get down." That's it for today.

Mary-Lou

Thursday, May 7, 2020

Finally finished my cityscape painting. (I'll do anything to avoid memoir writing these days.) So y'all liked my cat painting? I don't have any more small canvases lying around but I'm happy to paint any one of you a mini watercolor 3 x 3. Here are a few topic suggestions:

- Butterfly
- Tree
- Flowers/bouquet
- Fruit or vegetable
- Teacup and saucer or teapot
- Cactus
- Palm tree
- Cupcake
- Your pet
  First come first served!

I relaxed my quarantine boundaries today. After hours of gardening my back and neck needed an adjustment. I went to see my chiropractor, Dr. Kenny. His is a family-owned practice, Mom, Dad, and son. Kenny is a sweet, adorable 28-year-old young man. He asked me what I missed most about being quarantined. My answer was not immediate. I almost said, "my routine," and then I remembered all that it entailed: hitting the gym in the morning, attending to phone calls, paperwork, errands, and memoir writing every day by 2 PM. The truth: I don't really miss it. I have my kids within hug's reach. We've been eating like royalty, and I have a writing group with whom I can share my innermost thoughts. Every day is new, some up, some down, but never predictable. I've also relaxed my restriction on alcohol consumption. Could it be I've let go?

Morgaine

Friday, May 8, 2020

I complete an analysis of the valuation of a directory distribution company. They are in deep trouble with the customers moving to digital directories. Very depressing.

Make chicken and rice for dinner with chicken thighs and leftover rice from The Little Kitchen.

Gina

Friday, May 8, 2020

The Week in Review:

On *Tuesday* I went to Whole Foods. It was uneventful and I don't know why it made me so tense, but it did. I got home and thought I'd try gardening to relax. When I went to turn on the hose, I discovered the hard way that the splitter had cracked in two—a blast of water right to the face. I resolved that, then got my shoes soaked when I realized too late that the same thing happened to the nozzle. Then the spigot to the house started leaking all over the place so badly, we had to turn the valve off from inside the basement. A plumber will need to be called. The Get Goldman Office is obviously still staffed with essential employees.

On *Wednesday* I spent the entire day at my desk, doing nothing, picking my ear, and grumbling about the weather.

On *Thursday* I woke up with water-on-the-knee, which happens when I sit too long—ever since I dislocated my knee when I was 16, playing baseball. (BASEBALL?! What's that?!) I decided that maybe I could avoid the plumber if I got a new splitter, so I called Westport Hardware. They sold me a splitter and nozzle, cheaper than Amazon, and left them outside their door for pickup in 20 minutes. Once I picked that up, I decided to be a naughty girl and make a day of it.

! I got curbside wine, & in-store cat food, which I contemplated shoplifting since there was absolutely NO ONE in the store, not even an employee, and I had to shout like an idiot, "ANYBODY HERE?!" to get someone to ring me up. Then I hit Stop & Shop looking for yeast. There was none, but they did have the popsicles my husband likes, and some usually elusive pancake mix. And what they hell, while I'm all dolled up with my mask on, I might as well try Fresh Market on my way home. No yeast, but they did have the half-n-half I forgot to buy at Whole Foods on Tuesday. After visiting five places in one day, I was quite energized.

I resumed gardening when I got home. A purple flowering plant sprawled across the garden bed, yet over the winter it died in the middle, leaving a sort of groundcover donut. Ridiculous looking. I hacked it into sections and straightened it into a border. My mother-in-law would have loved my spadework. I set up the new splitter; I didn't get wet. It was a miracle. The spigot is still dripping, though not as badly. I might still call the plumber. He is a good-looking older man with very dry humor. I enjoy seeing him, though from six feet away my enjoyment might be diminished. I'm hoping he'll come, since it's an outside job.

At 5 PM, my husband wanted coffee and my son wanted "pies-n-fries" (which makes me McSick, but to each their own...) so I went out again. What excitement will tomorrow bring?!

Friday: Made bread; started it last night. This recipe took 16 hours to make. The whole thing will be eaten in under 16 minutes, I think.

This morning, my husband got mulch from Lowes even though it's too cold to plant, and we don't have anything to mulch. But he has had mulch-envy for weeks. Many of our neighbors get giant heaps of mulch delivered; mountainous piles stand in their driveways. My husband wants to be king of the mulch-mountain. But our garden bed is smaller than our sleeping bed, so a bag or two is all we need. Today, my husband bought six. But he also took me to Speedy Donuts in Norwalk, so I let it go.

The plumber is coming at 2 PM. I cleaned up a little & vacuumed in his honor.

Lynn

Lynn, your virally writing could be a book, a sitcom, or a mini-series! Love them.
Maria

Friday, May 8 ,2020

Today the Ahmaud Arbery killing got to me. He was three years older than my oldest grandson, Langston. It could have been Langston—or his 18-year-old brother, Ezra. Newscasters talk about the shooting dispassionately—and go on to the next breaking news story that gets an equal amount of time and is, by implication, equally important. And my soul aches.

I decided to immerse myself in Blackness. One of the few advantages of this quarantine is the availability of groups that I don't have to travel to. I'm reading *How to Be an Anti-Racist* since I'll be part of the panel to interview Kendi next Thursday on the Westport Library website. To my delight, I discovered he grew up in Queens not far from where I was raised. He describes the streets that I knew so well—Jamaica Avenue, 164th Street. More amazing, he gives a succinct description of Black English or Ebonics, a course that I researched and taught to Columbia graduate students on the way to the Ph.D. I was flooded with the familiar references, with the excitement of having been at the forefront of that exploration into a burgeoning linguistic field when everyone thought—and still thinks—that claiming Black English as a separate language rather than incorrect English—is foolish and unfounded. It was like sinking into a warm, welcoming tub of water that I hadn't known I missed.

Then I signed up to watch a Cornell Black Alumni Association talent show. For two hours I watched poets, a game show host, singers, comedians display their talents—a Ph.D. engineer read her protest poetry, an academic counselor sang a cappella, an English major and MFA candidate read her very personal poetry, a retiree asked us to choose one of two audition tapes that she will submit for admission to an acting class. Who knows what other talent was lurking in the background, watching, clapping, chatting—like me?

Now I'm quitting for the night, still mourning, still smiling.
Judy

It never ends, does it? We're good at hounding prominent white people for wearing black face at fraternity parties, but when it comes to the crime of "Black while jogging" we show our true color—white.
Mary-Lou

Our nation/world is obsessed with race. Why the fuck does it even matter? Heart breaking.
Morgaine

Friday, May 8, 2020
Food, which is always important in this household, has become super important during the pandemic. It doesn't help that both of us are home all day and evening, except when we're out walking or shopping for food. The day builds toward dinner. Hors d'oeuvres are chips dipped in melted nacho cheese, sometimes alternating with crackers and triple creme, accompanied by red wine. A typical dinner, especially on a gloomy day, is a fandango of artery-cloggers: steak; a salad, which sounds healthy, except

when the leafy greens are supporting an entire avocado; and a baked potato that must have sour cream, bacon, cheddar cheese and butter, tucked into its mealy innards. Oh, and a chopped scallion. Then the ice cream. This diet troubles me, but not enough.

Mary-Lou

Saturday, May 9, 2020

The five of us take a ride to the Gillespie Center to drop off bags of food. Then we go to Sasco Beach so Frances can take a photo on her iPad for a science class assignment.

Finish analysis of the valuation for an insurance agency. Their company risk is the highest I'd ever seen.

I get an email from H Salon. They will be reopening soon. Operators will be in full protective gear and customers must wear masks. No waiting area, no restroom, no coffee, tea, or water, and most of all, no hair drying. They will call me to set up an appointment sometime this summer.

It snows briefly around 5:45 PM.

A bouquet of Mother's Day flowers arrives from Maria and Chris.

Delivery from Golden Pizza. The voice on the other end of the phone now calls me by name and keeps saying thank you.

Monica works on kitchen cupboards until 5 AM.

Gina

Saturday, May 9, 2020

I've been sitting at my desk much of the day between a two hour Zoom writing workshop and then revising a chapter in a middle grade novel to send to a writing group that will meet on Tuesday by Zoom. I couldn't believe my eyes when it snowed earlier in the day and as I was on Zoom, I couldn't rush outside to check. I decided the wind was so strong I was seeing petals from a nearby magnolia tree. This afternoon when whatever it was started whipping by again, I went outside to see the snow. I, too, had to take a video. I also needed to feel it on my face after a day inside.

The writing workshop I had today also met Tuesday and Thursday for two hours. There were twenty of us who wrote to a prompt for five or fifteen minutes and then took turns reading aloud. It was a group of writers from all over the country and many I know from previous in-person workshops. The three sessions were a welcome diversion.

I'm impressed with all that the rest of our group can accomplish each day. I think two things that would enhance this at-home experience for me would be a small garden and a cat. This will be my first summer since 1971 that I've not had at least one beloved cat. Twenty-year-old Lexy died last July. I never thought she'd be the one to outlive her sisters and brother. It's so tempting to start all over with an adorable kitten, but I like the freedom and lack of responsibility without a pet. I am jealous, though, of those of you who have a dog or cat for company. I've promised myself when I no longer want to travel, I'll welcome a little feline into my heart.

Yesterday in conversation with a 95-year-old friend who lives on her own in Harvest Commons, she inspired me to get a hummingbird feeder. I never trusted my cats enough to have one. I stopped by Wilton Hardware and bought myself one. Once winter ends (ha!), I'll fill it and hang it out on my deck. Any advice from hummingbird veterans is welcome. They'll be my teeny-tiny, hyper-active companions this summer. We should get along well. We all love sugar.

I try not to be undone by the horrific news of the week. The bizarre snow in May seems to fit right into the pattern of unbelievable events. I can't help but wonder what this pandemic would have been like for us if we'd a real leader in the White House. I also want to believe, that the increased racism, anti-

Semitism, and sharp divisions in our country would have been mitigated by a leader who embraced all Americans. I watched *Becoming* the other night on Netflix and what a pleasure it was to see how adored our former first lady is. Tomorrow it's going up to 60! Good news.

Donna

We used to have a hummingbird feeder with sugar water. We now have a hummingbird sculpture made from recycled wood furniture by New Hope, Pennsylvania artist Adam Capone.
Gina

Saturday, May 9, 2020

This morning we braved 40-degree temperatures and brutal winds. Hardly anyone was at Sherwood Island, which suggests that the sane walkers stayed home. In fact, properly dressed—and we were—the walk was delightful, if bracing. It was so windy that the feathers on the Canada geese were ruffled, but that didn't stop each one of them from dropping its daily pound of green goose poop. Their droppings make for a vigilant walk—lots of side stepping, hopping, and jumping.

"Are Canada geese good for anything, like maybe *fois gras*?" I asked Larry. He's a good person ask such questions, because if he doesn't know the answer, he makes one up that seems reasonable. But this time he drew a blank.

When we got home, I googled "Canadian goose recipes." It turns out their breasts are good for eating, especially with teriyaki sauce, if you add a great number of ingredients such as cabbage, pineapple, and garlic; probably to kill the taste. And forget *fois gras*. Wrong kind of goose.

Mary-Lou

Saturday, May 9, 2020

I've moved from CT to the state of Overwhelmed. It's not the lockdown. Still feel pretty content with its restrictions. Maybe it's karma. If so, I've not lived a good life.

I can testify from the racket in the ceiling above me that squirrels do not get coronavirus. I listen to them and my usual extremely low blood pressure rockets. I heard today that the voice needs to be exercised because we're staying home and talking less. It justifies my screaming at the bushy-tailed assholes to either pay rent or get out. They could care less.

I woke up this morning as an ice cube. I knew immediately that the heat was broken.

All the above adds to the feeling that I will never sell my house or get a job and will end up living with my mother— something that I never found particularly easy to do.

Plus, I risked coronavirus exposure to satisfy my craving for mussels but cooked them a new way. Dismal, inedible failure. If you need a mussel recipe to show you what not to do, I'm happy to share. Just don't make it.

Now I'm about to have a quick Zoom meeting with Miggs Burroughs in advance of a Zoom interview and studio tour showcasing my work. It will become part of the library's *Artists and Residences* project. It's a great way to get my name, work, and website out to the entire library mailing list. I have our illustrious leader to thank for letting me know about the project and making sure Miggs and I got together on it.

Deb

Saturday, May 9, 2020

Yesterday, two months after my son returned home for what was supposed to be a week of spring break, we drove to Syracuse to pick up his belongings; his senior year has come to an anticlimactic end.

Daniel was in the driver's seat for the first 4 ½ hour leg. The only vehicles on the road were delivery trucks and police cars. Was warned of countless speed traps along our route, but my son, having received a speeding ticket his freshman year, obeys the speed limit. I, who drives an average of 80 mph on open road, was at the wheel for the ride home. A sudden snowstorm… *What the hell, it's May,* and faulty windshield wipers slowed me down a wee bit, but better yet the treacherous weather sent law enforcement back to their desks to tally up ticket revenues. While I held steady on the gas pedal, Daniel played Beatles music on Spotify: "Sergeant Pepper," "When I'm 64," "Let It Be," "Blackbird," "Eleanor Rigby," "Yesterday," "Getting Better," "Hey Jude" and on and on. Snow blinding, music blaring we sang together the entire ride home. A road trip to remember. At one point he looks over at me and says, "I love you Mama!"

Today my one cup of coffee had me speeding around the house, cooking, cleaning, running in circles. I need a massage!!!

Morgaine

Sunday, May 10, 2020

Sunday, Mother's Day was our eighth family weekend brunch in quarantine. Daniel made French toast with Trader Joe's brioche (my favorite). Michelle wrote me the most heartfelt poem and created a shadowbox sculpture of our family made from stones.

Morgaine

Monday, May 11, 2020

Item #1—This morning Morgaine and I submitted excerpts from our March and April virallies as assembled by Gina, to the Westport Historical Museum.

Item #2—I'm not happy to tell you that I've been phoning Bernadette for the past 3 days and have only been able to leave a message on her voicemail. I have not heard back.

Item #3—Larry is devoted to spending some of his spare time roaming around on iTunes. Last night he landed on Dame Vera Lynn singing morale-boosting songs associated with World War II. The melody and lyrics to this one brought tears to my eyes: "We'll meet again, don't know where, don't know when, but I know we'll meet again some sunny day."

Mary-Lou

Monday, May 11, 2020

You guys, I'm the worst. I'm so sorry to have alarmed you.

I recently received a diagnosis for yet ANOTHER autoimmune disease—a bonus disease if you will. I'm pissed off that I don't believe in God and can't shake my fist at anyone. I feel robbed.

I've mostly had my phone off and haven't been checking in with the world much.

I'm okay in that I'm not in the hospital stroked out. I'm also not all that okay in that my autoimmune stuff has flared, I'm sleeping all the time, my mental health is iffy at best. I'm sick of being sick, sick of being stressed, and sick of being so mad.

I wish I was feeling better and participating in this email chain but even just checking my email is hard right now. Frankly I'm barely functional.

I'm so sorry to have concerned anyone, and also sorry to be in TAKEN TO MY BED drama queen mode.

This hermit shit is a terrible ancient coping mechanism that I thought I had outgrown. I can't even believe I've reverted to this bs. Sometimes I'm such an asshole.

Super embarrassed to have worried anyone.

Bernadette

Monday, May 11, 2020

So happy to have connected with Bernadette. She has nothing to apologize for. Even in all her pain, she shares a bright, zany spirit with all of us.

Zoom with my sisters, Maggie, and Nell. They are up at Three Lakes, Wisconsin with Maggie's husband, Art setting up the cottage for renters. Nell has brought the Whispering Sisters wine I got at her AAUW auction so we can share it when I come up next summer, if I do.

Gina

Monday, May 11, 2020

My nephew arrived without incident at his new house in Atlanta. Whew!

I talked to a waitperson who used to work here; we became friends when she told me that she'd "only" gotten a B in her college statistics class. I admired her smarts; I talked my way out of a "required" statistics class at Columbia because I knew I'd never get a B and would lose my fellowship money if I got less than that.

I talked to Langston and Rosabelle, the two grandchildren who missed the Zoom meeting yesterday. Langston had been out with this girlfriend planting 600 saplings, a kind of spring festival with social distancing. He's finished his first year in a nursing program. Rosie is writing her last project for the post-graduate boarding school program she was enrolled in. After telling all of us for years that she hated writing, she admitted she sort of, kind of, maybe liked this writing: "What I've learned about being Black at boarding school." I'm glad she couldn't see me grinning.

I started brainstorming with two staff members about how to continue the Meadow Ridge college courses that I've organized for the past two years. My first thought is Zoom but about 1/3 of the population don't have computers. No resolution yet.

I learned that Data Tech was able to retrieve all my data from the malfunctioning hard drive. Among the files is a pen and ink sketch of Bill and me at a private jazz party in 2014. I'd forgotten it was there. It's worth the price of retrieval. Maybe that's the book cover? But I don't know who the artist is.

I finished revising a chapter of the memoir that some of you've seen, *Coupled I,* not an inspiring title. I'd retyped it last week and was preparing mentally to retype all the chapters according to which ones I wanted to work on. I followed some of the comments that you made. It's better than it was but not as good as it can be.

I joined a Zoom meeting of the Unitarians at Meadow Ridge. The topic was *Threshold*s. Three of the women are 90+. Two of them said they were ready for the next threshold, death. I am learning not to try to talk people out of their feelings that I don't want to hear. Instead, I listen and learn and understand that I'll get there soon enough.

Then I joined another Zoom meeting to determine how a group of us will talk about Ibram X. Kendi's book, *How to Be an Anti-Racist*, at the library on Thursday evening. The meeting is already full which scares me since I thought (hoped) only a few people would sign up. Maybe I'll hide my face like I did at the Cornell Black Alumni Association meeting last week. I have to push to finish the book—I do know how to do that.

Judy

Tuesday, May 12,2020

Larry is getting antsy. We will need paper towels in a few days, and our 1 cup Pyrex measurer is broken. We already took our walk today and stopped at Trader Joe's for my favorite bag of salad, which was out of stock, plus milk, eggs, avocados, bananas, flowers and hot dogs and headed home.

An hour later, Larry determined to go to the hardware store to replace the 1 cup broken measurer. (We have another 1 cup measurer, but Larry didn't want to hear about that. He wanted "out," although we promised ourselves at the beginning of the pandemic that we would severely limit our outing to a walk and once a week shopping.)

I balked. "It's bad enough that we went shopping; that's always a risk." He insisted. I finally talked him out of it by escalating into my drama queen mode. "Maybe you don't care of you die, but I care if I die." That did it for now, until I stupidly told Larry that I have a salon appointment on May 22 for a cut and color. He pounced, even though Gov. Lamont has given me permission.

Busted.

Mary-Lou

Tuesday, May 12, 2020

Wake to the sound of a wooden jackhammer. Seems to be coming from the yard next door.

One of the masks I ordered weeks ago arrives today. We pass on the giveaways at Bedford Middle School this morning.

Ordered printer ink from Staples. They were out of stock on XL, so I had to get regular. Getting supplies is a challenge with so much out of stock.

Get email from Stitch Fix and order a pair of pants that I don't need. Did I do it for the entertainment value, or what?

My sister Nell emailed me a list of books from the cottage that she and Maggie are planning to donate to the Three Lakes Library. Many titles are from the early 1900s through 1935. Some were even from the late 1800s. Musty. No one has opened them for years. I asked for a few that were gifts between my parents.

The American Society of Association Executives is canceling its August meeting. The Republicans are not. Get a bill from The ESOP Association today. My dues have gone up from $400 to $675.

Gina

This guy wakes me up many mornings with his jackhammering! He bangs on the gutter too, like a steel drum. That must hurt.

Lynn

Tuesday, May 12, 2020

We hadn't heard from Polly for a while, so I reached out to a mutual friend for news. Polly is recuperating and doing well but doesn't have the energy to join us in these exchanges. We miss her but it is comforting knowing she is OK.

Ken

Tuesday, May 12, 2020

I'm still having a problem with time, as if I'm perpetually going through a Daylight Savings adjustment, except I'm springing forward whole days instead of one hour. I feel like Rip Van Winkle: I worry that by the time the all-clear is sounded, I will be sporting a long white beard of un-tweezed chin hair and I won't know what the hell happened.

It's sunny and windy and the breeze smells like lilacs, and I can almost be happy—if I can stop thinking about the future, and the people dying, and 45's unhinged-ness. For many days, I've been able to keep a lot of it at bay. I stay upbeat, I think small. If I get to have a latte, I count the day as a success. But lately I fear I'm faltering. I find myself thinking, "I've got a bad feeling about this." I worry that more people are going to get very sick. I worry that unemployment is going to be a difficult problem to fix, along with hunger, homelessness, and poverty. Those problems were not solvable before, under better circumstances. How's it going to go now? I worry that people will disconnect from each other even more and view each other as threats. I worry that we will forget how to smile at each other from behind our masks. I worry about the election in November.

And I worry about the sun, as I have for a few years now. When I was a child, I could be outside, all day, in SPF 8, and not even tan. Now, 15 minutes in the yard without SPF 30, and I pay for it across my nose. The light seems glaringly bright. My husband thinks I'm nuts. I squint at the sky and worry.

And then, I stuff it all to the back of the closet and try not to think about it. I can ostrich with the best of them. Fingers in the ears, la la la, I'm not listening. I go back to playing video games, and baking, and coloring, and marching, and I try, again, to hope for the best.

Lynn

Stages of Quarantine

Ditto. The pandemic has grotesquely magnified everything that has been wrong with this country: racial divisions, economic insecurity, healthcare, greed as epitomized by Greenwich CT and Westport, corruption, to shootings, to burgeoning anti-Semitism, to disrespect for the truth, to gerry-

mandering and suppressing the vote, to recog-nizing climate change, to women's rights, to fill in the blanks, unless you're as depressed as you care to be. There are many more. And presiding over the brutal shredding of America is Donald Trump whose approval rate is still in the 40s. How can that be?

Mary-Lou

Tuesday, May 12, 2020
You need a morning smile…
Ken

Wednesday, May 13, 2020
Nell sends me an email with a picture of documents she found from 1991 relating to a condo transaction that never took place. I tell her to shred them. My sisters are cleaning up a lot of shit that has been in the family since my grandmother bought the cottage in 1946. My two sisters now own it and hope to rent it out to pay for replacing the roof.

Place delivery order with Peapod. The earliest slot I can get is Sunday, May 24th. I take it. I can always change it up until the day before.

Get delivery within the hour from Fresh Market—second one this week. Many items not available. The "Sinfully White Cake" is SO GOOD. I finally figured out that bulk items like nuts and candy from bins are not available. No touching the scoops, etc. No olive bar, either. I try to game the system by ordering what I couldn't get from Whole Foods Market via Amazon Smile.

My Stitch Fix pants arrive. Don't need them. I really like them. Glad I got them.

Gina

Wednesday, May 13, 2020

I apologize for being a minimalist contributor to our (your) growing collection of interesting, wonderful accounts of life under quarantine. Let me bring you up to date.

I have never had less to do but unaccountably, the time flies by. We have been in lockdown for weeks, but it seems like only a few days. I have little evidence of what I did with the time and even less recollection of it. For a short interlude, my reading pile shrunk but it has been restored. My backyard birds and squirrels have never been happier. The mallard family and Canadian geese couple that reside across the river have become parents. The local beaver seems to be constructing a small obstruction that attracts the interest of sporadic kayakers and fishermen. Most days it is noon before I realize the morning is gone. If there is any consequential guilt, another distraction relieves me of it.

As much as I love my friends, I don't look forward to Zooming with them beyond learning they are safe; small talk is not something I enjoy and the inevitable inclusion of something involving Trump is depressing.

Apart from the hour I spend each morning absorbing the depressing news, I am managing the ensuing guilt, concern, and frustration well.

With Lynn's encouragement, I am learning how to bake bread from scratch so I can surprise Sam with a homemade sample on her birthday next week. My trial run included buying Trader Joe's beer bread, managing to mix the ingredients, turning on the oven, and not spilling it on the floor; so, come the 21st, I may be ready for the real thing.

Notwithstanding all the above, I am still involved with real world matters. Most days I get calls and emails from clients, though fewer than in the past, which if I can, I refer to my partners, an arrangement that works for all of us. I remain a legal advisor to six not-for-profits, something that is rewarding for me and by their accounts helpful to them.

We are all so blessed. Hugs to all of you,

Ken

Wednesday, May 13, 2020

So nice to hear from you and know that I haven't dropped off your radar screens. I read your entries which remind me that there is a near-normal in this way of living—complaining, being grateful, and eating—mostly the eating part.

I continue to recover, slowly though it may be. My visiting nurse discharged me from her care yesterday and I drove to the drug store, although at 20 MPH which infuriated other drivers. I am getting weaned off the massive doses of prednisone. That's the upside.

My husband had fallen and cracked a rib while I was in the hospital. Our roles are now reversed as I am doing most of the caretaking, cooking etc. while he recovers. His cardio issues are recurring, so that means tele-visits with his cardiologist. We do NOT want him to have to go to the hospital.

The two weeks I was in complete quarantine at home have given me the strength to do what needs to be done here but on a minimal basis. We will get through this—there is no other way to think. Our son and daughter have been immensely supportive. They drive two hours each way to deliver our groceries but are not allowed in the house. We're in a protective bubble for now—no one comes in; no one goes out. I intend to start curbside pickup at our local grocery store next week.

Yes, I have much to write and will do so sooner or later. Right now, it takes too much energy/stamina to work on it, but fear not, it's all in my head and ain't going away soon.

So, keep including me in your virallies. I will continue to read them and may interject a few thoughts now and then. And yes, now that our days are calming down, I can see the boredom/restrictions trying to take hold of my psyche. Your descriptions give me an understanding of what to expect. With that said, I continue to be grateful that I came through that dark tunnel and am hopeful that I will make a full recovery to what will be a new and more simple way of living, but I am alive, didn't have to go on a respirator and am surrounded by caring and thoughtful people.

Please take care of yourselves and don't rush this return to living as we used to know it. What angers me most these days is seeing people flaunt the rules, face masks and social distancing. When they get the Covid virus, and some will, they will demand/expect the same fine care I received in the hospital.

Polly

Wednesday, May 13, 2020

I went to Trader Joe's today with no line. I went a little crazy getting food for the summer. I didn't even get hives of anxiety while shopping. Everyone was masked, and it didn't have the hushed, foreboding feel it did when I went five weeks ago. How did that much time slide by?!

Sunshine and a walk at Sherwood also lift the spirits. AND—I got my Compo Beach sticker in the mail. As a Westport teacher for forty years, it didn't matter that I lived in Weston or currently in Wilton. A beach sticker always feels like a nice perk.

Zoom with four sisters at 5:00. A perk of Covid-19.

Donna

Wednesday, May 13, 2020

We opened the pool today—an act of optimism that verges on the insane. Temperatures, for the most part, have been way below normal—remember the snow a couple of days ago?—and yet we hope that climate change will give us something resembling summer. We built the pool 45 years ago when our children were young. It was for them, not for us. We were young and devoted to long swims at the Y, doing laps, or in the Sound, swimming from the cannons to the jetty and back. Now, 4 ½ decades later and that much older, it is we who look forward to swimming in our smallish backyard pool. We turn the heat on June 1. Ally ally in free!

Our shoulders are shot, even the cortisone injections don't work the way they used to, and we are humbled and a bit amused by the way the wheel has turned full circle. Now we're the old folks, struggling, as our kids did, to make it from one end to the other.

Today, while the pool was busy filtering itself—it won't be ready to swim in for a few days—we sat poolside, six feet apart, chatting with old friends in 60-degree sunshine, drinking water from plastic cups and taking turns stabbing plump strawberries with toothpicks. It was such a pleasure to be un-virtual. What's missing from Zoom or even FaceTime is the totally lack of intimacy, even 6-foot apart intimacy. It was one of the finest pandemic days ever and it served to remind us of the joys of friendship.

Mary-Lou

Wednesday, May 13, 2020

Because my high school, Hackley, is not having a traditional graduation, the head of the Alumni Office sent an email out to older (really just OLD) graduates to reply with advice on life to share with graduates. I couldn't resist the invitation to reply.

Below is what I submitted. Much of this is borrowed from what I absorbed from a Westport business friend… there is nothing new. I claim no unique perspective! The "nothing good happens after midnight," I absorbed from the speaker at my grandson's graduation from middle school. The one "don't miss an opportunity to be kind" is a learned one. Did I miss anything you would have added??

Business advice:

1. Under promise, over perform.
2. Arriving 15 minutes early is arriving on time, arriving on time is late, and arriving late is unacceptable.
3. Treat school like a job... get up early, take early classes, go to bed at a decent hour.
4. Everything is an interview.
5. First impressions are lasting impressions.
6. Read everything you can.
7. Be prepared for meetings, don't "wing it."
8. Ask follow-up questions.
9. Never pretend to know something you don't. Say, I'll check on that and get back to you.
10. Send a personal thank you letter. No abbreviations. Spell everything correctly. Send it the same day.
11. For boys, always wear a dark suit, crisp white shirt, conservative tie, good but not fancy shoes. No cufflinks, no suspenders, no expensive watch, or jewelry. For girls, something akin.
12. Never sign anything you haven't read. If your signature is on something, you own it.
13. Don't screw up. You know what that means.
14. Be humble.
15. Be careful about what you put on Facebook. Nothing online goes away.

Personal advice:

16. You can't get if you don't ask. Be polite but not shy.
17. Everyone is insecure, you are not alone. Don't let your insecurities handicap you.
18. Almost nothing good happens after midnight.

19. Set goals and keep them in mind when making even daily decisions. You can always change them, but don't forget them.
20. Never pass up an opportunity to be kind.
21. If you pass a test, over time, you probably won't remember it. If you get caught cheating, it will scar you forever.

Ken

Son and Mother. Breathe no evil. See no evil.

Gina

That's hilarious! So sly of you.
Mary-Lou

Thursday, May 14, 2020

I have been in Slumpsville. Not feeling like writing. Not feeling like doing much of anything. Even so far as to let a thin layer of dust cover the furniture. Today is a new day, however. I forced myself to do yoga with Jack, and glad I did and now I'm going to enjoy a strong cup of coffee before meandering around my garden, possibly pull some weeds, perhaps just enjoy the beauty of my years of tending to it.

Inspired by Mary-Lou's poolside happy hour with friends, I invited a couple to *our* poolside to share a bottle of wine. We all agreed we need to do this more often. I managed to avoid CNN and the like. Most of the day was spent pulling weeds and trimming shrubs. The dust will have to wait for tomorrow.

Morgaine

Thursday, May 14, 2020

Today, a friend I haven't seen since February invited me to socially-distance walk with her and her dog in Weston. I went. It was beautiful. Weston is *the country* compared to Westport. I'd never been there, aside from the post office. My friend lives on top of a hill and on our walk, I saw craggy cliffs, a waterfall, a herd of deer, a black frog, a fox, and too many chipmunks to count. The chipmunks riled up my friend's beagle/basset hound, and the dog kept making a pathetic whine like, "I wants! I wants!"

It was so lovely to see my friend. She is the first person to invite me to do anything since mid-March. I wonder if people are afraid to meet, or if they were sick of me anyway and social distancing was a welcome break. I teased my friend and called her "my gateway drug back into society." I had so much to say to her, my throat hurt. I already long for another playdate. I'm like the whiny beagle: Who can I see next?! Who can I see next?! I wants!

My husband got into poison ivy last weekend. He's highly allergic and is miserable. The calamine lotion we had in the linen closet expired in 2007. We had two tabs of Benadryl in the first aid kit. They probably expired in 2005. For some reason, my husband has decided that it's okay for me to walk with my friend, and it's okay for me to go to Whole Foods, but CVS and Walgreens cross a line, and he is adamant that I should not go. He stands there arguing with me, while scratching his arms like a crazy person. I decided that he can be adamant, and I can do what I like.

So, on my way to pick up Indian takeout lunch today, I stopped at CVS in Norwalk. There was a man outside, panhandling. He had a mask on, and he asked me for a dollar. I lied and said I had no cash. To give him some would have meant getting too close. I felt bad about it. He told me to have a nice day. I wished him the same. I drove home, thinking I should have given him the money.

As I turned into my driveway, my husband came out to greet me. He laid down in the grass, flung his itchy arm onto the blacktop, and said, "Please. Make it stop. Just cut it off. Run it over. End my misery."

Oh, the drama! I rolled my window all the way down and hollered, "Come a little closer! Get your whole head in there! If we're doing this, we're doing it right!" He looked alarmed and stood up. I pulled the car all the way in and hucked the box of Benadryl at him as I drove past, but I carried in the calamine lotion like a civilized person.

Lynn

Friday, May 15, 2020
Today was another weeding frenzy. Three hours in the garden, digging madly with claw, trowel, clippers, and rake. Again, I threw myself into it and will no doubt pay the "Help! I can't get up" and "Help, I can't get down" price tomorrow morning. But while I was furiously digging out and pulling out unwanted ivy and Japanese anemone by the fistful—I filled an entire garbage can—I was reminded of a conversation I had at a party with a guy at college decades ago. I didn't know him, but he seemed lonely, so I approached him. We chatted for a while until I realized that he was boring, and I was regretting that I'd engaged him since it seemed as if I were in charge of keeping things going, not a job I'd signed up for. Desperate, I asked him what he wanted to do after

he graduated. He replied that he wanted to be a dentist. I couldn't imagine why anyone would want to be a dentist.

"Tell me," I asked. "Why do you want to be a dentist?"

His entire demeanor changed. Suddenly he was interested. His eyes lit up. He learned toward me. "Because," he said with great energy, "I hate decay."

I feel the same way about weeds. I can't get enough of digging down and yanking them out.

Mary-Lou

Friday, May 15, 2020

Today, on our walk, my husband gave a heavy sigh and said, "Well. This is about the least amount of fun you could have while still having fun." That made me laugh. A few steps on, he put his blistered, rashy, disgusting arms out in front of him, lolled his head to one side and started walking down the street making zombie noises. I followed in kind, except my arms looked pretty. We did our *Walking Dead* act past a few houses until our neighbor's dog went ballistic, charged the fence, and scared the hell out of us. We jumped and clutched each other, laughing. My husband said, "Wow. That dog *really* doesn't like zombies."

We might have had a little more fun than the least amount.

Lynn

Friday, May 15, 2020

My state of mind equals how busy I keep myself.

Today began with a drive to the Westport yard waste facility where I emptied the truck load of tree branches I dismantled last week. Home by 9 AM, I had a cup of "Rev" coffee and then went for a run, a mile and a half loop through the neighborhood.

Without showering I geared up for a shopping trip to Costco and arrived before the doors opened. After 15 minutes in line the caffeine on an empty stomach had kicked in; I went racing through the isles like a supermarket sweep. An hour later I was following the arrows at ShopRite where I completed my grocery list. I was home, at the sink singing Happy Birthday by noon. With clean hands I put the groceries away, had my smoothie and was out in the garden with my wheelbarrow digging out the roots of the uninvited. It was 3:15 by the time I showered and collapsed in front of the TV where I watched the final episode of season one of *Succession*. It did not disappoint. A margarita topped off the day.

State of mind: *EXCELLENTÉ!*
Morgaine

Saturday, May 16, 2020

Home Colleagues,

I am going to do what I usually don't do, make a TV recommendation. On Netflix we just finished watching Ricky Gervais' series called, *After Life*. It is a light comedy filled with pathos. Gervais wrote, produced and stars in it. The basic theme is Ricky's wife has just died and the plot is how he deals with the loss. It is sentimental without being maudlin and the characters are unusual and interesting. Sam and I loved it. There you go, I did it.
Ken

Saturday, May 16, 2020

Sorry I've been MIA. The last two days have been stressful, but I didn't know it until I stayed in bed today until noon, wondering why I was so tired, why I didn't have the energy to get up.

I went through the usual questions since I still don't know myself all that well.

"Did you have too much to drink last night?" No, just the usual one glass of wine, but maybe my system is not used to alcohol since I ran out of wine on Tuesday and the liquor store delivers on Friday.

"Too many carbs?" Probably, since I'm watching my tummy expand. Meadow Ridge delivers a roll and butter with each dinner, and I feel compelled to eat the roll. I could cancel the bread, but I'd feel deprived. I could also freeze it. Perhaps tonight I will.

"Worried about money?" Of course. Talked to one of two financial planners this week. She sold a fund that was tanking. Do I need the cash, or should I reinvest? I don't know. She's more solicitous than the other CFP; should I switch everything to her? I conclude I should look at performance. This is not a popularity contest.

Then I remembered the probable causes of the exhaustion. I overprepared for the Westport Library discussion on Kendi's book on Thursday night. Being super prepared has always been my answer to doubting my abilities, to the voice that says, "You're not that smart, you just work harder than everybody else." I have no proof that either statement is true, but those beliefs drive me.

P.S. I got all the information back from the corrupted external drive—the book! The pictures! The tax info! Yeah!!

Judy

Ah for the days of typewriters, where the hardest job was changing the ribbon and the only downside was waiting for Wite-Out to dry. We didn't know what we were missing. Now we do.

Mary-Lou

Saturday, May 16, 2020

I have been MIA also. Lots to do this past week.

For Mother's Day I had a first sighting of my mother since early March. That's pretty much what it was, with me in the driveway and her propped on her wheelchair in the front doorway. It made her happy. Like a child, she doesn't understand the pandemic and why I don't visit.

For my bereavement group I was tasked with writing a letter from David to me, telling me what he would hope for my life without him. I found it hard to separate my voice from his. It kept sounding as if I were putting words into his mouth. But the more I started over, the more I could hear him talking to me, could remember things he said during our many years together and in his last five months. His voice, his bare bones phrasing, his inability to not crack a joke about hard truths, all came back to me. I even heard him anticipating my reactions to his words.

I knew, of course, what he would have wanted for me. Nothing new there. But there was an odd comfort in hearing his voice in my mind, talking as though we were sitting together on the couch. As "he" addressed the big decisions and changes in my life, I felt calmed by his support, just as I had when I realized he was *that* guy, my guy.

Deb

Sunday, May 17, 2020

It is exactly two months—MARCH 17th—since I wrote my first virally. A lot has happened and yet nothing at all.

I recently learned that my precious Riley has diskospondylitis (an age-related spinal deformity.) Sounds like me with osteoporosis. Besides backaches, we share a birthday, January 31st. I love my fur-ball!!!

It's almost mulch time. I've recruited the help of Daniel, who sits at a computer for most of the day and Michelle's boyfriend, Greg, whose weightlifting regimen since he left NY consists of a fork to his mouth. I don't think either of them realize what a job it is to shovel and wheelbarrow 15 yards of mulch to the various gardens around the property. Of course, I will be the one to *spread* the mulch, as it must be done right. Such a control freak!

I've been thinking about inviting the family to join me in a fast. Not long, four or five days maybe, where we would each give up our individual vices since being quarantined. For Daniel it would be screens, Mark the game Dots on his phone, Michelle her nightly cocktail, Greg weed, and me... it would have to be cleaning. Would that include not making the bed? I don't know if I could do it.

Word has it Michelle and Greg are letting go of their NYC apartment; the lease expires on July 1. It makes sense; it's costing them $2,500 a month and there's nothing there for them anymore. They'll be moving their stuff into the basement in June, and it will be official, Daniel, Michelle and Greg will be living with us. Who was it that asked when the pandemic really hit you? It's now hitting me on a whole new level.

Morgaine

Sunday, May 17, 2020

I hope you all received the backyard photos sent from my iPad. Too exhausted to say mulch this evening, except to note that mulch is a serious annual expense around here, and I'm beginning to resent it. In the fall we must rake out the leaves from the beds, or at least we think we do. The mulch leaves with the leaves, and so it goes, year after year. There's not mulch more to say, except that after 3 days of weeding and mulching, Larry and I, who have been living in this house for 52 years, paying for snowplowing, window washing, lawn mowing, tree and bush pruning, painting were pitched into yet another very serious "should we move to a condo" conversation.

Mary-Lou

Sunday, May 17, 2020

It seems I've not been alone in being MIA, and I don't really know why I haven't participated in our communal news, except that I've not been in a good place, and I hadn't anything worthwhile or jolly to say. Things are the same, the condo gets vacuumed, dusted, I eat, I wash clothes, I feed Archie, I read. But inside, I can't get out of my own way. One thing that doesn't help is my computer acting up. Just now, I was going back to read any virally I'd missed and for no accountable reason, the emails are presented as if I mean to delete them. WTF?! Then, I'll type something, and I'm advised, the email can't be sent. Again, WTF!? I give up, I let the machine "rest." What I really feel like doing is throwing it out the window. Except for virallies and a few messages from other friends, emails are mostly ads or donation requests, many of them political. No matter how often I unsubscribe, they don't stop.

I was happy to hear that Bernadette, while still not well, is better, as is Polly.

The back of the condo building, that includes my unit, abuts town land and it seems that that space has been used as somewhat of a dumping ground for leftover bricks and concrete blocks, broken jars, along with Nature's own debris. But there, among all the weeds and debris is a patch of what I learned is ajuga, which for the last two years has adorned my view with small, perky dark blue/purple spikes of flowers. I fertilized them and I hope they know that I'm rooting for them. (Ha, ha.) A gardener I'm not so I limit myself to pot gardening. Last year I had some lovely pots blooming—until the deer found them. This year, my pots contain succulents, which I love in any case. So far, the deer have left them alone.

I wish you all a happy Sunday, a safe Sunday, and for Bernadette and Polly, continuous healing. Hugs to all,

Maria

Sunday, May 17, 2020

Yesterday, for dinner, we grilled—shish kebabs and veggie dogs. It was the first time we had used the grill in almost two years, so it needed a thorough going-over. The grill had become a hotel for spiders and stinkbugs, and my no-kill-policy-husband kept flicking them into the shrubs as he cleaned.

I also subscribe to the no-kill policy, but it is nice to have help. Inside the house, I leave spiders if I find them, or encourage the creepier ones out the window; Brian is usually the one called upon to catch all manner of other insects in Tupperware and take them outside. Except for ants. We both hate ants and relish their demise. Our son subscribes to the "I hate all bugs and am blessed with parents who will get them out of my sight" policy. I wonder what he'll do when he's out on his own.

As I was typing this story, my son walked in and said, so sweetly, "Mom, can I get your help with something?" He led me to his room and pointed at a stinkbug lurking on his ceiling. He said, "I will never be able to sleep with that guy up there!" This time I was the one who went and got the Tupperware. Be free, stinkbug! Be free! My son had better find a nature loving life-partner, or at least someone braver than he is.

Anyway, watching my husband flick the bugs off the grill reminded me of a story from almost 20 years ago: Brian and I had just started dating. We were working at the same soulless investment bank, and we were having lunch in the cafeteria with a hundred other people, when a little brown mouse ran across the blue carpet. The crowd in the lunchroom panicked. It was like people doing the wave at a sporting event: each person stood up as the mouse ran past. Choruses of, "Kill it! Kill it" erupted. Traders were trying to stomp on it or hit it with trays. The mouse ran for its life. My husband—then boyfriend—stepped out of the crowd and caught the mouse in a coffee cup. He took it out on the terrace and released it, much to everyone's awe.

I remember feeling so amazed at that moment: that he could be so kind; so gentle; that the mouse practically ran right to him, like he was the Pied Piper; that he stood up to a bunch of murderous frat boys to save a field mouse. It was the first time I knew, for sure, that he was special. I almost told him then that I loved him, but I was too shy, and I didn't want him to think I was weird.

So, tonight, nearly twenty years later, I thought I would tell him. I said, "I was thinking about the time you caught the mouse at UBS."

He said, "I remember that."

I said, "I loved you that day."

He gave me a sly smile and said, "I know."

Lynn

I may sound like Gypsy Rose Lee's pushy stage mother, but the mouse story would make a great, short "Modern Love Story" for the NYTimes. As for Brian, is it okay if we fall a tiny bit in love with him?

Mary-Lou

I'm with you on live and let live except for cockroaches. In Florida they're called palmetto bugs and they're huge, and they fly! Everyone has a limit and that's where my loving kindness stops.

We once had a gecko in our bathroom in Florida. He wouldn't cooperate and let me take him outdoors. We had one of those spa tubs with an overhang around the top and the little bugger kept hiding under there That tub was never used, we liked showers instead, so I set out some pieces of lettuce and a bottle cap of water. Geckos were always getting into the house, and I'd find them all dried up in some corner when I vacuumed. I was determined this one wouldn't die a slow thirsty death. He

disappeared one day and I never did find him. Guess he didn't like the menu.
Maria

Monday, May 18, 2020
Yesterday evening I heard a robin sing as I walked up the hill. The birdsong brought to mind the springs I'd had in my childhood home in Jamaica, Queens, NY. I knew that robin song and the song I learned from my mother about it.

"I heard a robin sing today / 'Cheer up, cheer up, cheer up'/ No matter skies be clear or gray / 'Cheer up, cheer up, cheer up.' "

I heard the robins singing then, when I woke up in the morning. I heard it when I went to bed before dark at 7 PM. I heard it when my father pushed the hand lawn mower against our front lawn that sloped to the sidewalk. The cut grass accumulated in a bag open at one end to receive it; I inhaled that sweet smell, wishing I were outside rather than in bed. He dumped the grass cuttings behind our one car garage, I think, but I'm not sure of that. I know there was no compost heap, just a grass heap somewhere.

My sister and I knew that spring had come when my father took the rolled-up canvas awning out of the garage, spreading it on the grass in our backyard and hosing it down to dislodge the spiders that had wintered in its folds. Once it dried, he and my grandfather stood on ladders to hoist it up onto the awning frame attached, at a slant, to our house. They unrolled the awning, starting in the front and reaching higher and higher until it met the back of the house, just above the first story windows. Using special rope, they lashed the sides and the front of the awning to its frame. The awning's scalloped edges hung over the frame, concealing the girding that supported it.

Yesterday the robin reminded me of that ritual. I did my own small part to welcome spring. I scrubbed down the patio furniture and laid out the rug that turns the patio into a kind of extra room. Then I put out the potted geranium whose faint scent I've never liked but whose flowers are generous, a gift from Meadow Ridge for Mother's Day. Voila! Spring has arrived.

Judy

Monday, May 18th

New York florists who, because of the pandemic, have lots of leftover blooms, generously decorated the public cityscape. Here's just one example of their big-hearted bounty.

Mary-Lou

Monday, May 18, 2020

Yes, I did… take out the trash, water plants and do laundry before our PFS team call. Finished the valuation analysis that I started yesterday. Got a delivery within an hour of placing it from Fresh Market. You get what you get, and you don't get upset! No ground sirloin, red onion, raspberries, dark chocolate almonds, mini corn muffins, or glazed vanilla donut holes. My latest technique is to order more than I need, expecting that I will not get a lot of it.

I had no tortillas on hand, so I make a taco hot dish instead using taco seasoning in the ground sirloin and adding a packet of black beans and peppers that I had made and frozen. The kids love the Fritos corn chips and cheese topping.

Gina

Monday, May 18, 2020

Highlight: Power planting with Bob Marley blasting on my little Bluetooth speaker. Sun, black soil, squirmy worms, mingled scents of my favorite herbs.

Work: Finished the header and footer for Stephanie Thomas' campaign video.

Low point: Television set caught "Covid" and succumbed. Sound, but no picture.

Love prevails: Arlo running and squeaky barking in his sleep as he dreams at my feet.

Deb

Monday, May 18, 2020

Today was a declared day of rest for both of us. No gardening. No walking at Sherwood Island. Lots of reading and some emailing. Later this afternoon I gave Larry a much-needed haircut. Turned out pretty well considering I didn't know what I was doing.

Can you tell I haven't got much to say? Do you want to know what we ate for dinner? Of course, you don't.

Maybe this will be of greater interest. I'm a fan of a daily news report called WTF, as in What————. Remember those armed Yahoos who gathered to protest continued closings? Well, here's what WTF had to report about them. *"Cellphone location data suggests that demonstrators at anti-lockdown protests may have spread coronavirus hundreds of miles after returning to all parts of their states. The anonymized location data was captured from opt-in cellphone apps and was used it to track the movements of devices present at protests in late April and early May in Michigan, Wisconsin, Illinois, Colorado, and Florida." (The Guardian)*

So how do I process this information? Two ways. "Serves them right" and "C'mon, we're talking about human beings here."

Mary-Lou

Monday, May 18, 2020

When the kids were young, to help encourage them to pick up

after themselves I invented "the box of no return." If an item was left on the floor, draped over a bar stool or outside the closet where it belongs, it went into the old chest at that top of the stairs, never to be seen again. The kids' treasures eventually resurfaced, but it wasn't overnight. Michelle learned her lesson when her Uggs went into the big wooden box; as for Daniel it was a miniature skateboard that he played with for hours, weaving it through his fingers, spinning its wheels and launching it from every surface.

This morning I tacked a list of chores on the refrigerator. Next to each one I made a box for initialing, to see who has done what. This was not some passive aggressive move on my part. Everyone knew the list was coming, in fact they welcomed it. The initials were Michelle's idea.

I did an hour of yoga, had my kale smoothie, and went out in the garden. I didn't come back in until two in the afternoon. Michelle was at the counter pulling ingredients from the fridge to make turkey sandwiches, the first task on the list.

"I'm not exactly sure how you do it," she says, "but I'll figure it out."

"Why don't we make them together," I say. "This way you'll know to toast the bread and always put cheese on before the tomato, so the bread won't get soggy." *Is this me being helpful or controlling and methodical?*

I walk by the fridge and glance at the list. To my surprise every other box is initialed. Chores are done. We could be onto something now that we're all living together for the unforeseen future.

Morgaine

Monday, May 18, 2020

With five kids, we had alternating chore systems. Alternating because we were advised that systems only hold up for a few months. The first, *Chore du Jour* assigned a particular chore to each child for a week. Chores would rotate on a weekly basis. The second was *Groom a Room*, where each child would be assigned a room and need to perform the necessary cleaning for the week.

And then, always, we had *The Dungeon*. Each child had a basket cubby in which they could leave things downstairs in public territory. But anything that was left around and not stored in the cubby, went into a brown paper bag with a name and date. The bag was stapled shut and put in the basement. It could not be retrieved until the date marked on the bag. Not under any circumstances. Your homework? Sorry. Your winter coat? Better wear a lotta layers. Your point shoes? You'll have to explain to your ballet teacher. No exceptions. A few items remanded to The Dungeon and the downstairs remained tidy.

Deb

Monday, May 18, 2020

That is a good idea and a great incentive if you don't want to have something you treasure go missing. It sounds like it worked. In my defense, I will say that at the end of each week, I did clean my room and as I got older, helped my mom clean the apartment—she was a demon about cleanliness! I remember one time a mouse got into the apartment and Mom ran around with a broom chasing the poor creature. (We could have used Lynn's Brian that time.) She never caught it, but it never showed its face again—must have crawled back where it felt safer.

A former boss said I was anal about things. Well, sometimes. I used to be messy as a kid. You could tell what I'd worn all week by looking at the clothes I dropped over my chair. I'm not tidy about all things, just some things, and sometimes I throw things in a drawer—if you don't see the mess it doesn't exist, right? That would be like if we don't perform Covid tests, then the number of

cases is low, right?
Maria

Monday, May 18, 2020

I am so impressed with your very creative methods of discipline. I just remember a few rules for the household of three daughters and a dog.

After I found a half-full glass of moldy orange juice in one of their bedrooms, one rule was "no food in the bedrooms." That seemed to work, or else they cleaned it up before I found it.

Another was that I would only wash clothes that I found in their hampers. If it was anywhere else—the floor, a chair, under a bed—it wouldn't get washed. "You have no clean underwear? Oh, well."

But they didn't need to keep their rooms straight; all they had to do was close the door so I wouldn't see the mess.

Toys were permitted in the playroom, not the living room (Marty and I needed a space where we could sit.) Each night we picked up the toys and put them willy-nilly into a toy box. If a toy had small pieces, its owner would have to stow it somewhere—I don't remember where—Lego pieces were always escaping our notice.

Our Labrador retriever was not allowed in the living room or downstairs (the main level of the house was on the 2nd floor). We let her outside through the door off the playroom. She learned to sit on the door sill that led to each room, wagging her tail and looking mournful.

Nor could she ever, ever sit on the furniture. I reasoned that she was a dog, not a person. One day I went up to Jill's room—my youngest daughter fed, walked, and trained her—and found her asleep on Jill's bed rather than in her cage, probably a common practice. When I grabbed her collar and ordered her off, she growled at me! We had a very serious heart-to-heart that day and she never growled at me again. As for sleeping on Jill's bed, who knows?

I also labeled the fruit that had inedible skins—bananas, oranges. Once I found that Jill would eat two bananas and then claim she hadn't—there was one piece of fruit per person per week—I only had time to shop weekly. That worked moderately well.

We kind of made up the rules as seemed appropriate since we didn't really know what we were doing. Think it's known as muddling through!

Judy

Monday, May 18, 2020

I'm so impressed by the various creative ways in which you disciplined your kids. Our son, Adam, had to be well-disciplined, because our household had to orbit around his younger brother Peter. For many years the situation was demanding and chaotic and he bore more of his share earlier in his life than was good for him. He married a woman for whom neatness and discipline were not a priority, and I mean that in the nicest possible way. As a result, his three children are slobs and Adam who no doubt suffered from too much discipline, is the person in the house who's in charge of picking up, putting away and cleaning. He waits until his wife and kids are elsewhere and goes at it hammer and tongs.

Mary-Lou

Monday, May 18, 2020

If you have never heard Adm. William McRaven's commencement speech, I highly recommend that you go to YouTube. It is terrific. He recites the 10 lessons he learned becoming a navy SEAL. The first lesson was the importance of making your bed each morning and he explains why. He wrote a book, *Make Your Bed* which is terrific.

Whenever we have young guests staying over, they are told that we have one rule, "You must make your bed." It amazes me how many of them confess that they rarely do that.

Ken

Monday, May 18, 2020

Hmmm... Did Monica have company last night? Her bed is not made.

Mine is. It always is.

I never get dressed without first making my bed. We six kids always made our own beds growing up. I don't ever remember seeing an unmade bed anyplace, anywhere unless the sheets were being changed. My grandmothers, great aunts, and aunts never had unmade beds. Even the beds at Gram's lake cottage were always made. I never saw an unmade bed at any of my friends' houses either when we'd have sleepovers. The homes of all my siblings also have made beds. After my mother died many years ago, my father always made his own bed.

When Stan and I were first married, we had a Murphy bed, which had to be folded up and closeted in a wall in our apartment living room. Over the years there were more Murphy beds and hide-a-beds to come.

When my kids were little and I was a stay-at-home mom for a few years, I always made up all the beds before starting the household chores for the day. Leaving a bed with rumpled sheets and blankets would drive me nuts. I love the serenity of getting into a bed with smoothed sheets, blankets, and a pretty spread.

And yes, my closets and bureau drawers are organized down to the last pair of shoes or earrings. I know where to find everything.

As for my kids and grandkids... that's a different story. My paramedic son and his nurse wife have often worked night shifts. My son was on call as a volunteer firefighter and often had to leave on a moment's notice when his buzzer went off. Monica makes a gorgeous bed with artfully draped throws and sparkly pillows when she's in the mood. Maria almost always makes her bed, but her two teenagers never leave their rooms.

The three granddaughters with whom I live almost never make their beds, although twelve-year-old Ryan can make up a really neat, perfectly made bed when she washes her own sheets. When I walk past the girls' bedrooms, I sometimes pull up the covers on their beds. I just can't stand to look at an unmade bed.

Gina

Now that compulsions have entered the conversation, bed-making is at the top of my list, or at least it was until I realized that keeping the bedroom door shut during the day was a partial remedy. Probably you don't remember, but one of my earlier virallies was about how Alec Guinness in Bridge on the River Kwai *insisted that his POWs continue to march and brush their teeth, as a way of maintaining disciple and raising spirits. I brush my teeth, I march around Sherwood Island, but I don't make our bed, except once a week when I change the sheets. I apply another dicta to that activity—"out of sight, out of mind."*

Mary-Lou

In our house, last one up makes the bed. That's almost always me. I do a poor and uneven job of it, which my husband comes in and fixes later.

Lynn

I confess I make my bed. Always have, don't know why, except I like the look.

Maria

I always make my bed. I like climbing into cool sheets at night and letting my body just sink into support. But I will put off emptying the dishwasher if I possibly can. Just hate doing it.
Deb

Sometimes I make mine, sometimes I don't, sometimes it's just too late to bother because the day has slipped seamlessly from morning to afternoon to the 7 PM news on PBS. Oh, well.
Judy

The morning bed-making ritual helps me feel organized and energized and ready to tackle the day. Approaching a made bed at night helps me feel soothed and relaxed. Even in hotels, I can't work or relax in a room with a completely unmade bed, so I always straighten up the covers. I wouldn't want to have room service or watch TV on a bunched-up bed.
Gina

I agree with you entirely... making one's bed is an essential part of the morning... and like you, I also tidy up beds at hotels. I would hate coming home and finding a messy bed.
Ken

In defense of the unmade bed. See how you can simply slip right in?
Mary-Lou

When I walk through my bedroom during the day, I need the peace and calm of a bed made. I even like to see the two stuffed animals from my kids' childhoods that get a quick kiss and "I love you!" each  morning when I place them on the bed. Some seasons I'm more decorative with bedding and pillows, but they'll be fluffed and in position before I head to the shower or down to breakfast. And I enjoy the process of unmaking the bed each evening. Making and unmaking the bed are rituals that bookend my day—a signal that all's right with the world—even when it isn't.

Donna

There's something very calming about a made bed. I love sliding into soft, smooth sheets.
Maria

Bed made every morning! :)
Morgaine

Colleagues in Bed-Making Preferences,

Tonight, I am going undercover to expose the refreshing truth that lies beneath these layers of authentic revelation. There must be a soft, yet firm, sanctuary resting below these clean and unmade layers of untidy honesty. For sure there are hidden feelings that blanket and rejuvenate the human spirit.

Ken

I love my bed. When Dave died, I rarely slept until early morning. My daughters and cousin and best women friends were all at my house. Sometime around 10:00 AM. they would all pile onto my bed for a "bed-in." It was, first and foremost, a means of comfort for all of us. But it soon became a thing that anyone who attended the bed-in was in store for a great treat because

my bed with its foam topper is incredibly comfy. I love making it so I can unmake it and fall into it at night. In a world, personal and public, that seems so disordered, it's one small piece of order I can count on.

The headboard is made from an antique fireplace. I made the velvet insert out of a vintage piece of fabric.

Deb

The collaborative bed-room—Bill liked red, I liked silk, he liked blue, me too, we loved art—every wall is filled with it.
Judy

The little critter in the forefront is Midnight, an amusement from Stan to our first grandchild who is now 21 years old.
Sweet Dreams!
Gina

Pretty pattern. Looks inviting.
Maria

Wow—Eye popping wonderful!
Mary-Lou

You all have such grown-up beds!

I am embarrassed. My bed is very college-student in comparison!

And I have to say, when I signed up for a writing class, never did I ever think I'd get to see everyone's bedroom! 😊
Lynn

Well, we didn't see the hospital beds of two of our classmates.
Glad they are in their own beds by now.
Gina

Tuesday, May 19, 2020

Those among us who must continue to live alone and in virtual lockdown have the hardest burden to bear.

We need one another physically. We long for touch. It's innate to our species. We are social animals. We are meant to be together. Trump wants to open up the country to commerce, dining out, movies, sporting events, and rallies, at the risk of what he calls little "embers" popping up here or there. His quasi-patriotic call to "liberty" is seductive. The more we hear about states opening even as their Covid-19 sicknesses and deaths rise, the more we have to steel ourselves against the temptations of closeness, the very thing we most crave.

To bring this message home, for the past few days I've been debating whether I should take the chance of getting a much-needed haircut. ("Vanity working on a weak head, produces every sort of mischief," Jane Austen wrote.) I doubt she had death in mind. When the pandemic struck, my salon encouraged me to book an appointment three months hence, for May 22nd. I did. Surely the epidemic would be over by then!

It wasn't, but Gov. Lamont declared that salons could open on May 20th. I was still debating whether to show up when he delayed salon openings for an indeterminate amount of time. A wise person wrote that when you're trying to decide between two apparently equally appealing or unappealing options, you should flip a coin, after determining that heads is one option, and tails, the other. Now here's the cool part. As the coin is still in the air, you will find yourself wishing for one and not the other. You may not have been conscious of your preference as you conducted what you thought was an even-steven, rational competition but your unconscious mind did. Luckily, Governor Lamont cut me some slack.

Mary-Lou

Wednesday, May 20, 2020

State of Connecticut partially reopens… but not my hairdresser yet! Today is a particularly difficult day for me. I am not traveling to Washington DC today to attend the three-day annual ESOP conference. It is canceled. It has always been a highlight of my year.

I miss the educational sessions, meeting up with colleagues, brunch with old friends, concerts at the Kennedy Center, theatre at the National, visiting the Smithsonian, walking around Georgetown, and riding around on the upper deck of Gray Line bus tours. I miss traveling on the Acela train between Stamford and DC Union Station.

I am beyond grateful to all those who have crossed my path in person or behind the scenes in years gone by—Uber drivers, conductors, engineers, reservation clerks, food servers, taxi drivers, housekeepers, cooks, waiters, bus drivers, ticket takers, ushers, performers, sanitation workers, security guards, and docents.

Instead, I listen to a webinar on valuing stock of privately held companies that could be involved in mergers and acquisitions as well as the ins and outs of applying for a Small Business Administration loan under the Payroll Protection Plan. To my great relief, cartridges of HP printer ink show up on my doorstep.

I relax with my first gin and tonic of the season. Cook fillet mignon, twice baked potatoes, and roasted asparagus for dinner, topped off with a key lime pie from Fresh Market.

Gina

Wednesday, May 20, 2020

Went to my son's home to witness the transaction of their refinancing their home. Their backyard was filled with sun and their dogs vied for my attention, except for Bella who would have liked a piece of me, literally. Bella is their latest rescue, a five pound, blind, deaf, Chihuahua. She isn't always this vicious, but today I was not to her liking. Jeter and Mango, their other rescues, make up in love what Bella refuses.

After the signing, I said my goodbyes since Elizabeth had to return to her online teaching, and Ron needed to get back to work. Next was a visit to Castle Wine to pick up my order—curbside— then the pharmacy to pick up a prescription. As I left the Walgreens parking lot, a call from my daughter let me know my groceries were in so I changed directions, much to the annoyance of the car behind me, and picked up my loot. Home at last to be greeted joyously by Archie. "Where have you been? I'm so happy you're back!" Lick, lick. Puppy kisses are so delicious.

Now it's my favorite time of the day when chores are done, and dinner is yet to be. A glass of wine and an appreciation of all the good the day held.
Maria

Wednesday, May 20, 2020

I'm so tired of planning dinner every night for five people.

When it was just Mark and me, he would cook substantial meals on the weekend. He enjoys cooking when he has the time; me, not so much. In fact, not at all. We'd enjoy his creations for two nights in a row and then stick the leftovers in the freezer. During the week there was always something to defrost, heat up and serve; dinner was over and done with in no time.

Now, it's shopping, planning, preparing, and cleaning night after night, after night, after night... Michelle loves to help, and even volunteers to cook for all of us. Like her dad she enjoys puttering around in the kitchen, and she has made some incredible and unique dishes. The only problem is the guys need a solid meal which means meat. Michelle, bless her heart, will spend hours in the kitchen making her tuna tartar appetizer, a killer crusted salmon, and other healthy dishes such as cauliflower rice with veggies, kale, and Brussels sprout salad. I fear if she cooked for the guys, they'd be hungry an hour later.

We're also on different time schedules. Mark, when he commuted to work, would be home by 6:00, we'd eat and be snuggled on the couch by 7:00. Daniel too prefers an early dinner, but he doesn't cook. He comes down to the kitchen around 6:30 and says, "What's the dinner plan?" Michelle and Greg, when in NYC were used to eating dinner around 8:00.

Tonight, we had burritos, which Michelle doesn't generally eat, but she said to hell with the calorie counting and began piling refried beans, peppers and onions, roast chicken, and cheddar cheese on top of a flour tortilla. It was bulging with ingredients and impossible to roll up into the tight little cocoon I am used to serving. I take charge and roll it as best I can. "Just eat it. It'll taste the same." Suddenly she has anxiety and has lost her appetite. I throw my napkin, scrape the contents of her meal onto a new tortilla and throw it in a pan. She leaves the room.

Why such a strong reaction on my part? Refer back to my lede.
Morgaine

Thursday, May 21, 2020

When I go down to the kitchen to make a cup of coffee, I notice a pair of men's sneakers by the front door and a dark blue SUV parked in our driveway. For the past few days, our class has shared glimpses of the most private of places—our bedrooms—and whether we make our beds or not. We haven't talked about who exactly is in them.

For two of our classmates who have been so sick, there's hardly been an opportunity to get out of bed, much less take a photo of it. For them, it must seem like more of a jail cell than a nightly resting place for sweet dreams. At times, they must feel very much alone.

Some of our classmates are married (still!!!)—Mary-Lou, Morgaine, Lynn, Ken, Polly—and others—Judy, Deb, Maria, and me—are widowed. Some of us have been married more than once or twice. Bernadette recently went through a painful divorce, but as of March 20th, *"On the bright side I'm quarantined with my hunky boyfriend of 8 months—in my postage stamp of an apartment. If we survive corona and each other I shall continue to update."*

For more than twenty years, my only bedfellows have been my little granddaughters. But, for my 51- and 47-year-old recently divorced daughters, it is a different story driven by an urgent need for intimacy. Having boyfriends who are not members of the household poses an exposure challenge where the circle is not completely closed. Who do the boy-friends meet—children living with ex-spouses, parents, workplace colleagues, clients? Both daughters have been social distancing with friends and neighbors in outdoor settings, but the dating situation takes it to a whole new level.

Today, our landscape crew showed up to care for the lawn. Ah, the sweet smell of fresh cut grass… and gasoline. The men practiced social distancing while enjoying their lunch break in the shade of a tree.

Gina

Thursday, May 21, 2020

I think I started this bed thing, but that's as intimate as I intend to get.

It also occurs to me that most of us have all but abandoned the pandemic theme that was the genesis of these virallies. Do we mean to? Are we sick of it? I suspect there will be more to write about as we move towards Connecticut's "re-opening." How far and how soon we dare to go, how faithful we are at sticking to the rules, how tempted we are not to. Who are the people we'd most like to see once we can hug? What about changes in eating and sleeping habits, the political stuff, wondering what the new normal will be, what we would like the new normal to be, changes we will make in our lives because of the pandemic. Are we worried about our children and grandchildren's future, our jobs, our money?

For instance, I know that the confinement and the attendant slowing down of time has been good for me. I read more. I sing more. I laugh more. I'm calmer. I've been offered a writing job that under pre-pandemic circumstances I'd covet, but having so enjoyed this leisurely time, I am thinking of turning the job down. I'm not as achievement oriented as I used to be. I don't want to be busy. How has this pandemic changed you?

So, dear class, what do you think? Do you want to stick closer to the pandemic theme, or would you rather just exchange whatever thoughts, feelings and news that engages your interest?
Mary-Lou

Thursday, May 21, 2020

I like the broader focus. My life doesn't revolve around the pandemic anymore. I've grown accustomed to being more solitary (that's always been my default anyway); I spend lots of time in Zoom gatherings, sometimes hidden, sometimes participating; I read more since my French teacher can't access Zoom to conduct classes; I haven't spent as much time playing the piano as I'd planned to; I spend more time writing. I miss seeing the East Coast daughters so I can hug them and the grandchildren, but I love it when the family Zooms together from all over the country. And speaking of Zoom, that word has now entered our everyday vocabulary just like "social distancing"—wonder when it will turn up in online dictionaries, especially the OED.

I guess I'm adjusting to the new normal that Meadow Ridge has superimposed over the general Connecticut orders. I'm relieved in some ways not to have to choose whether I'll go somewhere I can imagine an historian in 100+ years pouring over our individual entries, coding the topics that we've touched on, and drawing conclusions about how a group of privileged suburban residents reacted when the world turned topsy-turvy. Or maybe our writing won't interest anyone; at least it amuses us. That's fine with me too. I don't have enough pandemic related reactions to write about daily—although I haven't exactly been doing this daily either.

Judy

Thursday, May 21, 2020

My immediate reaction was like Judy's. As with any kind of grief—and I believe we are all grieving in this time of fear, death, and incompetent leadership—I know I need moments to get away from the pain. Mary-Lou, I think your note brings us back to a reflective place. We may be sharing pictures of our beds, but it doesn't mean that there isn't a relationship to the pandemic. For me, it's relief from being seriously concerned, as well as a marker of the different kind of relationships being built in our group that might not have happened in a non-Covid environment. And the fact that the unthinkable has become routine, as Judy said.

Also, I'm a bit of a peeping Tom. I love seeing how other people express themselves in the way they've built their nests.

Deb

Thursday, May 21, 2020

The pandemic inhabits our daily life, but it's hard to listen to the numbers, cases rising, deaths multiplying, without wanting to shout STOP! For the last two nights I've turned on the news and quickly turned it off. It's not good to be uninformed as to what goes on, but the bombardment of bad news is unrelenting and occasionally, a third viewing of *Sleepless in Seattle* seems preferable. We each know how much is tolerable and when to shift our focus so yes, I agree with Judith and like the broader view.
Maria

Friday, May 22, 2020

Spent another 4 hours gardening, slathered in sunblock, having a wonderful time planting and weeding. Since one of the gardens is invaded by an evil species called Japanese anemone, one has to dig down deep and follow the roots. Impossible. I did as much as I could. But while weeding I found myself wondering why gardening gives me so much pleasure when it's such a pain in the butt and back. I was carefully shaking the soil from the roots of the weeds when I swear, I heard my mother's voice saying, "Be sure to shake the soil from the weeds." Then I pictured the two of us side by side, digging, weeding, and shaking the soil.

My mother was very unhappy, and not a very loving woman— unhappy to start with and unhappily married. I assume that my parents married for love, but it didn't stay that way for either of them. Both of my parents loved me and my older sister strictly, as much as many parents of the 1940s did. Lots of tap, toe and ballet, piano lessons, thank you notes, and discipline. She demanded made beds (ha, ha, there's a clue) and sent us up to our room weekly to "straighten our bureau drawers." (There will be no photos of my drawers forthcoming.) Still, if there's one thing my mother loved passionately, it was gardening. She was even the president of her gardening club. When I got old enough to join her kneeling at the flower beds, I did. That was when we were at our best together. That's when her love was most evident and accessible. That's where I felt most loved.

Mary-Lou

Friday, May 22, 2020

Yesterday I took a meandering walk. I was bored with walking the ring road and decided to visit the pond with the screened-in gazebo. I've thought about sleeping in that gazebo under a full moon, but I'm not as daring as my bushwhacking older daughter. It remains just an intriguing idea. I even chickened out of sleeping in the hammock on the deck of the house I used to own after promising a neighbor that we would both do it and compare notes in the morning. "Too buggy," I concluded.

On my way to the pond yesterday, I noticed a footpath off the main path that I had intended to follow. The main path is mowed and groomed; fallen trees are removed; it's wide enough for three people to walk abreast. The footpath that intrigued me was barely wide enough for one person. I expected to climb over fallen trees; clumps of grass seemed to beckon me to follow a way that was paved with fallen leaves.

I was torn between the call of a path whose end I couldn't see and what was "age appropriate." I was dressed for it—long leggings, long sleeved shirt, trusty sneakers. *Check.* I had my cell phone in case I tripped and fell. *Check.* (I did fall 8 years ago on another path—tripped over a tree root and came back to the apartment, saying to Bill as I held the end of a bloody tee shirt up to my chin, "It's not as bad as it looks. I'm not going to the hospital.") Would the phone get a signal if I needed help? *I decided not to check.* Could I describe where I was? *No.* I'd forgotten that my phone has a compass.

I disturbed squirrels and birds as I clomped along, crunching twigs, and watching carefully for tree roots. I climbed over fallen trees and through openings in stone walls. I noticed lichen on the tops of boulders and a large outcropping of

rocks. I heard my father explain that glaciers deposited rocks like those millions of years ago. I took him at his word; I couldn't understand the concept of *million*. I told myself, *If you get really lost, you can always go back the way you came*.

This is where I ended up—a stream that I took my granddaughters to when they were young. I let them swing out over the water on a tree branch that is no longer there. Once there yesterday, I recognized a familiar path back to the Meadow Ridge meadows.

I've started thinking about following another path on the other side of the property. Will I?

Judy

Saturday, May 23, 2020

In response to our virallies having veered off topic, **everything** I've written over the last two months has to do with the pandemic.

Had we never been struck with quarantine I'd be two or three more chapters ahead in my memoir writing. I wouldn't be sitting down in front of a blank page daily examining my compulsive behavior, my love of gardening, my aversion to meal planning and the dynamics of my family relationships, let alone sharing my frustrations, my angst, and my pleasures with all of you.

Writing about my twenties now seems frivolous. Does anyone really care that my father sexually abused me, that I responded with promiscuity, that I read every self-help book I could get my hands on to stop using food to numb my feelings? Who gives a shit that I did EST, Enlightenment Intensives, spent two weeks on a retreat at Mt. Shasta with a spiritual teacher trying find myself? What good did it do me? I still react when my belief system is threatened, have feelings of insecurity and doubt, use food and alcohol (now and again) to take the edge off, and feel lost when the world as I know it has been turned upside down.

Confinement has not slowed me down. I get up every day and hop on a hamster wheel. I work out because I have to, I worry for my children's future, their health and welfare, the state of our country, our planet, our values. I mentally obsess. I cry more, write less, read depressing news articles instead of inspirational literature. When I lay in bed at night I often wonder, *what is it all for?* And yet, I am *not* so anxious to go back to the old way of life.

I know… I need to get out more.

Morgaine

Saturday, May 23, 2020

I so relate to what Morgaine wrote. I feel similarly about my memoir writing. All I write these days are pandemic diaries and responses to classmates.

Right now, I have no interest in writing about my dysfunctional childhood family, especially when I have my very functional and lovely family with me all day, every day. Who wants to wade through the swamp when you can stand in the sunshine? Life is too short.

And I too wonder if anyone cares/wants to read about the poor sad little waif I was 40 years ago. Does any of it matter? I guess it matters in the sense that it brought me to where I am now, but aside from that, what was the point of all that suffering? And why memorialize it? Is memoir a bad idea?

And when there are so many more pressing matters/important things going on globally, who is actually going to care about my childhood?! *I* don't even care about my childhood that much anymore!

I spent most of my life dwelling on my sad past or dreading my uncertain future. I seemed to never stop asking, "What's the point? What's it all for? Why? Why? Why?" The one good thing to come out of this pandemic for me is that I've mostly quit that. And I have never felt more serene.

Having a lot of time to think about this over the past two months, I realize that I dwelled on the past because I still needed healing from it. I think I wrote about it because I wanted someone to say, "That's terrible! What a hard time you endured! And look how well you turned out!" I wanted someone to say, "You are important!" Writing memoir is our own declaration of that, I think.

What I really wanted most was someone to say, "I'm sorry. That wasn't fair, what happened to you."

I think losing all three of my parents—two in the past 6 months—has freed me somehow and has enabled me to find forgiveness and release. Maybe I don't have to muck around in the swamp.

I want to thank you all for being there for me these past few months. You have all been so important in helping me figure a lot of this out and I am very grateful.

Lynn

Saturday, May 23, 2020

Reflecting on the most recent exchanges (writing memoirs, childhood trauma), and just in case you haven't already read it, I am halfway through *Educated* by Tara Westover. A remarkable memoir!

Great story, great writing, just wonderful!!!

Ken

Saturday, May 23, 2020

A fabulous day! Watched my granddaughter, Rosie, graduate virtually from Tilton, a prep school in New Hampshire where she did a post graduate high school year before going to college in September.

Then did an hour of Pilates broadcast by inhouse Meadow Ridge TV—felt invigorated and awake by then so I made up the bed.

Best of all, saw notice for a Cornell Reunion that a roommate and I considered attending and found out the university library is giving a virtual workshop on TONI MORISSON! Signed up immediately and volunteered to read a passage from *The Bluest Eye*. It's the 50th anniversary of that novel, her first. That book introduced me to the world of literature by Black women, became the basis of the Black woman's book club that I started with a friend in 1975, led to the anthology of short stories by African American women that Marty and I published in 1993 with a quote of hers, *Centers of the Self*, as a title. For 50 years I've wanted to take a seminar in her novels; I've read them all.

Couldn't find the book in my collection of Black women writers so I ordered it on Kindle because I needed it right away. I sank into her wonderful prose and have immersed myself all afternoon, doing what I love; read, read, read until my eyes are blurry and dry and my soul is sated. I'm so excited to revisit a book that's an old friend and then have the chance to hear scholars talk about it. YEA!

Judy

Saturday, May 23, 2020

No shoes by the front door this morning. Mr. Sneakers has his 11-year-old daughter for the weekend. But he'll be back—I was asked to add Truvia and San Pellegrino to the Peapod order that will come tomorrow after an eleven-day wait. I wonder how much of it I will actually get.

Monica promises to go to the store to see what she can get before the Peapod midnight cutoff for changing the online order. She doesn't go. Instead, she installs new faucets on the kitchen sink and finishes painting and hanging the cupboard doors. The transformation is magical.

I finally open a real book for the first time since I got back from Key West in February. The remarkable saga I am reading this weekend is *The Signature of All Things* by Elizabeth Gilbert.

Gina

Sunday, May 24, 2020

For Sam's birthday, one of her little gifts (and thank goodness I had some little gifts because my bread baking produced a doorstop rather than a taste treat) was a poetry book entitled *Love Poems (for Married People)*. With all our family interactions over the past six weeks, I think his poem "Yogurt" summarizes some of the familiar humor of our exchanges.

Ken

Sunday, May 24, 2020

Seriously, Ken, I love a love poem that turns around and bites you in the butt.

Mary-Lou

Sunday, May 24, 2020

Evelyn turns ten today. She's been watching the mail deliveries like a hawk and has already opened all her presents from me. She goes to the Fresh Market and Stop & Shop with her mother—her first outing since March 10th. They can't get either skirt steak or sinfully white cake at Fresh Market. They go to Stop & Shop. Monica comes home with most of the stuff I'd already ordered from Peapod and could no longer cancel.

Evelyn also gets her first real in-person Covid-19 play date as well. She is invited to swim at her best friend's pool where they observe social distancing.

Monica sets up the backyard for family birthday activities—bouncy house, cornhole, trampoline, and sprinkler as well as ping-pong on the back porch.

Mr. Sneakers comes over for a very short visit in late afternoon.

Monica grills filet mignon and asparagus for Evelyn's 10th birthday dinner. Peapod finally delivers right in the middle of the celebration. We now have dozens and dozens of bagels but are running low on paper towels and Kleenex. Trying to keep the pantry stocked with supplies during the pandemic is a real challenge.

Evelyn gives me a bunch of hair clips from a big bag she got for her birthday. Still blonde!!!

Gina

Sunday, May 24, 2020

Writers, at least good writers, are magicians—but you all know that. They draw us into worlds that live on the page and in our imaginings. Books that have brought on these musings are the first two books of Hilary Mantel's trilogy about Thomas Cromwell, his rise and his fall. The books are historical fiction, and the facts are well recorded and are not in question. What is magical about these tales is Ms. Mantel's gift for making this era and the characters that lived then so viscerally real. The actions and events take place in the court of England's Henry VIII. The second book, *Bring Up the Bodies,* which I finished two nights ago had my stomach in knots. I felt the tension and the terror of the woman in the Tower awaiting her death. The ending is no surprise; we all know what happened to Anne Boleyn when Henry tired of her and yet, I was right there with her as she was made to watch the execution of the five men accused of committing adultery with her and awaited her own beheading. Now I'm on the third and final book and I'm already dreading our hero's fall. (Thomas Cromwell is treated kindly in Ms. Mantel's stories, although not by history.) I love it when a book grabs you and won't let go!

During this pandemic, I've spent much time alone—and sometimes it has felt not unlike when I was young and kept in close quarters by my watchful mother. Not allowed to visit friends or play outside as most other young people did, I resorted much of the time to reading. Books were my haven, my friends. The books I read then—and I wish I could remember them all—fueled my imagination and took me away from a fairly solitary life. It was grand. So now, this pandemic has afforded me that same luxury.

Maria

Sunday, May 24, 2020

The hamster is on her wheel again today. Edging the gardens was the name of the game. A labor intensive but gratifying task. The boys and I will mulch after the holiday weekend. Mark gave me a back massage yesterday (Mary-Lou, you'd have been jealous.) I was a certified massage therapist when I lived in California, and I trained Mark well. After crawling around in the dirt all day today I am in desperate need of another. To receive a massage is my absolute my favorite pastime. Of course, it *must* be strong and deep; there's nothing worse than expecting to have your muscles ironed out and the masseuse starts petting you.

 Feeling a little sad for Daniel. He was supposed to leave for Japan today. He and two of his buddies were planning a five-week tour of the country after graduation. They had the trip all mapped out from accommodations to museums, attractions, anime studios and even recommended restaurants. When will any foreign country allow visitors from the U.S.? We're a disaster area, and by the looks of the Memorial Day Weekend crowds we're in for another sharp rise in Covid cases.

Morgaine

Wow, you're a whirlwind. Can you lend me some of that energy? So many plans and major milestones to be remembered as victims of the virus. These pics are terrifying. On a personal level, I feel furious looking at them. My daughter hasn't seen most of our family in nearly a year and would like to take a trip home from Belgium for her birthday in August. She can get into the US as a citizen, but because of our failed policies here it's unlikely Belgium would allow her to re-enter. Trump has succeeded in turning a natural disaster into a political one.
Deb

Sunday, May 24, 2020

Looking at those photos gives me mixed feelings. On one hand I think, "OMG. How stupid and inconsiderate are they?!" and on the other hand I feel jealous of the fun and closeness they're experiencing.

I have new neighbors who just moved in. The new neighbors are young—late 20s, and they PARTY—all the time. They moved in just three weeks ago and have been having tons of people (their friends from NYC) over for beers, barbeques, and midnight cornhole. The noise doesn't bother me, but the fun does. I want to play cornhole! I want to drink beer with friends! I want to have shenanigans!

Why do they get to be irresponsible? They claim they have a "Social Bubble" of six couples. (SIX?! WTF!)

Meanwhile, my grocery shopping suddenly looks angelic compared to midnight—beer-pong-parties-of-12.

Lynn

Monday, May 25, 2020

Memorial Day! I watch the Bedford Middle School/Staples High School band members give virtual performances on Westport's Channel 79. As I try to encourage Ryan to watch for her 7th grade classmates, Monica breaks in and tells the girls they don't have to watch if they don't want to. Her putdowns are becoming more frequent. She is getting ornerier by the day. She desperately needs to be back on the tennis court.

Two years ago, I rode in the Westport Memorial Day parade on the back of a classic convertible with a couple of officers from the Y's Women. This year we don't do anything—no grilling, no flags, no place to wear my nice new white shoes except between the front door and the mailbox at the end of the driveway.

The evening news has reports of George Floyd being murdered by four policemen in Minneapolis. The video...

Gina

Monday, May 25, 2020

Today was family brunch number ten. We were invited to my

mother-in-law's home. She is the only person who we visit w/o social distancing. Just for kicks I put on pants with a zipper, matched a pair of earrings with my outfit, glossed my lips and defined my lower lash line in pencil. I don't miss being fashionable. I don't miss retail shopping, annual galas, parties, or crowds of people. I don't miss throwing dinner parties or gathering at public spaces. What I do miss is the freedom to choose.

Morgaine

Monday, May 25, 2020

Hello there,

Please don't think for a minute that I haven't enjoyed reading your consistent and well-written messages during the past month or so. Your frustrations, joys, whines (and yes there are a few of those), and positive thinking has made me smile more than frown. After being focused on my health, pills, MD visits and calls and a husband who is recovering from a cracked rib when he fell while I was in the hospital (note, recognized run-on sentence but I don't care), I can well understand the monotony and boredom you faced then. Every day seems to be the same old, same old scenario. Dear God!

Now that I'm almost recovered, I am eager to rejoin you, but perhaps in a different way. I agree with some of you that I don't want to start writing memoir/essays at this time, but I do want to keep writing. Most of my article publishing gigs had gone into pause or non-function, but there is one column I have in a small weekly who is eager for my story. I usually just send him those articles that are already published, but he is suggesting something new. I mentioned to him that I'd like to write a short column warning the readers about what really happens when you have Covid-19 and are in the hospital. He has asked me to write more than one column describing my experience until my story is told.

This I have agreed to, so each week I shall have to write the next chapter and then the next and then…

If you agree, and I do need to hear that you are or aren't, I'd like to send these along to you. No hard feelings if you think they're not a good fit. Either way please keep me in your virtual loop.

Last thought. Bernadette, you're on this email. You've been in my thoughts. I'd love to hear from you. After all, "We're all in this together," another Covid-19 cliché.

Stay well, stay safe, and thanks for your friendship.

Polly

Dear Polly—Welcome home. Are you kidding? I, for one, would welcome such writing from you. It's what I've been waiting for. And great that it gets published, too.

Mary-Lou

Hi Polly, I'm all ears. Did you have Covid after 5 negative test results? Can't wait to read your story.

Morgaine

Hi Polly, so good to hear from you. I look forward to your installments about your Covid-19 experience. By all means, send it to us. Your experience is, gratefully, unique in our class.

Donna

It's great hearing your voice again! More, please. Big hug!

Maria

It's all been said. Nothing could be more relevant! And so great to have you back!!

Deb

Monday, May 25, 2020

Can This Marriage be Saved?

Staying home during this pandemic has exaggerated some areas of conflict in our marriage.

Me: I like to leave the wet, hand washed pots and other stuff that don't go in the dish washer on the counter to evaporate.
He: Likes to dry and put them away immediately.

Me: Before going shopping, I want to think up a few meals, check the fridge, the freezer, the pantry, and make a list of what's needed.
He: Thinking in advance of shopping cramps his style. He prefers to wander through the aisles, grabbing whatever appeals to him.

Me: I don't like salty or spicy food.
He: Does.

Me: I can barely get through the *NYTimes* Tuesday crossword puzzle.
He: He disdains Monday and Tuesday but does the rest of the week and all the puzzles on Sunday. Sunday is his day off from me.

Me: I worry.
He: Doesn't.

Me: I usually lose at Scrabble.
He: Usually wins, but that's because he knows all those bizarre crossword puzzle words that even well-read people never heard of.

Me: I'm a bad sport.

He: Of course, if you win most of the time it's easy to be a good sport.

Mary-Lou

This made me smile... oh, okay, I laughed. They say a good story should have some conflict to be interesting! :-)

Maria

Tuesday, May 26, 2020

Hello again,

*Here's the first chapter for my little column, **This and That**, which appears when I'm in the mood in a NH/VT weekly newspaper. The readership is uncertain, but they do deliver to every home in the Upper Valley area. (Read, it's free). Sometimes I get feedback, but that is rare. Many of the details won't be included. My goal in even writing this is to (a) stop dreaming about it at night, and (b) scare the living hell out of these stubborn New Englanders who don't wear masks and follow the guidelines. To date, there are very few cases in our area, but Hanover, about 45 minutes away is a different story.*

Polly

I Wasn't Going to Get Covid-19, but I Did

Throughout the month of March warnings about what was then known as The Coronavirus were becoming upsetting and threatening. I was confident that I wouldn't get it as I am a healthy and active senior citizen with no underlying health conditions, but I worried about my husband who is just the opposite. I followed the media's guidelines by wearing a mask and gloves for pre-dawn grocery shopping, washed my hands frequently, and stayed home. How and when I did get Covid-19 is unknown.

One morning in early April I woke up not feeling my best. It wasn't until I was brushing my teeth that I connected the dots—

tired and achy feeling, slight headache, and no yearning for coffee. Then came the cough which started out gently but soon got so comfortable in my lungs that it stayed with me for the next few weeks.

"I'll be fine," I told myself as I popped two Tylenol. I wasn't. By early afternoon I called my doctor. I described my symptoms to her which were all indicative of Covid-19. She wanted to know if I had a temperature. Well, it's been so long since we've needed a thermometer in our house that we couldn't find one that worked, so I told her I didn't think so. She suggested getting tested which at that time was in its infancy stages.

"No, I'm okay," I told her. "What's the point of getting tested? I know I have it. I'll ride this out at home. All the researchers want are the results for their statistics."

She reluctantly agreed and suggested that my husband and I self-quarantine from one another by sleeping and eating in different rooms, using separate bathrooms, and wearing masks. We tried our best which is to say it didn't always work the way it should have.

The next morning, which just happened to be my birthday, I was feeling worse. I called my doctor again. "I've changed my mind," I told her. "I think I do need to be tested." That wasn't as simple as it is now—she had to write a script. I had to fill out forms. An appointment was arranged for the following day at a hospital's parking garage for about 45 minutes from my house. That experience was surreal. Nurses covered from head to toe in outfits that looked like they were getting ready to walk on the moon approached my car, swabbed my nostrils and within minutes I drove home. The results would be available in 24-48 hours.

When they came back, they were negative. Now what? At this early stage, false negatives were unheard of. One was positive or negative. I was told to continue with the Tylenol, rest, drink fluids, and take the over-the-counter cough syrup.

I had met our neighbor at our mailboxes while I was waiting for the results. She told me that her husband was back at work after recovering from the virus. He had gone to the doctor and was told they didn't want to waste a test on him as they knew he had it. He was sent him home to rest unless he had trouble breathing.

Our neighbor loaned us her Fingertip Pulse Oximeter, "in case we needed it." I believe this simple device saved my life. She told us that any reading above 95 is good, but if it's 90 or below you go to the hospital.

Easter came. Easter went. I got worse. During the night I called the doctor's assistant twice. She calmed my fears and said that because I could string a sentence together without being short of breath, I was probably okay.

We talked again late morning. She was pleased and surprised that we had an Oximeter. When the oxygen reading hovered around 89-90, she said what I was hoping to avoid. "You need to go to the hospital. Call 911." People were being advised to stay off the roads because of hurricane type weather that was sweeping through our area.

Within minutes an ambulance was in our driveway. Without giving it much thought, I tossed a toothbrush, phone charger, face cream, and a magazine into an overnight bag. I was planning to come home the following day. Wrong.

If not, my husband could deliver the things I needed to the hospital. Wrong again.

Polly

Think this will keep me on the edge of my seat, well, really my couch.

Deb

Thank you, Polly, for sharing this experience with us. I'm looking forward the next chapter in your battle with Covid-19. Most

importantly is that you're back and well again!
Maria

Tuesday, May 26, 2020

The now former Minneapolis police officer who knelt on George Floyd's neck and killed him the night before was arrested and charged with third degree murder. Officials and pundits fill the airwaves. No talk of the coronavirus. The metric on the TV screen announcing global and US infection and death rates is gone.

We have our team call. It's hard to concentrate. There are protests going on within a short walk of my brother Mickey's Milwaukee condo—a neighborhood where I once lived.

In Minneapolis, protesters fill the streets where the lynching took place. I am shocked and dismayed at the crowds standing and shouting shoulder to shoulder with only some wearing masks. Will we end up with new spikes of coronavirus infections?

Nancy has worked the past two nights at Hennepin County Medical Center. The hospital is now full of patients with both Covid-19 infections and demonstrators' injuries. She and Christopher are supposed to be on vacation for these two weeks. Nancy is being called back to work. Chris doesn't want her in downtown Minneapolis. She stays home.

Maria calls. She is still staging her house to put on the market this coming weekend. She plans to drop off things she no longer wants.
Gina

Wednesday, May 27, 2020

I finish the valuation analysis for a nut butter manufacturing firm. They have made record sales because people are hoarding peanut butter during the pandemic.

Nell and I FaceTime. She lives fairly close to the epicenter of the Minneapolis protests, not far from where George Floyd was murdered. My son called her last night and told her to unlock her guns (she doesn't have any) and turn out her lights. She can smell the smoke and hear the pop of firecrackers or whatever is exploding. Chris relays information from his communication channels. There are outside agitators involved.

"Can I come and stay with you if we need to leave?" she asks Chris.

"You don't need to ask," he replies.

Gina

Wednesday, May 27, 2020

I try to keep myself from obsessing on this quarantine by keeping my mind and body busy:

I try to do the Meadow Ridge exercise program every day although repetition bores me. Today was better: a pregnant instructor led us in a series of basic ballet moves that challenged me (I had to hold onto a chair; now I know why ballerinas practice at the barre). When can I go on pointe?

I read several books at once—have a different chair for each. *The Bluest Eye* in a leather easy chair complete with footstool so I can sink into both the book and the chair, and Krugman's *Arguing with Zombies* in a straight-backed club chair, absorbing his righteous anger and some knowledge about economics.

I meditate with a Zoom group three times a week. At first, I thought they were just la de da ladies, but I'm growing into their Buddhist orientation.

I joined two other black ladies in a film club; we discuss a new film each week. So far, we've watched *Daughters of the Dust*, *Django Unchained*, and *Crash*. Next on the list: *Becoming*.

I tune into an investment webinar each week that my broker told me about. It forces me to think logically about investments. I find their assessments cold-blooded—projections of how many people will die in specific age categories given best case (continue to isolate), worst case (go back to business as usual) and middle of the road (open gradually) scenarios. Lower than 10% death rate in each category is acceptable; we'll never get to zero. Partly because of that, they predict that high yield bonds will outperform large cap stocks. A nugget I can chew on.

I try to work on the memoir right after the morning exercises, so my eyes aren't tired. Am rewriting the last chapter in the first section, Courtship/Wedding. I think there are two sections; the next is Marriage. This last chapter needs a total overhaul except for the ceremony itself—slow going until I hit the *flow* which is out there somewhere. I have to write my way to it.

Am editing my daughter's proposed blog that she hopes will drive readers to her book, *100 Acts of Love: The Girlfriend's Guide to Loving Your Friend through Cancer and Loss* by Kim Hamer. I love the editing: look at what Marty and I produced!
Judy

I'm amazed by how many interesting activities you pack into one day; such diverse interests; such energy! Were you this involved before the pandemic? I seem to have gone in the opposite direction. If you don't count the gardening, I pretty much shop, cook, eat, write, read, and binge. I feel more relaxed than ever, which is nice, but you make me feel lazy.
Mary-Lou

Wednesday, May 27, 2020

Mom went to have her hearing aids adjusted today. They took her temperature, new policy, only to turn her away because she had a one-hundred-degree fever. She puts a call in to her doctor, who is not seeing patients in the office. He will call her back. Meanwhile she calls me and says she's thinking of going to the hospital via ambulance. I can hear the fear in her voice.

"Nooooo! That's the last place you want to go," I tell her. She also has a scratchy throat, mucus, and the bottoms of her feet are so sore they wake her up at night. No cough, fever is low grade, breathing is fine.

"It doesn't sound like Covid, Mom. Let's wait and see what the doctor has to say."

After we hang up, it's not that I think she has Covid (although who knows with all the various symptoms people are having). What concerns me is the fact that she is alone. She once said to me, "Of all the girls," referring to her five daughters, "it's you I see by my side in the end." I'm a "calming, uplifting, reassuring voice," she tells me. In our present circumstances I can't run (drive) to her rescue, be by her side, rub her feet or even give her a hug if I wanted to. Whatever she goes through over the next... who knows how long, she will go through it alone.

It turns out she has a bladder infection, which explains the low-grade fever. She failed to tell me she's been peeing like crazy and experiencing a burning sensation. The scratchy throat is most likely from the pollen in the air, as she's been opening the windows since the humidity has kicked in. The sore feet—neuropathy. If only I could get a hold of the proper PPE gear.

Morgaine

Wednesday, May 27, 2020

I've given up keeping count. Just using the date now.

Things that I love in the era of Covid-19.

1. Scrunchies. Amazing how long I can go without hair washing if I just stick it in a ponytail.
2. Eggs. The all-purpose answer to dinner when I'm too tired or uninspired to cook.
3. Zoom. Let's face it, it's a godsend. And you only need to look OK from the neck up. Which leads me to number 4.
4. Sweat and yoga pants. Comfy and elastic waisted.

5. Yoga. Always love it but being able to have it led by my daughter in Belgium who is the best teacher I've ever had—priceless.
6. What I've spent on gas. Only slightly more than nada.
7. Long walks in Winslow Park. It's beautiful.
8. The mass migration of city dwellers looking for homes (like mine) with pools in the burbs.
9. Alexa calls me by my name now.

Have been working like crazy in between house showings to get my property looking as good as it can. My usual unusually strong body seems to be in protest. Poison ivy has taken over my personal surface area even more than it has spread across my property. My knee went out, my back aches and my right eye is swollen and red. Poor me. World's tiniest violin....

I'm in strive, working doggedly to remember pivot, then thrive. Turn it around. When option A is no longer possible, you've got to have an option B. Maybe I'm just not that great at the alphabet. Maybe if my stimulus check miraculously showed up it would be a little easier.

Yup, I'm bummed. But then I talk to one of my kids or grandkids, or gaze at the huge stand of ferns in the park, or stand back in awe at the beauty of the lupine and foxglove I've just planted, or read our journal writings, and there's option B. All that is still right with the world. Not what I expected, but OK. Or is it what I expected? That the circumstances are less important than the reality that I can love and be loved, see and express beauty, feel the gamut of emotions, and count on winter turning to glorious spring.

Deb

Thursday, May 28, 2020
Protesters and rioters rage for third straight night in Minneapolis. The third police precinct which is where the four involved officers

were based goes up in flames. I am glued to CNN watching the governor, mayor, anchors, and reporters.

I cook hot dogs for the girls and salmon filets for me and Monica. Monica puts more finishing touches to the kitchen.

Gina

Thursday, May 28, 2020

The first effort produced a "door stop," but this effort is a big success. Wish I could share some of it, but it will be gone by tomorrow.

Ken

Congratulations, Ken! It looks delicious. I'm one of the few who has not joined the bread baking troops— well, except for banana bread. Now I'm wondering if it would be a fun challenge.

Donna

Early on there was a yeast shortage. We finally acquired a fair amount; what'll be next. Raisin walnut or Challah? Maybe both. Nice work Ken!!!

Morgaine

Thursday, May 28, 2020

Yesterday I went up to Fairfield to play pickleball at Tunxis Hill. There were six other ladies there. We played for two hours and all of us agreed it was two whole hours where the world felt almost normal.

I had been so desperate for pickleball that two weeks ago we turned our patio (ie: concrete slab out back) into a mini-pickleball court. It's ten feet wide—the right size for a half court—but it is way too short lengthwise. We did our best, and at least we were able to chalk in kitchen lines and rig up a net made of duct-tape and garden trellis. The court does have some perils: cracks; weeds; anthills; a firepit in the back corner; cedar shingles and windows on the side of the house. It's not ideal, but it has been a great source of fun and stress relief, nonetheless. Smacking the hell out of a whiffle ball—and getting it past your teenage son—can be very therapeutic.

Speaking of teenage son: Zach turned 16 last week. All he wanted was lasagna for dinner and a chocolate torte royale—a family-tradition recipe of cinnamon meringue shell filled with a layer of melted chocolate, a layer of cinnamon whipped cream, and a layer of chocolate mousse. It is surprisingly easy to make; the lasagna was more work. My son was happy that his best-friend's parents allowed his best friend to come over to watch a movie. They had not seen each other since March.

Like most 16-year-olds, Zach wants to learn to drive. I am not at all keen on this. I think he is not ready, though I'm avoiding saying that to him outright. Sparing me the fight is another pandemic silver lining: the DMV is closed.

Lynn

Thursday, May 28, 2020

Today was a test of the new, not so normal, me. I've been carrying on about how the pandemic, horror though it is, has had a benign effect on my somewhat hyper personality. I experience myself as more relaxed, less driven.

I usually go shopping with Larry, but today he switched his allegiance to his vegetable garden, leaving me in sole charge of hunting and gathering. Armed with a list, I drove within the speed limit to Stop & Shop. I hate the place, but it's close and I figured I could buy what I needed there. I parked with care, I donned my protective gear and walked slowly from aisle to aisle, obeying the arrows* and examining the produce with great care, especially the peaches. I maintained a six-foot space between me and a shopper who took a good three minutes trying to make up his mind about which Talenti ice cream flavor he wanted. I did not sigh. I did not tap my foot impatiently. You get it. I was the new normal me. It wasn't until I got home that the old me emerged for a brief, anxious appearance: Ah! But will you lapse into anxious, impatient rushing when the pandemic is over?

Those up and down arrows reminded me that my older son, Adam, once explained to me that savvy supermarkets arrange their aisles in that up and down way. Stew Leonard's did that, although I don't know if they still do. That arrangement requires the shopper to  pass by all the displays, thus encouraging sales. That pattern of movement has a name: boustrophedonic—from the Greek, so sez Google. The "bou" part refers to an ox, the "stroph" refers to the line in which the ox plows the furrows—up one and down the other. For whatever reason, I've never forgotten the word and found myself thinking about it today as I shopped boustrophedonically. Make it your own. Amaze your friends!

I know I've mentioned our son, Peter, a lot. But I'm proud of Adam, too. So, here's a photo of the man I don't see often because he and his family live in Tucson. I miss him. His daughter took the picture.

Mary-Lou

A handsome man, your Adam. His smile is in his eyes, lovely.
Maria

Adam looks just like his dad.
Morgaine

Love the smile! I don't want to hurt your feelings, M-L, but I see a strong resemblance to Larry.
Polly

Lovely pic. Have to disagree with the rest a little bit. I definitely see Mary-Lou around his mouth—a combo kid. I love seeing family members. I think of Adam as a kid from reading Intensive Care. *Seeing him as an adult is like a tiny sequel to the book.*
Deb

I thought the same thing, Deb! I totally see Mary-Lou around the mouth! A combo-kid, exactly.
  Very handsome and distinguished-looking.
Lynn

I see Mary-Lou, too. This whole offspring deal is such a miracle!
Donna

Friday, May 29, 2020

One of my favorite plays is Thornton Wilder's *Our Town*. As often as I can, I try to remind myself of its basic theme to appreciate the beauty of the ordinary while one is able. This pandemic seclusion not only makes it easier to reflect on such things, but the "ordinary" is a shifting perception. As an example, yesterday I shared with you that I baked two loaves of bread. What I didn't mention was that in the process of energetically kneading my mixture of flour and water, I knocked over the bag of flour. In my hasty recovery effort, I also tipped over the salt container, which emptied onto the floor. Flour and salt were everywhere, on the countertop, underfoot, in the air, and very soon thereafter on my clothes, face and hair. The scene was worthy of an *I love Lucy* episode… like the one with the pies on the speeding conveyor belt. The only thing missing was the chef's hat.

I will treasure that moment for the rest of my life.
Ken

What a fun image. Did you return the flour to the bag and the salt to the shaker?
Donna

Now that would have been a picture!
Morgaine

Thank you, Ken. That made me laugh! Set a great tone for keeping a positive perspective. Wish I could have been a fly on the wall!
Deb

Friday, May 29, 2020

https://www.newyorker.com/magazine/2020/05/11/the-enduring-romance-of-the-night-train/amp

Under ordinary circumstances I doubt I would send a *New Yorker* article for others to read. As you all know and love beautifully crafted writing and you may have time to settle into a favorite chair and savor reading about night trains, here is such an article.

Just the other day a train roared by when I was walking with a friend. "I want to take the train," I wistfully told her. After reading Anthony Lane's exquisite prose, I long to take a night train—and to be a better writer.

I only happened to read this article because it followed one a friend had told me not to miss "The Greenwich Rebellion, how country-club Republicans learned to ignore their neighbors and love Trump." It almost set my hair on fire.

I'm obviously reading and not baking, but bed is made before

I'm allowed to break open a book or magazine. Now I'm heading back to my middle grade project to reread the first 50 pages after umpteen changes to the opening chapters. Rather than seeing myself as a dolt because of all the revisions after I thought it was finished, I reassure myself that I now know my characters so much better. I count them as friends at this point. And social distancing is not an issue.

Thank you for amusing and impressing me with your writing and active lives.

Donna

Friday, May 29, 2020

I get a call from a friend of mine at 11:30 this morning. I'm still in bed, listening to NPR, caught between facing the day and dozing. When I finally listen to her message, she says: "XXX (a Black commentator) suggested that white people should call a Black friend and talk about Minneapolis." I pause to ponder my responses: most people don't have Black friends so that's stupid advice; or why talk to Blacks when violence against us is a white problem, instead go "talk amongst yourselves"; or, I'm fine although every time I think about my two strapping grandsons, I say a silent prayer, *stay safe*; or put your money where your mouth is or just shut up.

Then I reconsider and call her back, but that's only because I like her, and she had a Black husband, and her kids are Black; she has some street cred. I explain my various reactions and why I returned her call. My logical brain tells me, *Start the conversation wherever you see an opening. Don't wait for the perfect entrance.* She tells me about a woman in a discussion group who said, "I don't see color." If I heard that comment, I'd have to suppress my instinct to strangle the speaker. My friend handled it more gently; maybe the woman heard her.

We end the conversation when I refer to John Donne:

Each man's death diminishes me,
For I am involved in mankind.
Therefore, send not to know
For whom the bell tolls,
It tolls for thee.

But that's me playing head games. Where I really am is in bed, imagining the real me, like *The Portrait of Dorian Gray* tucked away in the attic. Hidden in my heart is the two-dimensional Judy, a shadow with tiny pinpricks in it, one for each bullet fired at an unarmed Black man by the police or a bystander who imagined him a bogeyman. You can see through me. A little gust of wind will blow me away. No one will notice.

I'm going out for a walk. I hope I don't see anyone.

Judy

Oh my God Judy! Just wanted to reach out to you with a heavy heart. Watching CNN

Gina

Judy, that description is so desperate, so broken-hearted. little to say but how sorry and horrified I am. Just as each human is involved in mankind, each white is involved in racism. It IS our problem to fix, each of us, in whatever ways big or small within our reach.

Deb

Friday, May 29, 2020

I began the day in tears with the news that has veered off from the pandemic. We're on a fast train to fascism with a president encouraging violence and a police force that sees the world in black and white. Mark compared it to the "me too movement." As a man who respects women, he knew there was an issue with sexual harassment and abuse, but never imagined the depth and breadth of the problem, until every woman he spoke with knew firsthand. As white folk we can't even fathom what it's like to be born with black skin. It makes me sick to think of what has happened to our country on so many levels. I want to scream.

In comparison the issues closer to home seem trivial.

I shopped for and planted my vegetable garden yesterday.

Tomatoes, cucumbers, carrots, lettuce, arugula, eggplant, zucchini, peppers, and herbs. I was in another world digging in the dirt for most of the day, in my own little bubble.

Morgaine

Friday, May 29, 2020

Today was a sad day. The video of George Floyd played over and over again in my head. That he cried out for his mother who was two years dead, reduced me to tears. If that primal cry doesn't awaken the humanity that must dwell even in the haters, nothing will. That's what I'm afraid of. And that we have Trump presiding over this this nation at this time should feel like a knee on everyone's neck.

Mary-Lou

Gasp! Oh yes!!!
Gina

Ohh! What you wrote about Trump's knee to our necks made me gasp, as well. How awful. How true.
Donna

Mary-Lou, it's a perfect and perfectly terrifying image. My only shred of hope is that this is such a low point that we can only rise from it.
Deb

I wish I could believe that, Deb, but I despair. What horror! And it continues to happen. Over and over and over without change. When is enough, enough?
Maria

Saturday, May 30, 2020

I am so distracted watching the anchors, analyst, reporters, experts, public officials all weighing in on the protests across the country that I just can't think. I am stuck.

Maria calls.

"I talked to Aunt Nell this morning. She thinks I should break up with Paul. That relationship will never go anywhere if he's not willing to tell his kids about me."

"Nell is right!"

"I gave him an ultimatum. He tells his 11- and 13-year-old kids or we break up."

"How did he take it?"

"He wants to talk in person. He's coming out tomorrow."

Monica plays tennis on a private court in New Canaan with Mr. Sneakers. That evening she invites two other tennis friends to come over for a marshmallow roast and ping-pong. A man brings one of his kids. They all arrive masked. Monica tells them they don't need the masks in our house since they've been self-isolating for two months. Both are divorced, single parents. Both have kids going back and forth between households with ex-spouses. Where is the closed circle here? All this isolation is unraveling. No social distancing. All of them touch the wine bottles and ping-pong paddles and balls.

Gina

Saturday, May 30, 2020

My daughters are in tears and then they're off and running. Jill, in Harlem, joined a march that started at the office building on 125 Street, went east to the FDR and closed it down. "Will you post bail if I'm arrested?" she asks me. Of course, I will; if that's the worst that happens, I consider us lucky.

Kim in Los Angeles went to the LAPD and offered to conduct training—not sure in what: communication skills? Anti-racism? She's an HR trainer by profession. I offer to introduce her to a woman on TEAM Westport who's done that with the Westport Police Department. Her work surfaced problems but didn't solve them.

Fern and family are going to march in Boston tomorrow. I extend my offer for bail. Their daughters were the catalyst. Rosabelle, 19, had planned to go with friends; she needs to understand that this is more dangerous than the Women's March, that there's more at risk than there was when she started the Black Student Alliance at Tilton. There she just faced indifference.

I'd prefer that my grandsons not do anything since they're the most likely targets. But I can't control that either.

My sister and I are writing postcards to voters in swing states. We'll nurse the psychic wounds of our children and grandchildren as best we can. We are leaving them a world full of hate.

Judy

I have the same feeling about the world we are leaving children and grandchildren. So much hope in November 2008, So much desperation in 2020.

Deb

Pray hard, Judy, pray hard. I will too. Sending love,
Polly

Sunday, May 31, 2020

Chris and I talk:

"Well, between the pandemic and the protesters, two of the three legs of the stool keeping our civilization alive are splintered. All we need now is to throw in a natural disaster."

"Don't even say that, Ma. We had two tornados near here at the beginning of the week."

Chris has been deployed. He worked in the Minneapolis riot area the night before and in the state capitol in Saint Paul last night.

Monica, the girls, and I take a late afternoon walk. When we circle back home, they ask if they can go to Starbucks at Stop & Shop.

"Starbucks is filthy. That's probably not a good idea," I say.

"It's perfectly fine. It's totally clean. Come on girls. Get your masks," Monica says.

I have masks that I ordered from Amazon. I offer them to the girls. Monica had some in her car.

She is probably right about Starbucks. She's made a few trips to the store. I haven't been there since March 10th. But, when I went to that Starbucks every Monday afternoon with Evelyn after her tennis lesson some of the tables had trash on them, a couple of chairs had goo on the seats, and one of the lightbulbs in a hanging lamp was burned out.

I feel pretty burned out myself.

Gina

June 2020

Monday, June 1, 2020
Cut and Color

Another normal day in Trump's America: the pandemic continues to kill Americans at an alarming rate, the stock market goes up, the race riots are met with a presidential threat to use the American military on the homeland, and I got a haircut. What follows my lede is trivial. Feel free to check out.

I was born a redhead. It's a big part of my identity. That and being named Mary-Louise by a mother whose middle name was Mary, and a father whose middle name was Louis. As a little redhead, I garnered a lot of attention, since my parents both had dark brown hair. That provoked jokes about how our milkman must have been a redhead. (Clearly there were some recessives way back in the Ukraine where redheads with brown eyes are common.)

I arrived at the salon at noon, nervous, masked and rubber gloved. I was pleased to see that everyone was wearing masks and gloves and further, that each station was separated from the next one by a clear plastic curtain that hung from ceiling to floor.

I had an agenda. I had learned during the three plus months that my hair was pure white in the front, which I rather liked. However, I also learned that the back of my head was still red. I had toyed with the idea of "going white," but apparently that was out of the question. I also learned that I liked my hair a bit longer. I was also advised by my friends that my hair looked better lighter and longer. Apparently, that would add a "softness" to my features. I instructed the guy who dyes my hair to tone down the color to strawberry blonde. (I know it's *de rigeur* to say you have your hair "colored," but that has always reminded me of Crayolas, so I say "dyed.")

Instead, it came out flaming red. I was horrified. Do you remember Raggedy Ann and Andy? I looked like an aged Raggedy Ann. After driving around Westport aimlessly, I finally got up the nerve to go home. I was all ready to tell Larry not to panic, that red dye fades quickly and I would look a lot better after I washed it a few times. But before I could get the words out, he picked up my shirt and stared at my upper torso.

"What are you doing?" I said, befuddled.

He answered, "I just wanted to see if you had a little heart on your chest that says, "I love you."

Mary-Lou

We are in a perilous time, but Larry? He couldn't have said anything more perfect. Raggedy Ann and Andy were both quite lovable and so, I'm sure, are you!

Maria

Aw, Maria—That's so sweet of you to say.

Mary-Lou

Monday, June 1, 2020

I get a call from my 90-year-old cousin Marilyn from Florida. She wants to know if the July 31st cousins' reunion in Milwaukee is still on. She sounds game to fly out and would stay with her daughter who lives in Wisconsin. I told her I would check with my brother and sister-in-law who had offered to host before the pandemic set in. I don't know if they would want thirty plus relatives from all over the country traipsing through their house on the skirts of the pandemic.

Chris is still deployed and spends the night picking up patients who arrive at the airport by heli-copter and transporting them to Hennepin

County Medical Center. The helicopters can't land at the hospital right now because of police drones and laser beams.

Here are mother and son ready for work.

Gina

Tuesday, June 2, 2020

Am Zoomed out—eyes watering, nose running, stomach growling—glad this is a writing group.

Started early with Zoom meditation group this morning. I'm so tired that it was really a snooze group. Then I went to my go-to nap man, Brian Lehrer on WNYC, and napped through his always scintillating interviews. Realized at 11:45 that I had to make the noon deadline for ordering dinner—they're not able to read my mind yet at Meadow Ridge although sometimes I'm sure there's a tranquilizer drug in the water—so easy to control old people— why not? But I haven't got time to go down that imaginary rabbit hole tonight.

Then a Zoom meeting with a Black film group. We watched *Becoming*, a film that follows Michelle Obama on her book tour. Delightful, genuine—*Those were the days, my friend / We thought they'd never end...* I stayed awake for that one since I'd had something to eat. Coffee doesn't work anymore. At 3:30 joined friends from the grandmother's writing group that I've been in for 15 years to plan a Zoom presentation of sorts for the Congregation of Humanistic Jews on Friday. Why am I doing it? Because they asked—we're the Sister Grannies. Everyone's upset by the protests/riots/lynching. I'm sad but not devastated, maybe just hopeless. Mostly I see irony and hypocrisy, perhaps beyond anger and tears.

Decided to squeeze in a two-mile walk—have to be mobile in case the quarantine ends. Yesterday I exercised my car by driving it around the ring road. Today it was my turn. Saw a few people but didn't stop to talk. I'm rediscovering that I'm verbal but essentially reclusive. I used to write notes to my father instead of talking to him.

Got back just in time to end day with second meditation meeting. We meditate, read a book out loud, talk and end with meditation. Toward the end of the session no one could hear me although I could hear them. Perhaps a foretelling of death. Perhaps just a cosmic cyberspace joke. I prefer to think the latter, but who knows? If tomorrow comes, I'll be on an 8 AM call with TEAM Westport. If not, not.

Judy

Tuesday, June 2, 2020

It seems as though the world is in revolt. Pandemics, riots, murder, inequality. All plagues.

And my mother is dying. Not in the way we all are, but imminently. I went to see her today, not standing in the driveway, but entering her house. The first time since early March. It was crushing. She has wasted to the bare frame of the person she once was. Since she could no longer talk to me, I spoke to her. I listed the people who love her and walked her through some of my fondest memories of her mothering. I am sad about her; ambivalent about her. She is 98, and the woman who raised me has not been present for the last few years. I've watched her slip away.

I once attended a lecture given by a neurologist specializing in dementia. He made the progress of the disease graphic. If you think of the adult human brain as a cauliflower, dementia whittles the brain to one quarter the weight and volume. I've thought of that image, envisioning with each new cognitive deficit that another floret has broken away.

Tomorrow she will enter home hospice. It's déjà vu all over again. I feel guilty that the greatest pain is that it triggers my feelings about Dave's passing. But he was not 98, not more absent than present.

Yesterday my four-year-old grandson told me about his trip to Vermont to visit his other grandparents. His family stayed in the house that belonged to my daughter-in-law's grandparents. They were called Jolly and Bobo by everyone except my grandson, who can't pronounce "L."

Silas, "Weww, we stayed at Jowwy and Bobo's house. But they weren't there, reawwy. Weww, that's because they're dead right now."

Maybe he's right. Maybe they'll all be back one day.

Deb

Tuesday, June 2, 2020

Mary-Lou calls. She hears the down in my voice. My paramedic son says rioters throw rocks at anyone wearing a uniform. He wears a bulletproof vest to work. He does have a beefy, no nonsense, take-charge aura about him which puts him on the weird side of risk.

Lex calls. He is back at work at Starbucks. His store closes early at the end of each shift so he can deep clean to mitigate the coronavirus risk.

Gina

Wednesday, June 3, 2020
I Didn't Think I Was Going to Get Covid-19, But I Did (Part Two)

Our local hospital's emergency room looked as if it were a clip from the evening news rather than the place I've known so well throughout the years as a volunteer. The atmosphere was hushed and tense as the ambulance crew wheeled me into a small cubicle and shut the door behind them.

From my window into the hallway, I saw people working in the open area. They were all wearing a pale yellow paper gown that reached to their knees, gloves, and a mask underneath a helmet that had a pull-down plastic shield to cover their faces. Some wore goggles; some wore shoe coverings. Everyone had their hair tucked inside surgical caps.

One of the doctors on duty came into my room.

"We're full. We need to transfer you to another hospital in our network. Is this okay?"

"Sure. I just want to get better," I said letting go of the notion that I wouldn't be sick enough to be admitted. I called my family to tell them. We knew that no one would be allowed to visit me, so it really didn't make any difference what hospital I was in, but they were not happy with this news.

"Answer the phone," was written in large letters on a whiteboard on the wall facing me. Why? I wondered. Then it rang.

It was the doctor I'd just met who told me that because I might be Covid-19 positive all our communication would be via telephone. He took my health history showing special interest in my years as an on-again, off-again smoker. The next call was from the pharmacy about my medications.

My doctor called again. "We need to do another test."

"I've already been tested at a drive-through and it was negative," I assured him.

"Those results aren't that reliable. We need to do another one. You may have the virus, but your X-ray shows that you have severe pneumonia."

"Pneumonia?" I said. "How'd I get that?"

No answer.

Within fifteen minutes those test results came back. Negative.

"We still think you have Covid so we're putting you on hydroxychloroquine to treat it," my doctor said, "and strong antibiotics for pneumonia. You're a high-risk patient because of your age and because you were a smoker."

Then came the clincher. "We're going to admit you. Here. Either a regular room or the ICU." I was relieved to know that I wouldn't be going to another hospital but alarmed at the mention of ICU, which to me spelled respirator.

I called my family who tried to hide their concern. They didn't. We agreed that my son should be the contact person with whom the doctors would talk, and my daughter would take care of the logistics. Both would be in close touch over the phone with their father who was alone and terrified that I was going to die.

I needed all the support I could muster, so I texted a string of family and friends. "I'm in the hospital with what they think is the coronavirus and pneumonia. Prayers are most welcome as are your kind thoughts." Within minutes positive and reassuring messages came back as well as some from people who'd heard the news over the grapevine. There aren't enough words to say how much these meant to me.

New nurse, same old message. "We still think you have Covid-19. We need to do another test." It's important to remember that this all happened at the height of the crisis—mid-April. There was no such thing as a false negative reading.

"This will be two tests in one," the nurse said. "I'm going to walk one of them up to the lab, so there is no danger of it getting confused, and the other one will be sent to an independent lab."

Fifteen minutes later the test from the hospital lab came back. Negative.

I was so looking forward to getting to my room. I was told it would be ready at 9:00 that evening. It wasn't. "We don't have the personnel," I was told. "We're looking for another one. You can't be in a room with a Covid patient, in case you don't have it, and you can't be in with a patient who doesn't have Covid in case you are positive."

It was well after midnight when I heard the hollow sound of a portable oxygen tank being attached to my bed.

My nurse came in with a huge smile. "Your room is ready!"

As I was leaving the Emergency Room one of the doctors called to me. "Your test from the independent lab just came back. It was also negative."

Polly

Wednesday, June 3, 2020

Each day I sit down to write, but there are no words to express the deep sadness, the feeling of hopelessness, the utter disgust at the state of affairs in America.

Morgaine

I'm totally with you. There are no words. Having gone through the turmoil of the sixties, this seems so much worse. Maybe because the same things keep happening over and over. Our nation is in a very dark place and the man at the head just stokes the fires.

Maria

Wednesday, June 3, 2020

My grandson, Langston, has gone from New Hampshire to Philadelphia with a friend to join a protest march. Why Philly? I don't know. What I do know is that everyone in the family is texting messages that reflect their personalities. The pinging's been going on for hours.

Jill, my youngest daughter, the lawyer in Harlem: Langston, be sure to wear a mask and a cap. And cover your tattoos. Don't climb any statues. There are surveillance cameras everywhere— you don't want to be caught on camera. And take water. Hug your fellow protestors for me.

(I'd never have thought about the cameras. The tattoo that covers his shoulder and arm is in homage to his late father and links Langston with his brother and sister as a core family. There was no point in objecting to it once he did it, and I certainly love the sentiment. He has to cover it in his nursing classes.)

Fern, the middle daughter and her husband, Michael, in a Boston suburb: Be aware you're in mixed company. What white people can do is an arrestable offense for a Black man. Pray before you go out for direction and safety. If you need me, I'll drive down.

(Michael and Fern are rock solid. But if anything happens, it would be more effective to ask my sister's ex-husband, a lawyer in DC, to step in. That ex was once arrested for challenging a cop who was ticketing him over a broken taillight. At the station the ex demanded his one phone call. "Do you know who that is?" the desk sergeant asked the officer. They threw him out the back door of the station and locked it so he couldn't come back in.)

Kim, my oldest daughter, and Langston's mother in Los Angeles: Remember the great poet you're named after Langston. Speak for all of us.

(I thrive on poetry, but I don't know how it helps in a protest march. Maybe after the march.)

Cario and Tim, my sister and brother-in-law in a suburb of D.C.: *She*: it's best not to go out at night—that's when the trouble starts. *He*: Even an arrest could be productive if it moves us closer to a just society.

I find out that they've paid for Langston's hotel room. They're marching *in abstentia*.

I paid for a hotel room once for Langston. He was traveling by bus from Bangor to Boston and then flying the next morning to see his mother in Los Angeles. He told me he would sleep in the bus station overnight.

"No, you won't. The cops will pick you up for vagrancy." I wired him money for a room.

All of us surround Langston with love. It takes a village to raise a committed young Black man.

Judy

Wednesday, June 3, 2020

Nell calls. She talks about staging her Minneapolis house and getting it ready to put on the market by the 16th. Maria is also staging her house to put on the market this coming weekend. Both my sister and my daughter think their homes will move quickly because of the coronavirus—Nell because buyers want room for a home office—and Maria because of buyers who want to get out of New York City and move to the suburbs.

My stomach is in knots. Both daughters and one sister are going through various states of divorce. Two of them have houses going on the market and are facing what to do next. One daughter isn't speaking to her brother or sister. Both of my sisters are not speaking to the older of my two brothers. Maria's kids pretty much ignore me.

I get a lot of pleasure and comfort from the three grand-daughters with whom I live.

Gina

Thursday, June 4, 2020

My interview as part of the library's Artists in Residences series was uploaded to their YouTube channel today. Link is below if you want to check it out!

https://www.youtube.com/watch?v=OIeTyDC_Alg

Deb

Deb, thank you for sharing your interview. I loved hearing your process. You are a master at capturing light. I'm so inspired. Keep breaking the rules!!!

Morgaine

Thursday, June 4, 2020

The events of the last few weeks have sent me to a rather gloomy place. I do the usual chores, but underneath there is a pit of sadness, rage, and frustration at what keeps happening over and over again. I am, of course, specifically referring to George Floyd's murder, the latest in a long line of murders perpetrated against Black people and others of color, other ethnicities, other religions.

I've always thought of myself as non-racist, but as I've recently been taught, it is not enough to be non-racist, we must be anti-racist. This set me thinking about my own thoughts, feelings, and actions. And it brought to mind a woman I called Tia Mulata as a child.

I wrote the attached for her:

TÍA MULATA

Her name was Laura Fernandez, but they called her Mulata; I called her Tia Mulata.

My father's oldest sibling, Julia, worked in an orphanage in Sabanilla where Laura had been brought as an infant. She was the result of what was regarded as an impossible liaison. In the 1930s, race relations in Cuba were civil, even cordial, but each race kept to their own place. Children of mixed parentage were either raised by their Black families, hidden away, or placed in an orphanage.

Julia worked at the orphanage in 1931-1932. Laura was nine, maybe ten years old then; records of her arrival at the orphanage did not exist. She stood out from the other children with her soft voice, shy smile and quiet manner and she liked tagging along while Julia performed her duties. She helped Julia soothe the younger children when they cried or when they were frightened. She became Julia's shadow, and it wasn't long before the older woman came to depend on her.

Julia brought Laura home to her family and they adopted her. Whether it was a legal adoption, or not, from that point on, Laura was part of the family, but she was still called Mulata. Everyone accepted it as normal, including Laura. It's what she had always been called.

My grandparents, with whom she lived and with whom she stayed after Julia moved to Havana, were the only family she knew. From the time she was ten, she grew up in that house in Sabanilla. There was no outward appearance of bias, but it was there. Laura cooked, but so did my grandmother and my other aunts. Did she clean the house? I never saw that. From the vantage point of time, I must conclude that while she was treated kindly, affectionately, she was still "other."

By the time I was born, she was a grown woman. She would coax me to eat the small pieces of steak that she'd prepared. I was a poor eater, but she had infinite patience.

Laura was a romantic and loved poetry as did my Aunt Nené, another of my father's sisters. Perhaps they fueled each other's love for the form. My cousin, Gina and I giggled when we spied on her sitting on the front porch with her beau in the evenings, each reciting poetry to the other.

I have her to thank for my life. Had she not put out the flames that engulfed my small frame one afternoon, I don't think I'd be here today. The doctor thought I might not survive that conflagration, but she had given me those extra minutes that allowed me to survive. She never stopped to consider her own safety and later on, as I slowly recuperated, she was part of my healing.

The last time I saw my tía was in the summer of 1952, when my mother and I returned to Cuba for a visit. One day we went to see Tía Mulata—yes, I still called her that—and I asked her to join us at the beach where mom took my cousin, two young friends, and me every weekday morning. She was reluctant, but I pleaded until she relented and agreed to meet us there. We were playing in the sand the next morning, our blanket not far from the food and drink pavilion, when I spotted tía sitting at one of the tables, watching us. I ran to her, excited that she'd come, and took her by the hand, tugging at her to come join us. She refused in her own quiet way, saying that it would not be "proper"—that is the word she used. I had no idea what she meant, but I didn't question her remark. No matter how much I begged, she kept shaking her head. My mother came and spoke with her, but she still would not join us. Finally, wanting to go back to my friends, I kissed her cheek, gave her a quick hug and ran back to our place in the sand, looking up and waving every now and then. Tía stayed for a while, but when I looked back for her, she'd gone. Unthinking, I joined my friends in the water.

When I returned to Cuba in 1996 with my mother, tía was no longer living.

I honor the memory of her and the gifts she gave, not only to me, but to my family, to her own family, and to all who knew her.

In loving memory for my Tía Laura. She mattered. She had a name.

Maria

Maria, what a lovely piece of writing. It's a wonderful tribute to her that you have new understanding of the socially constructed differences that kept her sitting at a distance on the beach.
Deb

Friday, June 5, 2020

This is a text from my daughter, Fern, in Sharon, Massachusetts. They live across the street from a nature preserve—no houses there to witness anything that happens. Next door neighbors are hidden by trees which are fully leafed out by now. Michael is a 5'8" muscular karate black belt and an architect—not tall but big. He is standing behind a floor to ceiling picture window. Fern is an elected member of the town school board. She is known for being outspoken and occasionally confrontational—although what's "aggressive" for a woman is merely "assertive" for a man.

"Black in America—Report from Sharon

Michael was up late last night, working. A car drives by our house. Stops. Backs up and then drives in front of the house again. Michael gets up and stands in front of the living room window. Arms folded, ready to protect us and our home.

The person gets out of the car, steps onto our lawn, and proceeds to hammer in a local campaign sign—which I had asked for.

This is what racism does. Black men always have to be at the ready, expecting the worst even in their own homes."
Judy

Friday, June 5, 2020

I attend a Zoom meeting for the State and Regional Coordinating Council of The ESOP Association. The November annual meeting and trade show in Las Vegas in November is going forward as planned. Everything else scheduled before that is up for grabs.

I am grateful to be serving on the coordinating council—it contributes to my sense of professional self-worth.

Gina

Friday, June 5, 2020

I slipped up. I let my guard down. What was I thinking?

We had a couple over, Suzanne and Rosie, for a socially distant visit by the pool. They showed up in masks, which were soon down around their chins and eventually tucked away in a beach bag. We shared a bottle of wine in plastic cups, no harm in that. Michelle had made deviled eggs earlier in the day and before I know it, I'm serving hors d'oeuvres. The real clincher was when I put out a bowl of baba ghanoush and pita chips.

While I had an uneasy feeling as we dipped, munched and shared like old times, I ignored it. It was as though I had a lapse in consciousness. Or was it the kid inside that said, "Fuck it! I can't do this anymore?" After half the dip was consumed and there were two deviled eggs left on the plate, Suzanne says, "We went out to dinner last night. The place was hopping and there was a line outside the door."

That evening my 22-year-old son approached Mark and me asking, "What the hell?" I felt so bad. I let him down. Meanwhile, my daughter, who turns 25 in July is starving for social interaction. She has a handful of peeps who are recently six-foot distancing. One of them has antibodies, whatever that means. And what can I say when they have to use the bathroom? As the state of Connecticut begins to open, I grapple with my level of comfort, my own boundaries and those of the ones I love.

Morgaine

Friday, June 5, 2020

Westporter Mary-Lou Weisman said, "I'm in my 80s. My generation failed you. We have hope you can do what we didn't do."

—Dan Woog—06880 Blogger

Larry and I went to the Black Lives Matter rally that was held on the Ruth Steinkraus Cohen bridge at 1:30 today, Friday. With few exceptions—we being two of them—the rally was all about young people, both Black and white. I think Staples High School sponsored the gathering, so perhaps it's no surprise that most of the protesters were young. A contingent of Black kids from Norwalk and perhaps other nearby towns give the Westport crowd the appearance of racial diversity.

They were very well organized, and wonderfully loud and passionate. Young people with bull horns prompted the eager crowd to chant "I Can't Breathe" and "Black Lives Matter." Police closed bridge traffic during the demonstration, which was a very good idea, since, on command, every-

one lay down on the bridge, put their hands behind their backs as if in handcuffs. Shouting in ever diminishing volume, "I Can't Breathe." By the time the rally came to a close, there may have been 400 in attendance. The grand finale was a march to the police station where the chief of police delivered a brief but compassionate speech.

Larry was one of a few Westport lawyers who went to Mississippi during the horrific summer of 1964, as part of The Lawyers Constitutional Defense Committee. That was the summer of water guns, bullets, burning churches, menacing dogs, police brutality and the murders of civil rights workers Goodman,

Schwerner and Chaney. Larry's job was to remand those who were arrested by the police to hand themselves over to the federal rather than the state courts where they didn't stand a chance at justice.

None of the young people at this 2020 rally weren't even born. "Our" generation may have done our best to fight inequality and march for justice, but, clearly, we failed. I looked around at these kids and thought, now it's your turn. White kids are better integrated with Black kids than they were in what I hate to call "my day." They are multitudes, as we have seen in rallies and bridges all over this country. They know how to get the nation's attention. They give us hope.

Mary-Lou

Mary-Lou, I liked seeing you on 06880 and speaking for the older generation who did indeed fail. Here's to the younger generations and their wisdom and activism. Bravo to you and Larry for going.

Donna

I wish I could have been there. Not sure we failed. Change takes time. We laid the groundwork. It's been an uphill struggle, and I'm so glad that new, young energy is taking up the mantle to continue the climb. I believe the rock they are pushing up that hill is lighter for the civil rights generation of the 50s and 60s. Bravo for you and Larry for being there with them!

Deb

Saturday, June 6, 2020

My peonies popped today.

Like so much that is beautiful, they don't last long.

Mary-Lou

My daughter stripped out the peonies, rhododendron, azaleas, and lily of the valley from our yard because she wanted hydrangea and a clean uncluttered lawn. She is also afraid of bees—a friend of hers died from a bee sting. Now I have to get my peonies from Compo Farms Flowers.
Gina

Peonies ignite gentle summer memories for me. Thank you for the smiles.
Donna

Worth waiting for them no matter what! I am waiting for ours to bloom.
Polly

Saturday, June 6, 2020

I vacuum and dust for first time since the Saturday before Easter. Just got too tired to care about it. Glad to see the dust bunnies go for a little while. They multiply so fast they must be related to rabbits.

I call Kindred Spirits. Always get a friendly reception from them. They have two cases of Columbia Crest chardonnay wheeled over to our doorstep almost before I can hang up.

The badminton set Monica has ordered arrives. She sets it up in the backyard and plays with the girls.
Gina

Sunday, June 7, 2020

Bounced from the intellectual to the soulful this weekend. There was a virtual Cornell reunion on Friday and Saturday. Did much more online than I could have walked to if I'd been on campus.

Did the back half of a session on Friday, "Math and Crocheting." An older woman who confessed that she didn't hear well demonstrated 3D shapes that she crochets based on solid geometry. When people told her it couldn't be done or it wasn't worth doing, she kept at it. Now her pieces are in one of the Smithsonian museums. The crocheted results were like sculptures, convoluted, different from each angle, glorious. I didn't understand the math part—par for the course.

On Saturday I was at Cornell virtually for six hours.—The first session celebrated the 50th anniversary of Toni Morrison's *The Bluest Eye*. I did a crash re-reading of the book, selected a passage to read, then talked about how it spoke to me. Just as Pecola wanted blue eyes, I wanted straight hair. If a man had offered to turn my kinky hair straight permanently, I'd have gone with him just as Pecola did, caught as I was at 11 between still believing in magic with a child's hope and being grounded in the real world as a 'tween. The desire was so strong I can still taste it; straight hair would have made me beautiful.

Decided to join a Cornell Black Alumni meeting that dove into our rage and sadness at the unequal impact of Covid-19 and the continued police lynching of Black men like George Floyd—speakers, laughter, music, tears. That program was followed by an open chat about issues that apply to Black life at Cornell. There was no CBAA when my sister and I were there because there were only one to two Black students in each class.

The end of the weekend was similar to how it began. On Friday night I attended the Congregation for Humanistic Judaism as part of a panel to discuss personal experiences with racism in Fairfield County. This afternoon I was in a two-hour Buddhist spiritual retreat for Black women—300 women from all over the globe expressing present day suffering and personal healing techniques.

Shalom. Namaste.

Judy

What an amazing weekend. What an amazing woman. Holy cow! I'm envious. I'm in awe. I'm also exhausted! If I touch you, will some of that rub off on me?
Maria

What an amazing weekend you had, Judy. What exciting opportunities to learn, think, reconsider, etc. I must admit I'm a little jealous. About now I'm ready to go to college and be a student again. Just don't make me live in a dorm.
Donna

Sunday, June 7, 2020

Judy's last entry above is the last straw. It's official. It can't be refuted, denied, spun, or ignored any longer. It's no one's fault but my own, but you are all to blame. I joined our group with some confidence that I am a curious person and that I have devoted a reasonable amount of time pursuing an interesting life; however, during these past two months, the fog has cleared, the curtain has risen, the veil is removed. I am officially admitting to myself that I am a slug.
Respectfully,
Ken

Would that be a banana slug or one suited for escargot?
Morgaine

Sunday, June 7, 2020

My mother was born Hermione Frank on April 19, 1922. She was anything but a delicate flower, but as beautiful, complicated, and unique as one. She died as Nanny, forever thrilled by the name she acquired after the birth of her first grandchild. She was too tough and stubborn and strong-willed to pass before her 98th birthday. If I started to list the adjectives to describe her, I would be writing all day.

It's enough to say she was my mama, and I loved her.

Deb

Sunday, June 7, 2020

Lex calls and let me know his parents are now on vacation have gone camping. They are away from what remains of the Minneapolis protests, much to my relief.

Ryan attend's her bestie's Bat Mitzvah at a socially distant drive-by from twelve feet away. Monica prepares to take Ryan there.

Monica and Mr. Sneakers go off to play tennis. She comes back by herself and grills burgers. She sets up the badminton net and when it gets dark, sets off fireworks. The next-door neighbors' son and grandson come over to enjoy the pit fire and jazz music. Peapod arrives around 9:45 PM while they are all still there.

Gina

Sunday, June 7, 2020

A robin redbreast made a nest in a bush next to my back porch. I've been watching for a long time but aside from the robin visiting the nest every so often, I hadn't seen any movement.

Yesterday morning after I let Archie out as usual, I left the back door open to let the wonderful morning breeze inside. As I sat having breakfast, I became aware of a chirping noise. This was something new, and it was near! Could it be? I stepped as close as

I could to the bush and saw that somehow the small bird was not in its nest, but on a branch. I was worried. Had he somehow managed to tumble out? Would its mother be able to help?

I called my daughter-in-law, Elizabeth, our family's animal go-to person. Did I need to help the youngster? I was afraid to do that for fear that if I were to put it back in the nest, my human scent would keep the mother away. "Watch it," Elizabeth counseled. "If it's still there in an hour, I'll come over and we'll get him." (She has a young crow she picked up when he was found on the driveway, on his back, pedaling his legs as if on a bicycle.) Soon after I hung up with Elizabeth, I watched as the momma robin swooped to where the youngster was and fed some morsel into his open beak. Hurrah! I called Elizabeth and gave her the good news.

All yesterday, momma flew in at frequent intervals to check on and feed her little one. Last night, the youngster was back in the nest. I've not seen or heard any action this morning but am hopeful that all's well. The birds at least are carrying on with life.
Maria

The little bird may have become tired of the nest, which is how I can feel about my nest some days. Thank you, Maria, for the sweet story with a happy ending. Yay, Mother Nature!
Donna

Monday, June 8, 2020

There was zilch activity at the nest today, no movement and no appearance by momma. At 3:30, I decided to sit outside and perhaps I'd get lucky. About 20 minutes into my vigil, a small bird flew in and nestled into the bush where the nest sits, but he was face into the greenery so I couldn't see his front. He stayed silent and unmoving for a long time, over an hour. Perhaps he was the nestling who was now flying?

When I searched on the internet for robins, I learned that the nest is not the bird's home, just a place to lay and hatch the eggs and care for the young until they are able to fend for themselves. I'm hoping they're not through with their adolescence, so they'll come back for a little while.

In the meantime, the squirrels had their own fun, chasing each other up and down a tree and having a good tussle.

A good afternoon's watch.

Maria

Monday, June 8, 2020

I Didn't Think I was Going to Get Covid-19, But I Did (Part 3)

The first thing I noticed as my nurse wheeled me down the hallway to my room was most of the rooms had a large red plus sins taped to their closed doors, including the one I was entering. At first I was puzzled, and then I got it. They alert the staff that these rooms had Covid patients. Even though my tests were negative, I was still considered to have the virus.

My room was as fantastic as any hospital room can be. It was a double, but because of my isolation requirements, I was alone. It was middle-of-the-night dark outside, but I knew that once daylight came, the far-away view from the three large windows would be of Long Island Sound and I-95 North and when I looked down, I'd see the hospital's parking lot.

For the next few days anyone who entered my room, and there was a steady stream of them, had to remove their yellow gowns, gloves and mask, throw them in the trash and put on new ones.

I don't think I slept at all that night, but I must have as a tech from the lab gently woke me when it was still dark. She needed a blood test.

"Didn't I give you enough last night in the ER?" I asked. "They took so many tests I thought I'd run out of blood."

She tried to smile at my little joke, but I noticed tears in her eyes. I asked her what was wrong. She wanted to talk.

"Before I came into work this morning I stopped for coffee at Starbucks. A sign said first responders get free coffee. I had my money ready to pay, but when I saw that sign I put my five dollars back in my pocket.

"I am a first responder," I told the woman who took my order.

"Let me see your badge," she said. I showed it to her.

"No, you're not," she said in a nasty voice. "You're not a doctor or a nurse."

The tech held up a vial of my blood. "Without this, the doctors wouldn't know how to treat their patients. In order to get fast results we have about a hundred people working in the lab 24/7."

She wiped a tear from her eye and continued.

"Everyone who comes into this room or works in this hospital is a first responder from the doctors and nurses to the people who clean the rooms and deliver the food."

She patted her belly.

"My baby is due in June. I am so afraid he'll get the virus. When I get home, I take off my clothes and throw them in the wash before I give my family a hug."

All I could do was listen, nod my head, and tell her the words of appreciation she needed to hear. This was a pivotal moment for me. I had given a perfunctory thank you to those who'd helped me so far, but now this took on new meaning. I thanked everyone who came into my room with heartfelt words, and if they wanted to chat, so did I. No one was comfortable working on a floor with Covid patients. As my days in the hospital continued, I observed them doing their jobs with no sighing, no attitude, and no complaining. Most of them were working twelve-hour shifts.

The staff was stretched thin, but in spite of this, I received excellent care. I tried to limit my requests to the necessaries knowing that whenever anyone left my room, they had to strip off their PPE garb and put on new ones. The ice water in my bedside pitcher was often empty. I became a hoarder. I'd order several bottles of water with every meal and asked for a stack of towels, sheets and hospital gowns to store on the window sill to use when I needed them.

One day a nurse came into my room wearing a dark blue gown rather than the airy yellow one. It reminded me of a garbage bag. Beads of sweat dotted her forehead.

"New gowns?" I asked.

"We ran out of the others," she said. Another nurse told me she wore the same mask all day.

"There aren't any new ones."

One afternoon a loud commotion of sirens and horns from the street below made me go to the window. At first, it looked like a few ambulances, police cars, fire trucks and emergency vehicles driving up to the hospital, but soon there were hundreds of them circling the blocks around the hospital with their sirens blaring and horns blasting.

The evening news said that this was a message of support from neighboring towns and cities. I hoped that the pregnant lab tech who was turned away at Starbucks was near a window to enjoy this display.

At twilight, there was more noise from the parking lot. About fifty people of all ages were blasting their boom-boxes as they sang and danced to the music. Some held up signs of thanks to first responders. A few saw me standing at my window and waved back.

Polly

Monday, June 8, 2020

I understand how I'm reacting to my intense feelings—I'm isolating myself, which is my way of self-protection, of trying to heal. I'm deciding to talk when I feel like it instead of when people catch me unawares. I don't rush to the phone but instead listen to messages, only picking up if it's a close friend or a relative. I'll call back if and when I'm ready. That may not be soon.

I'm limiting my outside walks, not in any planned way but based on how ready I feel to face the Meadow Ridge public. I used to go out and bound up to anyone I saw, like an energetic golden retriever, imaginary fur waving each time two feet hit the ground, tail wagging, eager to exercise my voice. No more. I wave, head down, sunglasses on, tightly masked, and keep up my rapid pace.

Last night I twisted my hair so that now I look like Topsy. That used to be an insult—no one wanted to look like her with her Black face, wide nose, pink, heavy lips, and hair that looked like the spikes on the coronavirus. But now I am her with my unevenly knotted hair, tight and comfortable against my scalp. I don't care. I'll look the way I choose to, decide who to talk to and when, appear Black or white or however this world chooses to see me. What are they gonna do? Shoot me?

Judy

Tuesday, June 9, 2020

I've been a bit out of it, but now I'm back in. By out of it, I missed two MD appointments because in my pandemic daze I'm not supposed to have appointments. I didn't even bother to turn my month-in-advance calendar page over to June. Now I have, and now I have appointments and have re-booked the ones I had. Then more trouble. My toilet sometimes sings an ear-splitting aria when I flush it, but of course every time the plumber comes to fix it—3 times so far—he doesn't hear the problem. A lot is going wrong in our lovely tear down. We need a new driveway. Beaucoup bucks. We have a dead tree—a huge one—that has to come down. More bucks. Larry and I did what we usually do when we have to pay enormous bills at our late-ish stage of life. We sang a chorus of "It

must be condo time, it must be condo time" to the tune of "It's Howdy Doody Time" and then gulped and wrote the checks.
Mary-Lou

I've been living in a condo—two different ones since 2004—and I'm spoiled by the easier life. But I still drive by cute little houses and think one might be fun. Sometimes I forget my age. It may not be the best time for me to have a starter house. Most of the time I appreciate the sanctuary of my lovely condo. The longest I lived in a house was eighteen years. I can't imagine your attachment to your house after so many years. I say keep writing checks.
Donna

Tuesday, June 9, 2020

Now for an example of first class writing that appeared in an op-ed piece in the *NYTimes*. Notice how he builds momentum with short thoughts, so that when you get to the more complex thoughts, you are already hooked.

"This is an awful man, waving a book he hasn't read, in front of a church he doesn't attend, invoking laws he doesn't understand, against fellow Americans he sees as enemies, wielding a military he dodged serving, to protect power he gained via accepting foreign interference, exploiting fear and anger he loves to stoke, after failing to address a pandemic he was warned about, and building it all on a bed of constant lies and childish inanity."

—Robert Hendrickson, Rector, St. Philip's Episcopal Church, Tucson
Mary-Lou

Mary-Lou, Thanks for sending that fabulous sentence. A sensational summary of what happened
Donna

Tuesday, June 9, 2020

My brother Terry calls. He wants me to notify our cousins that the reunion planned for July 31st is definitely off because of the pandemic.

Other things are opening up. I email H Salon to see if they can fit me in for a haircut anytime soon. They can schedule me at 5 PM tomorrow.

It is Frances' eighth birthday. Monica makes her special pizza and we all eat it on the patio. I feel a crunch and then something loose while I am chewing. The damaged crown has come out. I put it on my plate and keep my mouth shut.

We go inside to sing to Frances while she blows out the candles on her ice cream cake. She is thrilled with the dozen slinky toys I got her.

Gina

Wednesday, June 10, 2020

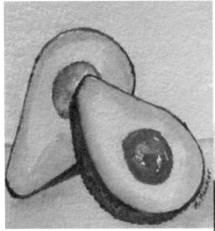

I love mornings. The stillness of family members in slumber. The anticipation of that first cup of coffee. The day ahead is full of promise. It's six thirty AM, the heavy gate to my vegetable

garden squeaks as I pull it open. It's time to put into the ground the tomato plants I started from seed. I dig deep, throw a banana peel into the bottom of each hole—tomatoes thrive on pot-assium. I bury the roots and most of the stem of five baby tomato plants. The soil is cool and damp and makes its way under my fingernails. I inspect the vines climbing up the mesh wall of my garden. Snap peas are ready for harvest, lettuce and arugula are not far behind. What shall I do next? Go back to bed and read, go for a run, do yoga. Ah yes, sip at my dark, bold, caffeinated palate pleaser and write today's virally.

Yesterday I got around to fulfilling my promise of mini watercolor paintings, the avocado for Mary-Lou, and Lynn's guinea pig, Rosie.

Morgaine

Wednesday, June 10, 2020

I call the dentist's office to get the appointment that had been postponed from last February. They can see me the next morning.

I Zoom into a New York/New Jersey ESOP Executive Committee meeting. It is good to catch up with colleagues. For now, we can't get out of the contract for our September conference at Hershey Lodge. Things may change with coronavirus over the summer.

I get my haircut. I just happened to get a lucky open slot. They are backed up for a month. Everyone is wearing masks and one of the owners is wearing a face shield. Every other shampoo bowl and workstation is empty. There is no waiting in the waiting room. I get a nice surprise—my stylist can blow dry my hair after all. I leave a cash tip in an envelope. I haven't used my handbag in months. It seems strange pull out my wallet and credit card. I Uber there and back for the first time since February 19th.

Mr. Sneakers' car is in the driveway when I get home. His car is still in the driveway the next morning.

Gina

Thursday, June 11, 2020

I wear mask and gloves in the Uber car to the dentist. I get there ten minutes early as instructed. I have to pull down my mask for my phone to recognize me. I stand outside the front door while the office texts me a survey. Then I take the elevator up, pressing the button with a knuckle. The dental assistant takes my temperature before escorting me to the open-door restroom where I am to wash my hands. She then takes me to the operatory and places my mask on a paper towel. She instructs me to hang my handbag on a hook. She and the dentist are totally gowned in personal protective attire. The dentist wears a triple mask. I am given a cup of antibiotic mouthwash which I am to swish without swallowing for 45 seconds. I last for 30. I get an X-ray. That goes well. They try to put some new anti-coronavirus plastic gismo in my mouth. I gag. They decide to go without it. The dentist is sympathetic. He is a gagger too.

The dentist administers a couple shots of Novocain before he begins to drill the tooth that is to accept the temporary crown. I wince when it gets too sensitive. It seems to be taking a long time. Then suddenly I feel a blast of pain and the assistant starts blotting blood from my mouth with gauze pads. Silence.

The assistant asks if the dentist wants a "four or a five" "Four," he answers. I get more Novocain. Then I see some long threads being pulled in and out of my mouth and feel tugging and tying. I realize I am having stitches. The base of my tongue has been nicked.

"Okay, now let's get back to where we left off," the dentist says. The drilling doesn't take much longer. Much to my relief, the impressions are taken with a camera. No more mouthful of trays with goo waiting to set.

Finally, we are done.

"Nothing salty or spicy for a few days," I am cautioned. The receptionist comes to the chairside to get my credit card payment.

The dental assistant escorts me to the door. No stopping along the way. I use my knuckle to press the elevator button and put on my gloves before touching the Uber door.

When I get home, I have to hold my jaw to take a sip of water. I am in pain. I welcome a distraction. I Zoom into the annual meeting of the New York Society of Association Executives. It beats taking the train to New York City, but I miss the ambiance of the Harvard Club where it was to have been held.

The pain takes hold. I wonder when I will be able to swallow again. I try soup and a pain pill for dinner.

Gina

Thursday, June 11, 2020

Just a little over three weeks until Michelle's twenty-fifth birthday. She loves birthdays. Yours, mine, hers; especially hers! Twenty-five is a big one. In the past we've gone out to an extravagant restaurant. The family, boyfriend, a bestie and Grandma—that's seven people. As of today, restaurants are limiting guests to five per table. "We can't go without Grandma," Michelle laments. She's all about tradition. Perhaps by July 5th the ceiling will be raised.

In another reality there would be a party. Fifty or sixty people gathered in our backyard, many of them musical theatre graduates. I adore my daughter's friends: interesting, smart, creative. There'd be tacos, tequila and a sound system. Her talented guests would entertain us well into the night. Michelle's request this year, five or six of her closest friends around the pool. One coming from NY, *Yikes!* Michelle knows to talk to her father when it comes to party planning. "Separate food stations for each person," she assures me. "I'll make fancy masks as party gifts." I hate saying "no" to Michelle, she's so deserving. Over the next few weeks, as Westport relaxes restrictions, the curve will be the deciding factor. Fingers crossed.

In the meantime, I'm toying with idea of going birthday shopping, at Free People and/or Anthropologie just to break the routine.

Morgaine

Thursday, June 11, 2020

Last evening we gathered at my daughter and son-in-law's home for dinner and a viewing of a Netflix documentary. My granddaughter, Callie, who lives and works in Maine, was the initiator of this gathering, and grandson Quinn here in Westport made sure everyone was notified. If you haven't seen this documentary, I urge you to do so. Its title is *13* which refers to the 13th Amendment to the Constitution, the one that abolished slavery. It is a powerful depiction of what happened after 13th was passed and shows how the very language of this amendment was twisted, leading to forms of slavery called by other names.

After the viewing we held a family discussion, Callie on FaceTime and the rest of us gathered around so she could see us. How to translate our beliefs into action was a lot of what we spoke of. How to shift the power from an all-white society to a more equal and just one was one of the themes that kept coming up. There is much work to be done. The demonstrations that are occurring in the US and all over the world are just a beginning. I feel there is hope that this time we can finally achieve a more perfect union.

Grandson Zachary's drive-by graduation "ceremony" happens tomorrow. We shall watch from the curbside with congratulatory banners when he and his classmates pass by. Something to be celebrating! Hoorah!

Maria

Friday, June 12, 2020

I Zoom into the NYSAE Engagement Lounge for a chat about

diversity and what associations are doing to make Black Lives Matter. I realize that when I've been attending one organization's conferences over the past five years, I have only come across one Black attendee and no Black speakers. The one attendee was a professional, not someone coming from a Black-owned business. Wow!

Monica goes to play tennis with a friend before Mr. Sneakers shows up at 10 PM.
Gina

Friday, June 12, 2020
Last year we had plenty of hummingbirds visiting our potted flowers. This season we bought a special hummingbird feeder and haven't seen a single one. Too gaudy? Advice?
Mary-Lou

It looks lovely. I wish I could help, but I have no clue. I have a hummingbird feeder, but no visitors, but then, I have no flowers. I assume you have the feeder filled with a sugar syrup?
Maria

What a lovely setting for the birds. My advice is patience. Word has not gotten out of your sugar water fly-thru. Your photo inspires me to get more flowers for my deck. Thank you!
Donna

Friday, June 12, 2020
Well, I'm terrified. Cases of the coronavirus are spiking in a number of states. For a while the federal government appeared to be in charge, although they were late and dangerously inept. Now

they're not in even there. The states are on their own. The hospitals are filling up, and it will take a brave governor, indeed, to take a giant step back and close up. But you know all this.

Meanwhile, Trump has moved onto his re-election. He's holding rallies. For him, the pandemic is over. He's not planning on dying, so what's the problem?

But I see hope on the racial front. This time does seem different. Of course, our record on white-Black relations is pretty dismal, but somehow the zeitgeist feels ripe for progress on both the racial and presidential fronts. I've been hopeful and consistently wrong so many times in my life, that it takes some nerve on my part and some incredulity on yours to give any weight to my predictions. Nevertheless, here goes: Trump is a dead man walking.

Mary-Lou

I take nothing as a fait accompli where DJT is concerned, but I like your prediction. As for progress on the "racial front," as you say, I am also feeling a seismic shift, a sense that this time will produce real change.

Maria

Oh! I hope so. I wish the election were next week! He seems to really have lost any sense of what it means to lead a country. Holding rallies? Now that is certainly head-up-your ass thinking.

I'm going to sit outside in the shade today and change the middle grade novel I've been working on from 3rd person to 1st person. That's how I know I'm a writer. I think that will be fun. Only a writer could think that.

Yesterday I added more exquisite flowers to my deck. Thank you, Mary-Lou for the inspiring photo.

Donna

Humpty Trumpty sat on his wall,
Humpty Trumpty had a great fall,
All the King's puppets and MAGA men
Couldn't put Trumpty together again.
Deb

This poster is from my ten-year-old granddaughter, Evelyn. She did this on her own.
Gina

Even your granddaughter looks like you!!! What powerful genes and what a good, conscious kid.
Mary-Lou

Love her! She has a very determined look.
Maria

What a sweetie!
Polly

Saturday, June 13, 2020
Please consider forwarding this ad to anyone who might even think about voting for Trump;
Lindsey Graham In New Ad: 'Joe Biden Is As Good A Man As God Ever Created' Senator's old comments come back to haunt latest video by Republican Voters Against Trump. Read in Huffpost: https://apple.news/AklC1ojxvRIu2np8EWecaIA
Ken

Ken, I had seen this. It says as much about Graham's lack of backbone as it does about Trump the monster. May they both go down in flames. and you're right—everyone should see it! And, I'm encouraged that an organized group calling themselves Republican Voters Against Trump even exists! I'm also surprised that Fox news is running it. The tweetmosphere must be going crazy.

Deb

Saturday, June 13, 2020

Am writing my way to semi-sanity—probably as close as I can get. Outlined the first half of my memoir yesterday. Found out in 4th grade that I can only outline what I've already written; the reverse doesn't work for me.

Then decorated the hat I'll wear to Zoom celebration of my grandson Ezra's graduation. I wore this hat for the first and last time 20 years ago when Fern got married—am not a hat person. But the name on it is new!

Judy

Love the hat, but especially love that grin! Congratulations to Ezra. Where was his graduation? Did his school do a drive-by like Westport. Zachary's drive-by was on Friday and we had the best time hooting and hollering at the curbside when the graduated passed by in their cars.

Maria

Love the hat and its history. It's a keeper!

Polly

Saturday, June 13, 2020

Mr. Sneakers has coffee and leaves by 10 AM. Monica packs

boxes and boxes of stuff and takes it to Goodwill by herself. She plays tennis with Jeff in the afternoon.

This evening we Zoom into the Music Theatre of Connecticut to watch Ryan play Dorothy in the *Wizard of Oz*. Each part was recorded separately. Ryan singing and stage presence were just lovely.

Gina

Sunday, June 14, 2020

Yesterday was my 27th wedding anniversary. We had the most idyllic wedding day imaginable. It was held in the flower garden on my in-law's property in Weston known as Byebrook. Surrounded by peonies, under a clear blue sky and a chuppah, Mark and I vowed to listen to one another, to support each other's dreams and to nurture the foundation of friendship that brought us together.

Every year on our anniversary we play the two-hour video of the ceremony, followed by toasts and precious moments like Mark's 90-year-old grandmother rising from her wheelchair to dance with her grandson, the groom. When the party is over, to my surprise, a trolley car pulls up in the cobblestone driveway, with "Just Married" plastered across the side panel. Twenty of our friends join us on a chauffeured drive through Westport, singing songs, telling stories and ringing the trolley bell. We make two stops, first at Longshore, where we acquire a bottle of champagne and the second at Stew Leonard's where in full wedding attire, we all disembark, and Mark and I are pushed in shopping carts past singing vegetables and gawking grocery shoppers. I smiled so much that day my cheeks hurt.

Thanks to a photographer friend of ours the entire escapade was recorded, and we have the day to relive and share with our children year after happily married year!

Morgaine

What a wedding! After hearing some of your memoir at our meetings, your wedding is so fitting. And how grand that you have the film to relive the day. Hap-py Anniversary to you and Mark. May your life be filled with champagne and lots of singing vegetables... happiness to you!

Maria

That would be the last chapter of my memoir. It is already written but needs some serious editing, I'm sure. My vegetables are in harmony! Thank you.

Morgaine

How joyous! Congratulations on 27 years together. Someday I hope to read how you met.

Donna

Sunday, June 14, 2020
Flag Day

I check my Facebook messages and discover that I have set off a family firestorm. I had posted something to the effect that I wanted to protect the rights of the LGBTQ community including my eldest transgender grandson from the monster in the White House. One cousin angrily lashes out at me (and Biden), while another who is gay retorts to her comments. I feel sick to my stomach.

Then Chris calls and chides me for my supportive comments.

He says I should tell Lex to get to a therapist. He adds that a lot of the stuff on Facebook is just reposted with no thought given to whether it is true or not or what the implications might be. He also questions another repost I'd made about how to identify an undercover cop in a crowd.

All his comments are made without anger or recrimination, and sound very level headed. After we finish talking, I remove every political comment I've made on Facebook, and resolve to stick to birthdays, anniversaries, friends, condolences and photos of flowers.

I talk to Nell about my family and friend Facebook trauma. She posts political stuff all the time. She sympathizes.

"You just don't poke a pig in the eye with a stick," she advises.

Gina

Monday, June 15, 2020

Did I watch the *Bachelor—Greatest Episodes*? Guess I did. What a lazy indulgence. Shame on me. This is what I'm reduced to. I am emotionally exhausted.

Gina

Wednesday, June 17, 2020

I gardened for three hours this morning, planting my one annual flower that I raised from seeds—zinnias. This pandemic has pitched me into gardening, something I hadn't taken to except at my mother's knee. I waited until they grew to about 3" and then transplanted them in various spots where perennials needed a color boost. I hope they'll get enough sun. I look forward to cutting them when they grow up. I felt rewarded afterwards by the appearance of our first hummingbird or at least the first one I got to see.

Mary-Lou

Yay, Mary-Lou! Your patience paid off. I'm still waiting, but as I've never had a feeder, it may take longer for them to find me.
Donna

Wednesday, June 17, 2020

More Facebook fallout. Monica has now exacerbated family fights by calling her aunt on Stan's side of the family a racist. The aunt thinks cops can do no wrong. The cousins support Monica, and one of them is estranged from this aunt who is her mom. I quietly unfriend the aunt. I am done with provoking family and friend fights.
Gina

Thursday, June 18, 2020

Today, during our morning beach walk, we saw two young women in bikinis emerging from a swim. When we were their age, we'd swim in Provincetown Bay in water as cold as 62 degrees. We lived on the edge of hypothermia. We were young and crazy. That was the water temperature today at Compo. Due to our tendency to deny the obvious—that we are old and that we keep our pool at 82 degrees—we wondered if we might try a swim tomorrow.

Then I remembered Grandpa. The scene was Provincetown, where we once lived in the summers, and where my Aunt Lily also spent her summers. My 96-year old grandfather was visiting his daughter, Lily. Grandpa loved to bob around in the water, but he was unable to get down the steps that led from Lily's deck to the beach. We offered to help him into the water, where he bounced happily in waist high water. We went in with him and helped him back up the stairs. He was elated.

That night he had a stroke and died. We never connected his death with his dip in the water until the following summer, when we were at a lobster party at Lily's beach house. Lily and I

438

overheard one of the guests, a medical doctor, say to someone, "Oh yes. Cold water can be very dangerous for older people. It can bring on a stroke." Lily and I instantly turned toward one another and mouthed the identical words at the very same time. "Oh my God, we killed Grandpa."

We're not going to try swimming tomorrow.

Mary-Lou

Absolutely do NOT go near the water! What a story! I think 80 degrees is the coldest temp for me at this point. Good to know that swimming in cold water is something I don't enjoy—and that it's probably my body's wisdom.

Donna

Thanks for the Long Island Sound advice. I think we can be counted on to act our ages.

Mary-Lou

Friday, June 19, 2020

New York City now recognizes Juneteenth as an official holiday. If this were a text instead of an email, you'd see confetti exploding. Change is happening, right under our noses. Dennis Adams, a master healer and teacher, with whom I did a two-week retreat with in 1987 called it a planetary shift in consciousness. We can only hope!

Morgaine

Friday, June 19, 2020

For me, what felt like despair when Aubrey, and then Floyd, were shot, has turned into real hope for change. Backlash against people of color after Obama's election has given way to backlash against the racism that always existed but has been so blatantly flaunted by the monster's administration.

My prayer is that heightened awareness of the means for suppressing Black votes will thwart attempts at suppression in November.

Deb

Friday, June 19, 2020

Forgive another political rant, but Maher boils it down to the basic question.

https://www.youtube.com/watch?v=9oEaK_ZR5zw

Ken

Friday, June 19, 2020

It was just a matter of time before we got sloppy, dangerously sloppy, and that time has come. It's turned me into a mean scold. In the early pandemic days, when we'd walk at Sherwood Island Park, everyone was wearing a mask and scrupulously keeping to the 6-foot separation rule. We waved happily at one another. We even spoke a muzzled "Hi" through our masks. We were all in this together. Then came an extended period of less enthusiastic but still good routine pandemic behavior. No more. The minute the rules were relaxed, so did our behavior.

These days, we walk at the beach. We follow the asphalt path from the cannons to Elvira's and back—a lovely walk if one didn't have to abandon the walking path and quickly detour onto the road when confronted with an unmasked gaggle of young people blocking our path. So far neither of us has been hit by a car. Even the more vulnerable among us—fat men with hairy bellies, probably diabetic and immune-compromised—strut about bald faced. I have a special way of dealing with them. I stop in my tracks and turn my back on them as they go by, a rebuke that I would normally consider rude, if their behavior weren't even more rude. They don't even notice my disdain. I fume behind my mask,

which fogs up my sun glasses, and take a reprehensible pleasure imagining them hooked to a ventilator.
Mary-Lou

...Along with all those at the Trump rally tomorrow. Who are these people?
Donna

Friday, June 19, 2020
Juneteenth

I talk to the girls about the significance of Juneteenth and order dinner from a Black-owned restaurant, Miss Barbara Jean's Soul Food Kitchen in Norwalk. The 7:30 PM estimated delivery doesn't arrive until 9:45 PM and is brought by the third Uber Eats driver who has been lined up. The first two cancel. The restaurant must have been overwhelmed.

We have baby back ribs and rice, pulled pork sandwiches and fries, deviled eggs, and potato salad. The cornbread is missing, but the food is really good.
Gina

Saturday, June 20, 2020

I get a Fresh Market delivery. They are out of a third of what I order.

I Zoom into my niece Molly's tiny backyard wedding in Portland, Oregon. It was to have been a much grander affair in Madison, Wisconsin today. The legal knot was tied this evening with about twenty digital guests. The in-person festivities will take place in Wisconsin in July 2021.
Gina

Sunday, June 21, 2020

Monica goes to Weston for an early game of tennis with Jeff. She turns off the location services on her iPhone. She invites all of us to go to Jeff's house for a midday swim and barbeque. We leave before his brother and family are due to arrive to celebrate fathers' day with him.

Peapod truck arrives early and is waiting in the driveway when we get home. Contactless delivery has speeded up the process. A glitch of that system is that I can't return substitute items that I did not order and do not want.

I get Fathers' Day greetings from my son and grandson—long story relating to my role as a single parent. They honor me on both Mother's Day and Father's Day.

Gina

Monday, June 22, 2020

Yesterday was Father's Day, the first day of summer and 100 days in quarantine. In lieu of the traditional Sunday brunch, the family, including Grandma, embarked on our first outing. Birchwood Country Club  is barbecuing. We're all showered and done-up. I have on the smallest of heels; they feel like stilts after months of running around in flipflops. Michelle put on makeup. As usual, she looks fabulous! Even Mark has finally gotten his haircut. I look around and see the eyes of those I love all peering over paper masks and—*BOOM*—the reality of pandemic life hits me on another level. Just as I'm getting used to my new reality.

The days have been quite nice here, at the Pauker resort.

Swimming, barbecues, frisbee, sun. Everyone is pitching in with chores, and I got smart, I put throw rugs in the high traffic areas of the kitchen. Scrubbing the floors every morning has come to an end. Instead I visit my vegetables friends.

Do I dare say my living situation is beginning to feel normal? I've even gotten back to memoir writing over the past few days. Confession: I've been avoiding reviewing my virallies like the coronavirus.

Out on the town...
Morgaine

Morgaine, I love your happy smile. Looks like a good time yesterday for everyone at the Pauker resort! It was for us, too, with my son-in-law's favorite meal: lamb. Son Quinn had a big hand in preparing the butterflied, marinated leg for his dad and grandfather. The grandmamas—that's Pattie and me—also enjoyed the festivities.

I dared today to get a pedicure! It felt so daring! All precautions were taken: separation, temperature taken upon arrival, etc. Now my Quasimodo feet don't look quite so gruesome, so I'm not embarrassed to wear sandals. Vanity, vanity, sigh...
Maria

The Pauker family clearly knows how to have a wonderful time together. Gotta admit to a bit of envy. Our family is far away, in Tucson, and there's no healthy way to bring us together. As for you, Maria, congrats on your pandemic pedi.
Mary-Lou

Tuesday, June 23, 2020

Monica is up early. She goes to play tennis at Staples High School. This is a change. She's usually not out of bed and at her desk until around 10:30 AM.

When I look out my kitchenette window, I see a red cardinal flying around the yard. I am so excited I tell the girls. They are totally nonchalant. They'd already seen one. Poof, there goes a chance for sharing some joy.

Evelyn and Frances have a playdate with friends who have a pool. Each of the girls has been paired with one friend with whom she can play. They don't see any other children face to face (unless Monica's tennis friends bring their kids over).

I am bored. I order five ¾ sleeve bateau neck tee shirts from Talbots. I am looking for yellow, but then... I see these other colors, too.

Gina

Tuesday, June 23, 2020

While Covid counts spike in so many states and localities, due to pandemic fatigue, sheer stupidity, and Trump's killer face-mask example, I'm relieved to know that Norwalk Hospital is being super careful. Larry is scheduled for elective surgery on his shoulder that was put off from April. He's in considerable pain and unwilling to wait any longer. Covid, more than the operation itself, is the major concern. He's has had to see every one of his doctors to tend to his various pre-existing conditions to get a pass for the op, itself. Now he has to have a Covid test on Friday—the operation is on Monday—and must quarantine during this coming weekend. All of this caution is very reassuring. He's a guy who doesn't like to stay home, so I anticipate some domestic drama. Bar the door? Take the car keys? Maybe just be extra nice?

Mary-Lou

I vote extra nice.

Morgaine

Peanut butter cookies and pie.
Gina

How about chocolate chip cookies and extra nice? Thanks for the advice.
Mary-Lou

Wednesday, June 24, 2020

I haven't cried for a long time. But I remember what it's like to shudder when the sobbing stops. I often shudder like that these days.
Gina

( ) ( ) Consider these as standing for big hugs.
Mary-Lou

Thursday, June 25, 2020

Four residents are having a wheelchair/walker party in the courtyard below my third-floor apartment. Since no one has food or drinks, I assume they've gathered spontaneously. They sit on benches under a tree on the circular brick patio. Rose bushes blossom in the center of the patio and surround a weather rusted globe, a gift from a resident. Two residents have Black aides who stand, ready to serve. All seem to be talking amicably. I won't join them.
Judy

Thursday, June 25, 2020

Landscapers are here to cut the grass. Clouds of dust blow up—the lawn is mostly brown.

I get a call out of the blue from a Jesuit friend. Karl and I met in high school and went out a few times. No romance. He had decided in 4th grade that he was going to be a priest. We have remained friends for over sixty years. He is now in the memory care unit at St Camillus in Milwaukee where a dwindling number of retired Jesuit priests live. Karl has his temperature taken three times a day. So far, no coronavirus outbreaks at the center.

Karl confides that the day after the last presidential election, a fellow Jesuit came to him and announced that we had just elected a total narcissist to the presidency.

I tell him about my recent Facebook confrontation with our mutual friend, Maripat who took me to task (saying she'll "pray" for me) for criticizing the "doctor-in-chief" because he suggested the internal ingestion or injection of disinfectants to prevent or cure the coronavirus. Karl gasps when I tell him that I'd had a little boy patient who'd swallowed Lysol and had to have his esophagus dilated. I never did respond to Maripat's comment. She's now sending out Facebook posts supporting the police. Well, I support the police, too, but not police misconduct.
Gina

Friday, June 26, 2020

Monica has an early evening round of tennis with three of her divorced single friends. They and their kids aren't seeing anyone outside their families (except us, of course!). The tennis group comes back to our house for margaritas and a pit fire in the backyard. Monica lights up the trees with sparkler like lanterns. It is magical.
Gina

Saturday, June 27, 2020

Taking up gardening late in life, with an injured tendon in my right wrist and arthritic knees may not have been the most best hobby choice, but it has given me enormous pleasure. As those of you who read my virallies may remember, I even enjoyed weeding, although there is a special place in Hell reserved for invasive species that continue to pop up in spite of my efforts to remove all rhizomes. The peonies are gone, but I've got pink daisies to enjoy. I wasn't counting on watering, which I don't enjoy, but I have bend to that need, too. I've been cheerful, even joyous, throughout this extensive project, including accepting as required, the price of mulch, but this morning I discovered a much larger than chipmunk hole in the middle of the garden, along with a couple of keeled over zinnia plants.

No more Ms. Nice girl. This is WAR. I stuffed the hole with a large rock. He (or she) won't get out by that route, but I suspect the frustrated varmint will create an exit hole.

I know there are some experienced gardeners among us. Any advice? I'm eager to take revenge. (Don't tell PETA).

Mary-Lou

When I lived in Florida, a large varmint (I never saw it) kept making huge holes in the front garden, tearing plantings, and just making a terrible mess. I dutifully went to a Home Depot and bought all kinds of mole (that's what it most probably was, I was advised) eliminators. Nothing seemed to work. I think it ate the stuff. Then a neighbor suggested I put down mothballs. Down I went to Ace Hardware and bought several boxes which I proceeded to scatter about. It didn't take long for the critter to disappear.

This worked, too, when I had an invasion of Cuban tree frogs (an invasive species that destroyed the local species) outside my covered front entrance. The frogs slept during the day and came out at night when they would poop all over the walls. The disadvantage to the mothballs is that they melt with water so, any rain or watering your garden and you have to replenish them. Yes, there is the smell, but it wasn't bad, and it was outside so I didn't mind. Good luck!

Maria

Saturday, June 27, 2020

I send celebratory Bitmojis to my son who turns 53 today, and to my brother and sister-in-law whose wedding anniversary is today as well.

Monica decorates the front door with 4th of July banners, a macramé flag, and a red, white, and blue wreath. I watch *Frozen 2* with the girls. Monica grills burgers and dogs. She deflects a sleepover at our house with Mr. Sneakers and his 11-year-old daughter who lives with her mother in a circle that is less than closed. Monica declines Mr. Sneakers' invitation to attend a party with a bunch of folks she doesn't know.

Gina

Sunday, June 28, 2020

I am in a total funk. I look up the real estate listings for Maria's and Nell's homes which have both come on the market this past week. Then I start to google the homes where I grew up and where Stan and I used to live. Am I looking back for comfort and safety or what?

The disaster-in-chief tweets that he hadn't been briefed about the Russians paying Taliban mercenaries to kill American troops in Afghanistan. I turn off the TV. Our tri-state governors want to monitor flights coming from states that have rising coronavirus infection rates. The vapid vice president defends the right to organize campaign crowds. In an about face Mitch McConnell is now touting masks. I want to order one of those masks that has your lower face printed on it.

Gina

You need a great big hug!!! I don't know how you do it, stay calm and not lash out. I hope July treats you well.
Hugs, hugs, hugs!
Maria

July 2020

Wednesday, July 1, 2020

Monica is up early to play tennis. I check with her before submitting a delivery order to the Fresh Market. She only removes one item that she doesn't want. The food is here within 45 minutes. Instacart drivers must be waiting in the store's parking lot.

The month is beginning on a positive note. The sun comes out. It rains. I call the girls to my skylight, and we enjoy a sparkling rainbow.

Monica and the girls finish decorating the front yard. She sets up folding chairs in the driveway so we can watch the cars that slow up in front of the house to catch the view. The girls draw flag designs and fireworks in chalk on the asphalt. A UPS driver stops and waves.

Gina

Thursday, July 2, 2020

Dear All—

The virallies have fizzled out. I miss them, but I think the lack of submissions makes it clear that they've come to their natural end. If I had my way, this is what I'd ask you to do.

I'd like you to write one more virally, no more than 150 words. It may come in handy to include at the end of the script. Nationally it seems as if we are back where we started. Locally, we have made substantial progress against Covid. Still, didn't we hope we'd be done with masks and distancing by now? Did we think we might travel? I was hoping my grandkids would come to visit this summer as they always do. Instead, they're in Arizona, the latest hot spot. I also thought we would travel. I had imagined London, but they're not imagining us. Feel free to ask questions about the future, or to imagine it. Be funny or sad, but whatever you write, think of your contribution as a kind of ending to the script.

It may be a long, long time before we get together again. I know that I will miss hearing from all of you, which is why I plan to continue to share thoughts occasionally with you on any subject and hope you will with me and all the others. Let Gina know if you are interested in a Zoom meeting. That may be another way to stay in touch. I know that I need weaning from what has been a fascinating writing experience.

Mary-Lou

I'd be glad to organize a Zoom meeting. 50,000 new cases today. Fauci expects it to go to 100,000 soon. Worse than when we started. Found out today from my sister that we aren't going to Wisconsin's north woods in August. Not going anywhere soon.

Gina

Have to say, my fizzling has more to do with zero time. Still trying to edit. My son-in-law, whose company turned to making masks early on, sent me 18 of them today. I'm afraid I'll need every one of them. Happy to write one more, or many more, times.

Deb

Sure, I'd be interested in a Zoom meeting if I can figure out how to make a connection. This is certainly a different, Fourth, but I'm hoping everyone has a memorable day no matter how you're celebrating, or in our case, not celebrating.

Polly

Friday, July 3, 2020

Larry did have his shoulder operation on Monday and he's doing fine. Thanks for remembering. Also, Polly, I'm with you when it comes to handling Zoom, but I've been promised a lesson and I'm sure Gina could help us, too. I'd love a Zoom meeting soon and will bring it up with Gina right after the weekend. We could use it to discuss the proposition below.

Right now, I'm changing my mind about the 150-word final virally. I propose that we back out (end) this presentation in the same way we entered it.

Mary-Lou

I'm fine with what everyone wants, but it feels sad. I know it's not ideal, but would you consider going back to offering the class, but on Zoom?

Deb

Friday, July 3, 2020

I clean up the kitchen while Monica shops for more fireworks. She comes home with armloads of flowers—puffy blue and white hydrangeas, and red tulips and roses. We have beautiful arrangements all over the living and dining rooms.

I oven roast marinated chicken thighs, mashed potatoes with sour cream and chives while Monica puts together a salad—greens, cranberries, almonds, croutons, and balsamic vinaigrette.

We top off the beginning of the July 4th holiday celebration by watching the streamed Broadway production of *Hamilton*.

Gina

Saturday, July 4, 2020

Monica and I are up early. She is working this morning at the Intensity Tennis Club where she has organized a mixed doubles match on three full courts. She comes home with cartons of Capri

Sun lemonade, Bubba burgers, and buns. She is delighted that her front door decorations appear on the 06880 Blog "Pics of the Day."

I spend the afternoon baking a NYT recipe for summer berry buckle, cooking seashell pasta salad, and par-boiling brats in beer and onions. A friend from Seattle baked the same NYT berry buckle recipe.

Around 6 PM, four "tennis friend" families come for barbeque and fireworks in the backyard. There are seven adults and ten children. No masks or social distancing. I bring out a few additional folding chairs so folks can spread out. The adults enjoy margaritas on the patio while the kids play badminton, volleyball, cornhole, and ping-pong and take turns making cotton candy and snow cones. Monica has a knack for drawing out shy adolescents and enlists their aid in putting on an extensive fireworks show. A sparkling end to a happy evening.

Gina

Happy 4th Gina. I hope today was happy day for you. You sure had it coming. I love my pinwheel toy. Thanks.
Mary-Lou

Pin your Good Mother Badge as close to your heart as you can!
Polly

Sunday, July 5, 2020

I've been working on my memoir, my garden, and my tan. Not necessarily in that order. Snap peas, fresh lettuce, arugula salads and kale smoothies (don't knock it 'til you tried it).

On the writing front... since my anniversary I've been editing the last chapter of my memoir. It's the story of my name change from Joanie to Morgaine and the weekend I met my husband, Mark. It's been fun, reliving a time full of promise, and challenging, to bring to a close the formative ten years of my life.

While states are hitting record numbers of coronavirus cases, Connecticut seems to be holding steady. I feel as though we're being careful, but it feels like I'm the only one of our group to take advantage of the Phase II reopening.

On Thursday night we went to an opera concert at a house near the beach; the performers are talented friends of my daughter. A six family, socially distant gathering out on the lawn. A good precursor to our own event celebrating Michelle's 25th birthday. Eight guests, all Connecticut residents and fully vetted. Tonight, we'll have dinner at Pearl.

Miss hearing from all of you!

Morgaine

Sunday, July 5, 2020

Monica and I spend a good part of the day cleaning up, putting away entertainment supplies, gathering recyclables and discarding trash. I tackle the dishes.

Monica takes Evelyn and Frances to a friend's pool for a swim. Ryan doesn't want to go.

Monica goes back to Longshore for tennis while I help the kids to leftover spaghetti and lo mein noodles. Ryan gets me out of bed to tuck her in tonight. A precious moment between us.

Gina

Monday, July 6 2020

We all get up early to be ready when Mark picks up the girls at 6:45 AM for their flight to Puerto Rico. The girls will be staying in Dorado with their father for seventeen days. Evelyn tells me she is both excited and scared. They all have their masks and hand sanitizer in their backpacks. Ryan is quiet.

"Who would take their kids on an airplane in the middle of a pandemic? The kids have no say. The adults have all the authority to make decisions." Ryan has been moody for a few days. This is what's on her 13-year-old mind.

She gives me a long hug and tells me she loves me. She and Monica have an even longer hug. Ryan acts like a lamb being led to slaughter. There is no negotiating with Mark.

Gina

Monday, July 6, 2020

I had my first virtual medical examination the other day. It was with my gynecologist. I was a bit bewildered about what, if anything, might be accomplished.

I called his office at the designated time. He picked up at his end. We exchanged "hello's" and "how are you's." Then, after moment of silence, I said, "So where do you want me to put the phone?"

Luckily, he laughed and went on to ask me a bunch of questions—chills? bleeding? pain?—you all know the drill except probably Ken, who doesn't need to.

Mary-Lou

Monday, July 6, 2020

June Recap:

I chopped off all my hair. I look like a cross between Rachel Maddow and Elizabeth Warren. My son cut it for me. He did a fine enough job; vanity has never been my jam anyway.

I started playing pickleball again, after a 3-month hiatus. It has been a sanity-saver. Several times a week, I get to be safely social, take out a little aggression, and have a reason to leave my house. It has eaten up a lot of my time though: once I drive to the court, play, drive home, shower, empty my water bottle and put my gear away, somehow five hours have gone by. Then I make a meal, or not, and the day is done. I don't know if this is good or bad.

My son has a girlfriend now and they have had to get creative to see each other. So far, they've gone to the beach, the Audubon Society, and the Aspetuck Land Trust. They hug hello and goodbye, but the rest of the time, they don't get close.

My teenage years were filled with movies, bowling, ballgames, pizza places, public transportation, malls, basement hangouts, and a lot of body-on-body time. In contrast, my son and his GF are watercolor painting e*n plein air*, six feet apart. They are running out of ideas of things to do and places to meet, but they seem happy. It's very sweet.

We finally broke down and bought a portable air-conditioner—mostly because the guinea pig was suffering from heatstroke. We put both pig and a/c in my son's room. My son said, "Oh. I see how it is. I complain for 10 years that *I'm* suffering and can't sleep in my room every summer, but *the guinea pig* is *uncomfortable* so *now* we have an air conditioner?!" Priorities, man. Priorities.

To celebrate the 4th of July, we bought an air-fryer, because nothing says America like fried food. We watched *Hamilton*, ate cherry pie, and took a moonlit walk.

I also set foot in Target for the first time since March. It was surprisingly boring and normal now that mask-wearing is normal. I bought a skirt, two towels and a box of cake mix.

That sums up the last four weeks.

Miss you all and hope everyone is well. Looking forward to

seeing you on Zoom.
Lynn

Wednesday, July 8, 2020

I'm in a Facebook war of words with my younger sister. A die-hard Trumpian it seems.

What I want to say is, "Wake up! He's a pathological liar, a cheat, a psychopath. How can you not see that?" Instead, I beat around the bush tagging her in my posts of articles on Trump's dangerous cutting of regulations, for instance.

What really got under my skin was her post that said, "Democrats are the Virus." That's personal. "It's divisive and hateful," is my comment, followed by, "I feel sad that someone I love is so blinded." She wrote back saying, "Block me if you feel that way." I think I'll do just that.
Morgaine

A comment that I'd posted on FB regarding the doctor-in-chief's suggestion to inject disinfectants, and another comment supporting rights for LGBTQs erupted in hateful family and friend warfare. I've deleted all political comments and now stick to flowers, birthdays, anniversaries, holidays, and sympathies. Like my sister says, "Don't poke a pig in the eye with a stick."
Gina

FB has become a battle ground.
Morgaine

Thursday, July 9, 2020
Zoom meeting!

Hi Everybody—(Bernadette, Deb, Donna, Gina, Judy, Ken, Lynn, Maria, Morgaine, Polly)

Those writers who want to, should please continue writing

virallies. I will. We need to keep on documenting what's going on as we venture into this brave "new normal." How far do you dare to go—the gym? elective surgery? social gatherings? We need to comment upon the incredible changes we've witnessed in the recent past—increased cases (are we back to square one?), polls showing Biden way ahead of Trump, Black Lives Matter, rebellions against wearing masks and distancing, and even small moments such as filling your gas tank for the first time in months, drive-by graduations, discomfort of wearing a mask in summer, or the drill you must go through before your long delayed dental appointment. Our Westport story has not ended. Let's Zoom again in a month.

Resumption of classes—looks like a fall session via Zoom is a real possibility.

Finally, I've missed everyone. I can't be the only one who feels sadly out of touch. Most of us are leading more social and more outdoor, summer lives. Still, even if we don't write as often, let's please write.

Mary-Lou

Thursday, July 9, 2020

I went to see an old, new Meadow Ridge friend yesterday. She's 97—hard of hearing, has difficulty walking but thinks clearly and is curious about everything. Naturally she has an aide; naturally that aide is Black.

"Would you like water?" my friend offered. "I have some specially packed cookies too." Turning to the aide, she said, "Alma, please get those for Dr. Hamer."

Alma and I looked at each other. She was stone faced. I smiled, an attempt at "sisterhood." I didn't want a Black woman serving me because that's the only thing Black women do at Meadow Ridge—serve and clean. I repressed the urge to run.

When my first husband, Marty, published his first story in

the *Atlantic Monthly* in 1963, a white writer, whose home Marty's mother cleaned, invited us to lunch at his Fire Island home. Probably curious—how could God "make a poet Black and bid him sing?"

I had never been to the private beaches of Fire Island although I went regularly to the nearby state park, Jones Beach. That afternoon we sat on the deck of the writer's house overlooking the sand and the surf. We drank; Marty and the writer chatted. Marty's mother, dressed in a crisp blue dress covered with a starched, white apron, appeared from the kitchen to serve us lunch. That's where I learned to repress the urge to run.

Judy

Goddam, Judy. your tongue must look like Swiss cheese after biting it so much.

Deb

Friday, July 10, 2020

"It was a dark and stormy night." That's how one of the essays in my college verbal aptitude test started out. Anyhow, not only is this a dark and stormy night, but it also feels to me as if we've reached a new nadir in the new normal. The so-called new normal seems more and more suicidal. Most of the states' Covid cases are right back where they started and still spiking.

And there's more. The Supremes handed Trump a free pass by sending the case right back where it came from, which means we won't know his finances before the election. Oh, and 85 children were sickened with Covid at a summer camp where they wore masks and practiced distancing, and our nation is trying to figure out how to school the nation's children in classrooms.

And one more thing: Any minute now Trump is expected to commute Roger Stone's jail sentence.

Mary-Lou

Trump has commuted Stone's sentence! And Covid is galloping through more states and still, people refuse to knuckle down. You're right, Mary-Lou when you use the term suicidal. Apparently, Dr. Fauci has been muzzled. He has not given Trump any briefings for quite some time now. Not that it really matters. After all, the idiot-in-chief knows more science than anyone. And his followers keep drinking the Kool-Aid, or in some cases, bleach. It is definitely a dark and gloomy night descending.
Maria

Somehow this reminds me of the Trump haters today. They don't seem to let up with their opinions. Luckily here in New Hampshire people don't slip Trump into every conversation. Everyone knows how others feel, but they don't seem to feel the need to comment on it. But many do not wear masks—could that be a silent political message or just stupidity?
Polly

Heard on the news earlier today that T will visit a VA hospital and plans to wear a mask. I'm sure he believes he's doing something heroic. So glad to see you the other day, Polly. You looked wonderful and I loved your haircut. NH air must really agree with you.
Maria

Friday, July 10, 2020
Yesterday afternoon, Pattie and I drove to Penders Field in Stratford to watch a baseball game: Westport vs Stratford. Zachary, our grandson, is on the Westport team, this time playing center field. After several games were canceled earlier in the week due to weather, we were finally able to attend.

The day had been stellar: brilliant sun, clear blue skies, even a breeze. The evening promised more of the same.

We arrived well before the start of the game scheduled for 5:45. Penders Field is beautiful, the artificial turf adorns the ground mimicking real grass and red dirt. The bleachers surround the field awaiting crowds. Lights, for night games, stand sentinel over it all.

The teams were readying to play, some of the players throwing a ball between them. The smack of the ball hitting the gloves was audible.

Ron and Elizabeth, Zach's parents, had arrived before us, but other than the four of us, the players, the coaches, and the two umpires, there was no one else. As the game proceeded, other spectators arrived, parents perhaps, or neighbors of the field, all scattered around, everyone respectful of the Covid protocols.

One of the fun things about attending these games—aside from the thrill of seeing Zach hit a home run—is the crowd. The yelling and encouragements that blare from the bleachers: for the pitcher, "C'mon, one more like that," when he's given us two strikes and we want another; to the batter, "Good eye, good eye," when he doesn't swing for a "ball."

All of that was gone. We did our part, but our voices were lost in that immense space. Even the teams in their dugouts were subdued. One of the umpires, usually behind the catcher at home plate, was instead standing behind the pitcher. He was observing physical distancing.

Top of the seventh inning, Westport 5, and Stratford with a score of 1, unable to score, the game ended.

Maria

I'm a huge Red Sox fan, and I've been missing baseball so much. The other day I was walking behind Kings Highway School, and I saw a group of people playing softball. I stopped to watch. The

batter popped it up but hearing that crack-of-the-bat noise made me smile.
Lynn

I'm not a huge baseball fan, but there's something about the crack of the bat. I also love the thunk of a solid tennis ball hit. The sounds of summer.
Donna

Saturday, July 11, 2020

The sum of my life right now is change. My house has been on the market for two years with hardly a nibble. With the great pandemic migration from New York City, in the last month I have had many more showings than in the last two years. On Friday I got three offers. The unheard of happened—a mini bidding war for my home.

This is good news, and terrifying, and terribly sad. I don't know where I will live. I have my mom's house to pack up and sell and endless paperwork for her estate. My car lease is up in three weeks. And when I close the door for the last time on my home of 35 years, I close the chapter on life with Dave. It is full of opportunity and sorrow.

And there's Covid. I am finding this new phase more challenging than the previous one. I struggle not to be negative— even put that in the negative! I struggle to be positive, but it's hard. Without a partner, I can't rely on going out to dinner, movies, and dancing to have a social life. These things are either not possible, or possible in limited ways. It's draining to calculate every move as to the risk and the logistics necessary to stay as safe as possible.

Wah, wah, wah. World's tiniest violin playing for me. Break it down to bite-sized bits. It's the weekend. On the weekend I allow myself to break it down to sip-sized bits. I'm opening the cabernet!

Deb

Tuesday, July 14, 2020

Mick Mulvaney calls U.S coronavirus testing abilities "inexcusable," now that it has affected his family directly. One more crony breaks from Trump.

I get my hopes up temporarily, and then wonder how in the hell are we going to have an election in November??? The country is in critical condition with no ambulance in sight. Trump is holding rallies, planning conventions, and demanding our kids go back to school, as early as three weeks from now. We're on a train racing down the track with no breaks.

Meanwhile. I'm writing memoir. YAY!

Morgaine

Hope springs eternal. Let's hope this is the start of people peeling away in greater numbers

Mary-Lou

Tuesday, July 14, 2020

Earlier today I went to my daughter's home at the invitation of my son-in-law. He'd been listening to a lecture series by his Union College history professor, Stephen Berk. Remembering that I am a history lover, Dick (my SIL) asked me to join him.

The lecture today covered the Russian Revolution, Lenin's rise, and the aftermath of his death. It was fascinating to hear of the jockeying for power between Trotsky and some of the other revolutionaries. Stalin, who was a lower ranked functionary ultimately became the supreme leader. He committed such atrocities, killing off, in many instances, the very people who could help face the menace of Nazi Germany. He made decisions that were quite insane.

I couldn't help but liken him to Trump because of the way in which the two men showed no compassion and understanding of the horror they inflicted/inflict on others.

I, too, worry about the November election. Unless mail-in voting is nationally done, I can only think chaos will result. Each state can mandate voting by mail, but some governors (i.e., the dimwit in Florida) will toe the Trump line.

I hope that parents will revolt against the insanity of sending their children to school in the midst of an increase in Covid cases.
Maria

Tuesday, July 14, 2020

Today, July 14th, is Bastille Day in France. I've been a Francophile and a wannabe Francophone for decades. To celebrate, I honked out *La Marseillaise* on my kazoo. At the same time, I realized that I might never travel to France again. That stage of my life is likely over. I can't even be confident that I'll see my son and grandchildren who live in Tucson.

This made me think about how Donna's early Covid remarks about the elasticity time during the pandemic prompted all of us to think about time: how dinner became the focus of every day, how every day was Sunday, how laundry day was any day, how, naively hopeful as we were back then, that April might release us to pre-pandemic days. We agreed that some days felt longer than usual, and how, surprisingly, some days seemed fleeting. Now, we are all in a new stage of life, the indeterminate future. Time stands still, as if it's holding its breath.
Mary-Lou

Philosophically speaking, the future is always indeterminate. but it doesn't usually feel like taking a stroll through a minefield, with

465

each step a movement towards the unknown. It is a more momentous change than we could have imagined, and it seems there are no coordinates on which to base our adjustment.
Deb

Tuesday, July 14, 2020

I had a false sense of security about the future before. Of course, I knew things could change on a dime, but I didn't expect them to. I anticipated that life would continue to be what it had been, with a glitch here or there.

Now it feels like all bets are off. There is no certainty—everything appears unknown.

"Everyone is marking time. We're seeing the best of humanity and the worst of humanity all magnified so we can get a good look at ourselves." (A quote from one of my favorite poets, David Whyte.) Today online he read one of his recent poems, "Getting Ready to Be Ready." A line says, "Just on the other side of that door someone is about to knock, and our life is about to change."

I do have that feeling of waiting for something. I have a sense of anticipation—although with the pandemic I'm not anticipating what I thought summer would bring—travel, tickets to plays and concerts, time outside with distant friends and family.

One highlight from yesterday was my visit to the Westport Library. It opened for the first time at 2:00 PM. I thought there would be a line into the parking lot the way it used to be at Trader Joe's. There seemed to be few patrons, which was fine with me

As I roamed along the shelves, I was suddenly ten years old again and back in the Stockbridge library in Kalamazoo. I remembered the thrill of the heft of the book, the rustle of the plastic cover, the promise it extended to me. Part of my pleasure was probably the bike ride through the neighborhood to the library. Such incredible independence. Another part of the appeal was no doubt the apples I could stick on my Johnny Appleseed

tree showing how many books I'd read during the summer. I wanted my tree covered with apple stickers for all to see. Back in the present, I checked out the books and left the library smiling.
Donna

Donna, your ten-year-old self threw me back to the St. James Elementary library where I read the entire series of All-of-a-Kind Family. *The adventures of five sisters. And YES! The Johnny Appleseed tree. OMG!*
Morgaine

Tuesday and Thursday, July 14 and 16, 2020

Is it summer? I'm at an online conference all Tuesday and Thursday afternoons this week. It's a real trip being on Zoom for four hours at a time. They gave us two ten minutes breaks to stretch etc.

I crave the mental stimulation and enjoy seeing the presentations by individuals I had met in the pre-Covid-19 era. It has been so long, it seems like an era, anyway.
Gina

I hope you have a very comfortable office chair. I'd also have to figure out a way to sneak snacks.
Donna

Laughing! Don't need to sneak. Breaks are for snacks, bathroom, email, phone calls. But the registration fee doesn't cover refreshments. You must bring your own.
Gina

Wednesday, July 15, 2020

Thoughts to Ponder
Chief Seattle, 1854

Humankind has not woven the web of life.
We are but one thread within it.
Whatever we do to the web, we do to ourselves.
All things are bound together.
All things connect.

Cree Prophecy
When all the trees have been cut down,
When all the animals have been hunted,
When all the waters are polluted,
When all the air is unsafe to breathe,
Only then will you discover
You cannot eat money.
Contributed by
Maria

If only Native American wisdom had prevailed. What we have done to them we are doing to ourselves.
Mary-Lou

Wednesday, July 15, 2020
Today began with a good cry...

Last week, a friend of my daughters got hit by a motorcycle on the street in New York. Yesterday, my nephew fell off a ladder and over the weekend a friend of mine was hospitalized after falling down a flight of stairs.

From Donna's recent post: "Just on the other side of that door someone is about to knock, and life is about to change."
Morgaine

What a nightmare! So sorry—a trifecta of horrible luck.
Deb

How awful. Sometimes a good cry is the only response that makes sense. Wishing your nephew and friends healing.
Maria

Scary and sad, Morgaine. Reading this reminds me of how quickly life can change and not always in a good way. I often don't take enough time to appreciate "normal" in spite of its radical changes to my life.
Polly

You are each a good knock at the door!
Morgaine

Thursday, July 16, 2020

I've "finished" what I thought was the last chapter of my memoir. It looks like there's going be an epilogue. My daughter gave it once over. She's my grammar girl. I anxiously await all your critiques.

Do I dare say, "It's looking BAD for Trump." 111 days until election day and he's changing campaign managers. Biden is up 12 points in the polls, the courts are closing in on Trump's tax returns and books are exposing his darkest secrets. But he's got his magic Goya beans.

Just when you think it's as bad as it can be... Today's headline, "Russian Cyber-Attacks on Covid-19 Research Centers."

On a lighter note. Early this morning, my neighbor Sue joined me for a swim in the pool.
Morgaine

There are many things I wish were over—first on my list is Covid and second is the election. I hope there isn't a third one to add to this.
Polly

Saturday, July 18, 2020

We try to watch Steve Hartman every Friday when he does the human-interest story at the end of the CBS evening news (6:30 PM). His stories are always touching and inspiring, while his commentary is always poetic.

If you have 20 minutes, or only watch a little of this, I am confident you will feel better about most everything. Great way to start the day and hoping you have one. Enjoy!

https://www.cbsnews.com/video/kindness-101-with-steve-hartman-service/

Ken

Sunday, July 19, 2020

Today I celebrated that fact that I swam a full mile at Compo Beach, from the canons to the jetty and back. Yea!

Change of subject. Later today I overheard a woman say the following to a sympathetic listener. "I'm 82 years old and I might have to spend the rest of my life living under the cloud of this pandemic. I won't be able to go to the theater in New York. Or the ballet. I had to cancel our vacation London—they won't even let us in! I hope they'll refund the theatre tickets. As it is, I have to play bridge on Zoom. If things get worse, I might not be able to eat out, or feel safe at the gym or socialize with my friends, except at a distance. How unlucky can you get!"

She doesn't know how lucky she is. She is healthy. She lives in a state that has been blessed by Cuomo's vigorous and early response, and the responses of our senators, congressional representatives and our governor. If she's worried, she can get a Covid-19 test and receive the results the next day. When she feels hot and fussy, she can turn on her air conditioning, take a dip in her pool, or go to the beach. She has lots of money. She can order in meals if she doesn't feel like cooking. She can even hire an entrepreneurial person to do her shopping for her to minimize her risks. Our local protests are peaceful, and no one will put his knee on her neck.

Mary-Lou

So well said Mary-Lou. After I canceled my flight to Michigan, I had to acknowledge that every Earthling is living with disappointment right now. That can't be my focus. It is a time to be Pollyanna. That feels so much better.

Donna

Sunday, July 19, 2020

I spent two days camping at a lake with my son and his best friend's family. Off the grid: No cell service. No internet. No news. No worries.

We walked in the woods. We played cards and croquet. We watched a baby deer watch us. Some of us canoed while some of us lounged on towels by the lake's edge, listening to the waves lap at the grass. We ate well: snacks all day, s'mores all night. We talked and laughed by the campfire. We saw the lightning bugs glow through the tent. We slept to the drumming of the rain. We woke up with the birds.

I felt like I was transported to a world that made sense. I wish I could have stayed longer.

Lynn

That sounds ideal. Just perfect.

Maria

Nothing like nature to ground you. I'm having a similar get-away at our lake cottage in NH. Alas I must return to "normalcy" this week.

Polly

Lynn, how lovely. even though you couldn't stay longer, I hope it served to fill up your cup! I take Arlo to a huge park with a lovely pond every day to swim. It also feels like a mini vacation, listening to birds and frogs and surrounded by ferns and trees. I love it.
Deb

Tuesday, July 21, 2020

I'm sure we're all gratified that this evening, at 5:00 PM, we can all watch Trump star in his new unreality briefing show, brought back by popular demand. At least by the popular demand of his counselor, Kellyanne Conway, the empress of "alternative facts." Remember that?

Standing on the White House lawn, she shamelessly told the TV reporters that she thought a Trump briefing revival was a good idea since his poll numbers had started dropping when he canceled his first briefings. Therefore, she reasons, once the briefings resume, his poll numbers will soar. She didn't consider the possibility that the more he spins, the lower he drops. Fingers crossed.

Mary-Lou

Wednesday, July 22, 2020

I get my second haircut of the season at H Salon in Southport. It feels great to be doing something "normal" again, even if I am wearing a mask during the appointment and don disposable gloves for the Uber ride there and back. I really want to walk along Post Road to visit Chico's, the Pantry, and the Fairfield Library, but don't have the nerve. And it is "too hot," I rationalize. I certainly don't need to visit the Chase ATM—I still have all the cash I'd had since the beginning of March.

When I get home, I dump the disposable mask and gloves,

shower and launder the clothes I'd worn for the outing. Creeped out about lurking virus.

Gina

Friday, July 24, 2020

I sit on my third-floor patio at 9 AM drinking coffee, watching the courtyard and listening to the birds whose songs I cannot identify. John Carter leaves the swimming pool wearing red trunks and a white t-shirt and a mask. "Why do white men wear red trunks and white t-shirts?" I wonder idly, recognizing the stereotype immediately, knowing that it's based on a sample of exactly two men.

I'm trying to mask the pain of remembering Bill who wore the same outfit. We swam together each morning. He circled the pool for 20 minutes without stopping. I swam laps—at first just two or three before I was breathless, and eventually 11 laps in 25 minutes. The fitness instructor told me that those laps were the equivalent of ¼ of a mile. "Good enough," I thought. Occasionally Bill and I fooled around in the pool—but that's a story for another day.

Whoever finished swimming first waited for the other, occasionally critiquing technique from the pool deck. I might say, "Your right arm is dragging when you bring it overhead. It may be slowing you down." Or he would comment, "No need to fight the water, Judy. Your goal is to get from one end of the pool to the other without drowning."

After the swim, I'd return to the apartment to shower. He'd relax in the locker-room sauna and shower there. Then he'd walk through the courtyard, following the curving path toward me. I'd be waiting on the patio, sometimes imagining myself to be Rapunzel letting down her long blonde hair to entice him. When he came within earshot, he'd look up and whistle at me. Or I'd call out, "Hey, good lookin'." We both knew the rest of that 1950s

song: "Whatcha got cookin'?/ How's about cookin' something up with me?" He'd be wearing red swim trunks and a white t-shirt—but no mask.
Judy

What a lovely recollection. I hope you'll keep it for your memoir.
Mary-Lou

Friday, July 24, 2020
A drawing for my friend who fell down the stairs.
Morgaine

Very deco/nouveau looking! She'll love it.
Deb

Love that drawing. I see deco and a little Matisse.
Mary-Lou

Saturday, July 25, 2020
It's been so hot, and I have so few summer clothes, I've been wearing the same two sundresses over and over, for what feels like months. My husband, who never notices anything, commented, "Didn't you wear that yesterday? And the day before?" I told him I'm like his idol Steve Jobs who wore the same thing every day; except I'm pretty sure Steve didn't buy his garb at Forever 21.
Lynn

Sunday, July 26, 2020
My house is bindered, inspection went well, septic inspected today and no problems evident. Buyer foresees signing contract on Tuesday. As we hear that the Covid era is here to stay, the era of living in my home, the chapter of my life that included Dave, are

coming to an end.

I looked forward to moving to Black Rock because of the close community and the number of artists I might meet living there. Now that move is becoming a reality and opportunities to meet and socialize are severely limited. The universe is a prankster.
Deb

Monday, July 27, 2020

This is my little cabin for three nights. I drove up yesterday to a *Highlights* workshop on picture books. (Honesdale, Pennsylvania) We are a total of ten—3 teachers and 7 participants. We all have our own little cabin, wear masks inside and social distance outside. This is so good for my spirit! Just to stand outside and have a casual conversation or have my meals served to me. There's plexiglass  between us at meals. And I'm learning! So glad I made the rash decision to do this. I always wanted my own little cabin in the backyard. Here it is!
Donna

Charming! Enjoy every moment.
Morgaine

How great is that! Idyllic!
Maria

Good for you, Donna! Can't wait to hear about what you've learned. And that cabin looks positively delicious! The whole experience seems so far away from Covid and politics, you could almost imagine the world was normal.
Deb

Another perk of this time away is being served 3 healthy and delicious meals each day. I've never appreciated it more. I will head back to reality with a deep gratitude for this stepping out of time. May there be a precious afterglow. I find there usually is after a writing retreat.
Donna

Monday, July 27, 2020

The ice cream truck has been coming around my neighborhood a few nights a week. My husband is usually the one to sound the alarm, "Lynn! Lynn! It's coming!" The two of us get very excited about the ice cream truck. It's a race to see who can get out the door first. Like little children, my husband is sometimes too shy to approach the truck and makes me order for him, and the last few times they've been out of my favorite—toasted almond—and I've pouted.

Yesterday, my nice neighbor Dennis and I happened to be at our mailboxes when the truck came by at 6 PM. He flagged it down and got me a chocolate éclair. I teased him, saying I couldn't remember the last time a man bought me dinner.
Lynn

Tuesday, July 28, 2020

Over breakfast we discuss dinner: Something from the freezer? Something from the fridge? Leftovers? Order a pizza? Pre-pandemic we were never so focused on "What's for dinner." Has the new normal pitched us into some atavistic hunter-gatherer preoccupation? It's as if the whole point of each day is dinner. Does anyone else relate to that fixation?
Mary-Lou

Tuesday, July 28, 2020

Since the beginning of the pandemic lockdown, I've been

shopping for groceries online—Stop & Shop's Peapod, the Fresh Market's Instacart, Whole Foods pickup, and Amazon Prime & Pantry. I am the only food planner in the family and am happy to do it, but I'd like more feedback or follow through. Monica keeps promising to go to the store and then doesn't until I've ordered groceries and it's too late to cancel. Then we end up with double the stuff we need, and she gets frustrated with me.

I think about dinner plans early in the day when I can make sure we have all the ingredients we need and time to defrost whatever we want. Monica's usual response is, "I can't think about that right now." She has a one-track mind and can't handle the stress of multitasking.

When it gets to be five or six o'clock and the kids are starving, I just go ahead and make them whatever they want or whatever I choose.

This is a lonely task. I wish there was more interest and less complaining. Arrgh!

When I'm really tired, I try to get consensus on from where to order. Ryan now is happy to look at menus on Uber Eats. Yay!
Gina

Tuesday, July 28, 2020

I wish I could blame it on the pandemic, but my husband and I have been arguing about food for 17 years. "What's for dinner" is *the* fight of our marriage.

He wants to not be involved at all, with any of it. He wants me to make something and serve it to him. Meanwhile, I'm rarely hungry, and I have this stupid idea that he should tell me what he wants so I can provide it.

He says, "Just make what you want!"

I say, "I'm not hungry! I don't want anything! You're the one who's hungry!"

He grits his teeth, "Just make whatever!"

I shout, "Tell me what you want, and I'll make it!" (For the sake of wordcount I've left out about a dozen f-bombs that would have peppered this conversation.)

In the marriage-counseling world this fight is known as an impasse. We are both looking for the other person to fix it, and we are both resentful because we believe the other person could fix it if they wanted to, but they're just being a jerk.

Usually, when my husband says, "What's the dinner plan?" I shrug. He scowls. I start listing things I wouldn't hate making: tacos, eggs, pasta. He keeps scowling. I keep listing. Eventually, he raises his eyebrows to the sky, sighs, and says, "Fine. Pasta." I trudge to the kitchen to make pasta nobody really wants.

Sometimes though, I give a pathetic list of things I know won't appeal to him: shrimp, falafel, anything with beans. Or I don't give a list at all. Like last night.

My husband said, "What's the dinner plan?"

I said, "Um... it's really hot!"

We ignored each other for a few minutes, then he said, "Five Guys?"

I said, "Oh, yes!" and ran to get my shoes on before he could change his mind. We took the top off the Jeep, picked up grilled cheese sandwiches and fries and split a chocolate shake. We drove to Sherwood Island and ate in the car. There was a nice breeze, and we were both very satisfied.

Lynn

"What's for dinner?" may be one of the most dangerous questions out there. Cooking every night is boooring! And when you live alone, you can't blame anyone for any catastrophe you might end up having to eat. On the other hand, there's no one around to see you pitch the catastrophe in the garbage. It's thinking up a menu that I find a chore. Once I know what I'm making, then I don't usually mind. Now with the pandemic, when I don't do my own

shopping, it's whatever is in the fridge. The other night I made a dish I saw Jacques Pepin prepare on one of his videos. It wasn't half bad, but sorry, Lynn, it contained beans and hubby doesn't like beans.
Maria

In my family, that's the norm. We're always talking food! But yes, more so now. It becomes a major decision when I'm trying to limit trips to a store and am underoccupied. Then there's the internal conversation about whether to do something about my expanding waistline or comfort myself with something forbidden and delicious. Given the waistline, you can guess which side of the argument wins!
Deb

Friday, July 31, 2020

Today would have been Stan's and my 55th wedding anniversary. I miss him terribly. He's been dead for 20 years. I grieve to think that he never saw our four youngest granddaughters. And he would have been a tremendous support for Lex during her/his transgender process.

Stan would have been horrified by Trump and his unimaginably irresponsible acts of cowardice during this pandemic. When Stan was president of the American Public Health Association, he met Dr. Anthony Fauci, and was a congressional witness in following years during the AIDS epidemic.

I toasted Stan by myself with a split of Veuve Cliquot. This is a photo of us on our tenth anniversary.

Gina

Beautiful photo; beautiful memories, well at least most of them.
Polly

August 2020

Saturday, August 1, 2020
Hi Deb,
    When does your move take place?
Gina

Still testing the septic system, so contract not signed yet. But the deal is strong, and I need to move by end of October. Lots to do!!
Deb

Sunday, August 2, 2020
"I don't know how much more of this I can take," Clare blurted out when our 45-minute free session issued its 10-minute warning. Clare is one of the most centered, positive, socially engaged women I know, so why, at the last minutes of our conversation, did she sound so panicked?

    After six pandemic months, Larry and I have adjusted to the new normal, so why hasn't Clare? For starters, Clare lives alone in a one bedroom Manhattan high rise. She leaves her premises only when she must because leaving requires that she ride in an elevator, distance herself in the crowded lobby, and then merge with others onto a crowded sidewalk. She limits her outings to grocery shopping, a trip which doubles as exercise. She is also fighting, against terrible odds, to mount virtual clothing shows to keep her international business afloat. It thrived when she was able to fly abroad safely. Now add to that the fact that her beloved husband died last year. For the first time in her long life, she lives alone.

    During the remaining minutes, we painted a much brighter and varied picture of how we live safely in Westport, enticing her with our low rate of Covid infections, the promise of walks at the beach, plus the pleasure of our company. We offered to drive to New York, bring her to our house for the weekend, and drive her home. She turned us down.

"I'm scared of you, too," she confessed.

Mary-Lou

My heart goes out to Clare for multiple reasons. Alone, with her husband gone a short year ago is an extra burden to bear. Grieving as she still must be, adds to the heaviness of day-to-day living. And trying to stay in business! She sounds very brave, but even bravery has its limits.

It's a shame she did not take up yours and Larry's invitation. Perhaps she needs a bit of time to let that percolate and she'll change her mind. I hope so.

Maria

Sunday, August 2, 2020

A hummingbird just came to my feeder! I'm thrilled. I hung out the feeder in May and recently changed the sugar-water. I am sitting on my deck writing and that didn't deter the hungry little guy! I'd almost given up hope—and then it appeared. There's a metaphor in there somewhere.

Happy August!

Donna

Renewal and patience pay off!

Deb

Sunday, August 2, 2020

I host a Zoom reunion for the first cousins on my dad's side of the family. Cousins from four of the eight Maier branches show up, including my sister Maggie. It is a technical disaster because all but one cousin has an echo when either listening or speaking. We give up after half an hour and decide to try again in a week. According to the family IT experts, the one cousin with no problem was probably the problem.

Gina

Sunday, August 2, 2020

Too funny a cartoon not to share. I suspect you will relate.

Ken

What wine goes well with watching too much TV and worrying about the end of democracy?

Tuesday, August 4, 2020

"Let's go down to the basement and have some fun," Monica says to the girls. "You can bring some blankets and flashlights, too, if you want." She's being really casual about the alarm that sounds on her cell phone warning of an imminent threat of a tornado in Westport. Frances makes a quick trip upstairs to rescue her loveys. We organize the stuff being stored in the playroom into comfortable spots to stretch out and watch the news on Channel 12. Then everything goes dark.

My cell phone still works. I text Monica's friend, Jeff.

"We are in basement. How are you?"

"Doing okay. About to go out for a swim in pool." (Laugh emoji)

We look out a basement window and see that a huge branch has fallen in our front yard. We timidly go back upstairs to check things out. We watch the wind blowing the mighty tree that sits on the lot line between the next door neighbor's house and ours. It turns out it is our tree. We watch as branches crack off and break the spikes on our neighbor's white wooden fence. Another limb lands on the roof of her enclosed sunroom. More branches blow into the street. One dangles from a power line.

We look out the backyard. A major branch has fallen at the edges of the lawn. A fake rock that covers an outdoor electrical outlet tumbles around in the grass. Monica goes out and fetches it. Moments later a grape arbor on a white trellis blows over. It starts to get hot inside. We go from window to window as the storm progresses. Where is the rain?

After the wind dies down, Monica turns on the grill. When the hot dogs and burgers are half done, the propane runs out. Monica goes to Stop & Shop to replace the empty tank. They have no propane and are dealing with wet floors in the produce department.

Monica has been texting Jeff. He has power. He invites all of us to come and stay at his four bedroom house. Monica and I empty the refrigerators and freezers in the kitchen and basement and load up the minivan with perishables and margarita fixings. We pack up our laptops, iPads, cell phones, chargers, swimsuits, pajamas and toothbrushes.

Monica backs the minivan out of the driveway and heads up to Post Road. We are very low on gas. None of the neighborhood gas stations are open. We go home, park the minivan in the garage and transfer everything to the smaller Porsche. Monica is able to manually open and close the garage doors. The girls see the tension on her face and try to offer comfort.

We get on I-95 and take the long way around to Jeff's because of all the road closures. There are no lights on I-95. Jeff calls me from his home phone to give detour directions. Monica's phone battery is dead, and Jeff has no cell service. Norwalk has street lights and open gas stations. We fill the Porsche's tank, so we aren't caught running out before we get to Weston. We make it to Jeff's and plug in all the chargers. We load his nearly empty refrigerator and freezer with all our food. He finishes grilling our half-cooked burgers and dogs.

Shake the pandemic with Hurricane Isaias for a perfect Covid-19 cocktail without ice.

Gina

Wednesday, August 5, 2020

A NY/NJ ESOP chapter officers meeting is canceled. Whew. I email the group about our power being out in Westport.

"Lots of work for Lewis Tree Service," I quip. (They are a client.)

"We are there," comes the reply from a Lewis Tree executive.

I have a good laugh.

Monica, Ryan, Frances and I go home to check things out and retrieve more food and clothes. The absentee ballot for the August 11th primary has arrived in the mail. I vote and return the envelope to the mailbox.

Evelyn stays behind to help Jeff clean up the pool and deck. We swim, relax, and have a smorgasbord of leftovers for supper. Jeff and Monica drink Corona beer in honor of the coronavirus pandemic.

Gina

Thursday, August 6, 2020

Evelyn and I team up to make guacamole and I make sour cream and onion dip for potato chips. Jeff grills more burgers and dogs. It looks like we might have power later tonight or tomorrow.

They all play board games before going to bed. I start to read Mary Trump's book about her uncle Donald.

Gina

Friday, August 7, 2020

Jeff and I watch CNN while we wait for Monica and the girls to wake up. More jaw-dropping tweets about the "non-problem" of the pandemic. Jim Shutto has written a new book, The *Madman*

Theory: Trump Takes on the World. I'll have to add it to the John Bolton and Mary Trump books I'm reading. Mary acknowledges a book by one of my exes, David Cay Johnston as a source. David has been investigating Trump for decades and is the author of *Temples of Chance, The Making of Donald Trump* and *It's Even Worse Than You Think.*

When Monica gets up, she shifts into high gear. We now have power. We pack up our belongings, unload the contents of Jeff's refrigerator, freezer and pantry and are on our way back to Westport. As we pull into the driveway, the girls squeal, "The lights in the basement are on." After a brief, spontaneous vacation, we are home. And the girls fourteen-day quarantine following their visit to Puerto Rico is now over. There may be no place like home, but there is no other place to go.

Gina

Saturday, August 8, 2020

The buzz of chainsaws and leaf blowers now replace the loud hum of generators. Our front yard is cleared. Monica and the next-door neighbor agree the big tree has got to go. The neighbor has scheduled a land survey to see whose tree it really is.

Eight-year-old Frances confides that she does not want to go back to Puerto Rico on Monday. She tells her father so. He deflects. She and her sisters know

they have no choice.
Gina

Saturday, August 8, 2020

It just dawned on me that I may be the only one in the group with power, internet, and cell phone service. We are lucky to live near Stop & Shop and got our power restored on Friday.

Hope you are all safe and coping all right.
Gina

We were only out of power and patience for 48 hours. But this is New York and a different supplier who was also lacking in advance planning. Still cleaning up the junk that fell in the yard.
Polly

Property trashed. still cleaning. Power back an hour ago, 10 PM on Saturday night. Ugh. So glad to be back to Covid "normal."
Deb

Still here. The "here" being my daughter's and SIL's home. Without power, the temperature in my bedroom at the condo can reach 85 degrees and sleeping becomes impossible. Here, there is a whole-house generator, so life has a semblance of normality, that is, what subs for normality these days. Where I live, we are still without power and no internet, cable, etc. Eversource advises we shall be restored by the 12th at 12 AM. Here at daughter's, power returned last evening along with cable et al. So here I'll stay for a few more days and happy to be.
Maria

Our power was restored tonight. Although we have a generator, so the biggest inconvenience was lack of internet and phone

service. The perk, NO NEWS for five days!!!
Morgaine

In my area of Wilton, we didn't lose power. I feel so lucky. It was déjà vu, however, not to be able to go to stores due to their loss of power or closed streets. Happy to hear many of you are having power, etc. restored.
Donna

Tuesday, August 4 to Sunday, August 9, 2020

The storm that uprooted trees and downed wires caused my family to lose its sanity and civility. The branches couldn't take the stress, and neither could we. It had been a long time since we fought with such ferocity. I don't remember ever bawling the way I bawled this week. It felt cathartic though, to howl.

I'm an atheist generally, but when that storm blew through so severely, and the sun came out about two hours later, I asked out loud, "WHY!?" I looked at the sky and yelled again, "WHY?! What was the fucking point?!" Suddenly it was all God's fault. Everything. All of it. This wasn't the Get Goldman Office. This was up the chain of command by several levels.

I spent the next five days like this:
1. Curled up like a shrimp on the living room floor, crying.
2. Leaning against the kitchen cabinets, sobbing.
3. Tossing and turning in the guest bedroom, wondering if I would ever want to sleep next to anyone ever again.
4. Sitting at my desk, staring at the giant tree that fell three feet from my window, and thinking, "Well, it could have been worse."
5. Walking red-eyed and zombie-like around the neighborhood, with my head on a swivel.

On Sunday afternoon I turned to silent prayer. *"Please. Please. I don't know what else to say. It's enough already. We've all had Enough."* I was sitting with my hands clasped into my forehead and my eyes shut. My husband chose this auspicious moment to ask me what the dinner plan was, at which point I converted from atheist to nihilist.

Twelve hours later, the power was restored. I'm sure I, and God, had nothing to do with it, but the relief was immense regardless.

Lynn

Tuesday, August 11, 2020

Communicating to you from the library where Wi-Fi is available. Life improved when the mouse nest was removed from the generator. Thanks, Gina, our communicator in chief. We may be among the last to get power since the tree that knocked out power in our neighborhood not only took down the electric wires but also the telephone pole. Eversource, we now call it "never source," cannot say when they can get their hands on a replacement pole. Fringe benefit from this latest disaster is that reading has replaced TV and we are increasingly grateful for what we do have. Think Beirut. Cheers to all.

Mary-Lou

Glad to hear that everyone is accounted for and mostly well. Still no internet. I'm so happy to have coffee and toast and hot showers again, I'm fine with the Wi-Fi taking its time.

Lynn

Thursday, August 13, 2020
A TREE FALLS IN WESTPORT

Last Tuesday, August 4th a large tree fell across our road, taking with it the electrical lines, the telephone pole, and all power to the neighborhood, making it impossible for cars to leave the area.

Westporters do not take kindly to inconvenience. One of our

neighbors hired a handyman with a chainsaw to clear the way. Since trees contain water, and since water conducts electricity, he was lucky he wasn't electrocuted. The noise of the saw was deafening, but no competition for the a cappella roar of many generators grinding awake.

Our generator wasn't working, we learned, due to a nest of mice that chewed through its innards and—no surprise—the necessary replacement parts were unavailable. Kind neighbors offered to put our perishable proteins and popsicles in their freezers. It was nice to meet them.

We took cold showers, lit candles, told time by the transit of the sun, and adapted to atavistic hunter-gatherer behaviors. We ordered pizza from Fairfield. From time to time our generated neighbors fed us. We prayed to the pagan gods of propane, Maytag, Netflix, and Kindle for relief.

Then, with no choice, we rose to the challenge, even as we couldn't stop turning on the light switches. After all, this wasn't forever. This wasn't the pandemic. We began to experience the pleasures of our pseudo pioneer life. It arrived in the form of peace: the phone didn't ring, emails didn't intrude, the TV screen stared darkly at us.

Stripped of all the modern comforts that preceded Edison's invention of the light bulb, we read books by the natural light of day, and by flashlights at night. We sat on the swing outside our front door and watched the stars come out and remembered how we used to catch fireflies in bottles. We took long walks at the beach, swam in the Sound, and played Scrabble.

When electricity was restored Tuesday night, August 11th, we were happy. We could cook. We could take warm showers and wash our clothes. We could talk with our friends and answer our emails, although we had to delete the 95 percent that were bids for money from swing state candidates.

Today is Thursday, August 13th. So far, we haven't turned on the TV except to celebrate Biden and Harris celebrating each other. We've curbed our enthusiasm for checking our email, most of which is unwanted, a lot like most of our phone calls. We recognize that we've wasted precious time watching unworthy TV. We hadn't noticed that it had become background noise in our lives. Reading, we had almost forgotten, is more satisfying. We hope we can hang on to at least a measure of the peace and relative simplicity we recaptured last week.

Mary-Lou

Sunday, August 16, 2020

It's been eventful. But is it Covid related? Yes. And no. But really, yes. Covid is impossible to separate from the rest of life. It's all one story.

It's the Covid flight from New York that has caused my house to sell. Contracts taking a long time, but only held up by small details. Deal is good.

Believe fully that my inability to spend time with my mom because of Covid led her to invite the death she had fought so hard to avoid. Don't feel guilty, but her life was less worthwhile to live.

It's because of Covid that I feel more isolated, and my connections with humanity have shut down. So I turned to Match.com. I've been viewed, liked, messaged, courted by phone, and broken up with before ever meeting a guy face to face. No problem, just pursue another viewer, liker, message-er.

My plate is full of a huge helping of change. That's a good thing, apart from the clear henna that turned my hair orange. Don't ask, and certainly don't look. Lots of messages on Match about my lovely, natural hair. Could be a deal breaker. The rest is good. Time to let go of the last threads that bind me to the past. Memories will come with me, but my feet need to go one in front of the other, not the reverse.

It's interesting starting to re-enter the weird world of

availability at my age. It feels like being an item in a vending machine. Look at the goods, read the ingredients, put in your coins, or pass over. But where else are you going to meet people during Covid? At this age, it's so much easier to read between the lines. There are clues in the way people choose to present themselves. Are their messages full of questions about what you've written about yourself, or all about themselves? Is the picture they paint of themselves as rosy as possible, or more realistic? Is it 'all good' or what an actual, living human being experiences in relationship? Are they focused on differences or similarities? Great psychological/sociological study. Salesperson's heaven.

I take Arlo swimming almost every day. Can see a difference in his mobility. Swimming is the best exercise for him. Clearly, he's a better conversationalist when he's feeling good. Gave me big kisses tonight for watching an obnoxious video about secrets to keeping your dog healthy. Hoping I can blame that one on Covid, like most other things.

Deb

Tuesday, August 18, 2020

I don't want to see this summer end, but the signs are everywhere. I found a tan, leathery oak leaf floating in the pool. You can see it in the light. That means that all too soon we'll be suffering from all that Covid brings; fear, sickness, death, economic ruin—have I left anything out?—Oh right, Trump. Too soon we'll be enduring all that in dark, cold winter. At least this summer we were blanketed in sunshine and warmth.

Mary-Lou

Thursday, August 20, 2020

Memo from Miss Goody Two-Shoes: Cool fall days will bring relief from the oppressive heat of summer. November is around the corner and our chance to begin correcting the damage done these past almost-four years.

Covid is still with us and will be for some time to come, but hopefully, the coming year will bring a vaccine.

Dark days are figuratively and literally ahead, but we have each other and that's a good thing.

Maria

Thursday, August 20, 2020

Bravo, Maria! Thank you for shining your beautiful light on the days ahead! It is so critical for me right now to stay in the present. We truly have no idea how the days ahead will unfold. I refuse to forecast the past into the future.

I have this reminder from Wayne Dyer on the wall in my office: "Resist being a pessimist. Resist with all your might, because we hardly know anything at all in comparison with what there is to know."

This morning my deck was being painted so I couldn't sit out there for breakfast and watch for my two hummingbirds. As I sat in my bedroom one level above the deck to write in my journal, I found myself listening for the sound of a hummingbird at the feeder below. Then this little poem arrived and surprised me with the last line.

My tiny high-speed hummer
A joyous sound of summer
Seeking nourishment at the feeder
How I have come to need her.

It's an ideal August day. Let's not lose any of it to our fears of the future. Or if we find ourselves in the grip of it—as it lurks even in the dust bunnies under the dresser—may we catch ourselves and return to the wonder of this glorious day. Do I hear a hallelujah?!

Donna

493

Sunday, August 23, 2020
Brunch for One

It had been more than five months since I'd been anywhere but the dentist and the hair salon and I longed to get out on this cloudless summer day.

Luckily, I was able to get a Sunday afternoon reservation at the Pearl Restaurant at Longshore. I donned my mask and pulled on a pair of latex gloves so I wouldn't have to touch the door handles or seatbelt buckle of my Uber. I arrived twenty-five minutes early and decided to walk around Longshore. An outdoor wedding was taking place on the lawn behind Pearl. A ringleader tried herding everyone into place for photos while a band played in the background.

I walked over to the nearly empty tennis courts where Covid-19 rules were posted on the fence. It had been several years since I'd watched one grand-daughter take a racket in hand while I chased her toddler sister and walked the newborn in a stroller. I'd get tuna sandwiches and ice-cold cokes for Monica and me from the snack bar while she laid out picnic blankets near the other families whose kids were also taking lessons.

Today, the snack bar was closed, and the picnic benches were tilted on their sides so no one could linger. The swimming and wading pools were empty except for the lone attendant providing maintenance. The shady tree under which the girls used to sit on the grass and listen to the Westport Library's story time was long gone—lost in a hurricane. The only busy spot was the golf course lined with carts traveling from tee to tee.

I walked back to Pearl where a hostess handed me a disposable menu and escorted me to a shaded patio table facing the Long Island Sound. A masked young waiter doted—bringing ice, bubbly Prosecco, fizzy water, salmon & beet salad, and for dessert, strawberry shortcake.

"Lucky you. That was the last one," he said.

Sailboats and kayaks rippled the water while spaced out restaurant tables filled and emptied. Laughter from the nearby wedding got louder with the flow of champagne and a DJ amplifying toasts and dances. Soon the wedding guests started to file out, walking past the flowering hedge that separated them from my table. It was time for me to leave, too. Brunch for one had come to an end. Uber, come take me home!

Gina

Wednesday, August 26, 2020

Hi All—You are about to receive an email from Jennifer Keller asking you to tell her whether or not you'd like to continue with the Advanced Writing class which will start in October. It will have to be a Zoom class unless the library is prepared to let us meet in our library classroom.

Mary-Lou

Friday, August 28, 2020

Now that the Republican convention is over, I can turn on my TV set. I'm sparing all of you as well as myself a lot of virally bombast. Instead, feel free to imagine what I would have written had I watched.

Instead, I'll focus on something abundantly beautiful, my zinnias. As you may remember, I started them from seed, the only time I've ever started anything from seed if you don't count my two children and my Chia Pet. Not knowing anything about horticulture, I had no idea, when I planted those seeds that they would reach the height of at least 4'. As they grew, they required staking. First, I raided the kitchen drawers and found steel skewers. But those guys kept growing, threatening to keel over if didn't stake them with longer and longer stakes, kind of like having to buy new shoes every two months for adolescent children.

If you're still reading this drama, you realize that I have established a mother-child relationship with these zinnias. Larry thinks it's an obsession.

The major storm we had earlier this month bent the stakes, taking the plants with them. I nearly lost my zinnias along with my power. Last night's storm came on fast. One minute the sun was shining and the next—KABOOM—thunder, lightning, and a simultaneous downpour. Caught unaware, I had to risk my life plus getting totally soaked and hailed upon to execute my save the zinnias strategy.

Larry: "Are you going to risk having our cars pockmarked by hailstones?"

Me: "Yes."

That required surrounding the garden with a barrier—Larry's car, my car, and a bench from our patio.

You'll be re-lieved to know that it worked. My zinnias are standing tall. Tonight, I may have to circle the cars and the bench again.

For those of you have not yet fallen into a coma, you will receive a photo of the garden from my iPad. The cars are still in the carport waiting to be called into duty.
Mary-Lou

Friday, August 28, 2020

I went to CVS to pick up a prescription. The pharmacy tech stood behind the counter, guarded with a plastic shield. She is, of course, wearing a mask. A guy comes up to the counter and leans over the shield. He's masked too, with a CVS nametag on his shirt. She turns towards him and lifts her head. They exchange a few words and kiss.

I start to laugh. "You kiss with your masks on?" I comment.

"We haven't got time to take them off," she says. "We're working." I continue to laugh as she selects the prescription, asks if I have any questions, and checks me out.

"Glad I could make you laugh, Mrs. Hamer."

"Me too." I'm still chuckling as I leave the store.
Judy

Saturday, August 29, 2020

Stormy weather is a good title for the political party conventions. I am what is called an undecided voter. To decide between the two poor choices, I watched both conventions with interest. I enjoyed the fireworks at both, the fashions, and in some cases the fashion oops, the testimonials, the speeches from the friends and family members, and noted what was missing from each. My takeaway was zilch for the Dems—they have no plan that I could discern except the mandate to VOTE. I don't need that reminder. What I do need to know is what are they going to do about the carnage destroying our cities, and on a personal level, the fear I now have about going to New York City alone. How are they planning to pay for their generous grandiose plans? What about China? What is their plan for relocating immigrants?

The Republicans were clear about these issues. I find Donald Trump obnoxious on all levels. Joe Biden a nice enough guy who radiates honor, honesty, and good manners, but I fear that if he's elected, we will really be voting for Harris who has the potential of being our next president for the next 12 years. YIKES! I didn't like her in the debates, and I don't like her now. I don't trust her.

Part of me says not to vote but I've never done that since I was 21—that was the voting age when I was growing up.

What I do know is that I can no longer be an election inspector because of Covid. And this was the election I was so looking forward to working at.

From your past comments, I believe that all of you are Democrats. I am proud to be an independent although to work at the elections you must state a party affiliation. I registered Republican, but that is seldom how I vote.

I would like your feedback on this issue without the pejorative jabs against Trump that so often sneak into your responses.

Stay well and keep those masks over your mouth AND nose. We're getting sloppy.
Polly

Sunday, August 30, 2020

Polly, I don't have your conundrum, but I appreciate that you are trying to make a thoughtful decision.

Biden was not a personal first choice, but I supported him from the beginning because he is a centrist—far from left. he's a statesman, and tremendously experienced. I heard in Biden's acceptance speech 23 suggestions for getting us on course. but it goes deeper than platforms for me.

I think our flawed constitution is a brilliant document. I can say respectfully, jab-free, that Trump is lawless, and our constitution and its processes have gravely suffered. I read a lot. Facts are facts, not alternatives. He has defied Congress, the courts, and now, science. Every one of his cronies is in jail or indicted, with the exception of Roger Stone, whom he pardoned to get Stone out of jail. These are the men who were piloting his ship. Manafort met many times before and during the campaign with a Russian operative whose sole job description is to interfere with the elections of other countries. This is from the final report of the bipartisan Senate intelligence committee.

If we have no moral compass, where are we? If we have no constitution, then the greatest experiment in democracy has reached its end.

So, you may get the idea—I would vote for anyone but Trump. I like that Biden will appeal to a wide range of folks, not just my own far left leanings.

As I understand it, the Democrats are predicating their agenda on creating jobs that repair infrastructure and increase our use of renewable resources. Biden wants to close tax loopholes in order to get major corporations that earn billions and pay $0 taxes to pay their fair share. Very importantly, he is very strong in international affairs, and we have a lot of mending to do globally.

In terms of Black Lives Matter, I too am saddened and frightened by the violence that has attached itself to peaceful protests. If one looks at the trajectory of hate crimes since Trump took office, it's alarming. I feel it as a Jew. I can hide behind the safety that no one need know I'm Jewish unless I tell them. I can only imagine what it would be like to be Black.

I don't condone violence but do feel it's years of poverty and a system that favors whites that ultimately is the cause. Better schools, more access to college, healthcare, home ownership— more opportunity in general—will go much farther than federal troops, which only fanned the flames. Biden is not perfect but has much of the Black vote. If we are to reform our police departments and judicial system, then Kamala Harris is a good choice. I found her to be strident in the debates—she IS a prosecutor. But I think she's a good choice. I am hopeful that if we have a president and vice president who are not fanning the flames of hatred, their leadership alone will send a message that people on the margins have been heard. Defunding the police is a terrible mistake in phrasing. But adding social workers and ramping up diversity training are good ways to help police focus on the part of the job they need to be trained to do.

I believe that one of the most important roles of a president is to exemplify a leadership style that people can look up to. We have had great presidents who exhibit different, but commendable styles of leadership. The president sets the tone. This president is someone my children warn their children about. He is the negative example. How do we explain to them that it is not right to gain and wield power by breaking laws, being hurtful and vengeful, and inciting hatred? What do I say to my fourteen-year-old granddaughter when the president of the United States says he can grab all the p***y he wants?

I have no trouble deciding.

Deb

Sunday, August 30, 2020

Like Deb, I read a lot. I read news when I should be resting or reading virallies. I read the news because I can't stop reading it, even as I recognize that it further damages my already incapacitated health. I believe this is the most important election of our lives.

180,000+ are dead from lack of federal response. Seniors and children are expendable to this administration, as we know via word and (in)action.

Four months after being discharged from the hospital I'm still in the throes of long haul Covid, with my business ravaged.

Brown people are in concentration camps where Covid rages unchecked.

Roughly thirty million are collecting unemployment due to lack of federal response.

Children are separated from families. Our institutions have been eroded. The current administration takes secret meetings with enemy nations, even when they place bounties on the heads of those who protect us.

Violence is perpetrated by secret police and white terrorists against protesters. Not the other way around. That's what makes it less safe to travel into New York City.

I know I sound like a drama queen, but this isn't even the half of it. While democracy gasps for breath the habitability of our planet teeters on a blade's edge. Watch what the current administration *does*, not what they *say*.

Joe Biden wasn't my first choice or even my 5th choice. However, he has experience with disease and disaster relief. He was part of an administration that rebuilt a devastated economy. He has a moral compass.

What I saw watching the Democratic National Convention was Biden building a unified coalition with former adversaries, during these most divisive of times. We need that. We need people who can unite rather than further divide us if we're to make the long return trip back from beyond the brink of fascism.

Please consider voting for Biden even if you're not wildly impressed.

Thanks for listening,
Bernadette

Sunday, August 30, 2020
Amen, Bernadette!

I believe in science. I want an administration that believes in science. I believe in clarity over chaos. I want a president who speaks from a compassionate heart and works to find unity. I believe a strong moral compass is sorely needed by our president. I've heard too many mean and ugly statements made by the current president. I believe in the power of words. I want a president who does more than dispense tweets and platitudes. I believe that experience is vital in this most important job—experience in running the government, not experience in grandstanding and denying facts that are obviously altered. I believe that who we surround ourselves with speaks volumes. How many of the current president's cohorts have been charged with criminal behavior or are already serving time?

Our personal beliefs come from what we value. The choice is crystal clear for me. I value integrity, kindness, intellectual curiosity, commitment to the ideals of our democracy. I have witnessed none of that in the past four years with Trump.

I always wondered how Germany could have ever have allowed Hitler to rise to power. I realize when there is a leader who says, "I am the only one who can solve your problems," a depressed electorate can buy into the slogans and fervor. Gratefully, the US is very different from post WW I Germany, but the chaos and bigotry espoused by Hitler echoes in some of the political language of the party in power.

Like Bernadette, Joe Biden would not have been my first choice, but he gets my vote. I honestly don't think our country could continue unscathed by another four years with Trump.

And, like Bernadette, I didn't expect to go off on this diatribe. (Good to hear your voice, again, Bernadette.)

Isn't it good that we don't have to agree with the opinions of others, but we feel free to express them in this group?

Donna

Sunday, August 30, 2020

Polly,

Like you, I am an Independent. I have voted in every election since I was 18. I don't believe in parties: I believe in people.

That said, what I expect from a president is what you described: honor, honesty, good manners. When citizens look to the president, they should be reminded that we are a community; that we can elevate ourselves in kindness and decency; that it matters how we treat each other. The president should call on all Americans to be better, to work harder, to participate in our own governance, to make sacrifices for the greater good—not only because it benefits us, but because it is morally right. This presidency has lacked all of that, and instead has unfortunately been a parade of greed, envy, pride, wrath, and other sins.

Six months ago, the president (and government) of my dreams would have stepped up and said, "We will not let you starve. You will not lose your homes. You will be cared for if you get sick. We will *all* wear a mask. We will keep each other safe. We will *all* take care of each other, because we are *UNITED* states, not red and blue ones." You asked about "the carnage destroying our cities," and I respectfully ask: who has been in charge as this carnage has worsened? Has our current leader's response been helpful? Who has been in charge as our citizens have become fearful, angry and have lost hope? His response has been to prey upon that fear and anger. I don't see anything improving if we stay the course.

While I agree that the Democrats might have vague plans at the moment, I do believe that Biden/Harris have values similar to my own. They seem hopeful and aware that there needs to be change and that it will take more than just the two of them to do it. I trust that they will select a cabinet of qualified people to help them.

No one government or election cycle has solved the healthcare crisis, or the housing crisis, or income inequality, or racism, or sexism, but every election is a chance to get a little closer to our ideals, even if that chance remains imperfect. Don't give up on voting now.

Lynn

Sunday, August 30, 2020

Well said Lynn.

When I began voting many moons ago, I was registered as an Independent. It bothered me that I could not vote in the primaries, but I stood by my choice and remained an Independent. Down through the years, I've voted for the person, not the party. In 2008, I changed my official affiliation to Democrat so that I could vote in those primaries in what I felt was an important crossroad in our history. But I am still an independent voter. I do not vote for a party; I vote for the person I think will do the job for our country. I abhor the "blue" and "red" states. I believe it was Obama who said that we were not blue states or red states, but the United States. I pray that we will endure.

Maria

Monday, August 31, 2020

Polly, I have read Bernadette's, Donna's, Deborah's, and Lynn's reply to your email on the presidential race. I won't repeat their points, all of which I agree with. Let me focus on what seems to be your primary misgiving about voting for Biden, which is not character but the issues. By way of full disclosure, I have been a Republican for most of my adult life until three years ago, and I would vote for a tomato sandwich before I would vote for Trump.

Trump's one selling point is his handling of the economy, but like most everything he touches, if you look beneath the "covers," you find much less than he tries to sell. The tax cuts (forgetting who benefited) were all put on a credit card. If the government pumps $1.5 trillion dollars into the economy (this is before the virus), of course you are going to get a bump in the economy, but it added to the national debt, something Republicans worried about until Trump was elected. If you deregulate how businesses are held accountable, then again, of course, businesses can profit, but at what cost to consumer protection, the environment, and health? As an example, do you think that all that pig waste now being deposited in rivers instead of being contained (as the pig farmers were forced to do before Trump's dismantling of that regulation) is doing good things, apart from adding to the company's profits? Or do you think deregulating the fossil fuel industries is good for our long-term health? Trump's claim to have grown the economy is built on his short-term thinking. Trump is essentially a "day trader" in the market. The price tag is in the future, and it is bleak.

But, back to the issues:

Climate change, an expression now banned from being used by the EPA. How the weather and science became a Republican political issue is still a mystery to me, but if you think it is a hoax, you can skip the rest of this paragraph. If not, Trump's pulling us out of the treaty signed by 190 countries (an extraordinary feat in of itself) was the single most disastrous decision of his presidency with the consequences being to put human survival in jeopardy. Do you think the storms in the Gulf, the fires in California, the floods in the Midwest are coincidences and normal despite the fact that science, the charts, and historical records all point to this being abnormal? How about the blistering heat in Africa, the Middle East and Phoenix? The US should be leading the world in addressing the problems, particularly since we are the most egregious contributor to the underlying causes of climate change. And, even if you want to dismiss the problems at the moment, wait till the heat, lack of water, and starvation in Africa, South

America and elsewhere get predictably worse; you can forget border control at that point because no wall will keep people out. Trump has ignored all of this even as our own National Security Agencies and military leaders have warned him of the unfolding disaster to the US.

North Korea. All of Trump's showboating and entertainment have done nothing to what Obama said might be the most serious problem Trump would have to deal with. Trump has ignored the ensuing and growing threat, while ignoring any concern for human values.

Iran. Trump has caused a lot of suffering in the country, but regime change hasn't happened, and they are building their nuclear weapons. What happens when they finally get them, and they remain hostile to us and others. All of Trump's bravado is making things worse, but to the gullible it sounds "tough."

China. We can agree that China's behavior is reprehensible, but no one can deny that it is strategic. Their long-term plan to be the most important, powerful country on earth is not a secret. But to deal with the underlying threat, it takes a coalition of countries working together to contain it. We can't do it alone, particularly when we offer nothing to entice other countries to join with us. We are actually forcing China's neighbors away from us and toward the Chinese because we give them no alternative. China has its eyes on the future while we dawdle with threats and useless tariffs. Did you know that China poured more concrete in the last three years than we did in the last century? Their infrastructure is advanced while ours is crumbling. Did you know that when the militaries do mock battles, China won 5 out of 6 times because "our best military in the world" is fighting the last war and they are planning on the next one?

Russia is now and has always been a threat to us and yet we have given them free rein in the Middle East, the Balkans, and the Artic. NATO is in tatters. What kind of leadership is it to remove

12,000 troops from Germany without advance notice to anyone because you don't like what Merkel said?

The dismantling of the Inspector General's offices. They exist for good reasons. They keep government accountable, transparent, and honest, all critical factors in keeping our democracy. Are you OK with this?

The appointment of "Acting Secretaries" to all the important departments to avoid Senate scrutiny/approvals, even as Republicans control the Senate.

The politicizing of the FDA and CDC to the point where people distrust the government agencies designed to keep us safe. Question: If the FDA brought out a virus vaccine today while admitting that they hadn't done the usual testing to ensure that it is safe (as they announced today), would you take it? Vaccines are given to healthy people. Personally, if I had my doubts that the government took all the precautions to ensure that I could take it without harming myself, I doubt I would be the first in line. And, if I feel that way, I believe others will as well. And, if most people won't take the vaccine, what is the point of announcing its availability apart from being an election gimmick.

The failure to appoint the fourth member of Elections Commission (that keeps oversight over elections and the integrity of the process) so that they don't have a quorum and can't even meet.

The dismantling of the Consumer Protection Bureau even as corporate greed is ever present. Think Wells Fargo.

I could go on and on and on (no more time), but I revert to **character** because at the root of all of Trump's horrible leadership is his lying to us, others, and himself. You can't rely on anything the man says. And, if you believe that to be true, even a little, what is it that he says that you trust? Until Trump appointed Barr as Attorney General, he scolded Sessions for not being his Roy Cohen, a disbarred, dishonest, and unscrupulous lawyer who gave him the advice that a lie becomes believable if you tell it loudly and you tell it often enough. Trump follows that advice every day. He sent out 70+ tweets this weekend alone. Even his own sister admitted that he is a relentless liar. Why would anyone want him, much vote for him, to continue lying to us? Think "tomato sandwich."

Ken

Monday, Aug 31, 2020

Polly, I really commend you for putting the 'civil' back in civil discourse. I hope you will ask questions based on what you've read or push back where you feel the need to. Respectful discussion is rare these days, and it has lifted my spirits to know it is still possible. Your decision is your own, but it took courage to reach out and I admire you for it.

Deb

Monday, Aug 31, 2020

Thank you, Deb, Ken, Donna, Lynn, and Bernadette for your thoughtful and intelligent responses to my question. I shall re-read them several times within the next few weeks rather than listen to what the media deems newsworthy. Anything else you want to add, or anyone else with an opinion is most welcome to join.

I am glad that we've risen above the name calling with factual data.

Polly

Monday, August 31, 2020

Polly, while it is no secret which candidate I will be voting for, as I've struggled over the past few months with the die-hard Trampers in my own family, I do appreciate your willingness to hear what your colleagues have to say.

There is nothing more I can add to the already rich commentary laid out by those of you who have responded before me. But what I will say is that I have never felt so angry, hopeless, scared, anxious and at times depressed than I have over past four years under this administration.

If Trump, by hook or by crook, gets a second term I don't know how I will cope.

Morgaine

Monday, August 31, 2020
Just Over Two Months Before the Election

I haven't weighed in thus far on the heartfelt and thoughtful responses to the dilemma posed by Polly, but I agree with all that has been shared. Here is my turn at the mic.

During July 2019, my siblings and I gathered for a pre-cousins reunion family dinner in Milwaukee at which I proposed an experiment. Starting with the youngest and ending with the oldest, I asked each of them to give me their top five congressional priorities. Knowing how explosive the political environment was (is), I wanted to deflect from administration angst, and instead focus on constructive steps that could be taken by Congress. No one was allowed to comment on anyone else's priorities. All of them jotted down their thoughts on the restaurant's paper placemats before taking their turns to speak. Here are their replies and their ages at the time:

Mickey, age 65, Milwaukee, Wisconsin
1. Legal immigration @10-15 million
2. Clean air and water
3. Climate change response
4. Reasonable fiscal policy
5. Educational support

Nell, age 68, Minneapolis, Minnesota

1. Fix the "gap"—the failure of low wage jobs to improve workers' standards of living
2. Loss of medical assistance
3. Loss of AFDC & loss of payments to single moms who then marry
4. Loss of disability payments when going to work

Solutions:

1. Negative income tax
2. Fixed payments for disabilities not reduced by employment
3. Increase, not decrease in family support where there is a live-in dad
4. Single payer healthcare not tied to employment

Maggie, age 71, Merrill, Wisconsin

1. Security
2. Environment
3. Healthcare
4. Legal immigration

Art, age 73, Merrill, Wisconsin *(Maggie's husband)*

1. Medicare
2. Education
3. Tax equity
4. No gerrymandering
5. Less spending on defense

Terry, age 75, The Villages, Florida

1. Enforce the rule of law
2. Protect our borders
3. Balance the budget
4. Protect the first amendment

5. Fix entitlements

Gina, age 77, Westport, Connecticut

1. Cyber-security
2. Climate change/global warming
3. Infrastructure repair
4. Universal healthcare
5. Full disclosure for presidential candidates *(birth certificate, curriculum vitae, educational transcripts, military service records, health records, tax returns, conflict of interest forms and investment portfolio)*

We finished our dinner in peace, with no acrimony or criticism and even posed for a group photo.

L-R: Gina, Terry, Maggie, Nell, Mickey

As everyone filed out, I quietly gathered up the paper placemats.

Gina

There is a way of canvassing called 'deep canvassing.' Each canvasser approaches a few people in his/her neighborhood and enters into a discussion in exactly the same way that Gina

proposed with her family. After ongoing discussions of the issues and solutions, the discussion turns to evaluating with solutions offered by the candidate the canvasser represents. It's brilliant in the way Gina was brilliant because it identifies common ground and generates real discourse. Gina, you're a natural deep canvasser!
Deb

Great idea, Gina. This was actually helpful for me. Sometimes all that needs fixing/attention feels so overwhelming that I can hardly put my thoughts in order.
Maria

What an elegant, sane way to invite people to share their views. Brava!
Mary-Lou

September 2020

Tuesday, September 1, 2020

Bernadette, are you gonna be with us for fall term?
Gina

I would really love to be but I'm still wading through post-Covid water and am afraid I won't be able to keep up with the assignments and reading. I'm really sad about it but need to focus on getting healthy and my energy/ability to focus is so limited right now.

I really miss being part of the group. 🙁 *Smooch!*
Bernadette

Friday, September 4, 2020

I thought I'd write about yesterday morning when I walked outside a side door of Meadow Ridge. I saw grass clippings on the walk and inhaled that sensuous, fleeting perfume of fresh cut grass as I heard the whirring motors of Elm Company's large lawn mowers. I remembered immediately the same smell from my childhood bedroom window when my father cut the grass with his non-motorized lawn mower. I think the blades were angled like the brushes in a vacuum cleaner. He cut the back and front lawns on the weekends, before he played tennis, early in the morning before the heat set in. I'd lie in bed, listening to the summer sound.
Judy

Tuesday, September 8, 2020

Westport Schools are open for in-person learning on a hybrid model. Limited groups in school, alternate with home-school days on

Chromebooks. Some moms organize small study pods. Students are placed in socially distanced groups at school and there is no cafeteria service. Masks are required for all teachers, students, and staff. The Westport superintendent of schools sends out daily infection rates for each school in the district.

Gina

Wednesday, September 9, 2020
A widow's guide to dating in the time of Covid-19

Ironically, this is the time I chose to put myself on Match, with the urging of a close friend and the mind-numbing effects of a couple of glasses of wine. Truthfully, I had been working up to it for a while.

It's quite an experience. There are a lot of people out there wanting to meet someone. I've had to set up my own parameters:

- Only one picture posted is a no-go.
- Minimal info posted, the same.
- Currently separated, forget it.
- In your 20s or 30s, tee shirt or muscle shirt, tempting, but no.
- In your 60s and 70s, muscle shirt, not so much.
- Messages akin to, "Hey babe, I think we should meet" means we shouldn't.

- Ditto "I think we have a lot in common" when all I know is that he's a foot taller than I am.

So, I have met some men who are kind, intriguing, funny, intelligent. We have messaged, then phoned, and now are up to meeting in person. As much as one can meet in person when masked and 6' apart and constrained by weather that will allow us to meet outside. Instead of being lost in conversation while walking along a beach or path, I can just see us yelling to each other across the void, saying nothing personal because we're in public (highly recommended in case one of us is secretly a serial killer) and practically screaming. My Friday prospect wants to go to Winslow Park with our dogs. Ah yes, just he and I, the two dogs, and a mighty bag of dog poop swinging from my hand. Nothing more romantic.

I am so out of practice. I haven't done this in 38 years. *Oy vey.*
Deb

Hilarious! I love your rules. You're going to be much too wonderful for almost all of the men you'll meet. Keep at it and you'll find your match. Sharing dog poop is a bit of a leveler for sure; so is screaming. But they're both great conversation starters. There are benefits. You'll find out right away if he's got a sense of humor.
Mary-Lou

Wednesday, Sept 16, 2020

I'm missing everyone's virallies, so I thought I'd heave myself off the sofa, push through my lethargy, sit down in front of my computer, and see if I can get all of you to write, too.

I am finding that staying vigilant against the coronavirus is hard to do. After nearly seven months, I confess I find my discipline slipping. I don't wash my hands frequently nor for long enough to sing two choruses of Happy Birthday. How about you?

I used to plan meals way ahead of time so that I could limit my shopping to once a week to minimize my contact with the virus. No more. I've been known to visit Stop & Shop twice in one day—first for the ice cream and then, since I'm a bit forgetful, the fudge sauce.

In the early days of pandemic, I got a kick out of being so organized, but apparently not enough of a kick to keep up the good habit. How about you? I have eaten out—out meaning out*doors*— a few times, but that treat is over now that the frost is almost on the pumpkin. All that's left of my good behavior is wearing a mask and observing six feet distancing when around people. On the plus side, I haven't been inside a bar, but then I never did go into bars, so I guess I don't get any points for that.

Along with the above cautionary slippage, I find that the sense of danger, adventure, freedom from obligations which had me so energized at the beginning of the epidemic has dissipated, replaced by that sense of endless time which so many of us found so soothing. Relaxed has become my new normal. I now look back at my old anxious, productive, super busy, worrying self as my old abnormal. I was sure the pandemic would give me the time to finally clean out the attic. It has, and then some. But I haven't. Accomplishing isn't what it used to be.

Mary-Lou

Wednesday, Sept 16, 2020

I got a new birdfeeder off the Westport Gift Economy Facebook group. The chipmunks have figured out how to climb the pole and sit on the feeder as if it is a giant dinner plate. It has been a banner year for birdwatching: an hour after I set it up, I counted ten different varieties.

I've been playing pickleball nearly every day, and I've become quite good. I play for several hours and then drive home, spaced-out, and almost high, reveling in my greatness. A few days ago, one of my partners said he always enjoyed playing with me because I was "so spirited." That comment pleased me and has become my favorite adjective to describe myself. On the court I feel strong, respected, confident and solid. Peppy and full of spirit. Off the court I feel like a bit of a hot mess or sad sack, depending on the day.

Like Mary-Lou, I'm losing some of my pandemic vigilance. I'm not scrubbing my hands to a kazoo soundtrack anymore. I spend less and less time at home, and more and more time outside, but with lots of people—which I know is "bad." People don't scare me as much as they used to, or as much as they should, though I do find myself backing away from "close-talkers." I'm not as freaked out about shopping anymore, but I've realized I have always kind of hated it anyway so I stretch the times between outings as long as I can. I've given up trying to be a good provider. The more I let the cupboards get bare, the more often my husband suggests we order pizza or pick up tacos, so what's the incentive to keep a full larder? My husband is still trying to drag me into Target every weekend, but I've put my foot down about it, more to avoid unnecessary capitalist consumption than to avoid contagion.

My son is back in school two days a week, and it's been weird to have him not be here. When he comes home, the first thing my husband says to him is, "Wash your hands!" My son rolls his eyes, but he rinses. Brian asked me, "Do you think he should change his clothes too?" I shrugged. "He's not radioactive. I hope."

Lynn

I walk at the beach about every other day. When I walk through the parking lot, I often hear the "pock, pock, pock" from the pickle ball courts. Next time I walk by I'll see if one of the players is Lynn.

Deb

Thursday, Sept 17, 2020

As always, I had smiles on my face as I read Lynn's latest virally. "Spirited" sounds like the perfect adjective for her, it shows in her writing, not only in pickleball.

I, too, have become complacent in my Covid diligence although I am faithful about wearing a mask whenever I'm out in public. Last week we had a poolside community gathering which was a big success. Everyone in the complex was happy to see their neighbors even if six feet apart. (We'd placed flowerpots at 6 feet distances so that it would be easy to do the social distancing.) Everyone wore masks. Everyone had a chance to speak, introducing themselves and telling a bit about their life.

We are having another gathering on October 7th, this time it's one with readings. Our leader, the indefatigable Joan, named me the moderator of this get-together and I am panicking. I thought we'd just read something to amuse, instruct, and/or intrigue our audience. I've been searching for a short story or essay that could be read in about 10-12 minutes, but no luck. Instead, I've decided to read a piece from the memoir I've been writing, the piece where I was burned. This could lead to some Q&A which would be good. I've done a little editing and shuffling to the piece so that it falls into the prescribed time allotment. Nancy, who has agreed to be an active participant, will read a few poems. We hope to have one or more of these gatherings before it gets too cold, or the light fails as daylight becomes shortened.

What I'm panicking about is moderating this hour of our get-together. I need an icebreaker of some sort, so everyone feels involved. Any ideas? Anyone? I think I should learn to keep my mouth zippered!
Maria

I have a lot of ice breakers from my workshop facilitator days. I can give you some ideas if you want to call me. Too hard to type it

all as I only have my phone. Computer in the shop.
Deb

Thursday, September 17, 2020

This morning, as I was dressing, my phone gave a ding, its indication that a message had been received. I looked at the screen and saw "Tina E," an old writer friend from Florida. I looked forward to her always chatty communication and thought I'd enjoy the read while having coffee.

So, I went about the chores that precede that morning cup: let Archie out, feed him, turn on the coffeepot (prepared the night before), stir the MiraLAX into my first glass of water of the day, pour the cereal, and finally, sit down to breakfast. I reached for the phone and pulled up Tina's message:

"Hello my friend. In hospital. Will be entering home hospice when I get out. Wanted you to know. Love you." Not the message I was expecting nor one I wanted to hear. I texted back and asked her if we could talk. A few minutes later, she called.

It was not the hearty voice of old, the one I remember, but a small squeak, sounding somewhat out of breath. Still, she was not morose and didn't sound sad or frightened. She'd had breast cancer a couple of years ago and it had come back, metastasizing into her lungs and other parts of her body.

She refused the treatments offered her: hormone therapy, surgery. Tina had always been—well, at least the years I'd known her in person—an enthusiastic proponent of holistic medicine. She refused any severe intervention for her father as his health deteriorated. She and her husband had moved to Florida from Long Island so they could see to her father's needs. She searched diligently for alternative methods so that his last days were calm and comfortable. For the most part, she succeeded.

Now it was her turn to travel that journey that we all must make and she was having none of that interference for herself. I wished her good travel and hoped that we could speak again, always if she felt up to it. Perhaps I'll hear from her. Perhaps not. She'll make this journey alone, as we all will, but she'll do it her way.

Maria

What a moving story. What a sad surprise. Your friend is a brave woman. I've often wondered whether I would "fight to the end" with what drugs have to offer or whether I'd let go of life gently. I so admire her. I'm glad you reached out to her.

Mary-Lou

Saturday, Sept 19, 2020

This will be my final outdoor swimming virally (actually, it isn't so much a virally as a bacterially). I wouldn't be a bit surprised if you're all relieved to be done with my swimming stories. At least I'm not going on about my zinnias.

Two days ago, Larry and I went to the Sound to see if the water was warm enough to swim in. We waded in. After much hesitation and conversation, "Can you feel your feet?" "Yeah, it's bearable," we decided to take what would be an abbreviated final swim. We didn't pay any attention to the man who called out "Watch out for the flesh-eating bacteria." We thought he was kidding. The water was cold and a bit choppy, but a wonderful, energizing, watery way to say "goodbye" to summer.

Mary-Lou

Saturday, September 26, 2020
Zoom by Yah Birthday

Several years ago, I had dinner at a Grand Central Terminal restaurant with five colleague who were all executives of New York nonprofits. During the conversation, we discovered that three of us were all born on September 26. In the years since, we've continued to get together for dinner around the time of our birthdays. Until this year. The year of Zoom.

One colleague and her husband got Covid-19 last spring. She says her husband caught the virus on a subway. The weeks of low-energy and difficulty concentrating dragged into months. She has lost all her hair. Her platinum wig mostly resembles her old chin-length blond bob. Her eyebrows are painted brown. She can't remember questions when she tries to facilitate a meeting.

This year on my birthday, there was a crowded, unmasked celebration in the rose garden of the White House announcing a nominee for the Supreme Court—"the heir to the late Justice Antonin Scalia." Who, I wondered, would be the heir to the late Justice Ruth Bader Ginsburg? How would the court deal with women's issues... women's rights? I fantasized that any justice who had ever been accused of predatory sexual behavior would have to recuse himself. Looking at you, Clarence and Brett!

My birthday gift to myself was a masked trip to Gino's Tailoring of Rome on Post Road in Westport to pick up some alterations that I'd put off since we were all locked up in March. Gino's shop was usually overflowing with racks of suits, shirts, slacks, gowns and jackets. Not today. The place was mostly bare. Just a few shirts waiting for a customer to pick them up. I was relieved to find Gino still in business... three days a week from 10:30 to 2:00.

Clothes that are manufactured for the average women don't work for the short arms and short legs that are my physical make up. I depend on Gino to take up sleeves or slacks and tuck in the gap on the back of my waistbands.

My birthday was beautiful, warm, and sunny. My sneaky little granddaughters asked if they could go to Starbucks inside Stop & Shop for their favorite Frappuccino's. Instead, they came home with a bouquet of creamy pink roses for me.

Monica arranged for Compo Farm Flowers to deliver a gorgeous arrangement. And yes, sometimes a picture IS worth a thousand words.

Monica's friend Jeff made margaritas while Monica ordered dinner from The Little Kitchen—something for everyone— Chinese, Japanese, Thai. And a Fresh Market birthday cake topped with fresh strawberries. I was delighted Jeff was able to join us. He had just completed two weeks of quarantine after a visit from his Covid-19 infected daughter who was on her way to graduate school in Ireland. Delta Airlines had to contract trace everyone who was on her flight from Montana to JFK which is where Jeff got the unwelcome news that she was positive. He'd spend months keeping to himself to avoid the virus and now it was right under his roof.

But I had a fun surprise on Facebook the next day. Maggie had baked a birthday cake and posted a video of her and her husband Art lighting a birthday torch and singing happy birthday to me. I'm sure Art enjoyed the cake. Maggie shipped a satin ribbon tied jar of her homemade raspberry jam—with fruit from her own bushes. A sweet ending to my 2020 pandemic-era birthday.

Gina

Monday, September 28, 2020

I am the vice president of the Coalition for Westport, a local, Planning and Zoning, political party dedicated to better long-term planning for the Westport community. As a community service, we are sponsoring a Zoom talk on subtle racism in Westport at 8:30 AM on Monday, October 5th. The speaker is Harold Bailey, the head of TEAM Westport, the town's diversity committee. Our fellow classmate, Judy Hamer is also a member. I'm sure his comments will be enlightening.

If you would like to join us, please reply to this note with a "yes" and I will have you included in the Zoom invitation.

Ken

Epilogue

Worried about the exponentially growing Covid-19 infection rates in September, the advanced memoir writing class "re-Zoomed" meeting every other week from the sanctuary of their own homes. Without the need for wearing masks in front of a computer screen, some even dressed up for the virtual gatherings.

Like the rest of America, class members were preoccupied with both the fall presidential election and the coming availability of an effective Covid-19 vaccine. The first inoculations were given in January of 2021, with most of the class members becoming age-eligible by February. The youngest of the classmates, Lynn, finally was able to get an appointment at the end of March. Hers is the last of the virallies.

Mary-Lou

Monday, March 29, 2021

Once I became eligible for the Covid vaccine, I went online and tried to get an appointment. I set up accounts on three different websites, created passwords with special characters that I can't remember, and was told "NO" over and over again in resounding red font. This went on for four days, and I almost decided, "Fuck it. If they're gonna make it this hard, I give up."

My neighbor told me about tricks and hacks and Facebook groups that would help to get an appointment. The whole thing sounded shady to me, and I didn't think one should have to go to such lengths, but I went home and logged onto CVS.com.

The map (again in red, why is it always red?) of 50 states took up the whole screen. I clicked "Connecticut." Fully booked, no available appointments, in any town, any distance away. I clicked

"Louisiana." Appointments available at most locations. I filled out the form. It asked to re-confirm where I wanted my appointment. I clicked "Connecticut." Bizarrely, seven slots in Stamford (my new favorite tongue twister...) opened up, and I booked one, then hauled ass through the whole Louisiana-loophole process again to book one for my husband—so we could get jabbed together, and then get donuts at our old haunt on Hope Street. On the one hand, I am thankful to the people of Louisiana who are foolish enough to fear science and brazen enough to think they are invincible, but on the other hand, I am nearly in their camp.

I was not/am not super-keen to get vaccinated. I'm young. I'm skinny. I'm healthy. My chances of dying are already pretty low. I hate doctors and all things pharmaceutical. My only medical experiences in the past two decades were stitches and a tetanus shot (begrudgingly) five years ago, and a C-section (willingly) twelve years prior. But getting vaccinated is the right thing to do. Not just for myself, but for an overwhelmed healthcare system, and for my community. I'm trying to keep up a positive attitude, but I am kind of frightened, silly as it sounds.

I'm not the only scaredy-cat: my husband, who is allergic to penicillin, erythromycin, pollen, and every detergent known to man, is worried that he will go anaphylactic. On the off chance, we have devised a plan for today: we're taking my car, so I can drive him home, or to the hospital, if I have to. We are having a potential "last meal" of cheese sandwiches prior to our appointment. We told our son that if he doesn't hear from us by 4 PM, he's on his own for dinner—maybe for the rest of his life. We have such little opportunity for drama these days, we are relishing this. You know it's a pandemic when the most exciting thing on your plate in a year is going to CVS and rolling up your sleeve.

We survived our appointment with our usual schtick:

After the shot, while we sat there waiting for our 15-minute-death-timers to go off, Brian teased, "My pharmacist said I shouldn't drive home." I said, "That's funny. My pharmacist said I shouldn't make dinner!"

As we walked out of CVS, we both agreed that we felt amazing and free. Our shoulders have come down from our ears. We're home now, and one of us is already asleep on the couch.

Lynn

Made in the USA
Columbia, SC
24 April 2023

15521407R00300